CRIMINAL JUSTICE

BALANCING CRIME CONTROL AND DUE PROCESS

THIRD EDITION

Matt DeLisi
Iowa State University

Kendall Hunt
publishing company

Cover image © Shutterstock, Inc.

Kendall Hunt
publishing company

www.kendallhunt.com
Send all inquiries to:
4050 Westmark Drive
Dubuque, IA 52004-1840

Printed in the United States of America
10 9 8 7 6 5 4 3 2

CONTENTS

PREFACE

I've taught introductory criminal justice courses for more than 15 years and used a range of textbooks. Almost without exception, I noticed that criminal justice texts included a brief section in the introductory chapter on the crime control and due process models developed by Herbert Packer as a way to show how the criminal justice system can be understood from these two competing perspectives. And then, the concepts of crime control and due process were never heard from again. Rather than using these models as a small part of an introductory chapter, I sought to write a criminal justice textbook whose central theme showcases the ways that criminal justice systems operate according to the at times conflicting, and at times complementary, goals of crime control and due process. With these models in mind, students can learn that the police, courts, and correctional systems can:

- Strive toward the goal of repressing crime or ensuring procedural safeguards
- Focus on police power or judicial oversight
- Operate with efficiency and finality or skepticism and deliberation
- Employ a law and order or civil libertarian mentality
- Operate with a presumption of guilt or a presumption of innocence
- Be likened to an assembly line or an obstacle course
- Appear to be conservative or liberal

Using Packer's classic formulation of the criminal justice system, *Criminal Justice: Balancing Crime Control and Due Process* (3rd Edition) can help students improve their critical thinking skills and evaluate why criminal justice practitioners make the decisions they do when processing criminal offenders. It is my hope that the crime control and due process models will help students organize and understand criminal justice as a system that is often characterized as decentralized, disorganized, and even chaotic.

In addition, *Criminal Justice: Balancing Crime Control and Due Process* (3rd Edition), to borrow the memorable line from the classic television show *Dragnet*, is a "just the facts, ma'am" kind of book. The essential materials of criminal justice are presented in 12 clear, concise, scholarly, and, at times, fun chapters. There is no fluff and there is no superfluous material that would be better served in a delinquency, criminology, or policing text.

Criminal Justice: Balancing Crime Control and Due Process (3rd Edition) provides students with a core understanding of crime, law, and justice and the ways that three big players (police, courts, and corrections) dispense crime, law, and justice. I hope you enjoy it.

Matt DeLisi
Iowa State University

PART ONE

JUSTICE, CRIME, AND LAW

CHAPTER 1

Justice and the Balancing of Crime Control and Due Process

CHAPTER OUTLINE

QUOTATIONS

"It is revolting to have no better reason for a rule of law than that so it was laid down in the time of Henry IV."—*Oliver Wendell Holmes, Jr.*[1]

"Mercy to the guilty is cruelty to the innocent."—*Adam Smith*[2]

"For the past generation, state and federal crime control policies have been based on the belief that law enforcement can solve the problem; more police, harsher sentencing laws, greater use of the death penalty. But today, with an unprecedented number of people behind bars, we are no safer than before. We are, however, much less free."—*American Civil Liberties Union*[3]

"'Just' or 'right' means nothing but what is to the interest of the stronger." —*Plato*[4]

"There can be no equal justice where the kind of trial a man gets depends on the amount of money he has."—*Hugo Black*[5]

"The anger of the crime victim as she watches her assailant walk free out of the courtroom must count as one of the great rages of a civilized society." —*H. Richard Uviller*[6]

INTRODUCTION

It is difficult to overestimate criminal justice as an area of interest in the United States. Nightly news anchors often begin their shows with the latest crimes that affect the community. Whether on the front page or on the local police blotter, crime figures prominently in our newspapers. Novice and expert criminologists and true-crime fans can watch television on networks whose entire roster of programming centers on crime and criminal justice. Seemingly, one could spend hours onto days watching criminal justice programs on television. Criminal justice is so popular, that on March 4, 2009, the United States House of Representatives established March as National Criminal Justice Month.

Criminal justice is more than intrigue; for some it is their school, work, and livelihood. Annually, more than 30,000 students earn crime-related undergraduate degrees at American colleges and universities. Since 1960, the amount of associate degree programs in criminal justice has increased about thirty-fold. The number of institutions offering baccalaureate degrees has increased nearly fifty-fold![7] The United States now spends more than $200 billion annually for police, courts, and corrections. Since 1982, this spending has increased 241% for policing, 321% for courts, and an astonishing 423% for corrections. Approximately 2.4 million local, state, and federal works are employed in criminal justice positions—a monthly payroll of $9 billion. From 1982–2001, the total number of criminal justice employees increased 86 percent.[8] "Cops and robbers" has never been more popular.

Why? Why is criminal justice so popular? Why do Americans find it so interesting? Why are American taxpayers so willing to pay so much for criminal justice? There are likely many answers. This book explores two of them: 1) our deep-rooted interest in justice, and 2) the ways that we entrust the government (or criminal justice system) to achieve justice. Justice is an abstract concept defined as the quality of being just, fair, equitable, or righteous. Justice denotes principles of moral rightness. Think of it this way: law is the codification of a society's morals, values, and beliefs—its goal is to achieve justice.

Although there is a basic human appreciation of what is just, there is sharp disagreement about the manner in which a society should create a system of justice. This disagreement, illustrated by Herbert Packer's crime control and due process models of justice, makes criminal justice such intriguing and controversial material. It is the tension of the crime control and due process models that serves as the basis for this textbook.

This chapter explicitly defines what is sometimes left unstated in criminal justice texts, namely the definitions of justice and criminal justice. A broad history of justice and societal attempts at achieving it is provided. As you will see, many of the criminal justice issues and concerns that we ponder today have existed for millennia. Also, this chapter outlines the competing Crime Control and Due Process Models featured in Herbert Packer's masterwork, *The Limits of the Criminal Sanction*, published in 1968. Although it is mentioned in virtually all criminal justice texts, this book argues that the balancing act between these two models captures the very essence of how criminal justice is practiced. Moreover, Crime Control and Due Process Models serve as the ideal types that pit consensus versus conflict, conservative versus liberal, and law-and-order versus civil liberty approaches to criminal justice. In other words, understanding the Crime Control and Due Process Models allows students to understand how criminal justice system works and, in some circumstances, why the system appears to not work. Prominent policies and initiatives that stress crime control and due process are also provided. Finally, an understanding of these competing models allows students to critically analyze the various components of the criminal justice system and appreciate how they function. See Box 1-1 for an example of crime control policy.

What Is Justice?

Imagine you are an anthropologist with a time machine. You are able to study tribes, people, cultures, and societies from around the globe over a span of several millennia. You would discover incredible diversity in the lives of these human groups that varied by epoch, location, economy, culture, race, etc. However, there would also be pronounced commonalities across observations. These consistencies in the human condition could be called human universals. Fundamentally, people recognize their own individuality and the benefits and

BOX 1-1

CRIME SCENE   DO NOT CROSS

CRIMINAL JUSTICE SPOTLIGHT

OPERATION FALCON CAPTURES MORE THAN 10,000 CRIMINALS!

Operation FALCON (Federal and Local Cops Organized Nationally), a massive coast-to-coast law enforcement sweep has been conducted six times since its inception on April 4–10, 2005. FALCON I captured 10,340 fugitives between April 4 and April 10, 2005 and included more than 3,100 police officers, sheriffs, and deputies from 959 local, state, and federal agencies participated in the largest coordinated dragnet in American history. The crime control measure coincided with Crime Victims Rights Week.

The 10,340 arrests cleared 13,851 warrants including 162 murder suspects, 553 rape suspects, 106 unregistered sex offenders, 638 armed robbery suspects, 68 kidnapping suspects, and 154 documented gang members. FALCON I also seized nearly 300 kilograms of drugs, $373,000 in cash, and thousands of other fugitives wanted for arson, assault, burglary, extortion, weapons violations, and auto theft. A staggering 71% of those arrested had prior arrests for crimes of violence. During the course of this operation, there were no serious incidents or injuries to either the law enforcement officers or to those who were taken into custody. According to the U.S. Marshals, "Based on the unprecedented success of this operation, there is no doubt that the Marshals will be encouraged in the future to conduct similar operations of this scale in order to reduce violent crime throughout the United States." Indeed, FALCON programs have been conducted five times since 2005 and resulted in 91.086 arrests and the clearing of 117,874 warrants. Initiatives such as Operation FALCON are likely the wave of the crime-control future.

Sources: Retrieved February 24, 2011, from http://www.usmarshals.gov/falcon/index.html. *Photo © 2011, joingate, Shutterstock, Inc.*

probable necessities of the collective or group. People, all people, appreciate that both individuals and groups (or societies) require respect for the maintenance of life. According to Plato, justice could be defined as a state of harmony between soul (individual) and the state. People who could not reign in their selfish needs would not last. They would devolve in what philosopher Thomas Hobbes called a war of all against all.

Part of the trade-off between selfish wants and societal necessities is the recognition and experience that our behavior has positive and potentially negative consequences. At a very basic level, people recognize that certain behaviors are good or bad in that their effects are good or bad. All people, even the most primitive human groups, conducted their lives in accordance with transcendent concepts like good and bad (or evil), right and wrong, helpful and harmful, action and reaction. Over time, these concepts coalesced into a social order that stressed the triumph of right over wrong, good over evil, equity, reciprocity, and proportionality. Importantly, the general human sense about rightful and wrongful conduct was not constructed. Instead it originated from our inherent human nature. Thus, the idea of justice, and our appreciation of it, springs from natural law.

What is natural law? Natural law is defined as the belief that the human world is organized by a positive or good natural order that should be obeyed by humans. First described by the Greek writer Sophocles, natural law is most famously attributed to Aristotle and its revival in the 13th century by philosopher St. Thomas Aquinas. Unlike the codified laws that we follow today, natural law is unwritten. Instead, it is tacitly understood and appreciated by human reason. Natural law is naturally authoritative over human conduct and the good of the order (referred to generally as "the good") takes primacy over individual rights and concerns. In short, natural law is obvious and unequivocal that certain behaviors are wrong and intolerable.

Evidence for natural law can be found in the universal human revulsion against specific negative behaviors or crimes. You would be hard pressed to find a society or group of people that did not morally condemn behaviors such as murder, incest, or even theft. These behaviors appear to be intrinsically wrong or *mala in se*. Of course, justice is not limited to natural law. As human organization became more complex and societies became more modern, justice evolved. The next section provides a brief historical primer showcasing how early civilizations dealt with the abstract but very real notion of justice and ultimately formulated the modern notion of criminal justice.[9]

HISTORICAL APPROACHES TO CRIMINAL JUSTICE

Throughout history, criminal justice has evolved in three important ways. First, the ways that justice is administered has evolved from informal to formal or bureaucratic means. In earlier epochs, the criminal justice system did not exist. Instead, family and community members responded to, sanctioned, and judged crimes and other behaviors that were deemed inappropriate. This is called informal social control. Informal social control still exists today. The ways that your parents, friends, and coworkers "correct" your behavior are informal means of social control. Being "grounded" for two weeks, lectured to by your boss, or given a stern gaze by your friends are just some methods that we police, judge, and punish others in everyday life.

A second point, and related to the first, has been the evolution of criminal justice from a personal to impersonal process. Although informal social control can be effective, it is also susceptible to biases and abuses because of the emotional connections between us. If the judge and the judged are members of the same family, then it is likely that evaluations of conduct will be marked by subjectivity. Subjectivity can compromise the lawful, equitable, and proportional goals of justice. It is thought that objectivity better serves the pursuit of justice since it is based on fact and evidence instead of on raw emotion. This is an exceedingly important point. A dispassionate, formal, professional system of criminal justice has evolved from the visceral, informal, personal methods of the past. This raises important questions about the ability of the modern, formal criminal justice system to harness the emotions elicited by criminal wrongdoing. Can formal criminal justice be as personally satisfying as former, informal methods?

The third major point of criminal justice evolution has been the dramatic change from brutal, barbaric forms of punishment to what are thought to be civilized measures of reasoned punishment (this will be explored in great detail in part four). A hallmark of the progression of civilization has been the diminution of violence as punishment. For example, although the United States still employs capital punishment, the ultimate sanction is rarely imposed and is administered in what is supposed to be a humane, medical procedure. By comparison, historical approaches to criminal justice were draconian and used the penalty of death for scores of crimes, even minor ones. In short, a hallmark of civilization has been the transformation of justice from something that was retributive and repressive to something that is more rehabilitative and restitutive. By and large, the personal vengeance inherent in justice was replaced by an impersonal bureaucracy.

Code of Hammurabi

Arguably the earliest important date in criminal justice history was the establishment of the Code of Hammurabi by the Babylonian King Hammurabi in 1780 B.C.E. The Code was fairly sophisticated and contained 282 clauses or case laws pertaining to a variety of social and legal issues. The Code of Hammurabi was guided by the doctrine of *lex talionis* meaning "an eye for an eye, a tooth for a tooth." The *lex talionis* embodied three principles that are applicable to the present day. First, law and criminal justice could be punitive and in part driven by vengeance. Second, crime and its punishment aimed to be proportionate. Hence, a person convicted of murder would be executed because the punishment equals the severity of the underlying criminal conduct. Unfortunately, because many non-lethal behaviors were punishable by death, the Code of Hammurabi often was excessive and not proportionate. Third, punishment was inflicted in the name of the community or city-state and not of the specific victim. The idea that all societal members suffer from crime, thus making it a social problem, is certainly salient to us today.

Judeo-Christian Tradition and Deuteronomy

Between the 16th and 13th centuries B.C.E., the Judeo-Christian traditions weighed in on criminal justice. According to religious tradition, Moses received the Ten Commandments from God. Containing most famously the proscription against murder, the Ten Commandments have heavily influenced cultures and legal systems within the Judeo-Christian tradition, such as the United States. A noteworthy contribution during this era was the book of Deuteronomy attributed to Moses. Deuteronomy is essentially a legal book containing the rights, laws, penalties, and proto-criminal justice system of Israel.

Like the Babylonians, the Judaic and Christian traditions of criminal justice were punitive and viewed death as an appropriate penalty for many transgressions. Consider two selections from Deuteronomy Chapter 17:6–7, "At the mouth of two witnesses, or three witnesses, shall he that is worthy of death be put to death; but at the mouth of one witness he shall not be put to death. The hands of the witnesses shall be first upon him to put him to death, and afterward the hands of all the people. So thou shalt put the evil away from among you." Another interesting and perennial criminal justice topic is the notion of evil, and by extension, evil people. From the Law of Moses to our modern concern about serial killers and other infamous criminals, people have struggled with the proper conceptualization and handling of criminals.

Greek and Roman Traditions

The Greek and Roman societies also made significant early contributions to criminal justice. In 621 B.C.E., the Athenian politician and magistrate Draco compiled the first comprehensive set of laws in Greece. Prior to this time, criminal matters were viewed as private matters and were resolved by the injured party or victim's family. Draco's laws were noteworthy for their severity as the penalty for many offenses was death. Poisoning, starvation, death by exposure, and banishment were just some of the sanctions employed during Draco's time. Indeed, the contemporary term draconian, often used to describe tough criminal justice policies, is derived from Draco and his legacy. Over the next century, as Greek society was plagued by dissent, the harsh criminal justice code of Draco was softened by reformists such as Solon and Cleisthenes. These progressive Greeks made only homicide a capital crime and instituted the widespread use of fines as a form of punishment. Fines served two purposes or constituencies. They were a form of restitution to the victim served as a tax for the public good. By paying both victim and community, Solon's use of fines helped bridge the private and public interests of criminal justice.

From the founding of Rome in 750 B.C.E. to 450 B.C.E., criminal justice was administered according to tradition of Roman patricians. Unfortunately, this informal, top-down form of justice was unfairly administered to non-elites. In 450 B.C.E., Roman magistrates created the Law of the Twelve Tables, a comprehensive and codified legal code to replace the oral, informal, and largely unfair prior tradition. The Twelve Tables would remain in effect for nearly one thousand years until the fall of Constantinople and the Eastern Roman Empire. An interesting facet of The Twelve Tables was the establishment of two sets of laws, one exclusively for Roman citizens and the other for non-citizens. The idea that law and criminal justice are applied differently based on individual characteristics exists to the present day.

Magna Carta and Common Law

A centerpiece historical contribution to criminal justice is the Magna Carta or Great Charter. Signed by King John of England on June 15, 1215, the Magna Carta was a codified set of laws that both delineated the set of behaviors that citizens could not engage in and limited the powers of the thrown. In many respects, the Magna Carta was the forerunner of the United States Constitution with its dual goals of cautiously empowering the state and granting rights and protections to the public.

In fact, the United States owes its entire criminal justice system and common law tradition to England. Common law is based on customs, traditions, unwritten norms, and general principles that ultimately find their way into codified or statutory law. Common law would characterize the burgeoning American colonies from the arrival of Columbus in 1492 to the Declaration of Independence in 1776 and the drafting of the United States Constitution from 1787–1789 to the ratification of the Bill of Rights in 1791.

On Crimes and Punishments

American justice also owes a tremendous debt to Cesare Beccaria's masterpiece, *Dei delitti e Delle Pene* or *On Crimes and Punishments*, published in 1764. An Italian nobleman and jurist, Beccaria was disgusted with the arbitrary, discriminatory, and largely barbaric system of justice that typified 18th Century Italy. Beccaria believed in the Enlightenment idea that people were rational and thus their behavior followed an almost economic weighing of the costs and benefits or pains and pleasures of action. Commensurately, punishment should be swift, certain, and severe (but proportionate) to hopefully deter or dissuade people from choosing to engage in crime.

On Crimes and Punishments contained a variety of ideas that seem obvious today but were revolutionary for their time. Some of these ideas were that laws should be rational, punishments should be in degree to the severity of the crime (thus capital punishment should not be widely applied), the presumption of innocence, law should apply equally to all people regardless of social class or other status, and long imprisonment is a more powerful deterrent than condemnation. The influence of Beccaria's ideas is discussed more extensively in Chapter 3.

Colonial America

The history of criminal justice in colonial America captured many of the themes that people and communities have grappled with throughout time. Consider this passage from legal scholar Lawrence Friedman:

> On the whole, life in colonial America was small-scale; it was life among neighbors in small, tight communities. Moreover, it was life lived in the shadow of a few powerful, regnant ideas about God, punishment, the afterworld, religion, and the social order. In short, life in the colonies was village life, orderly life, religious life. It was also a life dominated by ideas about hierarchy and subordination; about obedience to fathers, ministers, masters. The colonies had no real aristocracy on the English model, but the leaders of the settlements were neither anarchists nor democrats; far from it. These facts of structure and ideology made the criminal justice system what it was; they shaped types of punishment and the very definitions of crime.[10]

Of course, the history of criminal justice does not end in colonial America. The continued progression of criminal justice will be discussed in greater detail in Chapter 3 that is devoted to criminal law. What this abbreviated section has done is highlight the major historical contributions to criminal justice and touch on the philosophical, legal, and practical issues that criminal justice creates. Should criminal justice be a private or public matter? Is justice best served informally or formally? Should criminal justice be temperate or extreme in its response to crime? Should the pursuit of justice be deliberative and slow or decisive and swift? Is criminal justice best served by reason or emotion? Does vengeance have a place in criminal justice? Does violence have any place in a formal system of criminal justice? Finally, should criminal justice best serve the interests of the state or the individual? Can a happy medium be reached in these debates?

Many of these very questions were addressed in Herbert Packer's *The Limits of the Criminal Sanction*, especially regarding his competing crime control and due process models of criminal justice. In fact, these works are so important that they are the conceptual basis for this book. Every subsequent topic, police, courts, and corrections can effectively be evaluated from these competing perspectives. Most importantly, they provide a conceptual framework that helps to understand the history and current state of criminal justice.

HERBERT PACKER'S *THE LIMITS OF THE CRIMINAL SANCTION*

Crime Control Model

According to the Crime Control Model, the repression of criminal conduct is the most important function of the criminal justice system. If the police are unable to adequately control crime, public order will break down. A breakdown

CRIME SCENE   DO NOT CROSS

CRIMINAL JUSTICE NEWS

FIGHTING CRIME WITH FORCE

In *District of Columbia v. Heller* (2008), the Supreme Court held that citizens have the right to bear arms in the home to protect themselves, their family, and their home. At least 23 states in recent years have passed legislation that allowed people who feel threatened to "meet force with force" and defend themselves without fear of prosecution. The castle doctrine empowers individual's right to use lethal force without the necessity to retreat. Opponents of these laws suggest that it is reminiscent of the Wild West and has no place in modern society. Proponents argue that law-abiding citizens have the right to stand their ground and use force, even deadly force, in the face of serious criminal threats. What do you think?

Sources: *District of Columbia v. Heller* 554 U. S. 570 (2008); Boots, D. P., Bihari, J., & Elliott, E. (2009). The state of the castle: An overview of recent trends in state castle doctrine legislation and public policy. *Criminal Justice Review, 34,* 515–535. Photo © JupiterImages, Corp.

in public order poses a significant threat to human freedom. From this perspective, law-abiding people are doubly victimized by the wrongful acts of criminals and the unwillingness or inability of the state to stop criminals. In Packer's words, the criminal justice system is the "positive guarantor of social freedom."

To achieve this important objective, criminal justice must efficiently apprehend, prosecute, and dispose of criminals. Like an assembly line, justice should be driven by speed and finality. According to Packer, crime control could depend on informal processes of gathering information and ascertaining guilt (e.g., interrogations) and occasions for challenge should be minimized. Court proceedings are viewed as annoying "ceremonious rituals" that should be avoided. Instead, criminal justice personnel are viewed as experts who are competently able to process cases through the system by successfully screening out the innocent and the difficult to convict and capturing the guilty and likely to convict.

The Crime Control Model is driven by a presumption of guilt whereby being arrested or otherwise contacted by the criminal justice system is in itself a reliable indicator of probable guilt. According to this perspective, truly innocent people are not arrested. To be arrested is to be guilty. Since American law is based in part upon the presumption of innocence, the presumption of guilt might seem counterintuitive. However, according to the theory, the presumption of guilt is a mood or operating philosophy for the criminal justice system.

The presumption of guilt is not, of course, a thing. Nor is it even a rule of law in the usual sense. It simply is the consequence of a complex of attitudes, a mood. If there is confidence in the reliability of informal administrative fact-finding activities that take place in the early stages of the criminal process, the remaining stages of the process can be relatively perfunctory without any loss in operating efficiency. The presumption of guilt, as it operates in the Crime Control Model, is the operational expression of that confidence.[11]

Because the centerpiece of the Crime Control Model lies in the early, fact-finding stage, it is implicitly oriented toward the police and securing police power. Again, the subsequent stages of the criminal justice process are viewed almost as afterthoughts that serve to "rubberstamp" the diligence, expertise, and discretion of the police to initiate a criminal case. For example, from the perspective of the Crime Control Model, the courts should attempt to most cases via plea-bargaining (as they indeed do) because trials are resource-intensive and largely redundant since the police have already conducted their investigation of the defendant and arrived at a decision of guilt. At minimum, the courts serve as a check and balance to ensure that the police behaved appropriately.

There are many real world implications of the Crime Control Model that likely inform some people's views about the ways that criminal justice should operate. First, the model is based on a strident trust in the ability of government agents to tackle crime. This trust is based on the belief that nearly all people are bound by a similar set of beliefs, norms, and behaviors. The Crime Control Model is based on a culture of consensus. Sociology students will recognize a culture of consensus in Emile Durkheim's work and the idea of structural functionalism. Second, if the police are the keepers of freedom and the defenders of our morality, then there is a tendency to unleash the police to pursue their noble goals. "Law and order" are the goals, thus the police should have considerable means to maintain law and order. Third, the Crime Control Model denotes a fairly obvious value judgment of the state and criminals, good guys and bad guys. Criminal defendants are viewed as reprehensible at worst and probably guilty at best; these conditions make it easier to defend strong state powers to control crime. Ideologically and politically, the Crime Control Model is somewhat parallel to conservative and Republican viewpoints about criminal justice.

Due Process Model

Conversely, the Due Process Model resembles an obstacle course where each successive stage of the criminal justice system is "designed to present formidable impediments to carrying the accused any further along in the process." The Due Process Model holds as paramount the fair and formal processing of

CRIME SCENE   DO NOT CROSS

CRIME CONTROL AND DUE PROCESS MODELS

Item	Crime Control	Due Process
Goals	Repress crime	Ensure procedural safeguards
Focus	Police	Courts
Traits	Efficient and final	Skeptical and deliberative
Mentality	Law and order	Civil libertarian
Operating principle	Presumption of guilt	Presumption of innocence
Similar to	Assembly line	Obstacle course
Politics	Conservative	Liberal
Assumption	Society based on consensus	Society based on conflict
Sociology Theory	Functionalism	Conflict

criminal cases and the assurance of procedural justice. Proponents of the Due Process Model also find crime morally wrong and are committed to reducing crime; however, they tend to view the state's powers to process criminals as more important. It assumes that freedom is so important that every effort must be made to ensure that criminal justice decisions are based on reliable information.

Emphasis is on the adversarial process, the rights of the defendant, and formal decision making. According to the Due Process Model, the checks and balances of the criminal justice system are more than mere rubberstamps of police power they are separately important entities that evaluate and monitor the conduct of one another. Because the protection of the innocent is as important or perhaps more important than convicting the guilty, the criminal justice system must meet strict requirements and ensure Constitutional safeguards when processing defendants. This is another important distinction of the Due Process Model. Whereas crime control adherents have faith in the informal decision-making processes of the police, due process adherents hold as sacred the formal decision-making guidelines of the system. In this way, informal decisions and their susceptibility to biases are avoided.

Critics of the Due Process Model sometimes argue that the model is little more than a liberal, apologist perspective on crime. This is not necessarily true. Instead, the Due Process Model stresses the importance of the individual citizen as it relates to coercive powers of the state. In Packer's words, "the combination of stigma and loss of liberty that is embodied in the end result of the criminal process is viewed as being the heaviest deprivation that government can inflict on the individual."[12] It is particularly necessary to protect the rights of individuals since governmental power is open to abuses and criminal justice penalties are coercive, restricting, and demeaning.

CRIME SCENE   DO NOT CROSS

CRIMINAL JUSTICE RESEARCH

ARE SOCIOLOGISTS TOUGH ON CRIME?

Sociology and criminal justice are sometimes viewed as competing enterprises where the former is a progressive discipline which stresses the importance of social forces, and the latter a more conservative endeavor that holds individuals responsible for their conduct. Put bluntly, sociologists have been criticized for being soft on crime. Ironically, some of the theoretical foundation of sociology touches on the raw emotions that are stirred by crime, punishment, and justice. Emile Durkheim, the patriarch of sociology, wrote at length about the fundamentally moral tensions and functions of crime and punishment and was by no means soft on crime.

In a masterful study, criminologist Bruce DiCristina explored the nuances and ironies in Durkheim's work on crime and punishment. Durkheim viewed crime as a violation of the communal moral order, which he referred to as the collective conscience. Punishment was needed to restore the collective conscience and sanction the offender for violating it. However, as societies evolved their criminal justice systems transformed from repressive to restitutive (as Durkheim described them), or from punitive to rehabilitative in common parlance. As societies became more liberal in their criminal justice ideology so did their assessment of criminal offenders. Criminals increasingly became objects of sympathy and compassion. As such, it became increasingly unpopular and difficult to punish them.

What about Durkheim's fundamental point? If punishment is required to protect the common good and force the criminal to expiate, are modern, "civilized" societies up to the task? That is debatable. However, as Professor DiCristina points out, an accurate reading of Durkheim suggests that the most compassionate people who are most committed to the collective conscience or community are also the most committed to meting out deserved punishment to criminals.

Source: DiCristina, B. (2000). Compassion can be cruel: Durkheim on sympathy and punishment. *Justice Quarterly, 17,* 485–517. Photo © JupiterImages, Corp.

BOX 1–4

The Due Process Model is driven by the presumption of innocence and the idea of legal guilt. The presumption of innocence assumes that criminal defendants or accused citizens are innocent of wrongdoing until the state proves otherwise. Legal guilt, different from substantive guilt, is a higher standard of guilt whereby the accused was proven to be guilty by the state in accordance with law and due process. What is the difference between legal guilt and substantive guilt? For example, O. J. Simpson was found not legally guilty of the two murders for which he was charged. Whether Simpson was in fact guilty of these crimes in the court of public opinion is a lively topic of discussion.

Because of its skeptical orientation and emphatic concern about the rights of the individual versus the state, the Due Process is commonly likened to a liberal and democratic perspective on criminal justice. For due process champions, the criminal justice system and the state itself are untrustworthy Goliaths that could potentially harm everyday citizens. In some respects, the sheer power of the criminal justice system (and therefore the state) is reason enough for due process advocates to fixate on the procedural safeguards inherent in American law.

CRIME CONTROL AND DUE PROCESS IN ACTION

Herbert Packer's work has enjoyed considerable staying power because the Crime Control and Due Process Models, as polar arguments, are brilliant exemplars of the potential ideological divide on criminal justice. However, perhaps with the exception of election periods when opposing viewpoints on social issues tend to become increasingly polarized, most people recognize that the criminal justice system actually combines elements of crime control and due process. For example, the amount of resources we invest in fighting crime, the considerable power of the police, and the growing size of the correctional population are some examples of an American criminal justice system feasting on the Crime Control Model. The volume of dismissed charges, watered down lengths of stay in prison, and the snail's pace with which the death penalty is used highlight a justice system based on due process. Thus, students should appreciate that criminal justice can be simultaneously crime control and due process, punitive and forgiving, conservative and liberal. In fact, the criminal justice system itself makes considerable effort to combine the best of the Crime Control and Due Process Models. The next section explores some of these recent integrative efforts.

Improving State and Local Criminal Justice Systems BJA Report

Nationwide, there are many examples of collaborative efforts to create a more effective and efficient criminal justice system. Former Attorney General Janet Reno tasked the American Bar Association's Information Program to identify ongoing collaborations between public defenders, prosecutors, and other criminal justice agencies. Seven models were discovered:

Criminal justice planning commissions bring a multi-agency perspective to criminal justice within a single jurisdiction and are based on the rationale that a stable and balanced working relationship between criminal justice entities best ensures justice. Criminal justice planning commissions are in place in California, Georgia, Kentucky, and Nebraska. Some of the more innovative projects include drug courts to filter non-violent drug offenders into treatment; the use of video and satellite technologies to serve various court appearances and thus save on travel and administrative costs; resource and pay equity between prosecutors and defense counsel; and expedited, super-efficient court proceedings called "Rocket Dockets."

Cooperation in programs receiving federal funds seeks to disperse federal monies on a more equitable basis to serve the interests of both the prosecution and defense counsel. Officials in California, Delaware, and Minnesota use this model to create a criminal justice system guided by a balance between crime control and due process.

Task forces exist in Nebraska, Oregon, and Washington to address the resource and administrative limitations of indigent defense programs. Some of the more creative task force proposals include making many minor misdemeanors bail forfeitable offenses, reclassifying minor misdemeanors as civil infractions, and reclassifying low level or unclassified felonies as gross misdemeanors.

Fill the Gap coalitions in Florida and Arizona informed legislators about the likely effects of proposed legislative initiatives on the criminal justice system. The coalition teams include representatives from state attorneys and state defenders associations, and the state attorney general. Because police and prisons tended to receive most dollars, the coalitions pushed for greater resource allocation to the courts and generally instructed policy makers about how the various elements of the criminal justice system meshed.

Joint prosecutor/public defender unions exist in some jurisdictions in California and Minnesota. The unions seek salary parity between prosecutors, a central figure in crime control, and public defenders—the central figure in due process. On one occasion in California, district attorneys threatened the county board of supervisors with a work stoppage if public defenders salaries were cut. Joint prosecutor/public defender unions are a symbolic example of how criminal justice systems can be committed to balance.

Cooperation in case tracking and criminal justice systems are underway in Delaware, Florida, and Rhode Island to centralize computerized records systems so that various criminal justice agencies have work together and share information to efficiently and effectively combat crime.

Fiscal impact statements exist to better link criminal justice systems with state legislative bodies. For example, in Maryland, the fiscal services' research arm of the general assembly is required to collect impact statements from agencies that would be affected by proposed bills concerning the justice system.[13]

Project Safe Neighborhoods: America's Network against Gun Violence

In 2001 President George W. Bush created Project Safe Neighborhoods (PSN), a comprehensive gun crime reduction strategy that combines the efforts of law enforcement, prosecutors, and community leaders. Through its five core elements—partnerships, strategic planning, training, outreach, and accountability—Project Safe Neighborhoods is committed to building multiagency partnerships with criminal justice, community, and the media that create a strong and lasting coalition so citizens will become agents of positive change in their own communities. Since its inception, PSN has received more than $2 billion in funding from the Bush and Obama Administrations.

Initiatives like PSN combine elements of crime control and due process while reaching the larger goal of community safety and social good. The results have been impressive. In the Southern District of Indiana (Indianapolis) there has been a 154% increase in gun crime prosecutions and a 61% increase in convictions resulting in a prison term of more than five years. Moreover, the homicide rate dropped 30%.

In the District of Massachusetts (Boston), there has been a 157% increase in gun crime prosecutions resulting in a 47% increase in convictions resulting in prison terms of more than five years. Most impressively, the violent crime rate in the district reached its lowest level in 31 years! The Western District of Tennessee (Memphis) experienced a whopping 407% increase in federal gun crime prosecutions with 58% of convictions resulting in prison terms of greater than five years. The homicide rate declined nearly 20% and the gun-related aggravated assault rate dropped by nearly 11%.[14]

Comprehensive Communities Program (CCP)

The Comprehensive Communities Program (CCP) is a nationwide crime prevention and crime control initiative established by the Bureau of Justice Assistance in 1994. The program aims to bring together those most affected by crime, give stakeholders a meaningful role in solving crime-related problems, and apply a deliberate implementation process through community policing and community mobilization. To date, fifteen jurisdictions have participated in the CCP and have generally enjoyed positive outcomes. For example, CCP neighborhoods in Baltimore, Denver, Fort Worth, Hartford, Salt Lake City, and Wichita have enjoyed 50% reductions in violent crime. Significant crime reductions have also occurred in the most at-risk neighborhoods in Atlanta, Columbia, District of Columbia, Oakland, and Seattle.[15]

The Innocence Project

Perhaps the most important initiative that combines elements of due process and crime control is The Innocence Project. Established by attorneys Barry

Scheck and Peter Neufeld in 1992, The Innocence Project is a non-profit legal clinic that handles cases where post-conviction DNA testing of evidence can yield conclusive proof of innocence. The mission of The Innocence Project is to:

- Achieve the exoneration and release of factually innocent inmates through post-conviction DNA testing.
- Create a network of schools, organizations, and citizens that will effectively address claims of actual innocence.
- Document and study the causes of wrongful convictions.
- Suggest and implement policies, practices, and legislation that will prevent wrongful convictions.
- Train and educate future attorneys and advocates.
- Provide information and educational opportunities for the public.

To date, The Innocence Project has exonerated 266 persons.[16] That people can be wrongfully convicted and imprisoned, even condemned, is calamitous for the criminal justice system. How can such miscarriages of justice occur? The Innocence Project has identified a variety of factors that contribute to wrongful convictions. In descending order of prevalence, these include mistaken identification, serology inclusion, police misconduct, prosecutorial misconduct, defective or fraudulent science, "bad lawyering," and microscopic hair comparison matches. In many ways, The Innocence Project is a quintessential example of a due process policy. This is true; however, the Project also serves crime control purposes. Although many persons have been exonerated by analysis of DNA evidence, numerous other inmates have had their guilt affirmed by DNA technology. Thus, programs like The Innocence Project and the use of DNA testing can serve as watchdogs of justice: exonerating the innocent and affirming the guilty.[17]

Recently, The Innocence Project mobilized efforts to create Innocence Commissions to monitor, investigate, and address errors in the criminal justice system (much like the National Transportation Safety Board, or NTSB, investigates public transportation disasters). Several states, including Connecticut and North Carolina, are moving toward creating innocence commissions. According to Barry Scheck and Peter Neufeld, a federal Innocence Commission should have the authority to 1) investigate any wrongdoing conviction and recommend policy reforms, 2) order reasonable and necessary investigative services including forensic testing or autopsies, and 3) subpoena documents, compel testimony, and bring civil actions against any person or entity that obstructs its investigations. Moreover, Scheck and Neufeld advised that Innocence Commissions should be protected so that findings and recommendations are not bound to subsequent civil or criminal proceedings and be publicly accountable like other criminal justice entities.[18]

BOX 1–5

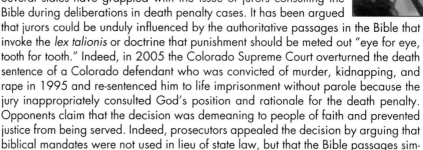

CRIME SCENE   DO NOT CROSS

CRIMINAL JUSTICE CONTROVERSY

THE UNCONSTITUTIONAL *LEX TALIONIS?*

Several states have grappled with the issue of jurors consulting the Bible during deliberations in death penalty cases. It has been argued that jurors could be unduly influenced by the authoritative passages in the Bible that invoke the *lex talionis* or doctrine that punishment should be meted out "eye for eye, tooth for tooth." Indeed, in 2005 the Colorado Supreme Court overturned the death sentence of a Colorado defendant who was convicted of murder, kidnapping, and rape in 1995 and re-sentenced him to life imprisonment without parole because the jury inappropriately consulted God's position and rationale for the death penalty. Opponents claim that the decision was demeaning to people of faith and prevented justice from being served. Indeed, prosecutors appealed the decision by arguing that biblical mandates were not used in lieu of state law, but that the Bible passages simply supplied the moral underpinning of the defendant's character and crimes. How might those from the Crime Control and Due Process Models debate this decision?

Photo © JupiterImages, Corp.

CHAPTER SUMMARY: BALANCING CRIME CONTROL AND DUE PROCESS

- People have grappled with the practical and philosophical issues related to justice (e.g., good and evil, rightful and wrongful conduct) throughout human history.
- Our timeless and perhaps innate interest in justice necessitates a balance between the rights and dignity of individuals and the coexistent powers of government.
- Systems of justice have evolved from informal to formal, personal/ private to impersonal/bureaucratic, and brutal to tempered.
- The pursuit of justice historically resulted in abuses of power, discrimination against classes of people, and resulted in subsequent reform.
- Two archetypal perspectives on criminal justice are the Crime Control Model (emphasis on combating crime) and Due Process Model (emphasis on preserving individual rights).
- Crime control is oriented toward strong police and state power.
- Due process is oriented toward both strong courts and checks and balances.
- Successful crime initiatives tend to combine elements of crime control and due process in their objectives.
- People have divergent viewpoints on justice which makes criminal justice such a controversial and vibrant area of study.

KEY TERMS

Classical   Informal social control
Code of Hammurabi   Justice
Common law   Law of the Twelve Tables
Conflict   *Lex talionis*
Consensus   Magna Carta
Crime   *Mala in se*
Crime control model   *Mala prohibita*
Criminal justice system   Natural law
Deuteronomy   Rehabilitative
Draco/Draconian   Repressive
Due process model   Restitutive
Exoneration   Retributive
Formal social control

TALKING POINTS

1. Why have societies tended to gravitate toward punitive, violent responses to crime? Does increasing civilization among current societies
   result in better or worse justice?

2. Is human conduct driven by natural law? What evidence can you
   provide?

3. If concepts such as natural law and human nature do in fact exist, do
   they help explain our fascination with criminal justice?

4. Look at the components of the Crime Control and Due Process Models.
   Which best typifies your views of criminal justice? Are you unilaterally
   in one camp? Or, do you support items from both perspectives?

WEB LINKS

American Bar Association Criminal Justice Section
(www.abanet.org/crimjust/)

American Civil Liberties Union
(www.aclu.org)

American Judicature Society
(www.ajs.org)

Bronx Defenders
(www.bronxdefenders.org/home/index.html)

Bureau of Justice Assistance
(www.ojp.usdoj.gov/BJA)

Bureau of Justice Assistance Clearinghouse
(www.ncjrs.org)

Office of Juvenile Justice and Delinquency Prevention
(www.ojjdp.ncjrs.org/)

Office for Victims of Crime
(www.ojp.usdoj.gov/ovc/)

Project Safe Neighborhoods
(www.psn.gov)

The Innocence Project
(www.innocenceproject.org)

FURTHER READING

Friedman, L. M. (1993). *Crime and punishment in American history*. New York: Basic Books. This is an outstanding socio-legal history of criminal justice throughout American history written by a distinguished legal scholar.

Garland, D. (2001). *The culture of control: Crime and social order in contemporary society*. Chicago: University of Chicago Press. This is a brilliant look at the roles that ideology, politics, and culture have in creating criminal justice policy, especially in the United States and United Kingdom.

Pinker, S. (2002). *The blank slate: The modern denial of human nature*. New York: Viking. Pinker, a distinguished professor of psychology, masterfully examines the politics and evidence pertaining to human nature, the nature versus nurture debate, and a variety of topics including crime and punishment.

Pound, R. (1954). *An introduction to the philosophy of law*. New Haven, CT: Yale University Press. Written by legendary legal scholar Roscoe Pound, this work explores the evolution of law from its philosophical roots. It is also relevant to history and philosophy courses.

Wilson, J. Q. (1997). *The moral sense*. New York: Free Press. Explores the classic and controversial argument that morality and thus our revulsion to crime are rooted in human nature. The author, a noted political scientist and moral philosopher, has enjoyed the greatest success at becoming a public intellectual on matters related to crime.

CHAPTER 2

The Raw Materials of Criminal Justice

CHAPTER OUTLINE

QUOTATIONS

"Something not very funny happened on the way to a formal system of justice. The victim got left out."—*William Doerner and Steven Lab*[1]

"That the sex variable in some form has not provided the starting point of all theories of criminal deviance has been the major failure of deviance theorizing in this century. In all, it appears to provide the single most powerful predictor of officially and unofficially known criminal deviance in this society and almost certainly in all others."—*Anthony Harris*[2]

"If sociological theorists of crime and delinquency were to use the 'clues' provided by known correlates of criminal behavior—in this instance, sex, race, and age group—as a basis for generating and modifying theory, theory and research might be able to advance more steadily."—*Michael Hindelang*[3]

INTRODUCTION

According to the most recent data collection, 13,636 people were the victims of murder or non-negligent manslaughter in 2009, for which 12,418 people were arrested.[4] Unless you were a criminologist or otherwise an avid reader of governmental publications on crime, it is unlikely that you would know this. Indeed, most people do not accurately quantify the crime problem. Consider the following example: Criminologists Margaret Vandiver and David Giacopassi administered questionnaires to 323 introductory students and 45 seniors majoring in criminal justice to determine how well they grasped the magnitude of the crime problem relative to other mortality conditions. They found that almost 50% of the introductory students estimated that 250,000 murders were committed annually in the United States. Fifteen percent of the students estimated that more than one million people were murdered each year.[5] For many reasons, perhaps most notably the extensive media focus on crime, students overestimated the likelihood of being murdered, but underestimated the prevalence of other causes of death that were less sensationalistic.

The purpose of the current chapter is to provide basic information about the "which, who, what, where, and how" of crime. Which behaviors constitute the most serious crimes? Who counts all of the crimes that occur in the United States? What are the assorted ways that crime is quantified? Where can you find crime-related statistics? How are crimes processed through the criminal justice system? Answers to these and other basic questions are provided.

To adequately understand criminal justice, it is crucial to understand the three essential players or components of the criminal justice process: criminals or offenders, crime victims (see Box 2-1), and the various agents of the criminal justice system, such as police. More dramatically, the sheer quantitative magnitude of the crime problem means that the criminal justice system cannot handle

BOX 2-1

CRIME SCENE   DO NOT CROSS

CRIMINAL JUSTICE NEWS

DON'T FORGET ABOUT THE VICTIMS OF CRIME

Due to the enormous attention that criminal offenders and criminal justice personnel receive, the other essential player in the crime picture, the victim, often is overlooked. Far from being disempowered, victims frequently turn the tables on criminal offenders and assist the criminal justice system. In March 2005, Ashley Smith was held captive for seven hours and ultimately convinced her abductor to surrender. The defendant, Brian Nichols, was on the run after killing four people while escaping from his trial on rape and other felony charges. Nichols was convicted of 54 serious charges and received multiple life sentences in prison without the possibility of parole. However, Ashley Smith received the most attention in this case because of the courage, strength, and cunning she showed in calming the escapee. For her efforts, Smith received more than $70,000 in reward money from the U.S. Marshals Office, FBI, Georgia Governor's Office, and various law enforcement associations in Georgia. Apparently, crime doesn't pay. Refusing to be a victim does.

Photo © JupiterImages, Corp.

all criminal cases. The state simply does not have the capacity or resources to process *all* crimes. Instead, cases are diverted or funneled through the criminal justice system for a variety of reasons that this book explores. In a way, the criminal justice system responds to crime similarly to the medical triage model: the most serious crimes get the most attention.

The imbalance between the volume of crime and the capacity of the criminal justice system to respond to crime necessitates that criminal justice personnel use their discretion in determining which crimes are most deserving of system resources. (For insights into the reality of crime, see Box 2-2.) In other words, at all points of the criminal justice system, personnel such as police, prosecutors, and detention staff must balance the objectives of crime control and due process in completing the course of their duties.

COUNTING CRIME

Uniform Crime Reports (UCR)

History and Scope of the UCR Program

For the first three decades of the 20th Century, the United States did not have a true systematic, nationwide policy on counting crime. Instead, crimes were recorded by individual police agencies across the country. In 1927, the International Association of Chiefs of Police (IACP) led efforts to create a national crime

BOX 2-2

CRIME SCENE   DO NOT CROSS

CRIMINAL JUSTICE RESEARCH

USING OFFENDER INTERVIEWS TO INFORM POLICE PROBLEM SOLVING

Criminologist Scott Decker has examined how tapping into the anti-social expertise of criminal offenders can yield payoffs as to how the criminal justice system combats crime. Funded by the U. S. Department of Justice, Decker's research produced a wealth of information about crimes, motives, and techniques among active criminals. First, most criminals are versatile in that they commit multifarious offenses. Drug offenders in particular are likely to commit violent, property, and drug crimes. Second, offending patterns follows peaks and valleys that are often unpredictable. Third, partying, status maintenance, group dynamics, and self-protection and retaliation are the primary motives for committing crimes. Few crimes are committed to meet rational economic needs such as rent. Fourth, lifestyle plays an important role in offending. Fifth, victimization is extremely high among offenders and often motivates further offending. In a certain sense, crimes can be understood as advances and retaliations between criminals/victims. Finally, offenders respond to specific criminal justice policies such as concentrated police stings. Otherwise, criminals are largely unfazed by the deterrent effects of the criminal justice system.

Source: Decker, S. H. (2005). *Using offender interviews to inform police problem solving.* Washington, DC: U. S. Department of Justice, Office of Community Oriented Policing Services. Photo © JupiterImages, Corp.

statistics initiative and formed the Committee on Uniform Crime Records. The Committee determined that the number of offenses known to law enforcement, whether or not there was an arrest, would be the most appropriate measure of the nation's criminality. From the beginning, the Committee realized that differences between state criminal codes precluded the mere aggregation of state statistics to arrive at a national total. Differences in state statutes also precluded accurate distinguishing between felony and misdemeanor crimes. To avoid these problems and to provide nationwide uniformity in crime reporting, the Committee formulated standardized offense definitions in which law enforcement agencies were to submit data without regard to local statutes.[6]

The Committee identified seven main offense classifications variously known as Part I crimes. Seven crimes were originally selected—murder and non-negligent manslaughter, forcible rape, robbery, aggravated assault, burglary, larceny-theft, and motor vehicle theft. In 1978, Congress mandated the collection of arson data and in 1982 directed the FBI to permanently count arson as a Part I offense. Part II offenses were less serious crimes and included 21 offenses, other assaults, forgery and counterfeiting, fraud, embezzlement, buying/receiving/possessing stolen property, vandalism, weapons carrying, prostitution and commercialized vice, sex offenses (other than forcible rape and prostitution), drug abuse violations, gambling, offenses against family and children, driving under the influence, liquor laws, drunkenness, disorderly conduct, vagrancy, "other" offenses, suspicion, curfew and loitering (applies to persons under age 18), and runaways (applies to persons under age 18).

Law enforcement agencies that participated in the UCR Program (it is voluntary) performed two important functions: classifying and scoring. Classifying is determining the proper crime category in which to report an offense to the UCR Program. Scoring is counting the number of offenses after they have been classified and entering the total count on the appropriate reporting form. The UCR Program relies on the hierarchy rule whereby only the highest offense in a multiple-offense situation is counted. The clearance rate refers to crimes known to the police that have been solved in the sense that a defendant has been arrested for the crime. Crimes cleared by exceptional means refer to cases where arrest is impossible, such as the death of the suspect, but police knew who had committed the crime.[7]

Congress enacted Title 28, Section 534, of the United States Code authorizing the Attorney General to gather crime information. The Attorney General charged the Federal Bureau of Investigation (FBI) with collecting the crime data from police departments, serving as the national crime data clearinghouse, and disseminating the crime information nationally. In September 1930, the UCR program began with 400 cities from 43 states participating in the data collection effort. By 2011, the UCR encompassed more than 17,000 law enforcement agencies that represented about 95% of the U. S. population. This data collection effort results in three annual publications, *Crime in the United States*, *Hate Crime Statistics*, and *Law Enforcement Officers Killed and Assaulted*. Additionally, the FBI publishes the *Preliminary Semiannual Uniform Crime Reports* and *Preliminary Annual Uniform Crime Reports*. The UCR data provide our basis for understanding the incidence of crime in the United States.

Over the years, the UCR Program has been revisited and improved to include more detailed information about the extent of the crime problem. There are several examples of the refinement of UCR data. In 1952, agencies began collecting data on the age, sex, and race of arrestees. In 1958, the FBI incorporated the concept of a national Crime Index, the total of six Part I offenses (excluding arson) and larceny over $50 to serve as the general indicator of criminality. The UCR was expanded in 1960 to collect statistics on law enforcement officers killed and again in 1962 to collect detailed information on homicide which constituted the Supplementary Homicide Report (SHR). In 1966, the National Sheriffs' Association (NSA) established a Committee on Uniform Crime Reporting to serve in an advisory capacity and to encourage county-level sheriffs throughout the country to fully participate in the program. The UCR program would continue to be revised in the 1980s, ultimately culminating in the National Incident-Based Reporting System (NIBRS) data collection program (described later in this chapter).

Definitions and Rates of UCR Index Offenses
Violent Part I Offenses
Murder and non-negligent manslaughter is the willful killing of one human being by another. As a general rule, any death caused as the result of an interpersonal fight, argument, quarrel, assault, or other crime is classified as murder and non-negligent manslaughter. Suicides, fetal deaths, traffic fatalities, accidental deaths, assaults to murder, and attempted murder are not classified as criminal homicides. Certain willful killings must be classified as justifiable or excusable. According to the UCR, justifiable homicide is the killing of a felon by a peace officer in the line of duty or the killing of a felon, during the commission of a felony, by a private citizen.

In legal parlance, first-degree murder refers to a homicide committed with premeditation, malice aforethought, intention, or one that is otherwise planned. It is the most serious crime. Second-degree murder typifies intentional but unplanned killings, such as a domestic killing during an intense argument (or "heat of passion"). Thankfully, murder is the rarest violent Index crime. The national murder rate is 5 murders per 100,000 in the population.[8]

Forcible rape is the carnal knowledge of a female forcibly and against her will. According to the UCR Handbook, carnal knowledge is the act of a man having sexual bodily connections with a woman or sexual intercourse involving penile penetration of the vagina. Other sexual-based offenses such as statutory rape, incest, rape by instrumentation, sodomy, or forcible fondling are not classified as forcible rape. Instead they are classified as assaults or other sex offenses. Because of its strict definition, males cannot be raped according to the UCR.[9] Forcible rape is about six times more prevalent than murder. According to the most recent data, the forcible rape rate was 28.7 per 100,000 females in the population.

Robbery is the taking or attempting to take anything of value from the care, custody, or control of a person or persons by force or threat of force or violence and/or by putting the victim in fear. Robbery is a vicious theft committed in the presence of the victim. Unlike thefts, robbery is aggravated by the element of force or threat of force. Because of the element or actual presence of force, robbery should always be considered a violent crime. The UCR delineates robbery in four ways depending on the means that the robbery was committed. In descending order of seriousness, robbery can be perpetrated with a firearm, knife or cutting instrument, other dangerous weapon, and strong-arm via hands or feet. Colloquialisms such as stickups, holdups, heists, muggings and related terms are robberies. The robbery rate is 133 per 100,000 in the population making it nearly 27 times more prevalent than murder.

Aggravated assault is an unlawful attack by one person upon another for the purpose of inflicting severe or aggravated bodily injury. This type of assault usually is accompanied by the use of a weapon or by means likely to produce death or serious bodily harm. Aggravated assault encompasses a variety of charges such as assault with intent to kill, assault with intent to murder, assault with a dangerous or deadly weapon, mayhem, maiming, and others. Reporting agencies must consider the seriousness of the injury incurred as the primary factor in establishing whether an assault is aggravated or simple. Generally speaking, injuries that require immediate medical care or hospitalization, such as broken bones or internal injuries, qualify an assault as aggravated. The aggravated assault rate is 263 per 100,000 rendering it nearly twice as prevalent as robbery.

Property Part I Offenses
Burglary is the unlawful entry into a structure to commit a felony or theft. The UCR Program classifies offenses locally known as burglary (any degree), unlawful entry, breaking and entering, housebreaking, safecracking, and attempts of these offenses as burglary. Persons who conceal themselves inside a building to commit felonies or theft and then exit the structure should also be described as burglars. Burglary is further classified by the means that entry occurs, such as forcible entry, unlawful entry without force, or attempted forcible entry. According to conventional wisdom, residential burglary is viewed as a more grievous offense than commercial or business burglary because of the potential that victims are home and could confront the burglar. In fact, about one third of burglaries target residences or dwellings during the day. The national burglary rate is 716 per 100,000 in the population.

Larceny-theft is the unlawful taking, carrying, leading, or riding away of property from the possession or constructive possession of another. Constructive possession is to exercise dominion or control over a thing. Larceny and theft have the same meaning and are used interchangeably. Larceny-theft encompasses many offenses such as stealing, pocket-picking, purse-snatching, shoplifting, and the like. Larceny-theft is the most prevalent crime in the United States, with a rate of 2, 061 per 100,000 inhabitants. The theft rate is 412 times greater than the murder rate!

Motor vehicle theft, defined as the theft or attempted theft of a motor vehicle (e.g., auto, truck, bus, or other vehicle), is a separate property Index offense. According to the most recent UCR, the motor vehicle theft rate is 259 per 100,000 in the population.

Arson is any willful or malicious burning or attempt to burn, with or without intent to fraud, a dwelling house, public building, motor vehicle or aircraft, personal property of another, etc. Arson is classified according to what was burned, such as structures, mobile units, or other property. Reporting agencies can only report arson or attempts to burn after an investigation has determined that the fire was willfully set. Fires of suspicious or unknown origin should not be reported as arsons. Arson is a unique crime. It is by far the least prevalent property crime. With a rate of 21.3 per 100,000, arson has approximately the same incidence as forcible rape. Additionally, arson is committed disproportionately by juvenile offenders. More than 47% of arsons are cleared by the arrest of a person under age eighteen.[10]

Part II Offenses

The UCR Program also collects data on 21 additional crimes. Part II offenses are considered less serious than Index crimes and are defined below.

Other assaults described as interpersonal attacks in which weapons are not used and the injuries incurred or minor. The following types of crimes should be classified as other assaults: simple or minor assault, assault and battery, stalking, intimidation, coercion, resisting or obstructing an officer, or hazing.

Forgery and counterfeiting is the altering, copying, or imitating of something without authority or right with the intent to deceive or defraud by passing the copy as an original. Forgery and counterfeiting are treated as allied offenses and include forging of public records, forging wills or other financial documents, and signing the name of another person or fictitious person with the intent to defraud.

Fraud is the intentional perversion of the truth for the purpose of inducing another person or other entity in reliance upon it to part with something of value or to surrender a legal right. According to the UCR Handbook, fraud involves either the offender receiving a benefit or the victim incurring a detriment. Both benefits and detriments can be tangible or intangible. Agencies should classify various acts such as passing bad checks (except forgeries), false pretenses, swindling, credit card /ATM/welfare/wire fraud, and impersonation as fraud.

Embezzlement is the unlawful misappropriation or misapplication by an offender to his or her own use or purpose of money, property, or some other thing of value entrusted to his or her control. Generally, the victims of embezzlement are businesses. Most people recognize embezzlement as "stealing from one's work or place of employment."

Buying, receiving, possessing, selling, concealing, or transporting any property with the knowledge that it has been unlawfully taken is classified as a stolen property violation. Many jurisdictions use the letters RSP as a catch-all for this violation, meaning receiving stolen property.

Vandalism is the willful or malicious destruction of property without the consent of the owner. Vandalism covers a wide range of malicious acts such as cutting tires, drawing obscene images on public restrooms, destroying school property, or defacing books.

The violations of laws prohibiting the manufacture, sale, purchase, transportation, possession, concealment, or use of firearms, cutting instruments, explosives, incendiary devices, or other deadly weapons is a weapons viola-tion. One of the most common weapons violations is carrying a concealed weapon (or CCW).

Prostitution and commercialized vice is the unlawful promotion of or par-ticipation in sexual activities for profit. To solicit customers or to transport persons for prostitution purposes; to own, manage, or operate a dwelling or other establishment for the purpose of prostitution; or to assist or otherwise promote prostitution is also illegal.

The generic sex offenses classification includes offenses against chas-tity, common decency, morals, and the like. Unlike forcible rape, which is defined as a male against female crime, sex offenses can include cases where males are the victim of sexual assault or abuse. The types of crimes that are viewed as sex offenses include adultery and fornication, buggery, seduction, sodomy or crime against nature, incest, indecent exposure, indecent liberties, and statutory rape.

Drug abuse violations include the unlawful possession, sale, use, growing, manufacturing, or making of any controlled drug or narcotic substance, such as marijuana, cocaine, heroin, morphine, methamphetamine, barbiturates, etc. The UCR specifies that agencies differentiate between drug violations involving mere possession or use and those involving manufacturing or sale. In this sense, a distinction is made between drug dealers and drug users.

Gambling violations include unlawfully betting or wagering money on something else of value; assisting, promoting, or operating a game of chance for money; possessing or transmitting wager information; or tampering with the outcome of a sporting event or contest to gain a gambling advantage. Reporting agencies divide gambling arrests into three categories: bookmaking (horse and sport book), numbers and lottery, and all other.

Offenses against the family and children are unlawful non-violent acts by a family member or legal guardian that threaten the physical, mental, or economic well-being or morals of another family member and that are not classifiable as other offenses, such as assault or sex offenses. These include non-violent cruelty or abuse; desertion, abandonment, or nonsupport of spouse or child; neglect; non-payments of alimony; or attempts to commit any of these acts.

Driving under the influence is operating a motor vehicle while mentally or physically impaired as the result of consuming an alcoholic beverage or using drugs/narcotics. Depending on jurisdiction, this offense is described as drunk driving (DUI, DWI, OWI, or OUI).

Four Part II offenses are commonly known as public-order or nuisance crimes that involve the public use of alcohol. These crimes frequently but not always are committed by transients. Liquor laws entail the violation of ordinances prohibiting the manufacture, sale, purchase, transportation, pos-session, or use of alcoholic beverages. Variants of liquor laws include boot-legging and the underage possession of alcohol. Drunkenness is to drink alcoholic beverages to the extent that one's mental faculties and physical coordination are substantially impaired. Disorderly conduct is any behavior that tends to disturb the peace or decorum, scandalize the community, or shock the public sense of morality. Vagrancy is the violation of a court order, regulation, ordinance, or law requiring the withdrawal of persons from the streets or other specified areas; prohibiting persons from remaining in an area of place in an idle or aimless manner; or prohibiting persons from going from place to place with visible means or support. Offenses included as vagrancy are begging, loitering, and vagabondage.

All violations of state or local laws that are not specifically identified as Part I or II offenses, except traffic violations, are termed other offenses. Some miscellaneous crimes in this category include blackmail and extortion, bribery, kidnapping, bigamy, trespassing, and the like.

Suspicion is an interesting thing. It is not a criminal offense; instead it is the grounds for many arrests in jurisdictions where the law permits. After law enforcement officers conduct an investigation, they either formally charge the prisoner with a crime or release him or her. Suspicion essentially facilitates law enforcement as they gather information to formally charge.

Finally, two Part II offenses pertain to juveniles or persons under the age of eighteen. Curfew and loitering laws are violations of specific ordinances that limit the times of night when youth should not be on the streets. Runaway is limited to juveniles taken into protective custody under local statutes. It is also known as "running away from home."[11]

Weaknesses of UCR Data

Over the years, a variety of criticisms of the UCR Program and official crime data generally have been levied. Some of these are that the UCR is voluntary and incomplete, omits many types of crime, and underestimates crimes because of its use of the hierarchy rule. In June 2004, it was recommended that the FBI discontinue the Crime Index and instead publish a violent crime total and property crime total. Over time, it was recognized that the Crime Index was not an accurate measure of the degree of criminality in a locality because larceny-theft comprised 60% of all crimes reported. Consequently, the volume of thefts overshadows more serious but less frequently committed crimes, such as murder or robbery.[12] For more information on the prevalence of crime, the arrest totals for all UCR offenses appear in Box 2-3.

NATIONAL INCIDENT-BASED REPORTING SYSTEM (NIBRS)

In the 1980s, the Bureau of Justice Statistics, the Department of Justice agency responsible for funding criminal justice information projects, initiated efforts to overhaul the UCR Program because of the limitations of its

CRIME SCENE   DO NOT CROSS

BOX 2-3

ARRESTS IN THE UNITED STATES

OFFENSE	NUMBER OF ARRESTS
Total	13,687,241
Murder and Non-negligent manslaughter	12,418
Forcible rape	21,407
Robbery	126,725
Aggravated assault	421,215
Burglary	299,351
Larceny-theft	1,334,933
Motor vehicle theft	81,797
Arson	12,204
Other assaults	1,319,458
Forgery and counterfeiting	85,844
Fraud	210,255
Embezzlement	17,920
Stolen property	105,303
Vandalism	270,439
Weapons	166,334
Prostitution and commercialized vice	71,355
Sex offenses	77,326
Drug abuse violations	1,663,582
Gambling	10,360
Offenses against family and children	114,564
Driving under the influence	1,440,409
Liquor laws	570,333
Drunkenness	594,300
Disorderly conduct	655,322
Vagrancy	33,388
All other offenses	3,764,672
Suspicion	1,975
Curfew and loitering law violations	112,593
Runaways	93,434

Source: Federal Bureau of Investigation. (2010). *Crime in the United States, 2009.* Washington, DC: U. S. Government Printing Office.

data. The Federal Bureau of Investigation awarded a contract to develop new offense definitions and data elements for the redesigned system. The goals were to revise the definitions of Index offenses, to identify additional significant offenses, to refine definitions of offenses, and to develop incident details for all UCR offenses. In short, the Department of Justice sought to create a national crime data collection effort that enhanced the quantity, quality, and timeliness of crime data and generally improved upon the methodology of the UCR. The result was the National Incident-Based Reporting System (NIBRS), which was introduced in 1989.

NIBRS has several advantages over the UCR Program. First, NIBRS contains incident- and victim-level analysis disaggregated to local jurisdictions and aggregated to intermediate levels of analysis. By comparison, the UCR was a summary-based system. Second, incident details the analysis of ancillary offenses and crime situations. By comparison, the UCR hierarchy rule counts only the most serious offenses. Third, NIBRS data permit separable individual, household, commercial, and business victimizations. Fourth, NIBRS offers data on incidents involving victims under age 12 (the NCVS only targets victims twelve and older). Fifth, NIBRS offers a broader range of offense categories. Sixth, NIBRS contains victimization information beyond which the NCVS provides. Seventh, NIBRS yields individual-level information about offenders from arrests records and victim reports and thus provides residual information on victims and offenders.[13]

As shown in Box 2-4, NIBRS contains 46 incidents in 22 categories for all incidents and eleven additional crimes for incidents that produce arrests. Although there is considerable overlap between the two crime data collection programs, NIBRS offers more information and, specifically, more contextual information about criminal events, as shown in Box 2-5. Since its modest beginning in 1989, more agencies are participating in the NIBRS program. For example, in 1991, 269 agencies participated in NIBRS covering a population of 4.1 million. By 1996, NIBRS participation increased to 1,082 agencies and covered about 15 million people. To date, 25 states participate in the NIBRS program with many other states in various stages of planning and development. This includes 5,271 law enforcement agencies and coverage of about 65 million people.[14]

Despite concerns about the quality of UCR data and the differences between the two programs, NIBRS and UCR data tend to paint the same picture about the incidence of crime in the United States. Ramona Rantala, a statistician with the Bureau of Justice Statistics, and Thomas Edwards, an FBI systems analyst, recently examined the effects of NIBRS on crime statistics. Overall, Rantala and Edwards found that when comparing data from the same year for the jurisdictions in this study, NIBRS rates differed only slightly from Summary UCR rates. Murder rates were the same. Rape, robbery, and aggravated assault rates were about 1% higher in NIBRS than UCR. The NIBRS burglary rate was a mere 0.5% lower than the UCR rate. Differences in theft were just 3.4% and motor vehicle thefts were just 4.5%. The convergence of NIBRS and UCR data suggests that both programs are worthwhile estimates of crime in the nation.[15]

CRIME SCENE   DO NOT CROSS

BOX 2-4

NIBRS OFFENSE CATEGORIES

GROUP A OFFENSES (REPORTED FOR ALL INCIDENTS)

1. Arson
2. Assault offenses (aggravated assault, simple assault, intimidation)
3. Bribery
4. Burglary
5. Counterfeiting/forgery
6. Vandalism
7. Drug/narcotics offenses (drug/narcotics violations, drug equipment violations)
8. Embezzlement
9. Extortion/blackmail
10. Fraud offenses (false pretenses/con game, credit card/ATM fraud, imperson-ation, welfare fraud, wire fraud)
11. Gambling offenses (illegal betting, operating illegal gambling, gambling equipment violations, sports tampering)
12. Homicide offenses (murder and non-negligent manslaughter, negligent man-slaughter, justifiable homicide)
13. Kidnapping/abduction
14. Larceny/theft offenses (pocket-picking, purse-snatching, shoplifting, theft from building, theft from coin-op machine, theft from motor vehicle, theft of vehicle parts/accessories, all other larceny)
15. Motor vehicle theft
16. Pornography/obscene material
17. Prostitution (prostitution, assisting/promoting prostitution)
18. Robbery
19. Forcible sex offenses (forcible rape, forcible sodomy, sexual assault with object, forcible fondling)
20. Non-forcible sex offense (incest, statutory rape)
21. Stolen property offense
22. Weapons law violations

GROUP B OFFENSES (REPORTED FOR INCIDENTS PRODUCING ARRESTS)

1. Bad checks
2. Curfew/loitering violations
3. Disorderly conduct
4. Driving under influence
5. Drunkenness
6. Family offenses, nonviolent
7. Liquor law violations
8. Peeping tom
9. Runaway
10. Trespass
11. All other offenses

Source: Rantala, R. R., & Edwards, T. J. (2000). *Effects of NIBRS on crime statistics, Special Report.* Washington, DC: U. S. Department of Justice, Office of Justice Programs, Bureau of Justice Statistics. *Photo © JupiterImages, Corp.*

BOX 2-5

CRIME SCENE   DO NOT CROSS

INFORMATION THAT NIBRS RECORDS ON EACH CRIME INCIDENT

ADMINISTRATIVE SEGMENT

ORI number
Incident number
Incident date/hour
Exceptional clearance indicator
Exceptional clearance date

OFFENSE SEGMENT

UCR offense code
Attempted/completed code
Alcohol/drug use by offender
Type of location
Number of premises entered
Method of entry
Type of criminal activity
Type of weapon/force used
Bias crime code

PROPERTY SEGMENT

Type of property loss
Property description
Property value
Recovery date
Number of stolen motor vehicles
Number of recovered motor vehicles
Suspected drug type
Estimated drug quantity
Drug measurement unit

OFFENDER SEGMENT

Offender number
Age of offender
Sex of offender
Race of offender

ARRESTEE SEGMENT

Arrestee number
Transaction number
Arrest date
Type of arrest
Multiple clearance indicator
UCR arrest offense code
Arrestee armed indicator
Age of arrestee
Sex of arrestee
Race of arrestee
    Ethnicity of arrestee
    Resident status of arrestee
Disposition of arrestee under 18

VICTIM SEGMENT

Victim number
Victim UCR offense code
Type of victim
Age of victim
Sex of victim
Race of victim
Ethnicity of victim
Resident status of victim
Homicide/assault circumstances
Justifiable homicide circumstances
Type of injury
Related offender number
Relationship of victim to offender

Source: Rantala, R. R., & Edwards, T. J. (2000). *Effects of NIBRS on crime statistics, Special Report.* Washington, DC: U.S. Department of Justice, Office of Justice Programs, Bureau of Justice Statistics.

NATIONAL CRIME VICTIMIZATION SURVEY (NCVS)

Perhaps the most damaging criticism of official measures of crime, such as the UCR and NIBRS, is that they omit crimes not reported to or discovered by the police. During the mid-1960s, criminologists such as Albert Biderman and Albert Reiss began to write about the "dark figure of crime," a term that describes the actual amount of crime that takes place but is impossible to detect because most crimes are neither reported to the police, nor result in arrest.[16] As part of President Lyndon Johnson's war on crime, The President's Commission of Law Enforcement and Administration of Justice conducted a pilot study of 10,000 households to assess the incidence of criminal victimization. The findings indicated that there was much more crime than the estimates produced by official data indicated. Inspired by these findings, the U. S. Bureau of the Census and the Bureau of Justice Statistics agency of the U. S. Department of Justice initiated the National Crime Survey (NCS) in 1972–1973. Now known as the National Crime Victimization Survey (NCVS), it is the victim's perspective on measuring crime.

The NCVS is a survey that obtains information about criminal victimizations and incidents from an ongoing, nationally representative sample of households in the United States. In 2009, 38,728 households and 68,665 people age 12 or older were interviewed. Nearly 92% of the eligible households participated in the NCVS.[17] The crimes measured by the NCVS are rape/sexual assault, robbery, aggravated assault, simple assault, and personal theft and constitute violent crimes. Murder is not included in the NCVS because it is impossible to interview murder victims, of course. Household burglary, theft, and motor vehicle theft constitute property crimes.

Of course, like any form of data, the NCVS has its limitations. By its very design, the NCVS does not measure the criminal victimization of persons younger than 12. Similarly, the NCVS is a survey, not a census, and thus is susceptible to sampling error. Finally, victims can inadvertently or intentionally report inaccurate information for a variety of reasons, such as embarrassment about being a crime victim, shame in hiding their own criminal activity, or simple misunderstanding of the definitions of various crimes.[18]

The Bureau of Justice Statistics has produced numerous reports based on NCVS data. In sum, the NCVS sheds further light on the quantity of crime and victimization occurring annually. Some of the highlights from these reports appear below.

- More than 20 million crimes occurred among U.S. residents age 12 and older.
- The violent crime rate was 17.1 victimizations per 1,000 persons age 12 or older; for property crimes it was 127.4 per 1,000 households.
- Males experienced 18.4 violent victimizations and females experienced 15.8 violent victimizations per 1,000 persons age 12 or older.

- African Americans experienced higher rates of violence (26.8 violent victimizations per 1,000 persons age 12 or older) than whites (15.8 violent victimizations per 1,000 persons age 12 or older).
- Strangers commit 55% of victimizations of males and 30% of victimizations of females.
- About 22% of all violent crime incidents involved an armed offender.
- Overall, 49% of violent and 40% of property victimizations were reported to police.[19]
- College students were the victims of nearly one half million violent crimes annually.
- Overall, college students have lower victimization rates than similarly aged non-students.[20]
- African Americans are six times more likely than Whites to be murdered and about eight times more likely to be murdered than other racial groups.[21]
- With a rate of 8.4 per 1,000 African Americans age 12 or older, blacks have a firearm victimization rate that is 40 percent higher than Hispanics and 200 percent greater than Whites.[22]

DO OFFICIAL AND VICTIMIZATION DATA MATCH?

Official measures of crime, such as the UCR and NIBRS, and victimization surveys, such as the NCVS, are most important in understanding the incidence of crime. To what degree do official and victimization data paint the same picture about the extent of crime in the United States? This is an important question. If official and victimization reports conflict widely, then we should have little confidence in our understanding about the true magnitude of crime (see Box 2-6). Moreover, there would be all the more reason to believe methodological criticisms of these methods. If official and victimization data converge, then we are likely measuring the crime problem with confidence, validity, and reliability.

Fortunately, official and victimization data match. For example, criminologists Janet Lauritsen and Robin Schaum recently compared UCR and NCVS data for robbery, burglary, and aggravated assault in Chicago, Los Angeles, and New York from 1980 to 1998. As the three largest cities in the country, this sampling method represents the bulk of crime that is committed in the United States. They found that for burglary and robbery, UCR crime rates were generally similar to NCVS estimates over the 18-year period. Police and victim survey data were more likely to show discrepancies in levels and trends of aggravated assault perhaps because of its susceptibility to domestic violence polices. Lauritsen and Schaum also found that even when UCR and NCVS data were different, the differences were not

CRIMINAL JUSTICE CONTROVERSY

What Is Controversial to Criminology May Be Irrelevant to Criminal Justice

Controversy has swirled around the validity of crime statistics since data collection began. Are crime statistics accurate, valid, reliable, or biased? In the academic criminology community, most of the controversy pertains to who is involved in crime. Official data like the UCR consistently show that youths, males, and racial minorities commit proportionately more crimes than older persons, females, and whites. Because official data are dependent on the discretionary decision making of police, it has been argued that certain groups, especially racial minorities, are discriminated against by law enforcement entities. If so, official crime estimates reflect these biased arrest processes.

Fortunately, it is relatively easy to examine the demographic correlates of crime (age, sex, and race) from various data sources to arrive at a triangulated answer. A variety of conclusions can be reached. First, official estimates of crime such as the UCR and NIBRS have been shown to be valid indicators of crime. In this sense, the correlates of crime that the data reflect are indeed the empirical correlates of crime. Second, victimization data such as the NCVS tend to match official estimates. This counters the claim that the police and official data generally discriminate against statistically high-crime groups such as youth, males, and minorities. Third, self-reports of crime still show significant differences by age, sex, and race for involvement in serious forms of crime, such as violent Index offenses.[35] In other words, crime data, whether measured by officials, victims, or self-reports, tell the same substantive story.[36] Fourth, there is almost universal understanding and acknowledgement that bias, most of it class-based, does exist in the criminal justice system. Consequently, it is naïve and simply incorrect to assert that justice is indeed blind to various social characteristics.[37] Fifth and concomitantly, most criminologists acknowledge the differential involvement hypothesis, which asserts that various groups (e.g., youths, males, minorities) are indeed disproportionately involved in criminal behavior. In other words, criminal justice system bias is far down on the list of reason why youths, males, and minorities disproportionately commit crime.[38]

When studying the correlates of crime, students should examine the empirical evidence and, of course, make of their own mind. Some classic and contemporary works on age[39], sex[40], race and ethnicity[41], and social class[42] are referenced here. Finally, while the correlates of crime are highly controversial to criminologists, they can be viewed as largely irrelevant to criminal justice practitioners. Suspects, arrestees, detainees, defendants, inmates, probationers, parolees, death row inmates, and the like *are processed by the criminal justice system for their legal status, not for their assorted demographic characteristics.* In other words, the statuses of murderer, murder victim, and material witness to the murder are infinitely more important to the criminal justice system than age, sex, race, and social class.

Photo © JupiterImages, Corp.

BOX 2-7

CRIME SCENE   DO NOT CROSS

CRIMINAL JUSTICE SPOTLIGHT

THE CRIME CLOCK

One violent crime occurs every 23.9 seconds
  One murder occurs every 34.5 minutes
  One forcible rape occurs every 6 minutes
  One robbery occurs every 1.3 minutes
  One aggravated assault occurs every 39.1 second
One property crime occurs every 3.4 seconds
  One burglary occurs every 14.3 seconds
  One larceny-theft occurs every 5 seconds
  One motor vehicle theft occurs every 39.7 seconds

Of course, crime does not occur at these regular intervals. The Crime Clock merely represents the annual ratio of crime and applies the data to fixed time intervals. Nevertheless, the Crime Clock does a great job of illustrating the sheer magnitude of the crime problem in the United States.

Source: Federal Bureau of Investigation. (2010). *Crime in the United States, 2009.* Washington, DC: U. S. Government Printing Office. *Photo © 2011, joingate, Shutterstock, Inc.*

statistically significant.[23] Substantively, the UCR and NCVS tell the same story about the magnitude of these three serious crimes in the nation's three biggest metropolitan areas. In fact, criminologists have examined the concurrent validity of official and victimization (and even self-reported) data for decades. With a few minor exceptions, researchers have found that official estimates like the UCR and victimization data like the NCVS are indeed measuring the same thing: the actual incidence or existence of crime.[24]

CRIMINAL JUSTICE STRUCTURE AND THE MAGNITUDE OF THE CRIME PROBLEM

The data presented in Box 2-7 and the schematic of the criminal justice system shown in Figure 2-1 convey two immensely powerful messages. First, there is a staggering amount of crime that occurs in the United States. If you were to boil the incidence of crime down to regular time intervals it would occur with frightening regularity. Indeed, as the Crime Clock shows, one violent crime occurs every 24 seconds and one property crime occurs every 3 seconds. Think of it this way: Your university criminal justice course lasts approximately one hour, which is 3,600 seconds. In the span of each and every one-hour criminal justice course that you take, 150 violent crimes and 1,200 property crimes occur!

What is the sequence of events in the criminal justice system?

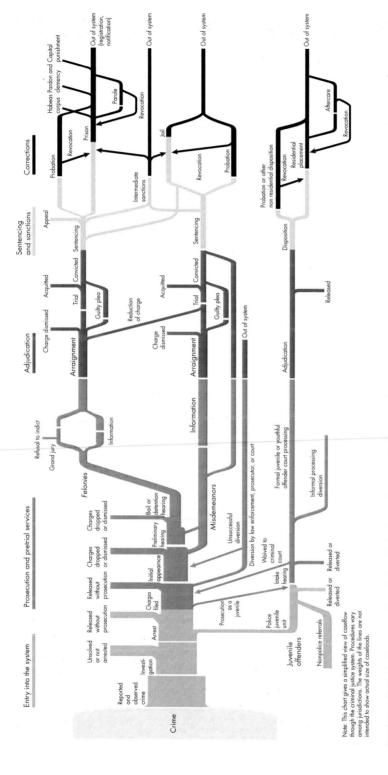

FIGURE 2-1 Schematic of the Criminal Justice System (Funnel)

Source: Adapted from The challenge of crime in a free society. President's Commission on Law Enforcement and Administration of Justice, 1967. This revision, a result of the Symposium on the 50th Anniversary of the President's Commission, was prepared by the Bureau of Justice Statistics in 1997.

Second, the criminal justice system has often been referred to as a funnel because cases are subjected to increasing levels of legal scrutiny as they pass from the possession of police to courts to corrections. As the UCR, NIBRS, and NCVS show, most crimes do not result in arrest because they never come to the attention of the police. The "dark figure" of crime is immense; the capacity of the criminal justice system is significantly more limited. Even if a crime is cleared by arrest, it does not mean that it will result in criminal punishment. There are many ways that a case can be ejected from the criminal justice system resulting in very few cases at the end of the criminal justice funnel. The next sections provide evidence for the sheer magnitude of the crime problem and the structural limitations and inabilities of the criminal justice system to address it.[25]

Federal Justice Statistics

Criminal justice often refers to local and state entities that combat crime across the country. Importantly, the United States has its own criminal justice system comprised of numerous federal agencies, such as the Federal Bureau of Investigation, the U. S. Marshals Service, the Drug Enforcement Administration, the Executive Office for the U. S. Attorneys, the Administrative Office of the U. S. Courts, the U. S. Sentencing Commission, and the Federal Bureau of Prisons. In one year, the federal criminal justice system investigated 124,335 persons for violations of federal law in which 124,074 were ultimately arrested. Of those arrested, 87,727 persons were actually prosecuted. In other words, U. S. Attorneys declined to prosecute more than one in four (27%) federal arrestees. Among those prosecuted, 71,798 were convicted and 53,682 were sentenced to prison. Of those originally investigated for federal violations, only 43 percent end in prison.[26] Although these data might seem unnerving, it is important to recognize that the federal criminal justice system is *tougher* than the various state-level criminal justice systems. As you will see, non-federal criminal justice is characterized by even more slack and leniency.

State Justice Statistics

Overall, similar funnel-like processes characterize state criminal justice systems. Thomas Cohen and Tracey Kyckelhahn, statisticians with the Bureau of Justice Statistics, examined the course of felony defendants in the 75 largest urban counties in the United States in a one-month period. Total arrests exceeded 58,100 of which 23% were violent felonies. Among the felony defendants, 60% are released on bond prior to their case reaching its ultimate disposition. Among the violent felonies, the conviction rate was a meager 50%. The conviction rate for misdemeanors and non-violent felonies was 68%. Almost all of these convictions are secured via guilty pleas. Among the serious violent felonies that result in conviction, 55% are sentenced to prison, 326% are sentenced to jail, and 18% are sentenced to probation.

The funnel-like nature of criminal justice becomes even clearer when you reduce these cases in scale. For instance, of 1,000 serious crimes, 500 go unreported and 500 are reported to the police. Of the remaining 500 cases, 400 are unsolved and 100 result in arrest. From the 100 remaining cases, 65 are adult cases in which 25 are dropped. Of the 35 cases that go to juvenile court, 30 of these result in summary probation or are dismissed. Only five juvenile cases will ultimately result in incarceration. Among the criminal cases (with an adult defendant), 30 go to trial and 10 defendants abscond on bail. Of the 30, 27 plead guilty, two are found guilty, and one is acquitted. Of the 29 guilty, 20 are ultimately incarcerated and nine are placed on probation.[27]

The volume of crime that goes unpunished can also be observed by simply analyzing data from successive stages of the criminal justice system. For example, recall that the FBI collects data on the percent of crimes cleared by arrest. Overall, these data tend to show that most crimes are not solved. The percent cleared by arrest for the Index crimes are relatively low: murder (61%), forcible rape (41%), robbery (25%), aggravated assault (54%), burglary (13%), motor vehicle theft (13%), larceny (17%), and arson (17%).[28] Moreover, the probability of being convicted and sentenced to incarceration, provided that a criminal is actually arrested, is similarly low. Just over 70% of murders, about 30% of rapes, 35% of robberies, 15% of assaults, and about 27% of burglaries result in imprisonment.[29] However, even imprisonment is adulterated or watered down. For example, the average sentence for violent convictions is 89 months of which only 43 months or 48 percent of the sentence is actually served. On average, murderers serve a meager 71 months of a 149-month sentence. Rapists serve 65 months of a 117-month sentence. Kidnappers serve 52 months of a 104-month sentence, and robbers serve 44 months of a 95-month sentence.[30]

CSI and the Iceberg of Unsolved Cases

The most popular show on television is *CSI: Crime Scene Investigation*. The show and its two spin-offs, *CSI: Miami* and *CSI: New York*, document the investigative role that forensic scientists and crime labs play in solving crimes. In addition to crime scene investigation, criminalists and crime laboratories perform a variety of important analytical responsibilities including ballistics, toolmark and footwear analysis, trace analysis, latent print analysis, fire debris, conventional serology, toxicology, and blood alcohol analysis. There are 389 publicly funded forensic crime labs in the Unites States that employ about 12,000 full-time employees. The typical lab has two managers, two secretaries, 12 analysts, two technicians, and a median budget of $1.3 million. On average, a crime lab begins the year with a backlog of 390 requests. Overall, labs outsource nearly 240,000 requests for forensic services to private laboratories. Criminologists Joseph Peterson and Matthew Hickman estimated that 1,900 additional full-time employees costing more than $70 million would be needed to achieve a 30-day turnaround for all forensic requests. Moreover, about 75% of the labs indicated that additional technological and equipment resources with estimated costs of $500 million would be needed to achieve the 30-day turnaround.[31]

However, unlike the television programs which operate with exceptional speed and finality (quintessential crime-control characteristics), real criminal justice forensics move much slower. For example, at the beginning of 2001, 81% of DNA crime laboratories had backlogs totaling 16,081 subject cases and 265,329 convicted offender samples. To complete DNA case and convicted offender sample analyses, 45% of crime labs contracted with private laboratories which in turn had a backlog of 918 subject cases and 100,706 convicted offender samples.[32]

The backlog of unsolved cases presents a host of problems that compromise criminal justice. For example, the National Institute of Justice appropriated funds to the Miami-Dade Police Department, Palm Beach County Sheriff's Office, and New York City Police Department to analyze DNA evidence from property crimes. They have found that using DNA evidence to solve seemingly minor property crimes often nets arrests for more serious violent crimes. In New York, DNA from murder crime scenes often matches DNA from non-related burglary scenes. The state's first 1,000 checks of DNA records showed that the vast majority of defendants were linked to other crimes. Indeed, 82 percent of persons involved in murder or rape were already in the Combined DNA Index System (CODIS) for property crimes like burglary. In Miami-Dade, 526 no-suspect DNA profiles produced 271 hits and in Palm Beach 229 profiles produced 91 hits. Of the 362 Florida CODIS hits, 56 percent came from evidence collected at burglary scenes.[33]

Fortunately, the national backlog of unsolved cases and the potential of forensic technology to solve crimes are increasingly being noticed by the criminological research community. Criminologists at Washington State University recently conducted a nationally representative survey of law enforcement agencies to examine the number of unsolved cases and barriers associated with case processing. They produced four major findings. First, the backlog of unsolved homicides, rapes, and burglaries with possible biological evidence is massive, about 700,000 cases. Second, nearly 25% of law enforcement agencies do not send DNA evidence to labs because they do not have a suspect. These are exactly the kinds of scenarios where the existing offender DNA database (CODIS) is most useful. Third, crime laboratories are overworked, understaffed, and insufficiently funded. This contributes to their inefficiency and law enforcement's reluctance to explore forensic angles to solving crimes. Pratt and his colleagues' corroborate the conclusions of the Bureau of Justice Statistics reports, which also found that crime labs are overburdened and saddled with case backlogs. Finally, the major policy implication from their study is that the federal government could play a larger role in reducing the national backlog of cases.[34]

CHAPTER SUMMARY: BALANCING CRIME CONTROL AND DUE PROCESS

- The volume of crime far exceeds the capacity of the criminal justice system.
- Most crimes go undetected, unsolved, and without notice of the criminal justice system.
- The UCR Program is the most venerable and validated source of crime data and provides the most coverage.
- The NIBRS program provides more contextual information about crimes and encompasses more offenses than the UCR.
- The NCVS is a nationally representative sample of 76,000 households of crime victims 12 and older and includes much information about crimes, criminal offenders, and crime victims.
- All sources of crime data, official, victimization, and self-report, have various strengths and weaknesses relating to coverage, validity, and reliability.
- According to all sources of data, youths, males, and non-whites disproportionately commit crime.
- Throughout the criminal justice process, cases exit the system for a variety of reasons. For this reason, criminal justice has been likened to a funnel.
- Most crimes are not cleared by arrest, for example nearly 40 percent of murders are not cleared or solved.
- Federal and state criminal justice systems ultimately punish a fraction of those initially investigated and arrested.
- Hundreds of thousands of serious unsolved crimes are backlogged annually.

KEY TERMS

Aggravated assault
Arson
Burglary
Dark figure of crime
Discretion
Forcible rape
Hierarchy Rule
Index Crimes
Larceny-theft

Motor vehicle theft
Murder and non-negligent
   manslaughter
National Crime Victimization
Survey
National Incident-Based Reporting
System
Robbery
Uniform Crime Reports

TALKING POINTS

1. What is the substantive significance of official, victimization, and self-report data producing the same correlates of crime?
2. How might strict crime control and due process advocates debate the various measures of crime?
3. Does the criminal justice system do an effective job at processing the appropriate criminals and crimes? Should certain criminal offenses be punished more harshly? Should others be treated more leniently?
4. How can shows, such as *CSI: Crime Scene Investigation*, actually help applied criminal justice?

WEB LINKS

Association of State Uniform Crime Reporting Programs
(www.asucrp.org)

Bureau of Justice Statistics
(www.ojp.usdoj.gov/bjs)

Combined DNA Index System
(www.fbi.gov/hq/lab/codis/index1.htm)

FBI Uniform Crime Reports
(www.fbi.gov/ucr.htm)

Justice Information Center
(www.ncjrs.org)

National Crime Victimization Survey
(www.ojp.usdoj.gov/bjs/cvict.htm)

National Incident-Based Reporting System
(www.ojp.usdoj.gov/bjs/nibrs.htm)

National Institute of Corrections
(www.nicic.org)

NIBRS Frequently Asked Questions
(www.fbi.gov/ucr/nibrs/faqs.htm)

Office for the Victims of Crime
(www.ovc.gov)

Office of Community Oriented Policing Services
(www.cops.usdoj.gov)

Office of Juvenile Justice and Delinquency Prevention
(www.ojjdp.ncjrs.org)

President's DNA Initiative
(www.dna.gov)

FURTHER READING

Note: Official statistics are traditionally criticized for ignoring "other" types
of crimes such as hate crime, organized crime, terrorism, etc. To the contrary, various entities within the U. S. Department of Justice have collected
data on these "other" crimes, producing reports and disseminating information for years. These can be accessed at: http://www.fbi.gov/stats-services/
publications.

CHAPTER 3
Substantive Criminal Law

CHAPTER OUTLINE

QUOTATIONS

"Even a sleeping dog distinguishes between being stumbled over and being kicked."—*Oliver Wendall Holmes, Jr.*[1]

"Law should be like death, which spares no one."—*Montesquieu*[2]

"No written law has ever been more binding than unwritten custom supported by popular opinion."—*Carrie Chapman Catt*[3]

"Throughout the history of mankind there have been murderers and tyrants; and while it may seem momentarily that they have the upper hand, they have always fallen. Always."—*Gandhi*[4]

"Laws are always useful to those who have possessions, and harmful to those who have nothing."—*Jean Jacques Rousseau*[5]

"Who thinks the law has anything to do with justice? It's what we have because we can't have justice."—*William McIlvaney*[6]

INTRODUCTION

The Mission of the American Bar Association (ABA) is to be the national representative of the legal profession, serving the public and the profession by promoting justice, professional excellence, and respect for the law. The ABA has eleven organizational goals:

- To promote improvements in the American system of justice.
- To promote meaningful access to legal representation and the American system of justice for all persons regardless of their economic or social condition.
- To provide ongoing leadership in improving the law to serve the changing needs of society.
- To increase public understanding of and respect for the law, the legal process, and the role of the legal profession.
- To achieve the highest standards of professionalism, competence, and ethical conduct.
- To serve as the national representative of the legal profession.
- To provide benefits, programs and services which promote professional growth and enhance the quality of life of its members.
- To advance the rule of law in the world.
- To promote full and equal participation in the legal profession by minorities, women, and persons with disabilities.
- To preserve and enhance the ideals of the legal profession as a common calling and its dedication to public service.
- To preserve the independence of the legal profession and the judiciary as fundamental to a free society.

Founded in 1878, the American Bar Association, with a membership exceeding 400,000, is the world's largest voluntary legal professional association.[7] Its goals reflect the importance of law to all citizens and indeed the importance of law for the maintenance of a functioning society. Of course, this has been the case long before the founding of the ABA.

Laws are the codified rules of society. In essence, legal statutes are a listing of behaviors that are proscribed or illegal. Law books contain not only crimes but also their punishments. Importantly, the values, beliefs, ideas, ideals, and norms of a society or culture are imbued in law. Recalling Chapter 1 and its exploration of justice, law is the written form of a society's views about justice, behavior, and limits on that behavior. This chapter explores the sources of American criminal law, legal classifications of crimes, the elements of crime, and the various ways in which the law limits the state or defends the individual from criminal prosecution.

HISTORICAL SOURCES OF CRIMINAL LAW

English Common Law

As shown in Chapter 1, the ideas of justice and law have existed immemorially. The roots of American law can be traced to the magisterial Magna Carta and the Enlightenment ideas of Beccaria and Bentham, which framed human behavior as rational, the outcome of free will, and responsive to punishment or deterrence. However, because the United States was once a colony of England, it owes its greatest debt to England and its legal traditions. The most comprehensive of these traditions is common law. Common law refers to the unwritten, traditional rules of conduct that are borne from everyday norms, usage, customs, and behaviors. In this sense, common law typifies the somewhat innate sense of justice, right-and-wrong, lawfulness and unlawfulness that we possess. Importantly, common law helped sway judicial decision making in English courts.

Statutory Law

Of course, a system of law is comprised of more than the somewhat diffuse common law. Statutory law, or simply law, is the official law of the land, the written or codified laws created by legislatures. Laws do many things and serve many functions, including the maintenance of social order, the enforcement of moral beliefs, the promotion of order, and the regulation of human interaction and behavior. Laws also showcase the separation of powers of American government. Laws are created by the legislative branch, enforced by the executive branch, and interpreted by the judicial branch.

Case Law and the Law of Precedent

Law is also built upon case law, the body of judicial precedent. Case law accumulates historically based on the legal reasoning, interpretations of the law, and outcomes of court decisions of statutory law. Case law serves as a guide or heuristic to future court decisions. The use of legal precedents is important because it ensures that previous judicial decisions are consistently and authoritatively used to decide future cases. Often referred to as the principle *stare decisis*, Latin for "standing by decided manners," the use of legal precedence guards against the arbitrary, inconsistent, erratic, and unfair enforcement of the law.

Procedural Law

All of these parts of law that define crimes and specify punishments are referred to as substantive criminal law. Procedural law refers to the methods used in enforcing substantive law. In other words, procedural law describes how the various elements of the criminal justice system must act when performing their duties. The United States Constitution contains some of the paramount verbiage about procedural law. For example, the Fourth Amendment limits the powers of the police to obtain evidence from suspects. *The right of the people to be secure in their persons, houses, papers, and effects, against unreasonable searches and seizures, shall not be violated, and no warrants shall issue, but upon probable cause, supported by oath or affirmation, and particularly describing the place to be searched, and the persons or things to be seized.*

The Fifth Amendment limits the powers of police and prosecutorial powers. *No person shall be held to answer for a capital, or otherwise infamous crime, unless on a presentment or indictment of a grand jury, except in cases arising in the land or naval forces, or in the militia, when in actual service in time of war or public danger; nor shall any person be subject for the same offense to be twice put in jeopardy of life or limb; nor shall be compelled in any criminal case to be a witness against himself, nor be deprived of life, liberty, or property, without due process of law; nor shall private property be taken for public use, without just compensation.*

The Sixth Amendment outlines procedural guidelines for the courts. *In all criminal prosecutions, the accused shall enjoy the right to a speedy and public trial, by an impartial jury of the state and district wherein the crime shall have been committed, which district shall have been previously ascertained by law, and to be informed of the nature and cause of the accusation; to be confronted with the witnesses against him; to have compulsory process for obtaining witnesses in his favor, and to have the assistance of counsel for his defense.*

The Eighth Amendment places procedural limits during the pretrial phase (e.g., bail) and punishment phase. *Excessive bail shall not be required, nor excessive fines imposed, nor cruel and unusual punishments inflicted.*

The United States Constitution and Limits on Criminal Law

The United States Constitution is the ultimate or supreme law of the land. All laws passed by legislative bodies, and indeed all state-level constitutions, must be in accord with the U. S. Constitution, otherwise they are invalid or unconstitutional. The process of judicial review is a constitutional doctrine that gives to a court system the power to annul legislative or executive acts that the judges declare to be unconstitutional.[8]

In addition to judicial review, assorted articles and amendments to the United States Constitution contain clauses that place limits on criminal laws. Additionally, there are other rights or doctrines that although not clearly de-lineated in the U. S. Constitution are inferred from the language therein. For example, the ex-post facto clause (Article I, Section 9, Clause 3 and Article I, Section 10, Clause 1) bans the creation of retroactive criminal laws. In other words, persons cannot be punished for actions committed before the law pro-hibiting the behavior was passed. Laws must follow due process (Article III, Section 2, Clause 3, also see Fifth Amendment) and provide equal protection under the law to all groups (Fourteenth Amendment).[9]

Generally, law is guided by the principles of rationality, justice, and fair-ness. Laws must be made public before they can be enforced. They must clearly define the criminal behavior in question (void-for-vagueness doctrine) and not at the same time prohibit legal conduct (void-for-overbreadth doctrine). The goals of the criminal law and the U. S. Constitution are clearly presented in the preamble. *We the People of the United States, in Order to form a more perfect Union, establish Justice, insure domestic Tranquility, provide for the common defence (sic), promote the general Welfare, and secure the Blessings of Liberty to ourselves and our Posterity, do ordain and establish this Constitution for the United States of America.*[10] Reading between the lines, the purpose of law is to strike a balance between crime control and due process.

CLASSIFICATION OF CRIMES

Imagine that a new neighbor moves in next door to you. During the course of introducing yourself, you learn that he had just been released from prison and was "beginning life anew" next door to your home. How do you feel about this? Probably, you wonder about the underlying criminal offense. Was your neighbor incarcerated for murder? Rape? Kidnapping? Forgery? Fraud? Income tax evasion? Child molestation? Habitual traffic offender?

Mala in se and *Mala prohibita*

The above example demonstrates that there are gradations or degrees of wrongfulness inherent in criminal behavior. Some offenses are seen as always

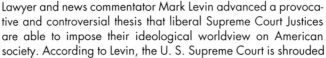

CRIME SCENE   DO NOT CROSS

CRIMINAL JUSTICE NEWS

IS THE SUPREME COURT DESTROYING AMERICA?

Lawyer and news commentator Mark Levin advanced a provocative and controversial thesis that liberal Supreme Court Justices are able to impose their ideological worldview on American society. According to Levin, the U. S. Supreme Court is shrouded in mystery and unchecked by the other branches of government. This renders the judiciary a more powerful entity than the executive branch (President) and the legislative branch (Congress). Unlike conservative justices who tend to be originalists, or persons who strictly conform the law to the expressed language of the Constitution, liberal justices employ great latitude in offering multiple interpretations of what the Constitution means and conform their decisions subjectively, inconsistently, and, according to Levin, tyrannically. *Men in Black* posits that in their majority decisions and dissenting briefs, justices drop seemingly insignificant phrases and words that will be invoked in future decisions. To wit, the Supreme Court has meddled in a variety of areas, including elections and fighting terrorism, not prescribed by the Constitution.

Men in Black is a national bestseller and one of the most talked-about books of 2005; however, its central idea is not new. Indeed, Levin quotes a letter written by Thomas Jefferson in 1825: "This member of the Government was at first considered as the most harmless and helpless of all its organs. But it has proved that the power of declaring what the law is . . . by sapping and mining slyly and without alarm the foundation of the Constitution, can do what open force would not dare to attempt."

Source: Levin, M. R. (2005). *Men in black: How the Supreme Court is destroying America.* Washington, DC: Regnery, p. 23. *Photo © JupiterImages, Corp.*

wrong, even evil. Other crimes are viewed as wrong but not necessarily grave. In other words, if your neighbor had committed certain offenses, you'd want him immediately to leave the neighborhood. Other crimes are viewed as less troubling. Crimes that are seen as intrinsically evil, wrong, and immoral are known as *mala in se* offenses. Acts such as murder, rape, or child molestation are wholly wrong and considered reprehensible. Persons who commit *mala in se* offenses elicit anger, fear, and revulsion. *Mala in se* offenses are punished by condemnation or death, precisely because they are so incontrovertible bad.

Although illegal, other crimes known as *mala prohibita* offenses are wrong by legislation, not by their nature. For example, most people would not be overly alarmed to find out that their neighbor had spent time in jail upon conviction for disorderly conduct or public intoxication. The criminal law necessarily prohibits these acts to maintain public order; however, disorderly conduct does not shock our moral sentiments and elicit outrage or great punishment. Compared to *mala in se* offenses, *mala prohibita* offenses are relatively benign and simply illegal.

Felony

Aside from their moral definition, crimes are defined according to their legal value. Felonies are serious crimes punishable by death or incarceration in a prison facility usually for at least one year. Although there is considerable variation across legal jurisdictions in the ways that crimes are classified, felonies are less subject to this discretion. Crimes such as murder, rape, robbery, aggravated assault, and the like are nearly always felonies. Although the sanctions for felonies are serious, the range of punishments is wide. Felonies are punishable by probation, fines, jail confinement, or a combination of these penalties. Felonies are graded or ranked in terms of their seriousness. For example, 1st degree murder is typically classified as a Class 1 or Class A Felony.

Misdemeanor

Misdemeanors are relatively minor crimes, such as shoplifting, that are typically punished by fines, community service, or deferred sentences in which the conviction is expunged if the defendant remains crime-free for a specified period of time. Misdemeanors can result in confinement, albeit in local jails, for usually no more than one year. Misdemeanors do not result in prison sentences. Like felonies, misdemeanors are graded or classified according to their seriousness, such as Aggravated Misdemeanor, Class 1 Misdemeanor, etc.

Petty

Petty offenses include very minor violations of the criminal law that are punishable by a ticket or summons. Petty offenses are sometimes described as offenses, infractions, or municipal violations. Behaviors such as jaywalking and loitering are often petty offenses.

Traffic

Traffic offenses also constitute violations of the criminal law. Of course, most violations of traffic code are not viewed as "crimes" per se. As many of you know, offenses such as speeding, driving without insurance, and failing to use a traffic signal can result in tickets and fines. Traffic violations are sometimes referred to as penumbral crimes. Penumbral crimes are acts characterized by a high level of noncompliance, little to no social stigma, and low level of police enforcement. Like all crimes, there are gradations of traffic crimes. At the most extreme, traffic offenses such as vehicular homicide under the influence are serious felonies

BOX 3-2

CRIME SCENE   DO NOT CROSS

CRIMINAL JUSTICE SPOTLIGHT

WHAT IS THE SINGULAR AMERICAN LAW?

There is considerable variation in state legal codes because law is a reflection of the values, beliefs, and norms of the community. Given the diversity of the United States, it should be expected that laws are not the same across jurisdictions. However, for all intents and purposes, there is a unified American law: The American Law Institute's Model Penal Code. Since its inception in 1962, the purpose of the Model Penal Code was to stimulate and assist legislatures in making a major effort to appraise the content of the penal law by a contemporary reasoned judgment—the prohibitions it lays down, the excuses it admits, the sanctions it employs, and the range of the authority that it distributes and confers. Since its promulgation, the Code has played an important part in the widespread revision and codification of the substantive criminal law of the United States. Indeed, 34 states reorganized their statutes according to the Model Penal Code and at least 8 other states are in the process of conforming their statues to the Model Penal Code.

Source: Robinson, P. H., & Dubber, M. D. (2004). An introduction to the Model Penal Code of the American Law Institute, Accessed February 25, 2011, from http://ssrn.com/abstract=661165. Photo © 2011, joingate, Shutterstock, Inc.

THE ELEMENTS OF CRIME (*CORPUS DELICTI*)

Criminal law contains the acts that are proscribed by society. These bad acts, called crimes, vary in their degree of seriousness. For the state to prove that a person did indeed commit a crime, they must show that he or she not only engaged in a guilty act but also intended to do so. This section describes the elements of crime or *corpus delicti* which is comprised of three factors, 1) *actus reas*, 2) *mens rea*, and 3) the concurrence of *actus reas* and *mens rea*.[11]

Actus Reus

Actus reus is the requirement that, for an act to be considered criminal, the individual must have committed an overt act that resulted in harm or failed to act when legally required. The action or omission must be voluntary and purposeful, not accidental. The *actus reus* or guilty act can encompass a variety of behaviors, such as possessing drugs, stealing money, damaging property, or punching another person.

Sometimes guilty acts are not consummated, but this does not mean that these acts were not crimes. Inchoate offenses consist of conduct that is a step toward the intended commission of another offense. Also known as anticipatory offenses, inchoate crimes include offenses such as criminal attempts, conspiracy, complicity, and accessory. Criminal attempts are acts or omitted acts that constitute a substantial step toward the culmination of a criminal act. Conspiracy is an agreement between two or more people to commit a specified crime. Upon acting in furtherance of the conspiracy, even if it entails legitimate acts such as meeting, persons are guilty of conspiracy. Complicity is any conduct on the part of a person other than the primary actor in the commission of a crime, by which that person intentionally or knowingly serves to further the intent to commit the crime; aids in the commission of the crime; or assists the person who has committed the crime to avoid prosecution or escape from justice. The person who helps another to commit a crime is known as an accomplice. The actual perpetrator of the crime is known as the principal or principal defendant. In some jurisdictions, persons who aid the perpetrator of an offense are called accessories. Inchoate crimes carry less severe penalties than completed criminal acts.

Mens Rea

The second element of a crime is the mental state of the offender when the act is committed. *Mens rea* or guilty mind refers to the intent that exists in the mind and actions of the offender when he or she offends. Thus, purposely elbowing a person in the face because you want to hurt that person is assault. Inadvertently elbowing a person in the face during a game of basketball is a mistake or accident, not a crime. Although the actions in these two scenarios are the same, the intent of the person throwing the elbow is different. The distinction renders one a crime and the other, a foul!

Of course, ascertaining the intent to commit a crime is difficult because *mens rea* refers to a subjective condition or state of mind. Fortunately, the Model Penal Code has delineated four states of mind that inform *mens rea*. In descending order of mental fault, these are purposely, knowingly, recklessly, and negligently.

"Purposely" describes the state of mind used when acting with conscious desire to cause a certain result, such as criminal injury or harm. In common parlance, this state of mind is referred to as premeditation or having malice aforethought. "Knowingly" describes the state of mind when acting with an awareness that something will likely occur. "Recklessly" describes the state of mind when acting with a conscious disregard of a substantial risk of injury or harm. "Negligently," sometimes referred to as vicarious liability, describes the state of mind when engaging in conduct that the actor should have known would cause harm or injury. In all of these circumstances, the courts make inferences about a defendant's state of mind based on his or her conduct.[12]

Importantly, there is a fifth "state of mind" where criminal liability may be imposed without the defendant having *mens rea*. Certain behaviors fall within a category known as absolute liability, strict liability, or, sometimes, public safety liability crimes. In these circumstances, only the criminal act or *actus reus* matters, *mens rea* is irrelevant. Thus, anyone who commits a strict liability crime, regardless of intent, can be found guilty. Examples of strict liability crimes include many traffic violations such as speeding, health and safety regulations, and other regulatory statutes.

Various sub-definitions of intent are employed in the criminal courts. General intent requires that the defendant intended to perform the criminal act. No additional intention or purpose must be reached. Assault is usually a general intent crime because the intent is to merely assault, not inflict some particular result or injury. Specific intent means that the prosecution must prove that the defendant had a requisite intent or purpose that is explicit in the statute books when committing a crime. Theft is a specific intent crime because it expresses that the perpetrator intended to permanently deprive the owner/victim of his or her possession. Constructive intent describes the situation where a person intends to commit an illegal act but, during the course of the crime's commission, injures an unintended victim. This is also known as transfer of intent.

Concurrence of *Actus Reus* and *Mens Rea*

The criminal act (*actus reus*) and criminal intent (*mens rea*) do not simply exist independently in time and space. They must coincide to constitute the *corpus delicti*. In other words, the intent to do criminal harm must immediately result in the criminal action to inflict that harm. The coexistence of the violation of law and accompanying culpable mental state is referred to as concurrence.

Additional Features of Crime

At minimum, a crime (*corpus delicti*) is comprised of the above three elements. However, some legal scholars contend that there are additional elemental characteristics that must be considered when describing the features of a crime. These are 1) causation, 2) harm, 3) legality, 4) punishment, and 5) necessary attendant circumstances. To some, causation is implied in the concurrence of *mens rea* and *actus reus*. However, the logical and temporal ordering of crimes is not always easy to establish. For example, an aggravated assault victim might, over a period of weeks or months, die from her injuries. The result, perhaps a charge of manslaughter or murder, was caused much earlier.

Legal causation refers to the legally recognizable cause of a criminal harm. Harm refers to the victim of a criminal act. Harm can be inflicted on tangible victims and seemingly victimless phenomena. For example, public-order crimes, such as prostitution and drug violations, are said to harm society writ large. Of course, crimes against persons and property harm people and their possessions. Legality and punishment hold that specific actions must be defined as crimes with specific punishments and located in criminal statutes prior to the commission of the offense. Finally, necessary attendant circumstances refer to any additional facts that must be present when identifying the commission of a crime. For example, kidnapping or rape charges could be necessary attendant circumstances to qualify a homicide offense as felony murder.

DEFENSES AGAINST THE LAW

Alibi
Latin for "elsewhere," an alibi defense operates on the assumption that the accused person is actual and factual innocent because he or she was so distant or removed from the commission of the crime. Those who offer an alibi defense can offer proven evidence that they were someplace else doing something else when the crime actually occurred. Because no one can be in two places simultaneously, alibis are compelling defenses against criminal charges.

Justifications
Justification defenses assert a moral claim that their conduct, although technically illegal, represented the lesser of two evils and thus should avoid prosecution.[13] Five general categories of justification defenses are 1) self-defense, 2) defense of other persons, home, and property, 3) necessity, 4) consent, and 5) resisting unlawful arrest. Self-defense is the protection of oneself from unlawful injury or the immediate risk of unlawful injury. It is the justification for an act that would otherwise constitute a criminal offense and that the doer reasonably believed was necessary to protect self from immediate danger. Lawful self-defense assumes that the minimum degree of force necessary be used when protecting oneself. This idea of reasonable force means that the amount or degree of force used in the self-defense should be approximately commensurate to the degree of force used in the attack. For example, the use of lethal force to respond to a shove from another person would violate the proportionality standard of reasonable force.[14] It would also result in criminal charges!

A related justification is the defense of other persons, home, and property. In most jurisdictions, persons can use reasonable, non-lethal force to prevent others from unlawfully seizing or damaging their homes and property. In some situations, the self-defense justification can be applied to the protection of a third person who faces imminent risk or injury from an unlawful attack. Those acting as good Samaritans can claim defense of others under certain situations. Relating to the defense of others is the alter ego rule, which asserts that a person can only defend a third person under circumstances and to the degree that the third person could act on his or her own behalf.

"Necessity" is the claim that some illegal action was needed to prevent an even greater harm. An example of necessity is the destruction of property to avoid the spread of fire. Consent describes conduct where the apparent victim gave permission to commit the act in question. For example, imagine that while walking through a parking lot you notice a person frantically screaming that they locked their keys inside their car along with their infant child. The person pleads for you to help them and asks that you break the car window to rescue the child. You do this. Because the car owner consented, you would not be charged with the property damage.

Resisting unlawful arrest is the final justification and describes situations where persons use non-lethal force to resist the unlawful actions or arrest attempts of a law enforcement officer. Resisting unlawful arrest must respond to unlawful force, in other words persons cannot initiate force against law enforcements officers because they perceive or anticipate that an unlawful arrest is imminent. An exceedingly important distinction should be made between resisting unlawful arrest and resisting lawful arrest. Many criminal defendants resist the police because they are angry or indignant that they are being arrested for their own violations of law. Resisting a lawful arrest is not only unjustified, but also frequently carries additional criminal charges such as resisting arrest, obstructing police, and so on.

Excuses

Excuse defenses assert that the person who commits an illegal act was not legally responsible for their conduct at the time of commission and as such should not be held accountable under the law. Basically, excuse defenses seek to negate criminal liability because of some condition, special circumstance, or disability that the defendant had at the time of the criminal action. There are several legal excuses. Duress is the unlawful constraint or influence used to force an individual to commit some act that he or she otherwise would not have committed.

Duress is sometimes referred to as compulsion or coercion. The textbook example of duress would be if you were forced at gunpoint to commit a crime because of fear for your life. For example, while standing in line at the bank, a masked gunman enters and orders everyone to the floor. The gunman points his gun at your head and orders you to take the jewelry, wallets, and purses from the other customers. Later, you would not be criminally liable for bank robbery, robbery, or theft because it was clear that your conduct was purely the function of the duress.

Age or infancy holds that persons cannot reason logically or rationally appreciate their conduct and the consequences of their conduct until age seven. In other words, young persons are viewed as incapable of forming criminal intent and, as such, cannot be held criminally liable for their conduct. The delineation of seven as the threshold for culpability descends from Common Law traditions. Indeed, as you know from your juvenile delinquency and juvenile justice courses, an entirely different justice system is built upon the idea that non-adults deserve special consideration in regard to their criminal conduct. Importantly, age, specifically youth, is used as a mitigating or exculpatory factor in numerous facets of criminal justice.

Mistakes infrequently can be used as excuses of criminal conduct. The phrase "ignorance of the law is no excuse" means that you can and will be held criminally responsible for unlawful conduct even if you were not aware that the conduct was illegal. Indeed, most claims of ignorance of the law are specious at best.

Involuntary intoxication can be invoked as a defense against criminal liability if it can be shown that a person's illegal actions were the direct result of unbeknownst intoxication caused by another person. The emphasis here is the word involuntary. Despite the efforts of many criminal defendants, voluntary intoxication is not a viable criminal defense. Indeed, the preponderance of criminal defendants are intoxicated by alcohol or some other illicit substance upon their arrest.

Unconsciousness and *provocation* are two additional excuses against the law. Unconsciousness describes cases where persons engage in conduct, even unlawful conduct, without being conscious. Somnambulism or sleepwalking is an example of a situation where a person could commit a crime, perhaps trespass into a home, without being conscious or even cognizant of their behavior.[15] Occasionally, courts have accepted provocation as a reasonable excuse for criminal behavior. For example, bar room brawls where one defendant reasonably responds to the overt provocation of another are potential cases where a provocation excuse would be offered. Generally, provocation excuses would only be attempted in relatively minor crimes.

Insanity

The defense that arouses the most interest among the general public is probably insanity. An insanity plea is a contention that a defendant is not culpable for the acts with which he or she was charged because a severe mental disease or defect rendered the defendant unable to appreciate the wrongfulness of his or her actions. In this way, insanity defenses assert that some defendants are either cognitively or volitionally unable to "achieve" *mens rea*.[16] Importantly, the law is largely unconcerned with the psychiatric features of insanity. Instead, the law has a simple goal regarding insanity: Could the defendant discern right from wrong and thus be held criminally responsible?

Early Insanity Defenses

Insanity defenses against the law are nothing new. Various forms of the insanity defense, such as the "Absolute Madness" doctrine, appeared as early as the Sixteenth Century under English common law. The "Wild Beast Rule" established in the 1720s asserted that criminal defendants could be found not guilty by reason of insanity if they were shown to be totally deprived of reason so as to be an infant or wild beast. In the early Nineteenth Century, the Hadfield Decision posited that defendants were not guilty by reason of insanity if a mental defect produced their criminal act. In many parts of Colonial America, the application and adjudication of the insanity defense was inconsistent and difficult to trace given the informal system of criminal justice that existed during that era.[17]

M'Naghten or McNaghten Rule

The 1843 decision that became known as the M'Naghten Rule established the first clear precedent for acquittal based on the defense of insanity. The defendant in the case, Daniel M'Naghten, was prosecuted for murdering Edward Drummond who was the secretary of British Prime Minister Sir Robert Peel. The murder was an intended assassination of Peel. The defense claimed that M'Naghten suffered from delusions (similar to what is today known as paranoid schizophrenia), was not of sound mind when he acted, and thus should not be held responsible for his actions. This established the "right-from-wrong" test of criminal responsibility: "If the accused was possessed of sufficient understanding when he committed the criminal act to know what he was doing and to know that it was wrong, he is responsible therefore, but if he did not know the nature and quality of the act or did not know what he was doing but did not know that it was wrong, he is not responsible."[18]

The Durham and Brawner Rules

The evolution of the insanity defense was updated in 1954 with the Durham decision. The Durham Rule altered the concept of *mens rea* by providing for a much broader test of mental illness as a legal defense stipulating that "an accused is not criminally responsible if his unlawful act was the product of mental disease or defect." Also known as the products test, the Durham Rule places the burden on the prosecution to show beyond a reasonable doubt that the criminal act was caused by the defendant's mental illness.[19]

The case of *U.S. v. Brawner* (1972) determined that a person was not responsible for criminal conduct if at the time of such conduct, as a result of mental disease or defect, he or she lacked substantial capacity either to appreciate the criminality of their conduct or to conform their conduct to the requirements of law. Importantly, mental disease or defect did not encompass the abnormality or pathology characterized by repeated or habitual antisocial behavior. The Brawner Rule also placed responsibility for deciding insanity in the hands of the jury.[20]

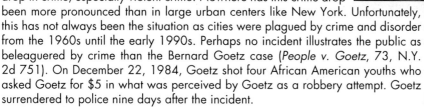

BOX 3-3

CRIMINAL JUSTICE CONTROVERSY

THE SUBWAY VIGILANTE

Since 1993, the United States has experienced an unprecedented drop in crime, especially violent crime. Nowhere has this crime drop been more pronounced than in large urban centers like New York. Unfortunately, this has not always been the situation as cities were plagued by crime and disorder from the 1960s until the early 1990s. Perhaps no incident illustrates the public as beleaguered by crime than the Bernard Goetz case (*People v. Goetz*, 73, N.Y. 2d 751). On December 22, 1984, Goetz shot four African American youths who asked Goetz for $5 in what was perceived by Goetz as a robbery attempt. Goetz surrendered to police nine days after the incident.

The incident created a media firestorm. Goetz, who is white, had previously been the victim of violent crimes, was active in community protection meetings, and made statements attributing crime to minorities. All four victims had prior criminal records, and three had been arrested since the incident, including one who was convicted of raping, sodomizing, robbing, and assaulting a pregnant woman. The remaining victim was paralyzed by the shooting and subsequently won a $43 million civil trial against Goetz, who filed bankruptcy.

Despite the potential racial dynamics of the case, New Yorkers of all racial and ethnic backgrounds responding with near-unanimity to the shooting. Goetz was portrayed as a heroic figure that stood up for the good guys in the face of criminals who were terrorizing the city. Indeed, despite his videotaped confession, the jury acquitted Goetz of the shooting except for a conviction for weapons possession for which he ultimately served eight months in prison and paid a $5,000 fine. Although vigilantism was not included as a defense against the law, the Goetz case showcased that, occasionally, persons who take the law into their own hands are viewed favorably in the court of public opinion and leniently in the court of law.

Photo © JupiterImages, Corp.

Other Insanity Defense Standards

Criminal defendants have used a variety of other insanity standards to attempt to absolve themselves of criminal liability. Many of these insanity defenses have been viewed as controversial because it is believed they were simply contrivances to avoid or skirt legal responsibility (see Box 3-3 for an example of this criminal justice controversy). For example, *the irresistible impulse test*, used since 1897, claims that defendants knew what they were doing and that the conduct was wrong but nevertheless could not stop themselves. Their mental condition made it impossible to control their conduct. In 1972, the Model Penal Code established the *substantial capacity test*, which claimed that, "a person is not responsible for criminal conduct if at the time of such conduct as a result of mental disease or defect, he lacks substantial capacity whether to appreciate his criminality (wrongfulness) of his conduct or to conform his conduct to the requirements of law."[21] According to the substantial capacity test, the prosecutor bears the burden of proof beyond a reasonable doubt. Present federal law employs the standard that the defendant lacked the capacity to appreciate the wrongfulness of his or her conduct. Under federal law, the defense bears the burden of presenting clear and convincing evidence of the reduced capacity.

Over the past two decades, variants of the insanity defense have appeared in statutory and case laws.[22] The 1984 federal Insanity Defense Reform Act stated that to find the defendant not guilty by reason of insanity, the defendant must prove, by clear and convincing evidence, that, at the time of the commission of the acts constituting the offense, the defendant, as a result of a severe mental disease or defect, was unable to appreciate the nature and quality or the wrongfulness of his or her acts. Mental disease or defect does not otherwise constitute a defense.[23]

Enacted in Michigan in 1975, the guilty but mentally ill doctrine (GBMI), made famous in the case of multi-millionaire killer John du Pont, established that the defendant must have had a substantial disorder of thought or mood which afflicted him or her at the time of the offense and which significantly impaired his or her judgment, behavior, capacity to recognize reality, or ability to cope with the ordinary demands of life. Whatever the effects of the mental illness, it falls short of legal insanity.

The GBMI doctrine has been controversial. Unlike insanity, which is an affirmative defense, GBMI is a verdict of guilty with a caveat "but mentally ill" that does not diminish the criminal responsibility of the defendant. The effects of GBMI verdicts on the criminal law are mixed. Some have found that defendants who plead insanity but were found GBMI received harsher sentences and less treatment, rendering GBMI a less attractive option for certain criminal defendants. Others have found that GBMI defendants are punished more leniently and that the entire doctrine is plagued by ethical, constitutional, and practical problems.[24]

Research Findings on the Insanity Defense

It is easy to become mired in the legal minutiae of the insanity defense. Fortunately, criminologists, legal scholars, and other social scientists have conducted much research on the insanity defense and its impact on criminal justice. Some noteworthy and interesting findings appear below.

- Nationally, the incidence of the insanity defense is extremely low. In many jurisdictions, the insanity defense is invoked in 1% or fewer of all felony cases. Juries appear to hold significantly more dubious assessments of the defense, as less than 10% of successful insanity defenses are disposed by jury. Testimony from forensic, psychiatric, and mental health experts can increase the success rate of insanity defenses.[25]

- Insanity defenses are successful about 15 to 25% of the time.[26]
- Defendants who successfully employ an insanity defense frequently spend longer in custody for psychiatric reasons than convicted defendants spend in prison for correctional purposes.[27]
- Criminal defendants with prior records of being found incompetent to stand trial and whose cases are brought before a bench trial (a judge rather than a jury) are significantly more likely to be found insane.[28]
- In jurisdictions where the insanity defense is an affirmative defense, the burden of proof shifts from the prosecution to the defense. The insanity defense was invoked in just 5% of cases. Shifting the burden of proof from prosecution to defense did not affect the frequency of the insanity plea or its success rate.[29]
- Defendants who commit crimes in "odd" ways rather than usual circumstances are more likely to be judged insane by prospective jurors. Similarly, defendants who commit crimes with unusual or seemingly unreasonable motives are more likely to be rated as insane.[30]
- Psychiatric and law enforcement personnel can sharply disagree about the veracity of insanity pleas from criminal defendants. Police officers are more skeptical of claims of insanity and can assist prosecutors in winning cases where the defense is invoked.[31]

Procedural Defenses

In the course of balancing crime control and due process, agents of the criminal justice system have, occasionally, themselves run afoul of the law while performing their duties. In the case of such grievous due process violations, criminal defendants can defend themselves in court by using procedural defenses. Procedural defenses assert that improper, illegal, discriminatory, or otherwise biased criminal justice system processing render null and void any criminal liability that resulted from the improper conduct even if the accused was indeed engaged in criminal behavior.

Entrapment is the illegal inducement to commit crime by agents of the law. Pure entrapment occurs when the police induce or coerce someone to commit a crime that he or she would not have committed without the input of the police. Various forms of police misconduct, whether egregious or "technical" in nature, can also be cited as procedural defenses. Examples of police misconduct include violating a defendant's Fourth Amendment rights by illegally obtaining incriminating evidence and overt acts of discriminatory conduct such as fraud or racial profiling.

The police are not the only entity that can be cited during a procedural defense. The courts must follow a variety of essential Constitutional safeguards that, if violated, can be used by defendants to aid in their defense. These include the Fifth Amendment's protection against being doubly prosecuted for the same offense (double jeopardy), the Fourteenth Amendment's equal protection under the law that precludes being prosecuted on the basis of some attribute, and the Sixth Amendment's right to a speedy and fair trial.

Innovative or Creative Defenses

The defenses described in this chapter attempt to invalidate the *mens rea* component of the *corpus delicti* and thus preclude criminal responsibility or liability. Over the years, a variety of innovative or creative defenses have been developed and advanced in the criminal courts as defenses against the law. These defenses share some commonalities. Fundamentally, creative defenses assert that emotional distress, a specific or generalized trauma, or some other condition or ailment produce a diminished capacity that compromises an offender's criminal intent.

In her book *Getting Away With Murder: How Politics is Destroying the Criminal Justice System*, legal scholar and media commentator Susan Estrich chronicled what she deemed the top ten sympathy defenses. All of these innovative defenses were attempted in the 1980s and 1990s; some were even successful.

Adopted child syndrome is an affirmative defense which asserts that the trauma of adoption, fear of abandonment, and feelings of powerless and rejection may produce a psychotic, insane rage which causes sufferers to strike out, often at their adoptive parents. *Battered child syndrome* and *battered wife/husband syndrome* are variants of self-defense. Both claim that due to years of physical and mental abuse, battered children or wives (women are more commonly the victims of such habitual abuse) may have a reasonable fear of imminent and severe abuse, even if that threat would be imperceptible to an outsider, because the defense is attuned to the stages of violence of the attacker. Thus, it is broader than the traditionally immediate time period of a classic self-defense claim. Cultural defenses occur when a member of a minority culture contends that he or she violated law because they were following the traditions or customs of their own culture. *Husbands who kill* claim that their wife's infidelity justified their murder; *mothers who kill* their children claim a proprietary right over them. The *mob mentality* or *riot syndrome* defense asserts a "group contagion" theory whereby individuals become lost in the collective behavior of the group and therefore are less responsible for their actions. *War-related post-traumatic stress disorder* (PTSD) and *urban survivor syndrome* posit that the violence, pressure, and disorder of war and modern urban environments become shocked and desensitized and, by extension, less responsible for their criminal actions. Finally, vigilantism or cases where citizens "take the law into their hands" and employ violence on alleged criminal offenders has also been employed as a criminal defense.[32]

CHAPTER SUMMARY: BALANCING CRIME CONTROL AND DUE PROCESS

- Law is the codification of a society's values, beliefs, and norms regarding justice and what is appropriate and wrongful conduct.
- Traditional common law, case law or precedent, legislated statutes, and the United States Constitution form the bases of criminal law.
- Laws encompass proscribed behavior that varies in its seriousness and the degree to which the criminal justice system will respond to its violation.
- An illegal act (*actus reus*) coupled with criminal intent (*mens rea*) that concurs in time and space results in crime (*corpus delicti*).
- There are numerous defenses against criminal liability, including alibis, justifications, excuses, and conditions, such as insanity, that compromise *mens rea*.
- A variety of doctrines, customs, and court cases have been developed relating to the insanity defense.
- Despite public hype and concern, insanity defenses are rarely attempted and often unsuccessful.
- Procedural defenses protect the accused from violations of due process by agents of the criminal justice system.
- Although law is codified and exact, the application of the law and defenses against the law are variable, subject to interpretation, and inexact.

KEY TERMS

Actus reus	Knowingly
Affirmative defense	M'Naghten Rule
Alibi defense	*Mala in se*
Brawner Rule	*Mala prohibita*
Common law	Mens rea
Consent	Misdemeanor
Corpus delicti	Model Penal Code
Defense of self, others, or property	Necessity
Duress	Negligently
Durham Rule	Penumbral crimes
Excuse defense	Petty offense
Felony	Procedural defense
Guilty but mentally ill (GBMI)	Purposely
Inchoate offenses	Recklessly
Insanity	*Stare decisis*
Justification defense	Statutory law

TALKING POINTS

1. Law is often described as "set in stone"; however, its application is subject to human interpretation. Does the malleable application of the law further goals of crime control and due process? Should widespread discretion characterize the mobilization of the law?

2. What is judicial activism? Why has it been viewed as unconstitutional? Does judicial activism favor crime control or due process agendas?

3. Should *mens rea* be a vital element of crime? Or, is the harmful criminal conduct the only issue of concern regardless of the intentions of the perpetrator?

4. What are your thoughts about the insanity plea? Is it a good or bad thing? Does the empirical evidence about the insanity plea alter your view? Should insanity pleas be abolished as they have in a handful of U.S. states?

WEB LINKS

American Bar Association
(www.abanet.org)

American Law Institute
(www.ali.org)

American Psychiatric Association
(www.psych.org/public_info/insanity.cfm)

Bazelon Center for Mental Health Law
(www.bazelon.org)

Find Law
(www.findlaw.com)

The People's Law Dictionary by Gerald and Kathleen Hill
(www.dictionary.law.com)

The United States Supreme Court care of Northwestern University Professor Jerry Goldman
(www.oyez.itcs.northwestern.edu/oyez/tour/)

FURTHER READING

Estrich, S. (1998). *Getting away with murder: How politics is destroying the criminal justice system.* Cambridge, MA: Harvard University Press. Scholarly yet accessible to the general public, this engaging book showcases some of the abuses of the criminal law and how political ideologies have seriously compromised the criminal justice system.

Levin, M. R. (2005). *Men in black: How the Supreme Court is destroying America.* Washington, DC: Regnery. This controversial and massively successful book shows how unfettered Supreme Court Justices are increasingly making the law via their judicial activism instead of interpreting the law.

Neubauer, D. W., & Fradella, H. F. (2010). *America's courts and the criminal justice system,* 10th edition. Belmont, CA: Cengage. This textbook is a comprehensive and detailed look at the criminal law and how it is practiced throughout the American courts.

Rehnquist, W. H. (2001). *The Supreme Court.* New York: Vintage Books. Written by the current Chief Justice of the U. S. Supreme Court, this book conveys the history and inner-workings of the court of last resort.

Walker, S. (1998). *Popular justice: A history of American criminal justice.* New York: Oxford University Press. This work traces the development of American law and criminal justice especially how it developed from English common law traditions. The book also showcases the competing goals of strict crime control and due process perspectives.

PART TWO

POLICING

71

CHAPTER 4

Police History, Function, and Organization

CHAPTER OUTLINE

QUOTATIONS

"[The public expects police officers to have] the wisdom of Solomon, the courage of David, the strength of Samson, the patience of Job, the leadership of Moses, the kindness of the Good Samaritan, the strategic planning of Alexander, the faith of Daniel, the diplomacy of Lincoln, the tolerance of the Carpenter of Nazareth, and finally, an intimate knowledge of every branch of the natural, biological, and social sciences."—*August Vollmer*[1]

"Like it or not, the police are in the social welfare business. They are the only 24-hours-a-day, 7-days-a-week agency open to address a wide range of social problems, such as domestic and social welfare programs."—*Jack Greene*[2]

"Although the police usually respond civilly or deal with citizens in a personal manner, regardless of their role, a disproportionate amount of uncivil behavior on the part of police is directed toward suspects or offenders."—*Albert Reiss*[3]

INTRODUCTION

More than any other component of the criminal justice system, the police are the object of public fascination and ambivalence. The police are the most visible members of the criminal justice system and the entity with which community residents are most likely to have contact. Irrespective of how much contact, experience, or education you have about the police, nearly everyone holds an opinion of them. To some, the police are the guardians of the common good, those who protect the public and maintain order. The police voluntarily wrestle the forces of evil. To others, the police are dangerous: a secretive group endowed with awesome legal power over other citizens. From this view, the police are a formidable agent of governmental power. Fundamentally, the police are the perfect conversation piece in the balance between crime control and due process.

Chapter 4 describes the history, various functions, and organization of the police. While digesting all of the information presented, you should take from this chapter two intertwined conclusions. First, the police have changed dramatically during the course of American history in terms of the relationships between police and the public, organization, political era, technological advances, the waxing and waning of crime rates, and the persons who are eligible to even serve as police officers. Indeed, there has been great change. Second, the more things change, the more they stay the same (for example, see Box 4-1). Despite the radical changes just mentioned, the intrigue surrounding the police has not changed. That the police are a fundamental requirement of a civilized society guarantees that they will be objects of controversy. The preservation of "law and order" is viewed by most as a good thing, but when people breach that law and order and come into contact with the police—things get interesting.

POLICE HISTORY

Informal, kin-based, pragmatic, and simple best describe early policing both in the English common law and early American traditions. As you will discover, many of the original ideas and methods of enforcement from nearly one millennium ago persist in some way to the present day. Throughout the Middle Ages, policing was the responsibility of all community members, the *posse comitatus*. Victims of crime raised a hue and cry to notify immediate community members that a crime had just occurred, and, in turn, able-bodied males responded and apprehended the perpetrator. Early law enforcement officers were not uniformed, were generally unorganized, and were led by the local leader of the county, an official known as the *shire reeve* or the constable known as *comes stabuli*.

The Norman Conquest in 1066 introduced the Frankpledge system with its organized members of protective groups called *tithings*. Tithings were headed by the patriarch of ten families who supported their organization or church with portions of their earnings and had responsibility for the behavior of all members over the age of 14. Ten tithings formed a hundred and ten hundreds formed a shire. Here we see some of the earliest signs of the hierarchical organization of policing. Another informal practice, the night watch system, involved watchmen or bailiffs who would monitor villages throughout the night to guard against thieves and other unwanted outside invaders.[4]

Once suspected criminals were caught, they were dealt with summarily. There was no presumption of innocence during this time. To be accused of a crime, it was assumed, was to be guilty of that crime. Unless one was protected by his or her family, kin-based feuds and protectionism was common during this era, punishment was swift and severe. Public forms of corporal and capital punishment were remarkably common. Modern ideas and vocabulary such as community watch, constable, and sheriff take their origins from these beginnings. In a way, the hue and cry was a forerunner of the police siren.

The Statute of Winchester of 1285 brought more organization to early policing. The Statute formalized the watch and ward system to encompass both day constabulary and night watch (even today, policing is a 24-hour occupation) and institutionalized the hue and cry and the attendant responsibility of community residents to respond to crime. Males were drafted into watch and ward duties. The Statute of Winchester not only delineated the functions that resemble law enforcement, but also stressed the importance of these early police officers to maintain community order. Around 1326, the justice of the peace was created to serve as the principal judicial officer in the county. In modern parlance, the justice of the peace was the county or district attorney who secured law and order with the sheriff (shire reeve).

BOX 4-1

CRIME SCENE   DO NOT CROSS

CRIMINAL JUSTICE HISTORY

TRANSPORTATION, BANISHMENT, AND EXILING
OF CRIMINAL OFFENDERS:

WANTED
DEAD OR ALIVE

REWARD 1.000.000$

An intriguing and often overlooked component of punishment from English Common Law was transportation or banishment. Persons charged with felonies were either convicted and executed, or acquitted. In 1615, James I ordered that clemency could be granted to some offenders, such as thieves, arsonists, swindlers, and prostitutes, and that they be relocated to the colonies, what is today the United States. The English Transportation Act of 1718 instituted banishment as the usual punishment for property crimes. From 1718 until the American Revolution, it is estimated that 50,000 criminal offenders were transported to the colonial United States from the United Kingdom.

You might think that transportation is an archaic form of social control; think again. Some police agencies transport troublesome persons, disproportionately those who are homeless, mentally ill, or intoxicated, out of a department's jurisdiction and then release the individual on his or her own recognizance. At times, the involuntary travelers escorted by the police or provided free train, bus, or cab fair to the city limits or even further.

A fascinating article by police scholars, William King and Thomas Dunn, examined the low-visibility, extra legal action they referred to as dumping or police-initiated transjurisdictional transport of troublesome persons (PITT). They found that organizational, community, situational, and individual-officer factors caused PITT, just as these factors cause or influence all police activities. Dumping or PITT incidents occasionally appeared in the news media and anecdotes of criminal justice practitioners, and even formed the basis of civil lawsuits against municipalities that transport troublesome persons. King and Dunn pointed to several adverse outcomes of dumping. For example, dumped persons are often high-risk in terms of offending and victimization, thus the police are displacing likely future offenders/victims onto another agency. There have been cases where dumped persons died as a result of heat stroke or freezing. Finally, dumping persons with serious mental health or substance abuse needs does nothing to address their problems. Moreover, involuntary placing them into a possibly new, bewildering environment may aggravate their behavior and current condition.

Then and now, transportation, banishment, exile, dumping, or PITT is an interesting, innovative, and morally shaky method of social control. It is also an alternative to arrest and illustrative of the considerable discretion that police officers can employ when performing their duties.

Sources: Wadman, R. C., & Allison, W. T. (2004). *To protect and to serve: A history of police in America.* Upper Saddle River, NJ: Pearson Prentice Hall; King, W. R., & Dunn, T. M. (2004). Dumping: Police-initiated transjurisdictional transport of troublesome persons. *Police Quarterly, 7,* 339–358. Photo © Yanta, 2011, Shutterstock, Inc.

These practices lasted for hundreds of years until the Eighteenth and Nineteenth Centuries when modern social forces such as vice, disorder, industrialization, and general urban strife necessitated change in policing. For example, the invention of gin in 1720 and its widespread availability created numerous social problems for European cities, especially London. However, alcohol abuse and its attendant problems were just the tip of the iceberg. The Western world was coming to grips with the Industrial Revolution whereby entire economies, cultures, and societies changed from mostly agrarian to industrial labor. The effects of industrialization and its sister concept of urbanization were nothing short of remarkable, as the entire social organization of society changed. This rendered obsolete earlier forms of policing and led to the birth of the modern police organization.[5]

Modern Policing

In 1829, the Metropolitan Police Act established in London the first organized police force. Shepherded by England's Home Secretary (and later Prime Minister) Sir Robert Peel, the London Police, known as Bobbies, was a 1,000-man force who replaced the watch and constable systems of centuries before. Despite the obvious problems that arise with the advent of a new institution, the Metropolitan Police were a success. By 1856, all boroughs and counties in England were required to have their own police force. Across the Atlantic Ocean, nascent police forces were created in Boston in 1838, New York in 1844, and Philadelphia in 1854. Since the formation of policing in the United States, police scholars have organized its historical development into three main epochs each in response to the other. The Political Era spanned 1840 to 1920. The Reform Era characterized 1920 until about 1980. The Community/Problem-Solving or Problem-Oriented Era has presided since 1980.[6] The main features of each are described next.

The Political Era, 1840 to 1920
The parochial, neighborhood image of the watch and ward system was still alive in early policing. During the Political Era, police forces were intimately connected to the neighborhoods and ward politicians of the local municipalities that they governed. Political machines played an active role in recruiting and staffing police forces, which in turn facilitated the political prosperity of the local politicians. In a way, policing was still kin-based as officers were recruited according to the dominant ethnic group in the ward (i.e., almost exclusively Caucasian) and multiple members of single families were common among police forces. Because of the obvious conflicts of interest inherent in this political arrangement, policing during the Political Era was rife with corruption.

Since policing was so tightly linked with neighborhoods, it was decentralized across a larger geographic area. First and foremost, the police served the interests of the political machines first and the public second. However, these constituencies were not mutually exclusive. Due to the probable political payoff, ward politicians directed the police to perform a variety of service and community functions, including helping in soup lines, providing temporary lodging for immigrants, and furnishing other social services.[7] Foot-patrol officers directly served the public by handling interpersonal squabbles and criminal complaints. With political and citizen satisfaction with the social order the paramount goal, criminal investigations were crude and heavy-handed. Police use of force and coercion was common to keep neighborhood residents and particularly outsiders—those from another ward, often of different ethnicity—in line.

The latter point about ethnicity is important because American policing has always been inextricably and dubiously linked with race and ethnicity. Indeed, you should notice that race is a substantial undercurrent in the three police chapters in this text. Police scholars Hubert Williams and Patrick Murphy have explored police history in America with a special emphasis on police-minority relations. Throughout the Political Era and indeed well into the Twentieth Century, the entire legal order and criminal justice system explicitly or implicitly sustained slavery, segregation, and discrimination against various racial and ethnic minorities. This negatively differential treatment was especially directed against African Americans. According to Williams and Murphy, the early political and social organization of the United States forged police behavior and attitudes toward minorities that exist to the present day. These include the idea that minorities have fewer civil rights, that the task of the police is to control minorities or "keep them in line," and that the police have little responsibility for protecting minorities from crime occurring within their communities.[8]

Despite these many negative characteristics, the political-based organization of the police was good in some respects. There was tremendous integration between police and community residents, something that modern-day community policing has strived to achieve. The police also performed many duties and served functions beyond simple law enforcement. In this way, the police were visible helpers, not an invisible entity that only arrives during times of trouble. Finally, the political arrangement of the police offered stability, neighborhood cohesion, and institutional familiarity—important ingredients for a bourgeoning police force and nation.

The Reform Era, 1920 to 1980

"Control over police by local politicians, conflicts between urban reformers and local ward leaders over the enforcement of laws regulating the morality of urban migrants, and abuses (corruption, for example) that resulted from the intimacy between police and political leaders and citizens produced a continuous struggle for control over police during the late Nineteenth and early Twentieth centuries."[9] First and foremost, the reform era altered policing by replacing politics with civil service bureaucracy and professionalism. The black eye that policing suffered due to the patronage and corruption from the Political Era was rectified with a strident fixation on the criminal law. Importantly, the criminal law not only served as the lawful basis for police power and legitimacy, but also guided the daily work of police officers. It was during the Reform Era that police officers became law enforcement officers above all of their other duties. Indeed, the various service functions were seen as onerous and the responsibility of social service providers, such as social workers.

Also during this era, the police were symbolically removed from the community in three ways. First, the newly centralized, civil-service type of organization voided the former ward-neighborhood approach. Now, police were not simply in the pocket and backyard of local politicians, but rather bureaucratic city workers. Second, the organizational culture of police departments in the Reform Era stressed professionalism, tact, and objectivity. In a way, the police responded to citizens as a polite yet aloof outside force. You will see the ramifications of this later. Third, the years spanning 1920 to 1980 were rich in technological advancement across all segments of society, including policing. The growing use of automobiles for patrol, 911 emergency service, and computer-aided dispatching meant that the police could quickly respond to crime while not necessarily living and working among the people that they served.

Two police reformers were especially responsible for professionalizing and modernizing American police, August Vollmer and Orlando Wilson. Vollmer is considered the father of modern American policing and the dean of American police chiefs. A former town marshal of Berkeley, California, Vollmer assisted in the creation of the California Bureau of Criminal Investigation and the founding of a police school of higher education at the University of California at San Jose. An academic who served on the faculties at the Universities of Chicago and California, Vollmer was responsible for a variety of innovations in policing, such as bicycle and motorcycle patrol, radio-equipped police cars, and police telephone-callbox systems. He also established the first scientific crime-detection laboratory and bridged the worlds of applied and academic criminal justice. Vollmer's protégé, Orlando Wilson, was another important police reformer with a dual academic and practitioner orientation. Among his many achievements, Wilson drafted what would ultimately become the code of ethics of the International Association, founded and later served as Dean of the School of Criminology at the University of California at Berkeley, and served as Chief of Police for Chicago. In his influential text *Police Administration* published in 1950, Wilson promulgated the theory of preventive patrol which hypothesized that omnipresent police automobile patrol would help detect crimes as they occurred, serve as a visible deterrent to potential criminal offenders, and promote feelings of safety among the citizenry. Such an approach was used for decades until experimental research highlighted the limitations of police patrol.[10]

Even with a cursory understanding of American history from 1920 to 1980, it is easy to see that despite the many positive aspects of Reform Era policing, its demise was inevitable. The staunchly professional, crime-fighting style of policing was reminiscent of the Joe Friday character from the television series *Dragnet*. Such a style was anachronistic in the 1960s and 1970s, decades characterized by social revolutions, urban unrest, malaise, and most importantly, surging crime rates. Crime boomed from the 1960s through 1980s, and it became apparent that the policing approaches of the Reform Era were failing miserably.[11] If one feature could be pinpointed as the symbol of the ultimate decline of Reform Era policing it would be the removal of the police from the community. Although removing the police from the people was mostly a function of administrative logistics and technological advancement, it produced an almost permanent detachment between the police and the public. Especially in areas with the highest crime rates, police-community relations were strained, volatile, and built upon mutual distrust. Rectifying this problem was the primary focus of the current era of policing, the Community/Problem-Solving Era.

The Community/Problem-Solving Era, 1980 to Present

The Community/Problem-Solving Era, sometimes simply referred to as the community policing era, combines and improves upon elements of the earlier eras. For example, community/problem-solving policing roots its legitimacy and authorization from the criminal law and values of professionalism, remnants of the Reform Era. However, the current paradigm has reattached to the community at the neighborhood level, reminiscent of the Political Era. Instead of being aligned with local politicians, the police have sought political alliances with community leaders, citizen groups, informal networks, and formal networks of social service agencies. Community/problem-solving policing is thus a collaborative effort between the police and the community that identifies crime and disorder problems and involves all constituencies to find solutions to these problems. Problem-solving policing assumes that crime can be controlled by uncovering and effectively addressing the underlying social problems that engender crime. Whenever possible, community resources and citizens are utilized. Education, negotiation, crime prevention, and conflict management are some of the tools that community/problem-solving officers employ.[12]

In a word, the current era of policing is *sociological*. Community/ problem-solving (interchangeably called problem-oriented) policing seeks positive, meaningful relationships between the police and public though collaboration and engagement. Fear of crime, public opinion, and quality of life, not just crime rates, are the outcome measures of interest to agencies engaged in community policing. Together, the police and the public seek to remedy the root causes of crime to provide a more comprehensive or systemic approach to crime control. As the earlier era demonstrated, simply responding to crime did nothing to address the social conditions that appeared to give rise to crime. Moreover, the public perception that the police are an aloof, secretive, ineffective agency that is not beholden to them is very problematic. By working with the community rather than against or for them, the current police era attempts to learn from the limitations of earlier approaches to American policing. (For a comparison of various approaches to policing, see Box 4-2.)

Some cities have utilized another variant of community/problem- oriented policing. This other variant is known to academics as enforcement problem-oriented policing but to the general public as zero-tolerance policing. Zero-tolerance policing is based on the "broken windows" theory promulgated by James Q. Wilson and George Kelling. Briefly, the theory asserts that neighborhood physical disorder engenders an environment in which nuisance offending and vice, which are precursors of more serious criminal behavior, are tolerated. If broken windows are left unattended, the police are in effect sending a message to the community that residents' physical environment and the criminal transgressions that occur there are unimportant. By connecting with the community to repair broken windows, the police establish the partnerships that are characteristic of the community/ problem-oriented approach. The point of departure is the method of zero- tolerance policing, which aggressively targets public offenses such as panhandling, prostitution, drug use and sales, vagrancy, and disorderly conduct. Zero-tolerance policing is a type of extreme order maintenance where all violations of the law are swiftly addressed and remedied (see Box 4-3). Zero-tolerance policing, especially in New York City, has been credited with the enormous reductions in crime that have occurred since about 1993.[13] By 2011, major cities including New York and Chicago were fresh of years with the lowest murder totals in 40 years.[14]

Community/problem-oriented policing has received widespread recognition from academic, practitioner, and political arenas. For example, the passage of The Violent Crime Control and Law Enforcement Act in September 1994 authorized $8.8 billion for the "Public Safety Partnership and Community Policing Act" and the creation of a formal agency within the U. S. Department of Justice called the Office of Community Oriented Policing Services (COPS) to administer and supervise

CRIME SCENE   DO NOT CROSS

VARIETIES OF POLICE ORGANIZATION, FUNCTION, AND PERFORMANCE

TRADITIONAL

Police Focus:	Law enforcement
Forms of Intervention:	Reactive to violations of law
Range of Police Activity:	Narrow, crime focused
Level of Discretion:	High and unaccountable
Focus of Police Culture:	Inward, rejecting community
Locus of Decision-making:	Police
Communication Flow:	Downward from police to community
Range of Community Involvement:	Low and passive
Linkage with other Agencies:	Poor and intermittent
Organization and Command Focus:	Centralized
Success Measures:	Arrests, crime rate reductions

COMMUNITY POLICING

Police Focus:	Community building through crime prevention
Forms of Intervention:	Proactive
Range of Police Activity:	Broad, crime, order, fear, and quality-of-life focus
Level of Discretion:	High and accountable to community and police
Focus of Police Culture:	Outward, building partnerships
Locus of Decision-making:	Community-police responsibility and assessment
Communication Flow:	Horizontal between police and community
Range of Community Involvement:	High and active
Linkage with other Agencies:	Participative and integrative
Organization and Command Focus:	Decentralized with community linkage
Success Measures:	Community linkages and use, safe neighborhoods, arrests

the grant programs. Moreover, nearly 100,000 additional police officers have been hired as a result of community policing initiatives.[15] Several studies attest to the current successes and likely continued growth of Community/Problem-Oriented Era. For example:

- COPS hiring and innovative grant programs have resulted in significant reductions in violent and non-violent crime rates in cities with populations greater than 10,000.

CRIME SCENE   DO NOT CROSS

PROBLEM-ORIENTED POLICING

Police Focus:	Law, order, and fear problems
Forms of Intervention:	Mixed
Range of Police Activity:	Narrow to broad, depending on problem
Level of Discretion:	High and primarily accountable to police
Focus of Police Culture:	Mixed depending on problem
Locus of Decision-making:	Varied, police and community identify problems
Communication Flow:	Horizontal between police and community
Range of Community Involvement:	Mixed depending on problem
Linkage with other Agencies:	Participative and integrative
Organization and Command Focus:	Decentralized with community linkage
Success Measures:	Problems solved, minimized, or displaced

ZERO-TOLERANCE POLICING

Police Focus:	Order problems
Forms of Intervention:	Proactive
Range of Police Activity:	Narrow, location and behavior focused
Level of Discretion:	Low, primarily accountable to police
Focus of Police Culture:	Inward, focused on attacking target problems
Locus of Decision-making:	Police directed
Communication Flow:	Downward from police to community
Range of Community Involvement:	Low and passive
Linkage with other Agencies:	Moderate and intermittent
Organization and Command Focus:	Centralized, but internal focus
Success Measures:	Arrests, field stops, location-specific reductions in targeted activity

Source: Adapted from J. R. Greene (2000). Community policing in America: Changing the nature, structure, and function of the police. In K. Heimer (Ed.), *Criminal Justice 2000*, Volume 3 (pp. 299–370). Washington, DC: U. S. Department of Justice (table adapted from p. 311).

- Specifically, a $1 increase in COPS funding per resident contributed to a decline of 5.26 violent crimes and 21.63 property crimes per 100,000 residents.
- A $1 increase in other innovative funding per resident contributed to a decline of 12.93 violent crimes and 45.53 property crimes per 100,000 persons.
- The above findings were based on analysis of 6,100 law enforcement agencies serving more than 145 million people. Overall, COPS grants have had no significant negative effects on violent or property crime rates.[16]

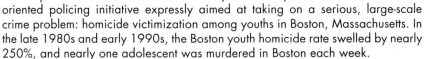

BOX 4-3

CRIMINAL JUSTICE SPOTLIGHT

PROBLEM-ORIENTED POLICING IN ACTION

Compared to traditional policing methods, problem-oriented policing has been criticized as being "soft" because of its focus on solving community level problems with residents. Based on the results of the Boston Gun Project, such a characterization is wildly inaccurate. The Boston Gun Project was a problem-oriented policing initiative expressly aimed at taking on a serious, large-scale crime problem: homicide victimization among youths in Boston, Massachusetts. In the late 1980s and early 1990s, the Boston youth homicide rate swelled by nearly 250%, and nearly one adolescent was murdered in Boston each week.

In 1995 and 1996, the Boston Gun Project launched Operation Ceasefire whose main elements were a direct law enforcement attack on illicit firearms traffickers supplying youths with guns and an attempt to generate a strong deterrent to gang violence. With ample funding from the National Institute of Justice, the Boston Police Department and federal Bureau of Alcohol, Tobacco, and Firearms directed a focused attack on known gangs, gun traffickers, and chronic offenders. Some of their methods were quite creative, such as disseminating posters to gang members informing them about Operation Ceasefire.

Operation Ceasefire resulted in a 63% declined in monthly youth homicides, 32% decline in monthly shots-fired calls, 25% declined in monthly gun assault incidents, and 44% decrease in monthly youth gun assaults. Clearly, severe police crackdowns on targeting youth gangs known to be involved in committing serious violent crime can dramatically reduce gun violence in the nation's cities.

The sudden police crackdowns used in Operation Ceasefire are similar to other police experiments or quasi-experiments that employed directed patrol. Directed patrol involves assigning officers to a specific area to engage in proactive investigation and enforcement via traffic stops. The traffic stops are focused in the areas with the highest crime rates, or hot spots, deter crime through increased police visibility, and incapacitate criminals who are likely to operate in hot spots. Directed patrols have been generally successful in reducing crime rates, especially when targeting toward reducing firearm violence.

Sources: Kennedy, D. M., Braga, A. A., & Piehl, A. M. (2001). *Reducing gun violence: The Boston Gun Project's Operation Ceasefire: Developing and implementing Operation Ceasefire.* Washington, DC: U. S. Department of Justice, Office of Justice Programs, National Institute of Justice; Koper, C. (1995). Just enough police presence: Reducing crime and disorder by optimizing patrol time in crime hot spots. *Justice Quarterly, 12,* 649–672; McGarrell, E. F., Chermak, S. Weiss, A., & Wilson, J. (2001). Reducing firearms violence through directed police patrol. *Criminology & Public Policy, 1,* 119–148; Sherman, L. W., & Rogan, D. P. (1995). The effects of gun seizures on gun violence: "Hot spots" patrol in Kansas City. *Justice Quarterly, 12,* 673–693; Sherman, L. W., & Weisburd, D. A. (1995). General deterrent effects of police patrol in crime "hot spots": A randomized controlled trial. *Justice Quarterly, 12,* 625–648; Wilson, J. Q., & Boland, B. (1978). The effect of the police on crime. *Law and Society Review, 12,* 367–390. Photo © 2011, joingate, Shutterstock, Inc.

- Nationally, about two-thirds of police departments employ community police officers and the absolute number of community policing officers increased nearly 600%.[17]
- Strategic problem-solving policing like that practiced in New York City has been widely adopted by police agencies across the United States.[18]
- Even in jurisdictions that have been committed to it, problem-oriented policing entails officers who generically apply problem-solving precepts to their patrol work.[19]
- Across the United States, community/problem-oriented policing has contributed to reductions in fear of crime, disorder, drug availability, and police-community relations.[20]

In sum, the history of American police contains revolutionary changes in terms of organization, technology, and function. From the Political Era to present day, American policing has become more sophisticated and professional; relied more on brains and innovation than brawn; become self-evaluative and responsive to change; and partnered with various communities rather than simply "serving them."[21] Like the criminal justice system that generally struggles with the balance between crime control and due process, the police have perennially struggled with the tensions between law enforcement and service. At various periods of American history, the police have focused more on one than the other. The following section highlights some of these various functions that the police perform.

FUNCTIONS OF THE POLICE

In his classic work, *Varieties of Police Behavior: The Management of Law and Order in Eight Communities* (1968), James Q. Wilson examined the relationships between politics, community structure, police departments, and the types of behavior that the police practice. Wilson evaluated Albany, Amsterdam, Brighton, Nassau, and Syracuse, New York; Highland Park, Illinois; and Oakland, California. These communities were marked by differences in crime rate, ethnic composition, community organization, and police-community relations. From his observations, Wilson developed three archetypal policing styles: the service style, the legalistic style, and the watchman style.[22]

Service Style
The service style typifies policing with a focus on community empowerment, help, and social assistance to residents. It typifies policing in more affluent areas and is indicative of well-paid, educated police officers. Of course, service style officers make arrests for violations of the law; however, the overarching goal is to help people. For example, instead of arresting a young adult for possessing a small amount of marijuana, service style officers might issue

the person a summons and direct him or her to counseling service or to a substance abuse center. The officer might even facilitate this by driving the person to the facility where he or she can receive the appropriate social service. It is easy to see that agencies that espouse a service style would be readily adaptable to adopting community or problem-oriented policing.

Anyone who has ever participated in a "ride-along" with a police officer usually makes a surprising observation: most police work is relatively boring! Indeed, the majority of a police officer's time does not involve strict law enforcement, but rather involves providing services to the community, such as working with other social service agencies, directing traffic at a sporting event, assisting a motorist with a flat tire, and providing information to residents.

So much police work is geared toward service that some jurisdictions have instituted a 3-1-1 non-emergency call system to free the traditional 9-1-1 call system for genuine police emergencies. It has been estimated that between 40 to 80% of calls placed to the 9-1-1 system were not emergencies requiring immediate police notice, but rather were mundane service requests. The National Institute of Justice recently sponsored an evaluation of the effects of the 3-1-1 non-emergency call system on various outcomes in Baltimore, Maryland. The implementation of 3-1-1 resulted in a 34% reduction in 9-1-1 calls, an 8% decline in total calls to either system, police response time actually increased despite the reduction in calls for service, and freed resources for other police duties.[23]

Legalistic Style

A legalistic style of policing is characterized by a strict enforcement of the precise letter of the law. Unless there is an identifiable violation of the criminal law, legalistic officers do not get involved in interpersonal situations that would nonetheless benefit from police intervention. In this way, the legalistic style would not be amenable to community or problem-oriented policing because of its hands-off or laissez-faire approach to issues and problems faced by individuals and neighborhoods. Legalistic policing voids officer discretion, which has pros and cons. For example, officers arresting people for speeding one mile over the legal limit is legally permissible, but does not make much sense normatively or from the position of public relations.

Watchman Style

Watchman style of policing places order maintenance above all other police duties. Disproportionately found in higher crime areas, watchman style officers use their discretion widely to handle citizen concerns via mostly informal methods such as intervention, persuasion, and, even, coercion. Maintaining public order, with and without the use of actual law enforcement, is the desired outcome of agencies that espouse the watchman style. Police scholar

Egon Bittner's study of police control of the "skid-row" population illustrates the divergent styles described by Wilson. According to Bittner, "patrolmen do not really enforce the law, even when they do invoke it, but merely use it as a resource to solve certain pressing practical problems in keeping the peace . . . thus, to implement the law naively, i.e., to arrest someone merely because he committed some minor offense, is perceived as containing elements of injustice."[24]

You can see how service, legalistic, and watchman style officers would differently respond to the above quotation, as well as differently respond to violations of the law. It is also clear that the very organization and local culture within a police department influence how individual officers perceive and respond to crime. Indeed, Robin Engel studied the attitudes and leadership styles of 81 patrol supervisors and discovered four types. The traditional supervisor favors aggressive enforcement, is highly task-oriented, is direct in their decision making, and has low expectations of community policing activities. Comparatively, the innovative supervisor favors community relations, holds more favorable views of subordinate officers, and supports innovations in police practices, such as community policing. The supportive supervisor protects or supports subordinate officers and is less task-oriented or fixated on other areas of law enforcement. This type tends to be inspirational in a sort of "union steward" way. Finally, the active supervisor scores highly on levels of activity, decision making, and perceived power. The active supervisor, previously likened as a street sergeant, often works with rank-and-file officers who often produce higher rates of arrest.[25] In short, the police on the street are often an extension of the police station and community.

POLICE PERFORMANCE

Scientific Policing

You have read how history, politics, levels of crime and disorder, community organization, and police department politics and philosophy influence how the police conduct their daily duties. For about 35 years, police performance has been enhanced by another factor: science. During the tumult of the 1960s, Congress created the Law Enforcement Assistance Administration (LEAA) as part of the Omnibus Crime Control and Safe Streets Act of 1969. The LEAA, the forerunner of the National Institute of Justice (see Box 4-5), was charged with disseminating funds for crime-fighting and crime-prevention proposals. One of the projects funded by the LEAA was the Exemplary Projects Program (1973) that was designed to promote innovative efforts toward crime reduction and prevention. A seminal program from this era was the Police Foundation. The Police Foundation is a private, independent, not-for-profit organization dedicated to supporting innovation and improvement in policing through its research, technical assistance, and communication programs.

The Kansas City Preventive Patrol Experiment

The gold standard of scientifically influenced policing is the Kansas City Preventive Patrol Experiment. This landmark experiment found that traditional routine patrol in marked police cars does not appear to affect the level of crime, a finding that countered the theorizing of police reformers such as Orlando Wilson. The Kansas City Preventive Patrol Experiment demonstrated that urban police departments can successfully test patrol deployment strategies and manipulate patrol resources without jeopardizing public safety.

The experiment was conducted in 1972–73 by the Kansas City Police Department and evaluated by Police Foundation. Patrols were varied within 15 police beats. Routine preventive patrol was eliminated in five beats, labeled "reactive" beats, which meant that officers entered these areas only in response to calls from residents. Normal, routine patrol was maintained in five "control" beats. In five "proactive" beats, patrol was intensified by two to three times the norm. The Kansas City Preventive Patrol Experiment assessed whether crime, as reflected by victimization surveys and crime data, varied by patrol type; whether citizen perceptions of police service varied by patrol type; whether citizen fear and behavior as a result of fear varied by patrol type; whether police response time and citizen satisfaction with response time varied by experimental area; and whether traffic accidents would increase in the reactive beats.[26]

Information was gathered from victimization surveys, reported crime rates, arrest data, a survey of local businesses, attitudinal surveys, and trained observers who monitored police-citizen interaction. A variety of interesting and important findings were produced.

- Citizens did not notice the difference when the level of patrol was changed.
- Level of police patrol had no significant effect on resident and commercial burglaries, auto thefts, larcenies involving auto accessories, robberies, or vandalism—crimes traditionally considered to be prevented by random, highly visible police patrol.
- The rate at which crimes were reported to the police did not differ in any important or consistent way across the experimental beats.
- Citizen fear of crime was not affected by patrol type.
- Citizen satisfaction with police was not affected by patrol type.
- "Ride-alongs" by observers during the experiment also revealed that 60% of the time spent by a Kansas City patrol officer typically was non-committed. This meant that officers spent a considerable amount

of time waiting to respond to calls for service. And they spent about as much time on non-police related activities as they did on police-related mobile patrol.

The overall implication is that resources ordinarily allocated to preventive patrol could safely be devoted to other, perhaps more productive, crime control strategies. More specifically, the results indicate that police deployment strategies could be based on targeted crime prevention and service goals rather than on routine preventive patrol. It is important to note that this experiment was conceived and executed by a local police department with technical help from outside researchers. The experiment demonstrates that, with the right kind of leadership and help, urban police departments can test new approaches to patrol. And they can use their patrol resources to conduct such experiments without jeopardizing public safety.[27]

The Newark Foot Patrol Experiment

During the Community/Problem-Oriented Era, police departments rejected foot patrol as antiquated, expensive, and irrelevant to contemporary policing. In most cities, it was not an integral part of police patrol strategy, carried low status among officers, was often regarded as a "public relations" activity, and was frequently used to punish poor performance. On the other hand, some citizens like foot patrol because they often associate foot patrol with the "good old days" when crime rates were low and they felt perfectly safe in their neighborhoods—recall the Political Era. Most citizens like frequent, close contact with the police; they may feel more secure when officers are visible and on the street.

The Police Foundation conducted an experiment from 1978 to 1979 to evaluate whether foot patrol improved police-citizen relationships; whether citizens felt safer when officers patrolled on foot; whether foot patrol reduced crime; whether citizens reported more crime when they had closer contact with the police; whether more arrests were made in foot-patrolled areas; whether foot patrol officers were satisfied with their jobs and had more positive attitudes about citizens; and whether citizens' fear of victimization declined.

Like the Kansas City project, a randomized experimental design was used. Eight foot patrol beats in Newark were matched demographically with foot patrol continued in four randomly selected beats and discontinued in four others. Foot patrol was also initiated in four beats where it had not previously been used. Researchers then compared reported crime, arrest and victimization rates, citizen fear and satisfaction with police services, as well as the attitude of foot patrol officers and officers on motorized patrol.

The Police Foundation found that introducing foot patrol in a mix of police strategies significantly enhanced citizen's perception of safety in the neighborhood. This is something no other police strategy had been able to do.

Although foot patrol seemed to have little effect on crime rates, it did have the following positive effects:

- Residents knew when officers were patrolling their neighborhoods on foot.
- Residents in areas patrolled by officers on foot thought that crime was less of a problem than did residents in areas with only motorized patrol.
- Residents in areas with foot patrol felt safer and less likely to be victimized.
- Residents living in areas with foot patrol took fewer steps to protect themselves against crime.
- Residents in areas with foot patrol were more satisfied with police services.

Overall, residents in areas in which foot patrol was introduced clearly changed their attitudes about crime and how they felt about the safety and livability of their neighborhoods. They also were more satisfied with police services. While foot patrol had no effect on recorded crime rates, it should be remembered that citizens feel threatened by nuisance behavior as well, and that this threat of victimization may dramatically alter their lives. Close contact between police and the citizenry helps the former develop first-hand information about crime and possible criminal behavior. Such information systems are likely to have a positive long-term impact.[28]

The Minneapolis Domestic Violence Experiment and Spouse Abuse Replication Program (SARP)

Until relatively recently, the police were reticent to arrest persons involved in disputes between intimate partners. Instead, police officers traditionally used informal counseling and other problem-solving techniques to attempt defusing the situation. However, it is also well known that various forms of physical abuse are common in American households, and that a "hands-off" approach from the criminal justice system was in effect enabling the problem of domestic violence. Today, all states have statutes that impact domestic violence and many localities have mandatory arrest policies in place for any domestic disturbance, verbal or physical.

In 1981 and 1982, the Police Foundation and Minneapolis Police Department with funding from the National Institute of Justice conducted the first scientifically controlled test of the effects of arrest on any crime, specifically domestic violence. Three traditional police responses were tested: 1) arresting an offender, 2) asking an offender to leave the scene of the assault, and 3) talking to both offender and victim and giving advice. Officers used a lottery method to determine which of the three responses they would use on each offender. Interviewers then re-contacted victims over a six-month period to measure whether the offenders continued to commit domestic assaults, how

BOX 4–4

CRIME SCENE   DO NOT CROSS

CRIMINAL JUSTICE RESEARCH

HIGHLIGHTS OF SCIENTIFIC POLICING

Boston Gun Project's Operation Ceasefire
Cincinnati Team Policing Experiment
Houston Targeted Beat Program
Indianapolis Community Policing in Action
Jersey City Drug Markets Analysis Program (DMAP)
Jersey City POP at Violence Places Project
Kansas City Crack House Police Raids Program
Kansas City Gun Project
Minneapolis Hot Spots Patrol Program
Minneapolis Repeat Call Address Policing (RECAP) Program
National Evaluation of Weed and Seed Programs
Newport News Problem-Oriented Policing
Reducing Fear of Crime in Houston and Newark
St. Louis POP in Three Drug Market Locations Study

Note: For an excellent summary of scientific policing, see Braga, A. A. (2001). The effects of hot spots policing on crime. *Annals of the American Academy of Political and Social Science, 578*, 104–125. Photo © JupiterImages, Corp.

were 30% less likely than minorities to be re-arrested for domestic violence, but 30% more likely to continue abusing according to victimization input. Overall, this recent evaluation affirmed the preventive effects of arrest on domestic assault while focusing on the importance of offender criminal history in explaining continued violence.[31]

As shown in Box 4–4, an array of scientifically informed policing initiatives have been conducted to remedy problems such as citizen fear of crime, gun violence, and crime and disorder in "hot spots," or areas that experience the bulk of crime problems in a single jurisdiction. In the spirit of the Police Foundation's research, the National Institute of Justice has been funding multi-site, multifaceted programs aimed to reduce crime and disorder and improve the lives of citizens. In 1991, the U. S. Department of Justice launched Operation Weed and Seed to demonstrate that a large number of resources can be mobilized in a comprehensive, coordinated effort to control crime and drugs and to improve the quality of life in targeted high-crime neighborhoods. Operation Weed and Seed offers a two-pronged strategy to "weed out" violent offenders through selective and intensive law enforcement and prosecution, and "seed" the neighborhood with prevention, intervention, treatment, and revitalization services. Community policing is an integral component of this strategy.

often they did so, and how serious the assaults were. Official
also reviewed.[29]

Domestic violence cases disproportionately involved unmarri⸍
with lower than average education. Most were minority or mix⸍
(black male/white female) relationships. Assailants were likely to ha
prior run-ins with police. Regardless of the race, employment status, e⸍
tional level, or criminal history of the assailants, however, the study sho⸍
that arrest was the most effective way to keep them from committing furth⸍
violence. As a result of the experiment, the Minneapolis Police Departmen⸍
changed its policy on domestic assaults. Officers are now required to file
written reports explaining why they failed to make arrests when it was legally
possible to do so. The new policy's initial impact was to double the number
of domestic assault arrests.

The Minneapolis Experiment prompted the National Institute of Justice
to fund replications in five additional cities: Omaha, Nebraska; Milwaukee,
Wisconsin; Charlotte, North Carolina Colorado Springs, Colorado; and Dade
County (Miami), Florida. The results from the Spouse Abuse Replication Program (SARP) were mixed. Arresting domestic abusers did not have a long-
term effect deterrent effect in Omaha, Charlotte, and Milwaukee, but did in
Colorado Springs and Dade County. The mandatory arrest policy appeared
to work differently for different populations. Those with a low stake in conformity, that is unemployed and unmarried, tended to escalate their criminal
behavior after their arrest. In this way, the domestic violence problem wors-
ened. For those with a stake in conformity, that is employed and married, an
arrest for domestic violence deterred future crime. Neither race nor a record
of prior offenses conditioned the effect of arrest on subsequent domestic violence. Thus, domestic abusers who are attached to society "get the message"
after being arrested and stop abusing their spouse. Weakly attached persons
only become more problematic after being arrested for domestic violence.[30]

Two decades after the Minneapolis Domestic Violence Experiment, scholars are still investigating the effects of various police responses to spousal assault. Christopher Maxwell, Joel Garner, and Jeffrey Fagan recently analyzed
4,032 cases from all five SARP sites. Maxwell and his colleagues were able
to conduct a more sophisticated and methodologically rigorous analysis to
examine the individual effects of arresting a batterer on subsequent recidivism. Their findings both affirmed and contradicted the earlier replications.
Most importantly, they found a consistent and significant deterrent effect
from arresting the domestic abuser across all sites once other important factors were considered. The deterrent effect depended on the characteristics of
the domestic abuser. For example, the odds of victimization decreased from
30 to 60% for each additional year of the offender's age. Abusers with criminal records were 250 to 330% more likely to commit new acts of domestic
violence after their most recent arrest! Official records indicated that whites

```
━━━━ ━━ ━ ━━ ━━ ━━  ━━━ ━━ ━━  ━━━━
        CRIME SCENE        DO NOT CROSS          BOX 4-5
```

CRIMINAL JUSTICE RESEARCH

NATIONAL INSTITUTE OF JUSTICE

The National Institute of Justice (NIJ) is the research and development agency of the U. S. Department of Justice and is the only federal agency solely dedicated to researching crime control and justice issues. NIJ's authorities are derived from the Omnibus Crime Control and Safe Streets Act of 1968 (42 U.S.C. §§ 3721–3722). The NIJ mission is to prevent and reduce crime, improve law enforcement and the administration of justice, and promote public safety.

The NIJ is committed to five challenges as part of its strategic plan:

1. rethinking justice and the processes that create just communities,
2. understanding the nexus between social conditions and crime,
3. breaking the cycle of crime by testing research-based interventions,
4. creating the tools and technologies for practitioners, and
5. expanding horizons through interdisciplinary and international perspectives.

The NIJ Director is appointed by the President and confirmed by the Senate. It has three operating units, the Office of Research and Evaluation, the Office of Science and Technology, and the Office of Development and Communications. The NIJ is part of the Office of Justice Programs, along with the Bureau of Justice Statistics, the Bureau of Justice Assistance, the Office of Juvenile Justice and Delinquency Prevention, and the Office for Victims of Crime.

As you will see, a substantial amount of research that is referenced in this book is sponsored by the National Institute of Justice.

Photo © JupiterImages, Corp.

National evaluations of Operation Weed and Seed have produced promising results. Janice Roehl and her colleagues evaluated the program at 19 sites and found that most weeding efforts targeted drug-related crimes, gun-related crimes, and violent crimes. A majority of cities also targeted street-level drug dealing. Weed and Seed increased coordination between various criminal justice agencies and social service providers. Interagency cooperation was strongest among law enforcement agencies. Seeding initiatives focused on prevention for youths, intervention for older adolescents, and the establishment of Safe Havens, multi-service centers that serve a variety of social service functions. Nearly 40,000 arrests were made between June 1992 and December 1993, with special emphasis on cases involving drugs, guns, and violence. More than 3,000 federal cases were initiated.[32] A more recent evaluation of Operation Weed and Seed from eight additional communities found significant reductions in serious crimes and improved resident perceptions of neighborhood safety. Effects varied across the sites; however, Weed and Seed thrived most strongly in communities characterized by grass-roots community resolve to combat crime and disorder.[33]

POLICE ORGANIZATION

It is clear that police organizations are a diverse bunch in terms of their mission, philosophy, and type of policing style that they employ.[34] A large reason for this variability is that the size and resources of police departments varies tremendously; indeed police departments exist in the smallest villages to largest metropolitan centers to the entire United States. This section provides some basic descriptive information about law enforcement agencies from the local, state, and federal level.

Agencies

The majority of law enforcement agencies in the United States are local. There are nearly 16,000 law enforcement agencies in the United States. Of these, 12,575 are local police departments, 3,012 are sheriff's departments (serving at the county-level), 49 are state police (Hawaii is the only state without a state police department, commonly known as state patrol since they patrol the state's highway system), 1,326 are special jurisdiction agencies, and 623 Texas constable agencies. Nearly all, 98%, of these agencies are located by municipal or township governments. Thus, local authority determines personnel, expenditures and pay, equipment, computers and information systems, and written policies.

Many of the more famous law enforcement agencies are not local, but federal. Nearly all cabinet-level agencies have law enforcement agencies. For example, the Department of Justice has the Federal Bureau of Investigation, U. S. Marshals Service, and Federal Bureau of Prisons. The Department of the Treasury maintains the Bureau of Alcohol, Tobacco, and Firearms and Internal Revenue Service Criminal Investigation Division.

Employees

There are more than one million full-time law enforcement officers in the United States. About 70% of them are sworn officers; that is, they have general arrest powers. The remaining 30% are full-time civilian employees. In addition, there are nearly 100,000 part-time law enforcement personnel, 56% of which are civilian with the remaining 44% as sworn part-time officers. Nationally, about 78% of full-time, local law enforcement officers are sworn personnel. Various federal entities employ 93,000 full-time sworn law enforcement officers and 72,000 civilian support personnel.

Personnel Characteristics

Law enforcement is a white-male dominated world. About 75% of full-time sworn officers are White with the remaining 25% constituted by non-whites. Men comprise nearly 88% and women 12% of all law enforcement officers. In large cities with populations of at least 250,000 people, between 40 to 50%

of officers are African American or Hispanic. Nearly all police agencies in the United States conduct criminal record checks, background investigations, driving record checks, personal interviews, medical exams, psychological evaluations, and drug tests prior to hiring personnel. Nearly 33% of all officers nationally are required to have completed some college education.

Operations and Services

The larger the population served the more resource-rich and greater service capacity of the law enforcement agency. Agencies serving more than one million people have considerable resources whereas agencies serving less than 2,500 people must often rely on outside agencies to provide services beyond rudimentary police duties. For example, all police agencies use automobile patrol and have calls-for-service dispatch system.

Overall, police services in the United States are exceedingly impressive. The preponderance of Americans is served by police departments that offer multiple forms of patrol, such as car, foot, bicycle, and motorcycle. These agencies have multiple investigative bureaus for specific crimes such as homicide, robbery, arson, and drug violations. Nearly half of the law enforcement agencies in the United States use video cameras and in-field computers to assist in their duties. Law enforcement officers use computers for records management, crime investigations, personnel records, dispatch, crime analysis, inter-agency sharing of information, automated booking, crime mapping, and other resource allocation. Police agencies are professional in the sense that they have officer handbooks, written policies and procedures pertaining to officer use of force and domestic violence policy.

Outreach

A recurrent theme of this chapter is the large amount of time that American law enforcement agencies devote to community outreach types of activities. According to Bureau of Justice Statistics statisticians Matthew Hickman and Brian Reaves, nearly 80 percent of law enforcement agencies regularly meet with neighborhood assistance organizations to facilitate the working relationship between the police and public. Police officers also regularly meet with a variety of other organizations (with percentages of agencies participating), such as school groups (75%), business groups (70%), senior citizen groups (60%), domestic violence groups (nearly 60%), local public agencies (55%), advocacy groups (50%), youth service organizations (50%), religious groups (50%), and tenant associations (about 50%). In terms of specific outreach devoted to community policing, between 76 to 100% of police departments serving communities with 250,000 or more residents perform tasks, such as meeting with citizen groups, conducting citizen-police academies, training citizens in community policing techniques, and surveying citizen views about local crime-related problems.[35]

CHAPTER SUMMARY: BALANCING CRIME CONTROL AND DUE PROCESS

- Policing has evolved from an informal, communal, and kin-based practice to a bureaucratic, formal, and professional organization.
- The police and the public have always been intertwined and their assessments of one another have varied from tight-knit and trusting to estranged and distrustful.
- Officer behavior and police departments are organized along three policing styles, service, legalistic, and watchman.
- The Kansas City Preventive Patrol Experiment showed that various levels of patrol did not affect the crime rate, suggesting that crime is not evenly distributed geographically.
- Police crackdowns, directed patrol, and other concerted efforts that target high crime hot spots and known offenders yield impressive results in terms of reducing crime, disorder, and fear.
- Most police time is spent performing services to the community and maintaining order, not making arrests.
- Police officers possess great discretion and often under-enforce the law.
- Police history has been marked at various times by corruption, politics, violence, a lack of professionalism, and troubled community relations.
- Most police in the United States are at the local level.
- Policing is largely decentralized.

KEY TERMS

311
911
Boston Gun Project
Broken windows theory
Comes stabuli
Community policing
Community/Problem-Solving Era
Directed patrol
Kansas City Preventive Patrol
   Experiment
Legalistic style
Minneapolis Domestic Violence
   Experiment and SARP
Newark Foot Patrol Experiment
Operation Ceasefire
Police crackdown

Police Foundation
Political Era
Posse comitatus
Problem-oriented policing
Reform Era
Scientific policing
Service style
Shire reeve
Statute of Winchester
Tithings
Traditional policing
Transportation
Watchman style
Weed and Seed
Zero-tolerance policing

TALKING POINTS

1. Why is the police-public relationship so complex? Which side is more to blame for police community relations, both good and bad? How might crime control and due process advocates respond to this question?

2. Is the current Community Policing Era the best approach to law enforcement?

3. Has zero-tolerance policing gone too far in enforcing the law? Is zero-tolerance policing deserving of its reputation for the crime reduction since the mid-1990s?

4. Nationally, should law enforcement agencies participate more frequently in scientific policing experiments? Are you impressed with the outcomes of the experiments described herein? Why might there be resistance to participate in police experiments?

5. Do police have any obligation to the citizenry? Are the police unfairly blamed for social problems? Provide some evidence to support your answer.

WEB LINKS

Police Foundation
(www.policefoundation.org)

Bureau of Alcohol, Tobacco, and Firearms
(www.atf.treas.gov)

Drug Enforcement Administration
(www.usdoj.gov/dea/)

American Association of State Troopers
(www.statetroopers.org)

International Association of Chiefs of Police
(www.theiacp.org)

National Association of Police Organizations
(www.napo.org)

National Sheriffs Association
(www.sheriffs.org)

Community Policing Consortium
(www.communitypolicing.org)

Vera Institute of Justice
(www.vera.org)

FURTHER READING

Raines, J. (2010). Ethics in policing: Misconduct and integrity. Sudbury, MA: Jones & Bartlett. A handy research-driven look at ethical issues in policing.

Reiss, Jr., A. J. (1971). *The police and the public.* New Haven, CT: Yale University Press

Vollmer, A. (1936). *The police and modern society.* Berkeley, CA: University of California Press.

Wilson, J. Q. (1968). *Varieties of police behavior: The management of law and order in eight communities.* Cambridge, MA: Harvard University Press.

CHAPTER 5
Police and the Rule of Law

CHAPTER OUTLINE

QUOTATIONS

"There is more law at the end of the policeman's nightstick than in all the decisions of the Supreme Court."—*Alexander Williams*[1]

"Nothing can destroy a government more quickly than its failure to observe its own law, or worse, its disregard of the charter of its own existence."—*Justice Clark*[2]

"Despite three decades to make their case, *Miranda* defenders have yet to provide research supporting the assertion that the decision's social costs are outweighed by its benefits ... the doctrine rests on apparently nothing other than the personal intuitions or unarticulated assumptions of Supreme Court Justices about how the rules have operated in the real world. Perhaps they are simply exercising their right to remain silent, but in the face of that silence the rest of us will draw the reasonable inference—an empirical case for *Miranda* does not exist."
—*Paul Cassell and Bret Hayman*[3]

"Nervousness, fear, confusion, hostility, a story that changes or contradicts itself—all are signs that the man in an interrogation room is lying, particularly in the eyes of someone as naturally suspicious as a detective. Unfortunately, these are also signs of a human being in a state of high stress."—*David Simon*[4]

"Sadly, this is where we've come: the point where a man who has committed a terrible wrong may not try to cleanse his conscience. There is no respect for the truth. And I challenge you to find the justice."
—*Judge Harold Rothwax*[5]

INTRODUCTION

The moment that the police come into contact with a citizen to investigate the reporting of a crime, the powers of the state and the individual collide (see Box 5-1). Moreover, the crime control and due process doctrines are poised for battle. The Framers of the United States Constitution were aware of this. For example:

The Fourth Amendment

The right of the people to be secure in their persons, houses, papers, and effects, against unreasonable searches and seizures, shall not be violated, and no Warrants shall issue, but upon probable cause, supported by Oath or affirmation, and particularly describing the place to be searched, and the persons or things to be seized.

The Fifth Amendment

No person shall be held to answer for a capital, or otherwise infamous crime, unless on a presentment or indictment of a Grand Jury, except in cases arising in the land or naval forces, or in the Militia, when in actual service in time of War or public danger; nor shall any person be subject for the same offense to be twice put in jeopardy of life or limb; nor shall be compelled in any criminal case to be a witness against himself, nor be deprived of life, liberty, or property, without due process of law; nor shall private property be taken for public use, without just compensation.

The Sixth Amendment

In all criminal prosecutions, the accused shall enjoy the right to a speedy and public trial, by an impartial jury of the State and district wherein the crime shall have been committed, which district shall have been previously ascertained by law, and to be informed of the nature and cause of the accusation; to be confronted with the witnesses against him; to have compulsory process for obtaining witnesses in his favor, and to have the Assistance of Counsel for his defense.

The Fourth, Fifth, and Sixth Amendments encompass the interaction between the police and members of the community, the requirement of a warrant and circumstances where warrants are not needed, the scope and limits of police powers when dealing with persons in an investigative manner, and the transition from investigating a suspect to charging the accused. In short, the Fourth, Fifth, and Sixth Amendments cover the "passing of the Constitutional baton" between the police and the courts.

WARRANTS

Warrants are an important example of due process at work because they involve the interchange between the police and local judges. Warrants are writs or orders by judicial officers, such as a judge or magistrate that direct law enforcement officers to perform specified acts and afford them protection from damage during the course of executing their duties. A warrant can only be executed by the officer to whom it is directed either by name or by description of his or her office. It cannot confer authority to execute it on one officer where a statute provides for its execution by another. The warrant cannot be executed outside the jurisdiction of the issuing court. Finally, the execution of a warrant necessitates that the warrant be in the officer's possession during the search and returned after the search or arrest.

As stated in the Fourth Amendment, probable cause is the evidentiary criterion and due process standard required for the issuance of warrants (and

CRIME SCENE   DO NOT CROSS

CRIMINAL JUSTICE NEWS

BOY GETS $6.2 MILLION FOR FALSE ARREST

In Chicago, Illinois, a boy who was falsely accused of killing an 11-year-old girl seven years ago will receive $6.2 million as a settlement in a lawsuit filed against the city and two police detectives. The boys, then ages 7 and 8, were the youngest murder suspects in the United States when they told police investigators that they killed the 11-year-old girl for her bicycle. According to the lawsuit, police ignored evidence that the boys were innocent and attempted to frame the young defendants. Semen found on the victim did not originate from the young defendants. Instead, DNA tests implicated a Chicago-area career criminal. That person awaits trial in the girl's death.

Illinois Department of Corrections records indicate that the latter defendant has served prison terms in Illinois for robbery, aggravated battery resulting in great bodily harm, aggravated kidnapping with infliction of harm, and three counts of predatory criminal sexual assault. The case is a cautionary tale for police to secure true confessions and tread carefully when dealing with suspects who are children.

Photo © JupiterImages, Corp.

indeed making any arrest). Probable cause is a set of facts and circumstances that would induce a reasonably intelligent and prudent person to believe that a particular person had committed a specific crime. Essentially, probable cause is the reasonable grounds to initiate a criminal investigation. Particularity is the other vital term from the Fourth Amendment. The particularity requirement means that warrants must specify precisely the places to be searched and the items to be seized. This prohibits the police from having unrestricted discretion to search for evidence.

The information that constitutes a warrant arrives from several sources. Frequently, victims, witnesses, or third parties report information of a crime to a police officer. These parties typically have first-hand knowledge that a specific person committed a specific crime (or number of crimes). Police officers conduct interviews, engage in other investigative activities, and produce a written document or affidavit that contains probable cause and the particular circumstances that an individual committed a crime. The report is then presented to a local judicial officer who then determines whether to issue a search warrant. In the field, these are commonly referred to as affidavit warrants.

The information that culminates in a warrant can also come from another interesting party, criminals or informants. Because criminal offenders are disproportionately likely to associate with other criminal offenders, they

5555555555

555

555

can often serve as a wealth of information to law enforcement officials who are investigating crimes. Of course, the validity and reliability of information produced by informants can be problematic. For example, informants could simply lie to police to deflect attention from their own criminal activity. Moreover, their testimony could be complete hearsay, and unable to be substantiated. Because of these concerns, the courts have addressed the use of informant information and "anonymous" tips. In *Aguilar v. Texas* (1964) the Supreme Court ruled that magistrates that issue warrants must be advised of (1) the underlying circumstances from which the affiant concluded that probable cause existed and (2) of the underlying circumstances from which the affiant concluded that the anonymous informant was credible or reliable. These two conditions constituted the Aguilar two-prong test for the issuance of warrants.[6]

McCray v. Illinois (1967) held that a reliable informant's identity generally did not need to be disclosed during court proceedings. This was an important preservation of the anonymity of police informants.[7] *Spinelli v. United States* (1969) applied the Aguilar two-pronged test to cases where the informant had not previously been proven reliable. However, it was asserted that some information was so highly specific that it must be accurate, even if its source was not revealed.[8] However, it was the case of *Illinois v. Gates* (1983) that expanded on the Aguilar case. *Illinois v. Gates* (1983) held that the reliability of an informant in search warrant cases should be based on the "totality of circumstances" instead of the rigid two-pronged test of Aguilar. Moreover, Gates established that prior reliability does not have to be established if the information is sufficiently detailed and has indications of credibility.[9]

THE EXCLUSIONARY RULE

The heart of the Fourth Amendment and by extension, warrants, is the lawfulness of the evidence that the authorities can marshal against a criminal defendant. The protection against unlawfully seized evidence is known as the exclusionary rule. The exclusionary rule is the principle that prohibits the use of illegally obtained evidence in criminal trials. This is an important due process restriction placed on the police. Even if they obtain information or evidence that incontrovertibly suggests guilt, the evidence cannot be used in court if it was obtained in violation of the Fourth Amendment.

The exclusionary rule was established at the federal level nearly 50 years before the state level. *Weeks v. U.S.* (1914) established that the Fourth Amendment barred the use of evidence secured through an illegal search and seizure by federal law enforcement officials.[10] The landmark case *Mapp. v. Ohio* (1961) held that the exclusionary rule was applicable to the states through the due process clause of the Fourth Amendment. Mapp overruled *Wolf v. Colorado* (1949), which applied the Fourth Amendment to the states but did not enforce the proscription of using illegally seized evidence at trial.[11]

A bastion of due process, the exclusionary rule is a judicial mandate designed primarily to further professionalize police behavior, not necessarily to serve as a guarantee of constitutional safeguards. It's a rather harsh rule, the reasoning being that it is better to let some of the guilty go free so that the majority of people would benefit from more thorough and professional police work. A related concept is the fruit of the poisonous tree doctrine, which established that evidence illegally seized is not only inadmissible, but also any evidence or testimony obtained later as a result of the illegally seized evidence is inadmissible. Established in *Silverthorne Lumber Company v. U. S.* (1920), the metaphor paints evidence as poisonous because of the illegalities of the underlying police search and seizure.[12]

In the decades since *Silverthorne*, the Supreme Court has generally softened the fruit of the poisonous tree doctrine. For example, in *Wong Sun v. U. S.* (1963) the Court held that defendant's statements were admissible in court because the connection between an illegal arrest and the statements had "become so attenuated as to dissipate the taint."[13] *Michigan v. Tucker* (1974) established that a witness's testimony against a criminal defendant can be admissible in court even though the initial statements made by the accused were without Miranda advisement and led the police to the witness.[14] The Court nearly reversed itself a year later. *Brown v. Illinois* (1975) held that the Miranda advisement does not reduce the taint of a defendant's illegal arrest and render admissible statements given after the arrest. In other words, the Miranda advisement is not a catch-all formality that covers for improper police behavior.[15] *United States v. Crews* (1980) and *United States v. Havens* (1980) further attenuated the poisonous tree doctrine. Crews held that in-court identification of a suspect was not made inadmissible solely because the defendant's original arrest was illegal. Havens held that illegally seized evidence could be used to impeach the defendant's statements made on direct examination during a criminal trial.[16] Two final cases linked the poisonous tree doctrine to confessions. *Taylor v. Alabama* (1982) held that a confession obtained through custodial interrogation, after an illegal arrest, should be inadmissible unless the confession is sufficiently an act of free will to purge the taint of illegal arrest.[17] *Lanier v. South Carolina* (1985) held that a finding that a confession was voluntary is merely a threshold requirement of Fourth Amendment analysis of confessions made after an illegal arrest. That Miranda warnings have been given is not enough, in and of themselves to purge the taint of illegal arrest.[18]

As this list of case law suggests, the nuances of the exclusionary rule are many. Although the exclusionary rule is a crucially important provision of due process, the majority of Supreme Court decisions since Silverthorne have tended to increase police powers in dealing with criminal suspects.

Indeed, there are many situations where the police are neither required to have a warrant nor bound by the exclusionary rule. These exceptions are reviewed next.

EXCEPTIONS TO THE EXCLUSIONARY RULE AND WARRANTLESS SEARCHES AND SEIZURES

There are a variety of circumstances where it is not reasonable to expect the police to require a warrant, wait on a warrant, or wait to conduct lawful searches during the course of their duties. Broadly speaking, these exceptions are known as exigent circumstances. Exigent circumstances are dangerous or emergency situations where it simply would not be prudent to force the police to wait on a warrant while exercising their professional duties. Situations where public safety is at risk, where evidence could be destroyed, and where the police are in "hot pursuit" are examples of exigent circumstances.[19] The courts have established a variety of exceptions to the exclusionary rule and circumstances where searches and seizures, without a warrant, are permitted. These exceptions with commensurate case law are reviewed next.

Good Faith

The good faith exception to the exclusionary rule is the principle that evidence that was collected via a faulty, erroneous, or technically illegal warrant may be used in court provided the police were acting in good faith. In other words, it does not penalize proper police behavior for the court's mistake. *United States v. Leon* (1984) established the good faith exception.[20] *Illinois v. Krull* (1987) further held that the good faith exception to the exclusionary rule applies to searches conducted by police officers acting in objectively reasonable reliance upon a statute authorizing warrantless administrative searches even though the statute was later found to violate the Fourth Amendment.[21] *Arizona v. Evans* (1995) held that the good faith exception applied to evidence seized incident to an arrest resulting from an inaccurate computer record indicating that there was an outstanding arrest warrant for the suspect. The exception applied regardless of whether police or court personnel were responsible for the erroneous record's continued presence in the police computer.[22] Given the proliferation of computers in society and criminal justice, *Arizona v. Evans* (1995) is sometimes referred to as the "computer errors exception" to the exclusionary rule. At minimum, it is an extension of the good faith exception.

The good faith exception is listed first here for an important reason. A recurrent theme in American case law is the consistent finding that as long as the police are acting in a lawful, reasonable, well-intentioned manner at the outset of their interaction with citizens, the courts are willing to grant them considerable legal discretion. This does not mean that the police have carte blanche to make mistakes and violate due process. Instead, it means that appellate courts favorably view crime control practices achieved via the tenets of due process. Acting in good faith matters.

Incident to Arrest

The most frequent type of warrantless search is one that occurs incident to or while the police are making an arrest. Of course, the arrest must be lawful and based on probable cause. The arrest must be custodial, that is the suspect is not free to leave. Also, the search must occur while the officer is making the arrest. Officers may search the defendant and the immediate physical area within the defendant's reach. The rationales for searching a suspect incident to arrest are to protect the officers (e.g., make sure the suspect does not have a weapon), prevent evidence from being destroyed, and prevent the defendant from escaping. The landmark case for the incident to arrest doctrine, sometimes also referred to as the "arm's length rule," is *Chimel v. California* (1969).[23] Since then, the incident to arrest doctrine has been further refined by the Supreme Court. For example, *Gustafson v. Florida* (1973) held that a full search may be made incident to a custodial arrest even though the officer had no fear for his or her safety and the offense was one for which there was no physical evidence that could be revealed by the search.[24] *United States v. Robinson* (1973) upheld that searches incident to full custodial arrests in which arrests had been made on traffic violations are valid regardless whether the search would produce a weapon, evidence of the crime, or contraband.[25] More recently, *Maryland v. Buie* (1990) held that incident to arrest, officers could look in closets and other spaces immediately adjoining the place of arrest from which an attack could be immediately launched. Such a search is precautionary. To go beyond the immediate area, there must be specifiable facts that would make a reasonably prudent officer believe that the area to be swept harbors an individual posing a danger to the arrest scene.[26]

Plain View

The plain view doctrine means that evidence in the plain view of police officers upon contact with a suspect may be seized without a search warrant. Early conditions for the plain view doctrine were that the officers have a legal right to be in the area where evidence was found, the sighting of the evidence needed to be inadvertent, and upon sighting, the officer must recognize the evidence as contraband, evidence, or the fruit of a crime (e.g., stolen property).[27] Over the past two decades, the United States Supreme Court has generally expanded the provisions of what is meant by evidence in plain view. For example, *California v. Ciraolo* (1986) established that warrantless aerial observation of the fenced-in cartilage (grounds or area adjoining a home) from an altitude of 1,000 feet did not violate the Fourth Amendment.[28]

Plain view also meant from the air as was also established in *Dow Chemical Company v. United States* (1986).[29] *United States v. Dunn* (1987) held that observations made from open fields did not violate any expectations of privacy and could be used to assess plain view evidence, in this case peering into the front of a barn.[30] *California v. Greenwood* (1988) established that the police may search garbage left outside of a home without a warrant. Importantly, such police action neither violates rights or expectations of privacy nor violates what is described as being in plain view.[31] Finally, *Horton v. California* (1990) held that evidence does not need to be inadvertently discovered in order to meet the plain view doctrine—this overruled the decision *Coolidge v. New Hampshire* (1971).[32]

Thus, the plain view doctrine has been expanded to include open fields. In a way, this has expanded the "jurisdiction" of what is viewable by police and thus encroached or limited the expectations of privacy from citizens. As long as police officers are acting lawfully in the first place, operating on probable cause, and can immediately identify the illegal nature of the seized material, the plain view doctrine is being met.

Automobile Searches

Among the earliest exceptions for the police to search without a warrant is the automobile exception. *Carroll v. United States* (1925) established that officers may search moveable vehicles if they have probable cause to suspect that the vehicle contains contraband or illegal materials. Because vehicles can be quickly moved away, the Court ruled that it was not prudent to expect the police to wait on a warrant before they searched the vehicle. In the eighty years since Carroll, the Supreme Court has largely expanded the scope of the automobile search doctrine. For instance, without warrants, the police may search vehicles that were impounded for the purpose of forfeiture due to transportation of contraband, drugs, alcohol, or unregistered firearms;[33] may search the entire passenger compartment including containers such as glove compartment, console, luggage, and clothing if incident to a lawful, custodial arrest;[34] and search mobile homes.[35] Several cases established that the police can search closed containers, such as backpacks,[36] and that the right to search a vehicle without a warrant was not contingent upon exigent or emergency situations.[37] A summary case is *Chambers v. Maroney* (1970), which established that if officers had probable cause to believe that if a mobile car contained evidence of a crime, it could be searched at the scene of arrest, after being moved to a police station, or after being impounded—all without a warrant.[38]

Inevitable Discovery

Nix v. Williams (1984) held that the body of a murder victim, which was found after the defendant was illegally interrogated, was admissible on the grounds that it would inevitably have been discovered even if no previous constitutional or statutory violation had taken place. The prosecution must show the inevitability of the discovery by the preponderance of evidence and need not show absence of bad faith in originally securing the evidence.[39] The inevitable discovery clause can be viewed as an "end around" the exclusionary rule.

Consent

Police officers will tell you that many of the searches they conduct are the result of citizen consent. Oftentimes, people voluntarily inform and thus empower police officers to search them. The Supreme Court has busily refined the conditions that must be present for a lawful consent search. *Schneckloth v. Bustamonte* (1973) held that advisement of Fourth Amendment rights was unnecessary as a prerequisite to a consent search in a non-custodial situation. The standard for the evaluation of consent is that the suspect consented voluntarily and without coercion.[40] Since 1973, the consent doctrine has been expanded to encompass searches based on the consent of a defendant's common law spouse[41] and an "informed third party" who it was believed had authority over the premises being searched.[42] Provided that the totality of circumstances reflect reasonableness, due process, and probable cause, consent searched can also encompass closed luggage, closed containers inside vehicles, and pertain to people before they are advised by police that they are "free to go."[43]

Stop and Frisk/Reasonable Suspicion

Arguably the most controversial exception to Fourth Amendment provisions was set forth in *Terry v. Ohio* (1968). In the 8-1 decision, the Court held that a person may be detained without probable cause to make an arrest if there is reasonable suspicion that criminal activity is afoot. Reasonable suspicion must be based on specific, articulable facts from which reasonable inferences must be drawn. When a reasonably prudent officer has a reasonable suspicion that he/she or others in the area are in danger, a "frisk" may be justified when its purpose is to discover weapons for assault of the police officer. The "frisk" must be limited in scope to a pat-down of the outer clothing of the suspect.[44]

Suspiciousness is a slippery term and the Supreme Court has arrived at a variety of decisions on the matter. As long as police officers are operating on the idea of reasonable suspicion, they can temporarily detain someone's personal luggage so that a narcotics sniffing dog can examine it, search a vehicle for weapons, and use a "wanted poster" as the basis for believing that crime was afoot.[45] *New Jersey v. T.L.O.* (1985) held that the Fourth Amendment applies to searches by public school officials. These searches are judged on reasonableness under all the circumstances and do not require probable cause if school officials believe that a student is currently violating, or has violated,

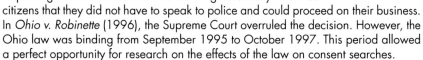

BOX 5-2

CRIMINAL JUSTICE SPOTLIGHT

VERBAL WARNINGS, CONSENT, AND POLICE SEARCHES: MUCH ADO ABOUT NOTHING?

State v. Robinette (1995) was an important Ohio decision, which required police officers to inform a motorist that he or she was "free to leave" before engaging in a consensual interrogation or requesting consent to search. The warning essentially informed citizens that they did not have to speak to police and could proceed on their business. In *Ohio v. Robinette* (1996), the Supreme Court overruled the decision. However, the Ohio law was binding from September 1995 to October 1997. This period allowed a perfect opportunity for research on the effects of the law on consent searches.

Illya Lichtenberg examined 800 consent requests made during the period. Prior to *Robinette*, the Ohio Highway Patrol requested consent to search an average of .80 times per day. After *Robinette*, the requests increased to an average of 1.03 consent searches daily. Unexpectedly, police officers sought consent more frequently after they were required to administer the warning than before when there was no requirement!

The lesson could be that alarmist claims about the "costs" of due process considerations do not necessarily handcuff the police. Indeed, due process could make the police more powerful.

Sources: *State v. Robinette*, 73 Ohio St. 3d 650, 653 N.E.2d 695 (1995); *State v. Robinette*, 80 Ohio St. 3d 234, 685 N.E.2d 762 (1997); *Ohio v. Robinette*, 519 U.S. 33 (1996); Lichtenberg, I. (2004). The impact of a verbal warning on police consent search practices. *Journal of Criminal Justice, 32*, 85–87. Photo © 2011, joingate, Shutterstock, Inc.

a school regulation or law.[46] This case expands the notion of reasonable suspicion from the police to other authority figures in other social institutions, namely schools. *Maryland v. Wilson* (1997) held that police officers may routinely order passengers out of vehicles that are legally stopped. No showing of suspicion or probable cause regarding the passengers' activities need be present. However, the Court did not address whether police could then search the individuals.[47]

The *Terry* decision and stop and frisk doctrine is a mighty indication of police power. By most standards, the police and the courts *must* operate from a principle of probable cause that criminal activity occurred. Otherwise, their conduct is not constitutional. That the police may stop and frisk people because of their suspiciousness, even when police suspicion is the outcome of training, experience, and professional expertise, is incredibly dicey. From a strict due process perspective, the reasonable suspicion doctrine is an invitation for police biases.

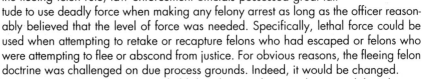

CRIME SCENE   DO NOT CROSS

CRIMINAL JUSTICE CONTROVERSY

THE EVOLUTION OF THE FLEEING FELON RULE

A dramatically interesting vestige of the English common law era was the law enforcement doctrine known as the fleeing felon rule. Under the fleeing felon rule, law enforcement officials possessed great latitude to use deadly force when making any felony arrest as long as the officer reasonably believed that the level of force was needed. Specifically, lethal force could be used when attempting to retake or recapture felons who had escaped or felons who were attempting to flee or abscond from justice. For obvious reasons, the fleeing felon doctrine was challenged on due process grounds. Indeed, it would be changed.

Tennessee v. Garner (1985) held that the Fourth Amendment prohibits the use of deadly force by police officers to prevent the escape of a suspected felon unless the force is necessary to prevent the escape and the officer has probable cause to believe that the suspect poses a significant threat of death or serious physical injury to the officer or another person. Thus, lethal force could be used in response to extreme levels of suspect force. However, the use of deadly force, whatever the circumstances, was viewed as constitutionally unreasonable.

After Garner, a variety of studies were conducted to examine its effects. Police shootings and use of lethal force declined considerably in Tennessee (where the case originated) and nationwide. Moreover, many police departments had already developed policies that softened the traditionally fleeing felon rule prior to the *Garner* ruling. Indeed, 70% of police agencies did not have to amend their deadly force policies in the wake of *Garner* because they had already done so. More recently, the Supreme Court held in *Scott v. Harris* (2007) that police pursuits that result in injury to the escapee do not violate the Fourth Amendment (Harris was rendered a quadriplegic as a result of the officer-initiated crash).

Sources: *Tennessee v. Garner*, 471 U.S. 1 (1985); Hall, J. C. (1988). Police use of deadly force to arrest: A constitutional standard. *FBI Law Enforcement Bulletin, 57,* 20–29; Culliver, C., & Sigler, R. (1995). Police use of deadly force in Tennessee following Tennessee v. Garner. *Journal of Contemporary Criminal Justice, 11,* 187–195; Tennenbaum, A. N. (1994). The influence of the Garner decision on police use of deadly force. *Journal of Criminal Law and Criminology, 85,* 241–260; Walker, S., & Fridell, L. (1992). Forces of change in police policy: The impact of *Tennessee v. Garner. American Journal of Police, 11,* 97–112; *Scott v. Harris* 550 U. S. 372 (2007). *Photo © JupiterImages, Corp.*

POLICE CUSTODY, INTERROGATION, AND *MIRANDA*

Perhaps the most iconic topic in criminal justice is the Miranda warning, the police advisement that criminal suspects have the "right to remain silent, anything you say can and will be used against you in a court of law, etc." The Miranda warning is a protection accorded criminal defendants once their interaction with police transitions from contact to custody and from mere investigation to bona fide interrogation. Similarly, the Fifth Amendment is the component of the Bill of Rights that marks the transition in criminal justice from the police to the courts. The Fourth Amendment applies strictly to police and the Sixth Amendment applies to court officials. The Fifth Amendment spans that middle ground where the police mobilize their resources to formally enter their arrest into the criminal justice system.

The Legacy of the Third Degree

A recurrent theme in this book is the evolution of criminal justice from harsh, even brutal, and capricious to its impersonal, bureaucratic, professionalized current form. A vestige of that earlier era was the use of heavy-handed police behaviors especially during the interrogation of people accused of crimes. Heavy-handed interrogation techniques, commonly referred to as the third degree, encompassed many forms of reprehensible police tactics, such as physical beatings, torture, extreme mental coercion, and interrogations that lasted dozens of hours. These tactics were disproportionately employed against African American suspects. (Movie fans might recall the scenes from the acclaimed film *LA Confidential*, which although fictional accurately portrayed third degree tactics). It was not until the early to mid Twentieth Century that the United States Supreme Court in cases like *Brown v. Mississippi* (1936), *Chambers v. Florida* (1940), *Ashcraft v. Tennessee* (1944), *Spano v. New York* (1959), and *Haynes v. Washington* (1963), deemed such egregious interrogation practices unconstitutional because the "confessions" they produced were involuntary and coerced.[48]

Although police interrogation practices became inarguably more civilized, their fundamentally coercive nature remained. Legal scholar Richard Leo has argued that police interrogation has simply shifted from coercion to deception as its operating tactic. "Where once custodial interrogation routinely involved physical violence and duress, police questioning now consists of subtle and sophisticated psychological ploys, tricks, stratagems, techniques, and methods that rely on manipulation, persuasion, and deception for their efficacy. Not only do police now openly and strongly condemn the use of physical force during interrogation, they also believe that psychological tactics are far more effective at eliciting confessions."[49]

The Road to Miranda

During the early 1960s, a handful of Supreme Court decisions laid the groundwork for increased suspect rights when taken into police custody and interrogated. *Massiah v. United States* (1964) held that no indicted defendant can be interrogated under any circumstances in the absence of his or her attorney without having his Sixth Amendment right to counsel impaired. The Massiah doctrine was applied to the states under the Fourth Amendment via *McLeod v. Ohio* (1965).[50] Essentially, the Massiah doctrine declared that criminal suspects are entitled to legal representation as soon as the police establish an adversarial relationship with the defendant. *Malloy v. Hogan* (1964) made the self-incrimination privilege of the Fifth Amendment applicable to the states through the due process clause of the Fourth Amendment.[51] *Escobedo v. Illinois* (1964) established the right to have counsel present during police interrogation once the investigation shifts into "accusatory" mode. At this point, the Sixth Amendment rights to counsel are actuated.[52] A landmark case in its own right, Escobedo established that upon interrogation, the entire adversarial system of American justice is initiated. *Griffin v. California* (1965) held that the Fifth Amendment forbids a state prosecutor's comments on failure of a defendant to take the stand and explain evidence and bars an instruction from the court that such silence may be evidence of guilt.[53]

Miranda v. Arizona (1966)

Miranda v. Arizona (1966) is among the most famous cases in American history.[54] In a narrow 5-4 vote, the Supreme Court held that the privilege against self-incrimination is available outside of criminal court proceedings and applied to police interrogations of persons in custody. Prior to custodial interrogation the following warnings must be given: (1) you have the right to remain silent; (2) anything you say can and will be used against you; (3) you have the right to have an attorney with you during the interrogation; and (4) if you are unable to hire an attorney one will be provided for you without cost during questioning. Fundamentally, the Miranda warning or advisement notifies suspects that they are empowered to be quiet in the face of police questioning. Citizens are not required to provide the police with evidentiary ammunition (pun intended) that could be used against them. Moreover, the police may invoke protections against Fifth Amendment self-incrimination at any time. Suspects may begin to answer questions, then change their mind and remain silent. Two conditions "trigger" the requirement of a Miranda advisement: custody and interrogation. These conditions make clear that the police behavior has moved from initial investigation to a custodial arrest that will bring criminal charges.

Many criminal suspects opt to waive their Miranda rights and agree to talk with police investigators about their case. If Miranda rights are waived, the waiver must be voluntary and knowingly waived. To assure this, officers ask a few short questions that the defendant must clearly and affirmatively answer. In other words, the suspect's answer must be "yes." These questions are:

- Do you understand each of these rights that I have explained to you?
- With these rights in mind, do you now wish to answer questions?
- Do you wish to answer questions without a lawyer present?
- If the suspect is a juvenile, an additional question is "Do you wish to answer questions without your parents, guardians, or custodians present?

BOX 5-4

CRIME SCENE   DO NOT CROSS

CRIMINAL JUSTICE HISTORY

THE CRIMINAL CAREER OF LEGAL MARTYR ERNESTO MIRANDA

WANTED
DEAD OR ALIVE

REWARD 1.000.000$

On March 13, 1963, Ernesto Miranda was arrested for a robbery that netted an $8 profit. During his famous confession, Miranda admitted to police that he also had kidnapped and raped a mildly retarded 18-year-old woman eleven days earlier. What transpired in that confession would culminate in the landmark *Miranda v. Arizona* in 1966. Miranda would become a household name and a symbol of the due process standards inherent in the United States Constitution.

His 20-year prison sentence was vacated because of the inadmissibility of Miranda's confession. Unfortunately for Miranda, he confessed to his wife about his perpetration of the kidnapping-rape. Even without entering his confession to police, Miranda was found guilty and sentenced to 20–30 years in prison. After four parole denials and 11 years in confinement, Miranda was paroled.

Prior to the 1963 event, Miranda was no stranger to the criminal justice system. His prior arrests or convictions encompassed crimes such as armed robbery, assault, burglary, motor vehicle theft, and attempted rape. Miranda was incarcerated at least four times between the ages of fourteen and eighteen. He was dishonorably discharged from the army and was incarcerated in military prison for AWOL and peeping Tom. In short, Ernesto Miranda's life was a series of antisocial behavior and confinement in reform schools, jails, penitentiaries, and military stockades.

His post-"Miranda" life was not much different. After his parole in 1972, Miranda was arrested and detained numerous other times for weapons offenses, traffic violations, and parole violations. For a while, he carved an existence selling autographed Miranda Warning cards for $1.50. The ignominy that was Miranda's life would end when he was murdered, stabbed to death in a bar altercation. Yet, from such a life came one of the greatest achievements in American legal history.

Source: Thomas, G. C. (1998). Miranda: The crime, the man, and the law of confessions. In R. A. Leo & G. C. Thomas (Eds.), *The Miranda debate: Law, justice, and policing* (pp. 7–24). Boston, MA: Northeastern University Press. Photo © Yanta, 2011, Shutterstock, Inc.

Post-Miranda Developments

Miranda was viewed as and still is a pinnacle event in American law and is a symbol of due process. It accords criminal defendants with substantial power against police investigations and the coercion inherent in custody and interrogation. Indeed, Miranda provides legal power to David in the face of the Goliath-like state. It should be expected then, that such an impressive due process measure would be challenged and indeed it has been. Myriad cases have revisited Miranda since 1966 and some of these are reviewed next.[55]

Orozco v. Texas (1969) held that if a suspect's freedom has been restrained "in any significant way" be it at his home or at the police station, the police are required to give the suspect the *Miranda* warnings.[56] *Harris v. New York* (1971) decided that confessions obtained without appropriate Miranda warnings could nevertheless by used in court to impeach the credibility of the defendant's testimony when it was inconsistent with the original confession.[57] *Brown v. Illinois* (1975) held that when a suspect is arrested without probable cause, any evidence obtained including confessions (even those obtained after the warnings are given) is inadmissible as evidence.[58] *Michigan v. Mosley* (1975) held that if a suspect asserts his right to remain silent during an interrogation, police officers have to honor that.[59] *Beckwith v. United States* (1976) held that when a person is not in custody, and is being interrogated in a relaxed atmosphere in the comfort of his or her home the full content of the *Miranda* warnings does not need to be given.[60] *Edwards v. Arizona* (1981) established that once a defendant requests counsel all questioning must cease until an attorney is present.[61]

New York v. Quarles (1984) was noteworthy because it established the public safety exception to Miranda. In this case, police officers frisked and handcuffed the defendant after receiving a tip that he was in possession of a firearm. When asked about the location of the gun, Quarles answered and the police seized the gun. Afterward, they read the defendant his Miranda rights. However, because of the exigent risks to public safety posed by the gun, the Court ruled that officers did not have to Mirandize the defendant.[62]

Along the same doctrine as *Orozco* and *Beckwith*, *Minnesota v. Murphy* (1984) held that interrogations held in "other potentially coercive environments," in this case, a probation office, may not generate the same necessity to give the *Miranda* warnings as when the interrogations are done in a police station.[63] *Berkemer v. McCarty* (1984) held that persons stopped for traffic violations are not in custody, thus, the *Miranda* warnings may not be given. If the motorist is arrested, however, and taken into custody, *Miranda* warnings have to be given before interrogation.[64] *Oregon v. Elstad* (1985) held that a properly obtained confession after a prior illegally obtained one is admissible in Court. However, the Court overruled this with their decision in *Missouri v. Seibert* in 2004.[65] *Minnick v. Mississippi* (1990) established that interrogation cannot resume after the suspect has contacted a lawyer and the lawyer is no longer present.[66] *Arizona v. Fulminante* (1991) held that a confession obtained by a prison informant, under circumstances where there was a credible threat of physical harm by other inmates unless the informant intervened, was coerced and violated due process. Confessions obtained through coercion may not necessarily amount to reversible error and are subject to the harmless error rule.[67] *Davis v. United States* (1994) held that police officers are not bound to stop interrogating suspects who make "uncertain" requests to have an attorney present.[68]

In sum, the case law since Miranda covers the many contingencies that arise when the police interrogate criminal suspects. Many of these cases have centered on what constitutes police custody, what constitutes police interrogation, and what are reasonable exigent exceptions to Miranda. One of the most recent cases is among the most dramatic in preserving the Miranda doctrine. *Dickerson v. United States* (2000) held that Congress may not legislatively overrule Miranda v. Arizona and thus govern the admissibility of statements made during custodial interrogations. Dickerson essentially invalidated a Congressional law passed in 1968 (18 U.S.C. 3501), which had eliminated the presumption that a confession was involuntary unless the Miranda warning was delivered prior to interrogation. In short, U.S.C. 3501 employed a totality of circumstances approach that was less restrictive than Miranda.[69]

THE COSTS OF MIRANDA?

Crimes Lost

If Miranda is a noteworthy achievement in due process, does that also mean that it is a crippling blow to crime control? After the Miranda decision, legal scholars debated whether the rights-laden decision would negatively impact the ability of the police to secure confessions from defendants. Legal scholar Paul Cassell, who is also a United States District Court Judge, has conducted much research on the empirical costs of the Miranda decision and has been a vocal critic of its negative effects. His research has produced some compelling findings. For example, Cassell examined confession rates in major American cities before-and-after Miranda. He found considerable decreases in suspect confessions to police after Miranda. These included:

- Pittsburgh   19%
- New York   35%
- Philadelphia   25%
- New Haven   16%
- Seattle   16%
- New Orleans   12%
- Chicago   27%

Los Angeles was the only major city where confessions increased (10 percent) after the establishment of Miranda. In additional analyses, Cassell estimated that about 3.8% of cases are lost because of Miranda safeguards. Using Uniform Crime Reports data, Cassell estimated that in 1993 28,000 suspects for violent Index crimes were lost due to Miranda. This amounted to:

- 880 killers
- 1,400 rapists
- 6,500 robbers
- 21,000 aggravated assaulters.

Additionally, Cassell found that 79,000 suspects for property Index crimes, burglary, larceny-theft, motor vehicle theft, and arson were also not brought to justice. Moreover, 67,000 pleas to reduced charges in property cases and 24,000 pleas to reduced charges in violence cases were adulterated because of missed confessions.[70]

Cassell's research caused a stir. Stephen Schulhofer reported numerous methodological flaws in Cassell's analyses and estimated that Miranda negatively impacted less than 1 percent of cases. Moreover, Schulhofer argued that rather than inhibiting police behavior, Miranda liberated the police to conduct lawful custodial interrogations and thus has vital symbolic value.[71] Motivated by these critiques, Cassell and Richard Fowles conducted a quantitative analysis of the effects of Miranda and found that without Miranda safeguards the clearance rate for violent crimes would increase between 8 to 20% and property crimes would increase 4 to 16%. Annually, hundreds of thousands of cases would additionally be cleared without the due process powers of Miranda.[72]

Legal scholars disagree sharply about the benefits and costs of Miranda, but what do criminal justice personnel think? Do law enforcement officers, police administrators, prosecutors, judges, and the like think that Miranda is a centerpiece of America's commitment to due process, or an impediment to effective crime control? Victoria Time and Brian Payne surveyed police chiefs in Virginia to assess their perceptions about Miranda. The produced a variety of interesting findings. For example:

- More than 90% reported that officers are sufficiently trained to ensure suspects' Miranda rights.
- About 40% felt that defendants would "get off easy" because of the protections inherent in the Miranda warning.
- Nearly 90% felt that suspects will routinely confess even after they have been Mirandized, that is, been formally been advised of their rights.
- Nearly 60% of police chiefs felt that Miranda should not be overturned; 40% felt that it should be overturned.
- About 60% felt that abolishing Miranda would have little effect on the day-to-day functioning of the police.
- About 90% of police chiefs believed that the public had misguided perceptions about the Miranda warnings (that is, it had to be advised for any police contact).
- About 80% of police chiefs reported little to no experience of seeing cases dismissed for Miranda violations.[73]

Waive or Invoke?

Additional research has provided evidence to buttress the putative costs of lost crimes that Miranda has created. Legal scholar Richard Leo observed actual police interrogations and arrived at a variety of interesting conclusions. First, among 175 police interrogations, suspects invoked their Miranda rights in only 22% of cases. The remaining 78% of cases involved suspects who knowingly and voluntarily waived their Miranda rights and talked with police investigators. Second, a suspect's criminal record appeared to influence whether or not they spoke with police. Persons with no prior criminal history were most likely to waive their Miranda rights and speak with police. Indeed, 92% of those without criminal records waived their rights. On the other hand, less than 70% of persons with prior felony records waived their rights and nearly 30% invoked their Miranda rights. This offers conflicting support of Cassell's thesis. The majority of experienced criminals actually talk with police, but they are nearly four times as likely as first-time arrestees to invoke Miranda.

After the police interrogation, the effects of waiving or invoking Miranda had variable effects on the case processing through the criminal justice system. Suspect's response to Miranda had no statistical effect on the prosecutor's decision to charge or the likelihood of conviction. However, a suspect who waived Miranda was twice as likely to have his or her case resolved via a plea bargain. Yet, waiving or invoking Miranda did not significantly affect sentence severity.[74] Taken together, the effects of Miranda and whether it is waived or invoked do not dramatically alter the progression of a case through the criminal justice system.

Leo's research touched on a tangential but important issue pertaining to who chooses to waive their rights. Compared to experienced criminal offenders whose prior interactions with criminal justice officials accorded them a sense of what to expect during interrogations, first-time, naïve, or novice offenders had no such experience. Yet, persons without criminal record were overwhelmingly likely to waive their Miranda rights and participate in custodial interrogations. Experimental research similarly conveys that factually innocent suspects, persons who presumably should have nothing to share with police because of their lack of involvement in crime, were most likely to waive their rights and talk with police. For example, Saul Kassin and Rebecca Norwick found that 81% of innocent people agreed to talk with police even in the face of a hostile, closed-minded interrogator where there was nothing to be gained by participating in the interrogation.[75]

Thus, whether a defendant waives or invokes Miranda speaks to the double-pronged nature of the Fifth Amendment protection against self-incrimination. For criminals who invoke Miranda, it is a powerful opportunity to shut down police efforts to marshal evidence against them. For innocents who waive Miranda, it places them in an undeniably coercive interaction with police.

Due Process Symbolism

As described earlier, interrogations have evolved from relying on physical coercion to psychological methods of deception. Today, police investigators employ a variety of subtle but powerful techniques when interviewing criminal suspects in an effort to lawfully secure a true confession. The two most common methods are appealing to the suspect's self-interest and confronting the suspect with existing evidence of guilt. When used in concert, these approaches can be quite effective. There are at least ten other tactics used by police during actual interrogations. These include: (1) undermine the suspect's confidence in his or her denial, (2) identify contradictions in the suspect's alibi or story, (3) ask specific "behavioral analysis" interview questions, (4) appeal to the importance of cooperation, (5) offer moral justifications and face-saving excuses, (6) confront the suspect with false evidence of guilt, (7) praise or flatter the suspect, (8) appeal to the detective's expertise and authority, (9) appeal to the suspect's conscience, and (10) minimize the moral seriousness of the offense.[76]

Of course, the criminal justice system must balance the twin goals of crime control and due process. As such, it is unrealistic to expect police custody to be a cozy environment and police interrogations to be a pleasant, facile experience. Fortunately, Miranda has likely facilitated both crime control and due process goals. Legal scholar Richard Leo noted that Miranda has had four profound impacts on American law enforcement. First, it has brought a civilized tone to police interrogations. Second, it has helped transform and professionalize police culture. Third, it interjected constitutional rights into American culture. Fourth, Miranda inspired police to develop more specialized, sophisticated, and seemingly more effective interrogation techniques.[77] In the course of cementing American due process, Miranda helped the police hone their crime fighting skills.

Symbolically, Miranda is perhaps the greatest example of due process in American criminal justice. Its ultimate social costs are a matter of great debate. To some, Miranda is the antithesis of legitimate police power. For example, Judge Rothwax recommended that Miranda be overruled because it placed unnecessary constraints on the police and inappropriately empowered criminal defendants in ways that were beyond the scope of the original intentions of the Fourth Amendment. According to Rothwax, Miranda (1) has sent jurisprudence on a hazardous detour by introducing novel conceptions of the proper relationship between a criminal suspect and police, (2) has accentuated the features in the criminal justice system that manifest the least regard for truth-seeking, such as the view that the process is a game of chance in which the defendant should always have some prospect of victory, (3) was decided at a time when effective alternatives for restraining unlawful police conduct were ripe for implementation but never pursued, and (4) the many exceptions to constitutional constraints on police behavior render Miranda ambiguous.[78] To some, the Miranda doctrine is a doctrine still under development.

CRIME SCENE   DO NOT CROSS

BOX 5-5

CRIMINAL JUSTICE RESEARCH

CONFESSIONS AND CRIMINOLOGICAL THEORY?

Having a confession increases the likelihood of conviction and can serve as the only piece of tangible evidence that police investigators possess. For these reasons, the stakes are high during police interrogations. At the same time, police custody and interrogations are meant to be unpleasant, deceptive, and coercive to the degree that these discomforts can elicit confessions. Deception can even be accomplished using criminological theory!

FBI Agent Brian Boetig, an instructor in the Law Enforcement Communication Unit at the FBI Academy has written about the use of criminological theory to entice criminal suspects into confessing. The logic is simple. Many criminological theories of crime, particularly if their scope is sociological, assert that social conditions, circumstances, and contingencies are often the root causes of criminal behavior. Phenomena such as social inequality, poverty, adversity, living in bad neighborhoods, coming from a non-intact family, associating with delinquent peers, racism, and sexism are some of the variables theorized to predict crime. Interrogators can cite these factors as the "real or genuine" causes of crime, which in turn deflects the perceived blame, culpability, and guilt from the suspect. Acting as a quasi-professor delivering a lecture, the interrogator presents himself as less adversarial and more understanding of the moral, practical, and ethical reasons why the suspect committed the crime.

Of course, this is deceptive. The investigator may believe these theories of crime but they are indeed irrelevant to the suspect at hand. However, if the suspect feels that the investigator is an ally, confessions are likely to occur.

Source: Boetig, B. P. (2005). Reducing a guilty suspect's resistance to confessing: Applying criminological theory to interrogation theme development. *FBI Law Enforcement Bulletin, 74*, 13–20. *Photo © JupiterImages, Corp.*

CHAPTER SUMMARY: BALANCING CRIME CONTROL AND DUE PROCESS

- The Fourth Amendment of the United States Constitution protects citizens from unreasonable searches and seizures and states that warrants based on probable cause are needed to justify police searches.
- The Fifth Amendment of the United States Constitution covers police and court functions especially the right against self-incrimination during police confessions.
- Custody and interrogation are the conditions that trigger the Miranda advisement of rights.
- The exclusionary rule prohibits the use of illegally obtained evidence to be used during prosecution.
- Due to exigent circumstances and other important contingencies, there are several exceptions to the exclusionary rule and situations where warrants are not needed to search suspects.

- *Miranda v. Arizona* is perhaps the most famous criminal case in American history and has great symbolic and applied due process value.
- Miranda has compromised and facilitated crime control depending on the evidence and perspectives of various legal scholars.
- Police interrogation has evolved from one characterized by physical coercion to psychological deception.
- Suspects who waive their Miranda rights can face adversarial police interviews.
- Persons with more extensive criminal history are more likely than innocents or first-time arrestees to invoke their Miranda rights.
- American case law exists in a continual state of development and refinement. Thus legal doctrines are in a state of flux.

KEY TERMS

Fourth Amendment	*Mapp v. Ohio*
Fifth Amendment	Miranda advisement
Sixth Amendment	Miranda triggers
Automobile searches/Carroll doctrine	*Miranda v. Arizona*
	Particularity
Confession	Plain view doctrine
Consent search	Probable cause
Custody/custodial arrest	Search and seizure
Dickerson v. United States	Self-incrimination
Escobedo v. Illinois	Stop and frisk/reasonable suspicion
Exclusionary rule	Tainted arrest
Fruit of the poisonous tree doctrine	*Terry v. Ohio*
Good faith doctrine	Totality of circumstances doctrine
Incident to arrest doctrine	Waive
Inevitable discovery doctrine	Warrant
Interrogation	*Weeks v. United States*
Invoke	

TALKING POINTS

1. Does the Bill of Rights equally serve the interests of crime control and due process?
2. Are the Fourth, Fifth, and Sixth Amendments still applicable today? What changes would you recommend that better serve the goals of contemporary criminal justice?

3. Has Miranda been a positive or negative for American justice? Should it be overruled? Why or why not? Do various exceptions to Miranda already reduce its legal significance?

4. Professor Paul Cassell has been a vocal critic of Miranda. Are the lost crime estimates that he has found reason enough to re-address Miranda?

WEB LINKS

United States Supreme Court
(www.oyez.org/oyez/frontpage)

Cornell University Law School Legal Information Institute
(www.law.cornell.edu/)

United States Supreme Court (Official Site)
(www.supremecourtus.gov/)

Miranda Warning
(www.usconstitution.net/miranda.html)

Police Employment (various information)
(www.policeemployment.com/)

FURTHER READING

Irons, P. (1999). *A people's history of the Supreme Court.* New York: Penguin Books. Subtitled "The men and women whose cases and decisions have shaped our constitution," this work is a great overview of the changing nature of case law. It shows the humanity behind Supreme Court decisions both in terms of the Justices and the defendants that gave rise to the cases.

Kassin, S. M., & Gudjonsson, G. H. (2004). The psychology of confessions: A review of the literature and issues. *Psychological Science in the Public Interest, 5,* 33–67. This journal article comprehensively reviews the scholarship on police interrogations, custody, and confessions. The authors are major contributors to the literature.

Leo, R. A., & Thomas, G. C. (Eds.). (1998). *The Miranda debate: Law, justice, and policing.* Boston, MA: Northeastern University Press. An excellent anthology of papers on various aspects of Miranda v. Arizona (1966). This is must-reading for students interesting in police interrogations and case law pertaining to the police.

Rothwax, Judge H. J. (1996). *Guilty: The collapse of criminal justice*. New York: Warner Books. This national bestseller is a brilliant, polemical look at the absurdities of the criminal justice system. The author began his career as a liberal defense attorney and card-carrying ACLU member, but after 25 years as a New York State judge, began to reconsider his positions on many legal and justice issues.

CHAPTER 6

Police Behavior, Discretion, and the Dark Side of Policing

CHAPTER OUTLINE

QUOTATIONS

"In the United States, anybody can pick up a phone, walk into a police station, or stop a police officer on the street and expect that an officer, armed and uniformed, embodying the full authority of government, will attend to the private problems of that individual."—*David Bayley*[1]

"The virtual absence of disciplinary control and the demand for discretionary freedom are related to the idea that patrol work involves 'playing by ear.' What the seasoned patrolman means, however, in saying that he 'plays by ear' is that he is making his decisions while being attuned to the realities of complex situations about which he has immensely detailed knowledge."—*Egon Bittner*[2]

"The police see people when they are dirty, angry, rowdy, obscene, dazed, savage, or bloodied. . .they are not in these circumstances 'equal,' they are different. . . .'Decent people' and 'bums' are not equal."—*James Q. Wilson*[3]

"No police anywhere has ever existed, nor is it possible to conceive of a genuine police ever existing, that does not claim a right to compel other people forcibly to do something. If it did not claim such a right, it would not be a police."—*Carl Klockers*[4]

"Brutality and the third degree have been identified with the municipal police of the United States since their inauguration."—*William Westley*[5]

INTRODUCTION

"The first contact between a law enforcement agent and a suspect is a moment alive with possibilities. Experienced cops know. Their customary cool and casual manner masks quivering antennae. Unexpected things happen and they happen fast. Why do cops draw their guns as they walk up to a strange doorway, why do they approach a stopped car from both sides, the cop on the right hanging back just behind the occupant's line of sight? Because the lore of the station house, in the cities, at least, is that most folks do not think of a conversation with a police officer as a pleasant social encounter. Bane or blessing, police carry with them an aura of menace. Without even trying to activate their threat glands, they instill an uncomfortable feeling that one's life is about to take an unexpected turn. And people who have recently committed a crime may feel the pang of panic. Those emotional ingredients can make a lethal adrenaline cocktail. Plus, the good cop knows that the first contact might shake loose an incriminating item—a surprised, unguarded acknowledgement or sudden guilt-inspired flight, perhaps a surreptitiously discarded object or a demonstrably false alibi. All good evidence of culpability. It pays to be alert."[6]

This paragraph, borrowed from legal scholar H. Richard Uviller, lyrically captures the essence of Chapters 5 and 6 in a mere 205 words. The moment that the police and the public come into contact, the doctrines of crime control and due process become activated. The police serve multiple concurrent roles as the guarantors of due process and crime control, preservers of the Constitution, and protectors against criminals. Police officers serve and protect the people and are simultaneously empowered to deprive the people of their liberty. The police are immensely powerful. For these reasons, and others that this chapter will explore, the public and the police have a complicated relationship. For the public and law enforcement insiders, the police are an entity characterized by danger, secrecy, power, and solidarity. They are the often self-imposed thin blue wall shut off from the rest of society. Chapter 6 looks behind that blue wall to examine what the police actually do, and by extension, what they often do not do, the place of discretion, and various sensationalistic topics in which the police occasionally are involved.

DISCRETION AND THE DETERMINANTS OF POLICE BEHAVIOR

Discretion is the latitude to choose one course of action over another. In the context of policing, an officer's discretion can produce a range of activities, from assisting a motorist, lecturing a citizen who has committed an illegal act, letting a suspect off with a warning, making an arrest, and using force against a resisting suspect. There are numerous determinants of police behavior and influences of officer discretion, such as department policy, legal characteristics of the arrest situation, the extra-legal characteristics of the accused, and the attitudes, behaviors, and presentation of self of criminal suspects. Discretion also depends on the "type" of officer. For example, Richard Wortley examined police officer attitudes toward discretion using the service, legalistic, and watchman styles developed by James Q. Wilson and found that service style officers advocated the use of discretion as a means to solve resident problems. Conversely, legalistic style officers disliked discretion because they were inflexible in their commitment to enforcing the law equitably. Watchman style officers, the most authoritarian type of officer, had favorable valuations of discretion because it accommodated their desire to appropriately "handle" citizens for serious law violations.[7]

In the end, what do the police actually do? Since most citizens have little to no contact with the police and thus zero police experience, they likely do not know. According to television, film, and the nightly news, the police engage in an array of scintillating, death defying, dangerous, and dramatic activities, such as engaging in high speed chases, getting into fights, exchanging gunfire with the bad guys, giving the third degree in an interrogation room, and the like. Of course, such activities occur, but how prevalent are they?

As Albert Reiss once wrote, "The conventional view of the criminal justice system provides almost no information on encounters and transactions between police officers and citizens, the microcosm that generates all cases for processing in the criminal justice system. The core of all these transactions... is a discretionary decision."[8] The lack of knowledge of day-to-day police behavior became a major research initiative in the mid to late 1960s during the era of intense tumult between the police and public. The work of social scientists during this era produced a rich knowledge base about police behavior and the use of discretion, descriptive information about arrests and other police-citizen contacts, characteristics of police officer personality and police culture, cynicism and other stressors associated with policing, and dramatic police activities, such as the use of force.

Reiss, Donald Black, and their colleagues conducted systematic observation of more than 5,700 police-citizen interactions in Boston, Massachusetts, Chicago, Illinois, and Washington, DC during the summer of 1966. They arrived at a number of important conclusions about normative police behavior, the influences of police discretion, and the determinants of arrest.[9]

Mobilization
Most arrest situations arise through citizen rather than police initiative. In this sense, policing is overwhelmingly reactive, not proactive. This is infinitely important to your evaluation of due process and crime control. Most criminal cases pass through the moral filter of the public before the police are mobilized. In this sense, it is the citizenry that determines whether one's behavior will result into entry into the criminal justice system. This finding generally counters the popular notion that the police proactively select targets for contact and arrest.

Complainants
Arrest practices sharply reflect the preferences of citizen complainants. According to Donald Black, this gives police work a radically democratic character. Thus, citizen complainants express whether they want a suspect to be talked to, taken away, given a summons, arrested, and the like. The police have no obligation to comply with the complainant, but they often do.[10]

Leniency
The police frequently use leniency rather than harshness or enforcement and exercise their arrest power with less frequency than they could. By and large, the police are good judges of when to resort to arrest when other discretionary avenues have been exhausted. Several other criminologists using various sources of data have also found that police are sensible problem-solvers who wield their legal power with constraint rather than overly aggressive law enforcers.[11]

Evidence

Evidence is an important factor in arrest. This finding is fairly obvious. The stronger the evidence that a crime occurred, especially if the police personally witnessed its commission, increased the likelihood of arrest.[12] However, even when the evidence against a suspect was very strong, the police frequently took action short of arrest.

Seriousness

The probability of arrest is higher in legally serious crime situations than in those of a relatively minor nature. This means that the police reserve arrests to serious crimes, such as murder, robbery, assault, etc., and is further testament to their discretion. Minor crimes, such as disorderly conduct, shoplifting, and the like, are then less likely to result in arrest.[13]

Intimacy

The greater the relational distance between a complainant and a suspect, the greater is the likelihood of arrest. In other words, the police are more apt to arrest when suspect and victim are strangers and less willing to arrest when they are friends, neighbors, or family members.[14] It is assumed that informal methods of problem solving are used for domestic disputes, which were traditionally viewed as private matters.[15]

Disrespect

The probability of arrest increases when a suspect is disrespectful toward the police. This underscores the larger relationship between citizen demeanor and officer behavior. By and large, police officers respond to incivility, belligerence, and contempt like other people; they reciprocate. Poor, negative, disrespectful, or hostile citizen demeanor not only increases the likelihood of arrest but also other forms of police action, such as use of force. (For an exploration of research in this area, see Box 6-1.)

Discrimination

No evidence exists to show that the police discriminate on the basis of race. Differential arrest rates by race reflect racial differences in disrespect shown toward the police and citizen reports to the police. The effect of race on police behavior is a controversial area that is explored further in this chapter. However, an important point should be considered. Recall that the preponderance of police behavior reacts or responds to citizen mobilization. In other words, victims, offenders, or witnesses to crimes call the police who then respond and conduct an investigation. According to Black, Reiss, and other early police scholars, this fundamentally counters the idea that the police are discriminatory in their enforcement practices.[16]

To summarize, early observational research on the police indicated that law enforcement officials are responsive and receptive to the public to a

BOX 6-1

CRIME SCENE ⬛ DO NOT CROSS

CRIMINAL JUSTICE RESEARCH

TALKING YOUR WAY TO JAIL? SUSPECT DEMEANOR AND OFFICER DISCRETION

Police scholars such as Albert Reiss, Donald Black, James Q. Wilson, William Ker Muir, and many others produced somewhat comforting findings about police behavior. As a whole, police officers' interactions with citizens were civil, professional, and involved relatively mundane services. Patrol officers generally showed restraint, good judgment, and tended to under-enforce the law while solving problems. However, extra-legal characteristics, such as demeanor and offender demographics, have also been important. Suspects who had poor demeanor and treated officers with disrespect were significantly more likely to be arrested for violations of law. In short, surly citizens can talk their way to jail via their actions.

How salient is suspect demeanor to the arrest decision? Scholars have produced conflicting information. According to the classic police article by Irving Piliavin and Scott Briar, between 50 to 60% of the police decision to make an arrest was the result of suspect demeanor. Youths who were disrespectful and seemed to adopt or play the role of delinquent were significantly likely to receive harsher legal treatment. However, Piliavin and Briar also found that prior criminal record was the most important determinant of officer behavior. Using an array of data sources and analytical methods, scholars have rather consistently found that citizen or suspect demeanor that was abusive, disrespectful, and the like resulted in more punitive outcomes, namely arrest. To illustrate, Joel Garner, Christopher Maxwell, and Cedrick Heraux found that suspects who used an antagonistic demeanor with police were 163% more likely to be handled with force. Persons who initiated physical force against officers were 1800% more likely to have police force applied to them!

More recent police scholarship has cast doubt on the demeanor doctrine with findings that once various situational, behavioral, and legal controls are considered, demeanor is not significant. Criminologist David Klinger found that early studies of police-citizen interactions were rife with errors. For instance, suspect "demeanor" was defined so broadly that it often encompassed explicit criminal acts. Moreover, prior studies often did not adequately control for criminal conduct. Of course, "demeanor" was predictive of crime—demeanor in many cases was crime. Klinger also found that many forms of demeanor were spuriously related to arrest outcomes. Only extreme forms of citizen hostility predicted arrest independent of other important factors.

What does it all mean? As Klinger himself has pointed out, the importance of extra-legal variables was likely inflated or even exaggerated by some police scholars working during the 1960s and 1970s. Studies purporting that demeanor, race, sex, social class and the like were what activated police behavior radically underestimated or even ignored the lawful considerations of offense seriousness and other important factors relating to due process.

Sources: Piliavin, I., & Briar, S. (1964). Police encounters with juveniles. *American Journal of Sociology, 69,* 206–214; Engel, R. S., Sobol, J. J., & Worden, R. E. (2000). Further exploration of the demeanor hypothesis: The interaction effects of suspects' characteristics and demeanor on police behavior. *Justice Quarterly, 17,* 235–258; Lundman, R. J. (1996). Extralegal variables and arrest. *Journal of Research in Crime and Delinquency, 33,* 349–353; Lundman, R. J. (1996). Demeanor and arrest: Additional evidence from previously unpublished data. *Journal of Research in Crime and Delinquency, 33,* 306–323; Reisig, M. D., McCluskey, J. D., Mastrofski, S. D., & Terrill, W. (2004). Suspect disrespect toward the police. *Justice Quarterly, 21,* 241–268; Sun, I. Y., & Payne, B. K. (2004). Racial differences in resolving conflicts: A comparison between black and white police officers. *Crime & Delinquency, 50,* 516–541; Garner, J. J., Maxwell, C. D., & Heraux, C. G. (2002). Characteristics associated with the prevalence and severity of force used by the police. *Justice Quarterly, 19,* 705–746; Klinger, D. A. (1994). Demeanor or crime? Why 'hostile' citizens are more likely to be arrested. *Criminology, 32,* 475–493; Klinger, D. A. (1996). More on demeanor and arrest in Dade County. *Criminology, 34,* 61–82; Klinger, D. A. (1996). Bringing crime back in: Toward a better understanding of police arrest decisions. *Journal of Research in Crime and Delinquency, 33,* 333–336; Terrill, W. Paoline, E. A., & Manning, P. K. (2003). Police culture and coercion. *Criminology, 41,* 1003–1034. Photo © JupiterImages, Corp.

considerable degree. Citizens are the ones who most frequently mobilize the law and the police balance problem solving and enforcement decisions with the complainant's wishes. Of course, offenses seriousness and evidence significantly increase the chances of arrest. Police officers show impressive judgment, considerable restraint, and employ leniency more frequently than they employ harshness. Indeed, citizens who are contrite and acknowledge responsibility for wrongdoing, such as for traffic violations, can expect to be "let off with a warning." Claims that the police discriminate widely or enforce the law zealously are incorrect. In fact, from a crime control perspective, the police let far too many potential offenders off rather than initiating their involvement in the criminal justice system.

CHARACTERISTICS OF POLICE PERSONALITY AND CULTURE

The preponderance of interactions between police officers and citizens entail courteous, unexciting action. The police are public servants who deal with the daily demands and stresses of their occupation like all other people who work. Make no mistake, however; there is no other job quite like being a police officer. First, although most police work is relatively mundane, some situations are not. Indeed, policing has been described as hours of sheer boredom interrupted my moments of sheer terror/excitement/danger. Second, unlike other jobs, police officers are legally empowered to make arrests, use force and coercion (when necessary), and initiate the processes of depriving human beings of their freedom (of course, upon convictions for violating criminal law). Third, police officers see the bottom of the barrel in terms of human behavior and the worst of cruelty with which people inflict on one another. It is they who manage the balance between the lawful and the unlawful. As a consequence, the police are different to a certain degree because of their unique and awesome powers and visceral experiences in responding to criminal behavior. This section explores some individual characteristics of police officers as well as the loose culture that in some ways typifies law enforcement. Recall, no culture, and that includes police culture, is monolithic. There are differences among officers and within departments and the characteristics described next are some of the recurrent commonalities that scholars have found when studying police officers.

Secrecy, Solidarity, and Violence

As William Doerner, a longtime police officer and police scholar at Florida State University, advised, "This sense of being different from civilians and the knowledge that a police officer can depend only upon other officers in a moment of need fosters a sense of security and occupational solidarity known as the police subculture."[17] A subculture, or referred to simply as police culture, is a subgroup differentiated by the police occupation that functionally unifies the group and acts collectively on each member. It also separates them from non-police officers, an out-group that is perceived as different. In the 1950s, William Westley was one of the earliest social scientists to study the subculture that separates police officers from civilians, the so-called thin blue wall. Westley found that a secrecy-based solidarity was a fundamental characteristic of the police culture. From interviews, he found that 73 percent of officers admitted that they would not report a fellow officer for stealing and 77 percent were willing to commit perjury rather than testify against a fellow officer. A primary way that the police ensure secrecy is to socialize rookie officers on the job and effectively inculcate the values, beliefs, and norms of their patrol unit.[18]

In addition to secrecy, Westley also found that the police culture in part endorses violence as a reasonable means to perform the duties of police work. Officers offered a variety of rationales for the legitimate use of violence against citizens. In descending order of prevalence, these were 1) to retaliate against someone who was disrespectful to the police, 2) when it was impossible to avoid violence, such as responding to force, 3) to obtain information, 4) to make an arrest, 5) to punish a "hardened criminal," 6) to inflict punishment when the officer "knows" the person is guilty, and 7) as an especially punitive treatment of offenders who commit sexually based offenses. Moreover, Westley found that police violence was illegal, acceptable, and at times even endorsed or expected by colleagues.[19]

The Working Personality

Jerome Skolnick's classic *Justice without Trial: Law Enforcement in a Democratic Society* is noteworthy for its description of the "working personality" that police officers employ during the course of their duties. According to Skolnick, the police officer's role contains two principal variables, danger and authority, which are the result of the police's constant pressure to appear efficient. The threat of danger makes the police extremely vigilant about protecting themselves and, as a result, they become highly suspicious of people who might be potential sources of danger. Potentially dangerous people are viewed as "symbolic assailants." The constant concern about symbolic assailants coupled with the unique arrest powers or authority of police officers tends to isolate them from conventional society. Taken together, the police personality is a constellation of traits that include danger, isolation (and thus alienation), authority and power, suspiciousness, conservatism, and a fiercely held solidarity with other officers.[20]

Coercion

William Ker Muir used coercion as the organizing principle of police work. Muir developed a typology whereby officers held either a tragic view of human behavior or a cynical view of human behavior and whether officers were content

CRIME SCENE   DO NOT CROSS

BOX 6-2

CRIMINAL JUSTICE BRIEF

DRUG USE AMONG LAW ENFORCEMENT OFFICERS

Since the police are guardians of due process and the law, many citizens hold police officers to a higher moral standard in terms of their behavior. Improper or illicit behaviors among the police can erode public confidence in criminal justice. One facet of this public concern is substance abuse among police officers. Does it occur? What is its prevalence?

Police scholars Kim Michelle Lersch and Tom Mieczkowski recently conducted an empirical study of drug testing within a police agency from 1990 to 1999. During the period of data collection, 48,704 random drug tests were administered to officers and 148 positive test results were produced. In other words, 0.31% of all tests indicated illicit drug use among police officers. Of these positive tests, more than 80% were for cocaine use. Lersch and Mieczkowski concluded that perceptions about drug use among police officers are much ado about nothing. Nearly 100% of officers were clean—estimates that are similar to prior research.

Source: Lersch, K. M., & Mieczkowski, T. (2005). Drug testing sworn law enforcement officers: One agency's experience. *Journal of Criminal Justice, 33,* 289–297. Photo © Phase4 Photography, 2008.

or conflicted about using coercion against suspects. From these constructs, Muir devised four types of officers. Professional officers, found to be the most effective, held a tragic view of humans and were able to use coercion with equanimity. Reciprocator officers held a tragic view and were conflicting about using coercion. Enforcer officers were cynical and certainly willing to use coercion. Avoider officers possessed a cynical view and were conflicted about coercion. According to Muir, "the basic condition of patrol work is that it is lonely, dangerous, and preoccupied with human suffering."[21]

Cynicism

Because of the "doom and gloom" situations that police officers face, it perhaps should be expected that these experiences would weigh on their mental health. Two additionally important lines of research pertain to socialization into police work and the resultant cynicism that emerges among police officers. There is considerable evidence that police officers "become blue" or fully develop into full-fledged cops via on-the-job training. Whatever their pre-existing characteristics and experiences, it is actual police work and importantly, socialization by veteran officers, that molds officer personality. Generally, police officers begin their careers motivated, energetic, and at times naïve about their ability to effect change in the lives of citizens. Over time, their experiences and exposure to the police organization and culture change them.[22]

One of the changes that police officers can undergo is the development of cynicism. In his classic *Behind the Shield* (1967), former New York City police officer and police academy instructor Arthur Niederhoffer suggested that cynicism occurs when officers "lose faith in people, society, and eventually in themselves. In their Hobbesian view the world becomes a jungle in which crime, corruption and brutality are normal features of the terrain."[23] According to Niederhoffer, cynicism was directed toward both the public and the police organization itself and developed along a path of pseudo-cynicism, romantic cynicism, aggressive cynicism, and resigned cynicism. His empirical analyses confirmed that police rookies were idealistic and that cynicism progressively increased for the first 7–10 years of the officer's career. It then decreases briefly and plateaus as officers become resigned to the fact that substantive improvement of society and their police department are not possible and they look toward retirement. The subsequent literature on cynicism has generally supported Niederhoffer's thesis but quibbled with the methodological properties of his cynicism scale.[24] In what has been a recurrent theme in Chapters 4, 5, and 6, cynicism among police officers is a result of conditions stemming from both the police organization and the public.

To summarize, police scholars have devised a variety of descriptions and even developed typologies to capture police characteristics and police culture. All of these approaches, such as the work by Westley, Skolnick, Muir, Niederhoffer, and others, were valuable. Over time, there was an increased acknowledgment that although there were important commonalities among police officers, there was also great heterogeneity. Different officers have different styles that are promoted differently by various police departments. Today, departmental culture, organizations, rank and tenure, individual style, and many other factors are cited as predictors of police personality and culture.[25]

USE OF FORCE

Police use of force against citizens figures prominently on the front pages of the newspaper, the lead story on television news, and in the minds and evaluations of persons who are critical of the police. Despite its notoriety, one empirical point about police force must be considered: It is exceedingly rare. Matthew Durose, Erica Smith, and Patrick Langan of the Bureau of Justice Statistics analyzed national data from the Police-Public Contact Survey, a supplement of the National Crime Victimization Survey (NCVS). According to the most recent data, 43.5 million residents age 16 or older (about one in five persons of this age group) had one face-to-face contact with a police officer. The total volume of police-citizen encounters exceeded 71 million. Of these interactions, more than 56 percent were the result of a motor vehicle

BOX 6-3

CRIMINAL JUSTICE INTEREST

DO COPS KNOW MORE THAN CIVILIANS?

A hallmark of a good police drama is the interrogation scene in which the savvy and street-wise police officer elicits a confession from the accused. Armed with their experience, training, and raw guile, the media often portrays law enforcement officers as having some extra-sensory power to detect deception and guilt among persons accused of crimes.

Anecdotally, police officers and other investigative groups suggest that guilty people behave in significantly different ways than persons with nothing to hide. For example, it is believed that persons who are attempting to deceive the police will not look them in the eye and are inconsistent and provide few details when recalling events. Moreover, "guilty" interviewees appear shifty, nervous, and use a different pitch of voice when responding to questions. A good detective, it is believed, just "knows" whether the suspect in custody is indeed the perpetrator of the crime.

Interestingly, psychological research does not necessarily match and at times even conflicts with the popular image of the keen police officer. For example:

- Most studies find that respondents, usually lay people such as college students, can detect liars from truth-tellers between 40 and 60% of the time. Chance alone is 50%.
- Experimental research indicated that liars carry a difficult cognitive load while perpetrating deception. Compared to truth tellers (and thus presumably innocent people), liars take longer time in between periods of speech, are gaze aversive, that is they avoid looking investigators in the eyes, provide fewer illustrations, have fewer hand movements, and hesitate more in their speech. These findings conform with police lore.
- Police officers have about the same (lack of) success in detecting deception. In fact, a meta-analysis by Christian Meissner and Saul Kassin found that across a variety of studies, "[criminal justice] training and experience had no significant effect on participants' ability to accurately discriminate truth from deceit."
- Leif Stromwall and Par Anders Granhag found that police officers', prosecutors', and judges' ideas about signs of suspect deception were remarkably inconsistent with the research literature about actual indicators of deception.
- Researchers have found evidence of "investigator bias" where criminal justice agents are significantly prone to rating suspects as deceitful or guilty even when they are not.
- Investigator bias can be a contributing factor in cases that are ultimately discovered to be miscarriages of justice.
- Persons under investigation for murder or rape perceive police attitudes characterized by either dominance (e.g., the police try to bully them) or humanity (e.g., the police are civil and polite). Suspects are more likely to confess as the result of police interviews characterized be humanity and more likely to deny crimes when interviewed with a police-dominant approach.

Sources: Vrij, A., Edward, K., & Bull, R. (2001). Police officers' ability to detect deceit: The benefit of indirect deception detection measures. *Legal and Criminological Psychology, 6,* 185–196; Meissner, C. A., & Kassin, S. M. (2002). "He's guilty!" Investigator bias in judgments of truth and deception. *Law and Human Behavior, 26,* 469–480 (p. 472); Stromwall, L. A., & Granhag, P. A. (2003). How to detect deception? Arresting the beliefs of police officers, prosecutors and judges. *Psychology, Crime & Law, 9,* 19–36; Leo, R. A., & Ofshe, R. J. (1998). The consequences of false confessions: Deprivations of liberty and miscarriages of justice in the age of psychological interrogation. *Journal of Criminal Law and Criminology, 88,* 429–496; Radalet, M. L., Bedau, H. A., & Putnam, C. E. (1992). *In spite of innocence: Erroneous convictions in capital cases.* Boston, MA: Northeastern University Press; Scheck, B. C., Neufeld, P., & Dwyer, J. (2000). *Actual innocence: Five days to execution and other dispatches from the wrongly convicted.* New York: Doubleday; Holmberg, U., & Christianson, S. (2002). Murderers and sexual offenders experiences of police interviews and their inclination to admit or deny crimes. *Behavioral Sciences and the Law, 20,* 31–45. Photo © Lo, 2008.

stop and the remaining for other reasons, such as the police responding to a complaint.

- Of the more than 71 million encounters between the police and the public, just 1.6% of these interactions resulted in the use or threatened use of police force.
- About 0.8% of motor vehicle stops result in actual or threatened use of police force.

Or, conversely:

- 98.4% of all police-citizen encounters are devoid of actual or threatened police force.
- 99.2% of motor vehicle stops are devoid of actual or threatened use of police force.[26]

Police-citizen encounters are, of course, interactive (for an interesting look at police-citizen interactions, see Box 6-3). To understand police use of force, it is vital to understand how the actions, comments, and demeanors of both the officer and the suspect affect one another. Using assorted sources of data, a number of criminologists have examined the causes and correlates of police use of force. William Terrill examined 6,523 police-suspect sequence encounters based on observational data of the Project on Policing Neighborhoods (POPN) in Indianapolis, Indiana and St. Petersburg, Florida. In increasing order of seriousness, suspect resistance ranged from none, passive, verbal, defensive, and active. Commensurately, police force ranged from none, command, threat, restraint, takedown, and impact. The police used the most severe level of force in a mere 0.5% of all interaction sequences. The second most severe option, takedown, was utilized in just 1% of the sequences. Overall, Terrill found that officers underused the amount of force that they could have legally and proportionately used against resisting suspects. When force was used, it was at the lowest levels on the force continuum.[27] In a separate study, Terrill and Michael Reisig found that police use of force was disproportionately used in neighborhoods characterized by extreme economic disadvantage and extremely high homicide rates.[28]

Peter Hoffman and Edward Hickey conducted a seven-year investigation of 1,863 use of force incidents and nearly 32,000 arrests. Overall, they found extremely low rates of police force. Under 6% of incidents involved any use of force and the preponderance of these involved unarmed physical force. Moreover, 506 incidents resulted in injury to the suspect from a total of nearly 32,000 arrests—a rate of just 1.6 per 100 arrests.[29] Finally, in his review of the literature, Kenneth Adams summarized what is known about police use of force. In addition to its infrequency, police use of force typically involves the lower end of force, such as grabbing, pushing, or shoving, and occurs when the police are trying to arrest a resisting suspect. An officer's demographic characteristics, such as age, sex, and race, are not generally predictive of use of force. Persons under the influence of drugs and alcohol and/or with mental health illnesses are more likely to have police force used on them. A small proportion of officers are disproportionately involved in use of force incidents.[30]

LETHAL FORCE AND POLICE KILLINGS

At the extreme, police-citizen interaction can result in the death of potential suspects, the officer, or both. Fortunately, justifiable homicides by police and police killings are exceedingly rare; however, they do occur. For instance, the number of police officers who were murdered in the line of duty increased sharply in 2010–2011.[31] Jodi Brown and Patrick Langan, two criminologists who work for the Bureau of Justice Statistics, examined both forms of homicide from 1976 to 1998. They produced several important findings:

- On average, the police justifiably kill 400 felons per year.
- On average, criminals murder 79 police officers per year.
- 1 in 6 murders of a police officer directly resulted in the justifiable killing of the murderer.
- Overall, only 3% of justifiable police killings are connected to the murder of a law enforcement officer.
- Young black males constituted 1% of the U. S. population but 14% of felons killed by police.
- Young white males constituted 7% of the U. S. population but 15% of felons killed by police.
- Young black males constituted 21% of felons who murdered a police officer.
- Young white males constituted 20% of felons who murdered a police officer.[32]

Police scholars have studied various aspects of the split-second phenomenon of killings between police and suspects.[33] A recent investigation of police officers involved in shootings by David Klinger produced some intriguing findings. Klinger found that officers manifested a variety of physical and emotional problems in the wake of shooting, such as insomnia, nausea, fatigue, anxiety, guilt, fear, numbness, and sadness. However, these feelings dissipated rather quickly within three months of the shooting. The other important finding was that officers often experienced perceptual distortions about the shooting and had imperfect recall of the event. Consequently, investigations of officer shootings should not necessarily conclude that officers are being dishonest when they could not recall details of the shooting.[34] David Klinger's research is particularly important because he is a former police officer who justifiably killed an assailant during the course of his duties. The combined academic and applied approach of his book *Into the Kill Zone: A Cop's Eye View of Deadly Force* coupled with Professor Klinger's harrowing experience offers a rich insight inside the use of lethal force.[35]

POLICE CORRUPTION AND MISCONDUCT

American policing can be viewed as a cyclic state of existence, reform, and transformation. During various eras, police organization, officer behavior, social conditions, and police-community relations have mixed to create conditions that seem to call for improved law enforcement. As mentioned in Chapter 4 with the Political, Reform, and Community/Problem-Solving Era, policing is always in flux and improvements in policing are frequently an outgrowth of dissatisfaction with previous approaches to policing. The following section highlights some of the important investigative commissions that sought to improve American policing and the social conditions that engendered police reform.

Chicago Crime Commission

Founded in 1919 by 35 members of the Chicago business community, the Chicago Crime Commission is a non-partisan, not-for-profit organization devoted to improving the quality of public safety and criminal justice. It is the oldest citizen crime commission in the United States and has an important and colorful history. In the 1920s, the Chicago Crime Commission rose to prominence during an era of intense public concern about organized crime and ineffective law enforcement. The new commission was especially interested in crimes against property, which it saw as the work of a highly sophisticated organized crime syndicate led by the infamous Al Capone. The commission stoked public anger and interest in organized crime with the 1930 release of a public enemies list, featuring "Public Enemy #1 Al Capone." Drawing on the work of its "Secret Six" investigative unit, the commission was among the organizations that called for the ultimately successful tax-evasion prosecution of Capone in 1931.

In addition to its work combating organized crime, the Chicago Crime Commission advocated a more efficient, rigorous criminal justice system that would deter with certain, harsh punishment. As public watchdog, it monitored the criminal justice system for lenience, laxity, and corruption. For example, it campaigned unsuccessfully against the widespread practice of plea-bargaining, which it portrayed as the product of judicial inefficiency and corruption. Today, the Chicago Crime Commission is as active as ever with over 200 business and professional leaders from Chicago contributing to the organization. The Chicago Crime Commission is the Community Engagement Partner for the Project Safe Neighborhoods Task Force, a massive Department of Justice initiative. The commission educates the general public about crime-related issues, reports to the Illinois legislature, implements programs and services to address crime and disorder problems (for example, violent youth gangs were recently rated public enemy #1), and, overall, ensures the integrity of law enforcement and criminal justice entities.[36]

During the Progressive era of the first decades of the Twentieth Century, the Chicago Crime Commission was successful in its role as watchdog of the criminal justice system. Similar investigations were developed in 24 other states and the National Crime Commission, founded in 1925, was viewed as an outgrowth of the Chicago Crime Commission's mission.

WICKERSHAM COMMISSION

As discussed in Chapter 4, early forms of policing were marked by corruption because the very organization of police departments was linked to local, ward politicians and political machines. For example, the 1894 Lexow Committee found that police protection of underworld activities in New York City resulted from the corruption-ridden organization between politics, police, and illicit businesses.[37] Indeed, there were very few standards for officer behavior, and officers relied extensively on physical abuse and coercion to force compliance. Citizens became increasingly frustrated with the lack of professionalism and wanton use of force employed by the police. Across the United States, there was widespread dissatisfaction and at times, open public hostility against the police.[38] There was another problem between the police and public in early Twentieth Century America: alcohol. On January 29, 1919, the ratification of the Eighteenth Amendment to the United States Constitution ushered in the era of prohibition. Beginning in 1920, the manufacture, sale, transportation, and importation of intoxicating liquors or alcoholic beverages were illegal. Prohibition was disastrous. Bootlegging of alcohol was relatively common and the police were suddenly forced to deal with a new, publicly unpopular criminal problem. The Prohibition era was noteworthy because it showed the difficulties inherent in the enforcement of standards of vice. In addition to the other points of conflict with the police, the public resented law enforcement meddling in their drinking habits. It was only the beginning of the indignant and hostile relationship between the police and the public.

These conditions culminated in the National Commission of Law Observance and Enforcement or Wickersham Commission (named after former U. S. Attorney General George Wickersham) in 1929. Mandated by President Herbert Hoover, the Wickersham Commission documented widespread use of illegitimate police force (known as the "third degree") and indeed a tone of lawlessness among law enforcement organizations. The Wickersham

Commission also found that Prohibition was largely unenforceable and that alcohol enforcement itself was highly susceptible to payoffs and other forms of corruption. Ultimately, the Wickersham Commission would serve as the major federal impetus behind systemic change to American policing. Indeed, the Wickersham Commission helped to hasten the Reform Era of policing. As a historical endnote, Prohibition would end, but not until the Eighteenth Amendment was repealed on December 5, 1933.

Commission on Civil Rights and National Crime Commissions

The middle 1950s to early 1970s were perhaps the worst period of police misconduct and corruption. Widespread allegations and observable evidence of civil and human rights' violations prompted the U. S. Commission on Civil Rights in 1957. Police abuses were disproportionately directed toward racial minorities, mostly African Americans, and included flagrant violations of African Americans' Fourteenth Amendment rights. The result was increased attempts to professionalize law enforcement including the creation of external review and civilian oversight of police behavior. Unfortunately, there was not widespread improvement. The late 1960s and early 1970s were characterized by rising crime rates, intense public protest over the Vietnam War and other national concerns, and continued strife between the police and citizenry. Several major urban centers, including Newark, Chicago, and most infamously, the Watts section of Los Angeles, experienced horrible rioting that was largely attributable to the mutual animosity between the police and minority residents. Although police-public relations are certainly on better footing today, the relationship continues to be tenuous at times.

Knapp, Christopher, and Mollen Commissions

Since about 1970, major scandals have served to initiative police reform and attempt to end police corruption and misconduct (see Box 6-4). For example, the brave testimony of Officer Frank Serpico, later immortalized in the film *Serpico* starring Al Pacino, exposed institutionalized corruption inside the New York City Police Department. The Knapp Commission delineated two general types of misbehaving officers, meat eaters and grass eaters. Meat eaters were officers who actively solicited bribes and vigorously engaged in corruption and misconduct. Grass eaters were officers who accepted payments for police duties. Grass eaters were viewed as more benign and interested in money; whereas meat eaters were viewed as more dangerous and willing to commit all types of corruption, even overt criminal activity. Corruption involves the misuse of police power for personal gain and it is a flagrant violation of police integrity. Misconduct refers to improprieties or violations of departmental procedures. There are gradations of police misconduct, such as malfeasance, misfeasance, and nonfeasance. Malfeasance is the intentional commission of a prohibited act, such as committing perjury during

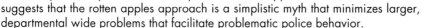

CRIMINAL JUSTICE SPOTLIGHT

BAD COPS: ROTTEN APPLES OR A SPOILED BUNCH?

Cases of egregious police violence, corruption, and misconduct inevitably lead to attempts to explain why the improprieties occurred. Two rival hypotheses have been advanced. The "rotten apples" approach suggests that a small number of rogue police officers engage in the preponderance of police misconduct and that there is not a systemic cultural or organizational problem with police departments. The "spoiled bunch" approach suggests that the rotten apples approach is a simplistic myth that minimizes larger, departmental wide problems that facilitate problematic police behavior.

Researchers have produced conflicting findings about both approaches. The spoiled bunch approach asserts that police subculture or other organizational/structural dynamics produce illicit police behavior; however, scholars have questioned whether a unified police subculture even exists. Moreover, others have advanced that there are many niches or types of officer within departments. As for the rotten apples approach, scholars have found that police officers are "average or normal people" who are not driven by dark, authoritarian impulses to control others. Since corruption and misconduct are rare phenomena in the first place, it is doubtful to expect widespread cultural or individual predictors of illicit police behavior.

When investigating the empirical data about problem-prone officers, compelling evidence for the rotten apples thesis is discovered, however. Complaints of police misconduct or use of force tend to cluster around certain officers. Kim Lersch and Tom Mieckowski studied "problem-prone officers" and found that a handful of officers tended to be repeat offenders that were recurrently the source of citizen complaints for their alleged misbehavior. Indeed, they found that nearly half of the officers in their study did not receive a single complaint, but 7% of the officers accumulated 35% of the complaints.

"Problem-prone" officers (all were males) tended to be younger and less experienced than other officers and likely to be accused of violent and non-violent harassment that resulted from proactive contacting of citizens. Most problematic police-citizen contacts were intra-racial. Interestingly, there is evidence that the most problem-prone officers are also the most productive cops because they stridently and proactively enforce the law and perform the duties of their job. Perhaps it should be expected that citizens would complain while they are being arrested.

Sources: Austin, T. L., Hale, D. C., & Ramsey, L. J. (1987). The effect of layoff on police authoritarianism. *Criminal Justice and Behavior, 14*, 194–210; Balch, R. (1972). Police personality: Fact or fiction? *Journal of Criminal Law, Criminology, and Police Science, 63*, 106–119; Bannish, H., & Ruiz, J. (2003). The antisocial police personality: A view from the inside. *International Journal of Public Administration, 26*, 831–881; Bennett, R. R. (1984). Becoming blue: A longitudinal study of police recruit occupational socialization. *Journal of Police Science and Administration, 12*, 47–58; Herbert, S. (1998). Police subculture reconsidered. *Criminology, 36*, 343–370; Sherman, L. W. (1980). Causes of police behavior: The current state of quantitative research. *Journal of Research in Crime and Delinquency, 17*, 69–100; Trojanowicz, R. (1971). The policeman's occupational personality. *Journal of Criminal Law, Criminology, and Police Science, 62*, 551–559; McElvain, J. P., & Kposowa, A. J. (2004). Police officer characteristics and internal affairs investigations for use of force allegations. *Journal of Criminal Justice, 32*, 265–279; Lersch, K. M., & Mieczkowski, T. (1996). Who are the problem-prone officers? An analysis of citizen complaints. *American Journal of Police, 15*, 23–44. Photo © 2011, joingate, Shutterstock, Inc.

BOX 6-4

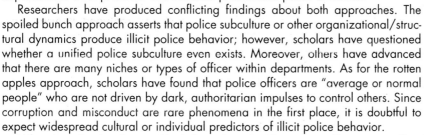

court testimony or accepting police gratuities. Misfeasance is negligent or improper performance of police duties and nonfeasance is failure or omission of police duties.

The reprehensible police beating of African American motorist Rodney King in 1991 led to the Christopher Commission headed by later United States Secretary of State Warren Christopher. Their charge was to conduct a comprehensive investigation of the recruitment and training practices, internal disciplinary system, and citizen complaint system within the Los Angeles Police Department. Their investigation produced a variety of important findings.

- From 1986 to 1990, about 1,800 officers were charged with excessive force. More than 1,400 of these officers were accused only once or twice.
- 183 officers had four or more allegations, 44 had six or more, 16 had eight or more, and one officer had 16 allegations.
- The top 5% of officers accounted for more than 20% of all allegations of excessive force or improper tactics.
- 25% of officers surveyed indicated that officer racial prejudice against African Americans and Hispanics contributed to poor police-community relations.
- 28% of officers agreed that an officer's prejudice towards the suspect's race may lead to the use of excessive force.
- The LAPD has an organizational culture that emphasis crime control over crime prevention.
- The emphasis on law enforcement contributes to isolation between the police and the public.[39]

Public concerns about police corruption relating to the enforcement of drug laws in New York City led to the Mollen Commission, a twenty-two month investigation conducted from 1992 to 1994. They too produced a variety of findings related to police corruption, including some of its potential causes.

- The "vast majority of New York City police officers are honest and hard-working, and serve this City with skill and dedication each day."
- Police corruption is a multifaceted problem that has flourished because of:
    - Police culture that exalts loyalty over integrity.
    - Silence among honest officers who do not want to "rat" out colleagues.
    - Willfully blind supervisors who fear the consequences of a corruption scandal more than the corruption itself.
    - Demise of the principle of accountability among police commanders.
    - Hostility and alienation between police and residents in high-crime precincts that fostered an "Us versus Them" mentality among police.

The Mollen Commission found that things had indeed changed since the Serpico scandal in the early 1970s. Gone was the pervasive bribery scheme that was systemic and institutionalized. The 1990s showed that corruption was significantly less commonplace, but where it did exist, it tended to be more venal and diabolical. Officers were acting as criminals to participate in and protect drug trafficking. More than 14 officers have been arrested and charged with crimes including robbery, burglary, assault, and various drug violations.[40]

It is difficult to estimate the negative implications of police corruption and misconduct. Corruption and misconduct are direct violations of the ideals of due process and crime control because the Constitutional rights of defendants are trampled and police can shift from crime fighters to criminals. Moreover, corruption erodes public support for the police and criminal justice generally and provides graphic confirmation for persons who already distrust state power. Michael Armstrong, who was Chief Counsel on the Knapp Commission, delivered this testimony before the Mollen Commission:

> The crooks, however, that you have uncovered, the criminals seem to be a different breed of criminals [than twenty years ago]...the guys you're digging up, these guys are walking around with lead-lined gloves and riding shotgun for organized crime people, it seems to me they have changed the nature of being a 'meat eater' in the Department. Instead of taking money to look the other way while someone else commits a street crime, they're out there competing with the criminals to commit street crimes themselves, and it seems to me that is a very big difference.[41]

THE POLICE-PUBLIC RELATIONSHIP

A recurrent and important theme in Chapters 4, 5, and 6 is the complex and, unfortunately, sometimes strained relations between the police and their various constituencies. The police-public relationship is multifaceted and blends resident concerns about the degree to which the police are achieving and balancing the twin goals of crime control and due process. As shown in Chapter 5, the police have an important Constitutional mandate (the Fourth Amendment) to perform their duties while observing and respecting the legal rights of citizens. The police do not simply run rampant, they serve and protect within the constraints of law. When the police engage in unlawful, improper, corrupt, or even reprehensible ways, public trust in them is eroded. Paradoxically, it is often the police themselves that are the greatest victim of police misconduct, and the resultant bad press, because it is they who must face a skeptical, distrusting, and even hostile public who might feel that police officers believe themselves to be above the law. Strained police-public relationships make for negative public relations. Real and perceived evidence that the police are not honoring due process provisions is an explosive problem. However, this is only part of the problem. Crime control, public safety, and the maintenance of social order are also important expectations of private citizens and vital responsibilities of police departments. While ensuring due process concerns, the police are charged with catching the bad guys and ensuring public order to the degree that citizens are not fearful to conduct their daily lives.

Since the inception of policing in the United States, the police-public relationship has been especially difficult as it relates to the nonwhite minority population. Indeed, given the Nation's history, the police were once officially and lawfully authorized to control African Americans who were then not even recognized as human beings! Unquestionably, American history is replete with examples of police officers applying differential treatment to various racial and ethnic groups.[42] Fortunately, there has been great progress generally in making all aspects of the criminal justice system more humane, accountable, and professional.

There is an important empirical issue that further complicates the tenuous relationship between the police and community residents. The very groups most likely to be the recipients of various negative and sensationalistic police actions, such as use of force, profiling, lethal force, and arrest, are also the groups with the greatest involvement in crime. That adolescents and young adults, males, and racial and ethnic minorities residing in neighborhoods characterized by extreme economic impoverishment have grievances with the police can be interpreted in many ways. Perhaps these groups are genuinely the victims of improper police tactics. Perhaps the police behave improperly against these groups because of deep-seated biases against youths, males, nonwhites, and residents of poor neighborhoods. Perhaps the police target these groups as a function of the groups' disproportionate criminal behavior. Perhaps there is no improper police activity, and groups that have high offending and victimization rates also tend to blame the police for their problems.[43] Two hot button contemporary issues, racial profiling and zero tolerance policing (discussed in Chapter 4), are explored next to examine the current state of the relationship between police and the public.

Racial Profiling

Racial profiling occurs when the police use a citizen's race or ethnicity as the sole basis for contacting the individual as if race or ethnicity was itself a proxy for criminality. Of course, at times a person's race is of great legal relevance such as when police are pursuing a suspect on whom there is descriptive information. Also, the police can and do contact persons who are behaving in suspicious ways that, given the experience, knowledge, and training of the officer, reasonably suggest that the person is engaged in criminal activity. Racial profiling is in effect a form of discriminatory harassment and an egregious violation of due process.

In the 1990s, racial profiling became a national social issue and anecdotal accounts suggesting that it was a pervasive form of police impropriety. For example, John Reitzel, Stephen Rice, and Alex Piquero studied perceptions of racial profiling among Whites, Blacks, and Hispanics in New York City. Citizens reported on whether they felt profiling was widespread, whether profiling was justified, and whether they had ever been profiled. African Americans and Hispanics were significantly more likely than Whites to believe that profiling was widespread and that they had personal experiences of being profiled. Blacks, but not Hispanics, reported that profiling was unjustified. Reitzel and his colleagues arrived at an interesting conclusion. Minorities believe that profiling is occurring regardless of whether it is true or not![44] In a related study, Rice and Piquero found that Blacks hold unshakable opinions about the widespread use of police profiling by race and that African Americans' viewpoints are not mediated by income or education level.[45]

As is the case with any criminological phenomenon, especially controversial ones, the observable as opposed to perceptual existence of a problem should be evaluated based upon empirical data. To date, evidence of racial profiling is equivocal at best. Using Maryland data, Stan Becker found interesting relationships between race and the type of drug seized during traffic stops. Whites were significantly more likely than minorities to possess marijuana, thus there was evidence of profiling especially against Hispanics. However, Becker also found that Blacks and Hispanics were significantly more likely than Whites, five to ten times, to possess hard drugs or drug money. In these circumstances, Whites were unfairly profiled.[46] Michael Smith and Matthew Petrocelli analyzed data from 2,673 traffic stops by the Richmond, Virginia Police Department in 2000. They produced a variety of vital findings. First, Black motorists were stopped by police more than their proportion of the driving population. Second, Blacks were not more likely than Whites to be searched. Third, minority motorists were more likely than Whites to be warned by police rather than ticketed or arrested. Fourth, minorities were 250 percent less likely than White drivers to be the subject of consent searches by police. Fifth, White police officers were no more likely than minority officers to stop, search, or arrest minority drivers. In a subsequent study, they found that neighborhood crime rate was the sole determinant of police stops. Police stops and searched were more common in mostly Black neighborhoods, but stops that resulted in arrests were less likely in predominantly Black neighborhoods.[47] Using data from a different source, Joseph Schafer, David Carter, and Andra Katz-Bannister found differential rates of police contacts for Whites, Blacks, and Hispanics, however these differences were largely mediated by the age and gender of the suspect. Furthermore, they produced no evidence that police prejudices or any police improprieties were related to officer discretion.[48]

In short, a recurrent finding in the racial profiling has been that there are often significant differences across racial groups in terms of their contacts by police. However, the reason why police stopped them is, curiously, often avoided.[49] Until researchers start measuring officer opinions, assessment, and viewpoints about racial groups and how these potential biases impact their discretion, the racial profiling question will be mostly conjecture.[50]

Zero-Tolerance Policing

A tangential recent issue in policing has been the adoption and proliferation of enforcement-based, problem-solving policing more commonly referred to as zero-tolerance policing discussed in Chapter 4. Recall that aggressive policing has been lauded popularly for reducing crime and disorder in many major cities around the United States. However, zero-tolerance policing has also been criticized for placing too much emphasis on crime control and possibly too little emphasis on due process considerations. How does the evidence bear on this debate? Heather Mac Donald, an attorney, journalist, and researcher at The Manhattan Institute compared police outcomes during the New York mayoral terms of Ed Koch and David Dinkins in the late 1980s and early 1990s compared to tenure of Mayor Rudolph Giuliani who staunchly advocated aggressive policing practices for the rest of the 1990s and to the present.[51] In terms of police performance, Mac Donald found:

- 75 percent reduction in gun homicides (2,200 to less than 683)
- 25% reduction in officer use of firearms
- 67% reduction in shootings per officer
- 1993: NYPD made 266,313 arrests and killed 23 people
- 1998: NYPD made 403,659 arrests and killed 19 people
- 1990 compared to 1998: 250% reduction in fatal police shootings per officer
- 1994 to 1996: 20% reduction in civilian complaints per officer
- In the spring of 1996, an Empire State Survey found that 73% of New Yorkers had a positive view of police, compared with 37% in June 1992.
- By 1998, a federal Bureau of Justice Statistics survey showed 84% of New Yorkers age 16 and older satisfied with the police, including 77% of black New Yorkers.
- Cops report that in 1998 they did 138,887 stop and frisks, 85% of them on blacks and Hispanics—less than the 89% of suspects identified as black and Hispanic by victims.
- Assuming that police stopped mostly young men and that they stopped everybody just once, that would mean that they stopped 11.6% of all minority males between ages 10 and 45.

An assortment of criminologists has also studied the effects of aggressive zero-tolerance policing on crime rates and other social outcomes in various areas across the country. Zero-tolerance policing has generally been found to reduce physical disorder and improve public morals, reduce crime and calls for police services, and generally contribute to improved citizen assessments of public safety and fear of crime.[52] Andrew Golub, Bruce Johnson, Angela Taylor, and John Eterno interviewed 539 New York City arrestees in 1999 and found that half of them had stopped or reduced their multifarious involvement in crime and disorder because of the aggressive tactics of the zero-tolerance approach. Among street criminals, the "word was out" that the police were not going to tolerate crime, vice, and disorder—and all of these problems were reduced as a consequence.[53]

Ultimately, police-community relations are a potentially volatile relationship that requires sustained attention from both the law enforcement community and the residents they serve and protect. Although the majority of citizens hold favorable views of the police, significant assessments exist between the White majority and racial minorities, particularly African Americans.[54] It is probable that racial differences in assessments of the police will never become equal.

Chapter Summary: Balancing Crime Control and Due Process

- Police behavior is a combination of problem solving, people skills, and law enforcement.
- Observational studies of the police illustrated that they exercise great restraint, are responsive to complainant wishes, and under-enforce the law.
- The police are mostly a responsive entity.
- Although police discrimination does exist, its prevalence is exaggerated and often convoluted by legally relevant variables.
- Various forms of police corruption have resulted in enormous scandals, investigative commissions, and attempts at genuine reform.
- Sensationalistic topics such as police use of force and lethal force and police killings are exceedingly rare.
- Racial profiling is a national concern for the threat it poses to due process for all citizens. To date, research has uncovered little tangible evidence that profiling explains racial differences in contacts with police.
- Zero-tolerance policing has resulted in impressive reductions in crime, disorder, and related social problems.
- The relationship between the police and the public is multifaceted and controversial.
- Strengthening community relations is a major law enforcement priority.

KEY TERMS

Blue wall
Christopher commission
Corruption
Cynicism
Demeanor
Discretion
Grass eater
Knapp commission
Lethal force
Malfeasance

Meat eater
Misfeasance
Mollen commission
Nonfeasance
Police killings
Police misconduct
Police personality
Racial profiling
Wickersham commission

TALKING POINTS

1. The early research findings by Reiss, Black, Wilson, and others were revelatory because they showed that the police responded to citizen mobilization of the law. What does this mean for those who assert that the police are biased toward certain social groups?

2. What are the implications of police behavior on the goals of crime control and due process? Which ideal is better served by actual police behavior?

3. Will relations between the police and the public ever be great? What are some of the barriers to better police-public relations?

4. Is police profiling according to any characteristics of citizens ever justified? Why or why not?

5. What are some characteristics of the police personality? Does the daily contact with criminal offenders produce some of the negative characteristics of police, such as cynicism?

WEB LINKS

Best Practices in Police Accountability
(www.policeaccountability.org/)

Bureau of Justice Statistics Law Enforcement Statistics
(www.ojp.usdoj.gov/bjs/lawenf.htm)

Chicago Crime Commission
(www.chicagocrimecommission.org)

Federal Law Enforcement Training Center
(www.fletc.gov/)

Los Angeles Police Department
(www.lapdonline.org/)

Mollen Commission Final Report
(www.parc.info/reports/pdf/mollenreport.pdf)

New York City Police Department
(http://nyc.gov/html/nypd/)

Office of Community Oriented Policing Services
(www.cops.usdoj.gov)

Police Executive Research Forum
(www.policeforum.mn-8.net/)

The Racial Profiling Data Collection Resource Center
at Northeastern University
(www.racialprofilinganalysis.neu.edu)

U. S. Department of Justice
(www.usdoj.gov/)

FURTHER READING

Bratton, W. (1998). *The turnaround: How America's top cop reversed the crime epidemic*. New York: Random House. A fascinating, insider look from the former New York City Police Commissioner whose policies resulted in the recent plummeting of crime.

Doerner, W. G. (1998). *Introduction to law enforcement: An insider's view*. Boston, MA: Butterworth-Heinemann. The author is a longtime faculty member in criminology/criminal justice at Florida State University in addition to his career in law enforcement. This introductory text provides all of the basics in law enforcement with the added advantage of an author who has lived the experiences. The book is lively, interesting, and highly accessible to undergraduates.

Muir, Jr., W. K. (1977). *Police: Streetcorner politicians*. Chicago: University of Chicago Press. This classic explores the art of policing based on interviews and observations of officers from a large city. According to Muir, successful police officers are able to use just forms of coercion to handle the "tragic nature" of human behavior. It is an interesting work that illustrates the intangibles and "artistry" of patrol work.

Walker, S. (2003). *Early intervention systems for law enforcement agencies: A planning and management guide*. Washington, DC: U. S. Department of Justice, Office of Community Oriented Policing Services. This 174-page summary report describes the important "early warning" systems in place in American law enforcement to monitor and supervise officers who may demonstrate assorted forms of misconduct.

PART THREE

COURTS AND JUDICIAL PROCESSES

CHAPTER 7
Bail, Jail, and the Pretrial Period

CHAPTER OUTLINE

QUOTATIONS

"As long as the process is itself the punishment, the adjudicative ideal will continue to conflict with the substantive goals of American criminal law."—*Malcolm Feeley*[1]

"The frequent exposure to the jail setting among repeat street criminals makes the jail an important place for the periodic reinforcement of subcultural values as the inmate re-experiences confinement and renews acquaintances with similarly situated people."
—*James Garofalo and Richard Clark*[2]

"It is at the pretrial stage that one's freedom is so often intertwined with one's money."—*Stephen Demuth and Darrell Steffensmeier*[3]

"The system is lax with those whom it should be stringent, and stringent with those with whom it could safely be less severe."—*Arthur Beeley*[4]

"Jail inmates may be serious repeat offenders, novices in crime, or even naïve traffic violators."—*John Klofas*[5]

"Three hots and a cot."—*Popular jail axiom which indicates that jail facilities provide free food, shelter, and a place to sleep, an improvement in living conditions for some jail inmates*[6]

"There is no place for the self-appointed public avenger in a professionally run jail."—*W. Raymond Nelson*[7]

INTRODUCTION

What happens between a defendant's arrest and his or her first appearance in court is probably the least understood area of the criminal justice system. Criminal defendants and their families often have many questions. Where do arrestees go after they are placed in police cars and driven away? Can they be released? What is bail? What is bond? What are the differences between bail and bond? What does "own recognizance" mean? Do they have to pay money in order to be released? Who has jurisdiction over arrestees once police officers bring them to municipal holding stations or county jails? How much time transpires before arrestees appear in court? Do arrestees receive due process even without appearing in court? The answers to these questions occur during the pretrial period.

Interestingly, the pretrial phase contains the greatest convergence between the three primary agents in the criminal justice system: police, courts, and correction. The police arrest people and initiate the accusatory and investigatory process that will send their case through the criminal justice system. As always, the police have great discretionary power in determining the treatment of a criminal suspect. Police officers can issue a ticket or summons for crimes ranging in seriousness from petty offenses to felonies. They can charge defendants with municipal violations or state charges. Most importantly, police officers write arrest reports that chronicle the legal reasons for the arrest, such as the bases for probable cause, the charges, a narrative of how the crime transpired, and a list of victims, witnesses, and co-defendants. The arrest report is the foundational legal document of a criminal case.

Once the police officer completes the arrest report and terminates their discussions (if any) with the defendant, judicial personnel assume responsibility for the case. Most large jurisdictions have judicial officers, variously referred to as pretrial service interviewers, pretrial officers, bond commissioners, and the like. Pretrial service officers serve two interrelated purposes. First, they interview criminal defendants and gather information about the offender's social and criminal history. Information on residency, family contacts, employment status, substance abuse, and psychiatric history are included. They do not interview defendants about their current charges as a way to influence guilt or innocence. Once the information is gathered, the judicial officer writes a report that summarizes the social and criminal history for the court and makes a bond recommendation. This is the second purpose of pretrial service personnel. As judicial officers, they decide the type of bond that a defendant should receive and serve as the primary way to alleviate jail crowding.

All of this activity usually transpires at a county jail. Jails are local correctional facilities that house persons who have been convicted of crimes and sentenced to less than two years confinement and those awaiting trial. Operated by the county sheriff's department, jails are a temporary form of incarceration, thus they are much different than prison. Importantly, persons who are unable to post bond or be released on their own recognizance are detained until their case reaches a resolution in court, such as dismissal or conviction. This creates a sort of paradox in American due process. The presumption of innocence ensures that defendants are considered innocent until proven guilty, yet tens of thousands of criminal defendants each day are detained during the pretrial phase. Think of it this way. Imagine you were arrested for drunk driving while vacationing out of state. Because your community ties would be weak, you technically would be transient or "passing through town," and would likely receive a secured bond. Imagine that you cannot pay the bond amount. Two weeks later, you meet with the district attorney and a public defender and they indicate that charges against you are going to be dismissed. You are free to go. You have not been convicted of a crime, yet you were in custody for two weeks!

This chapter explores the pretrial period, the misunderstood location where police, court, and correctional entities meet, and centers on three main areas. First, the historical and contemporary use of bail as a means of pretrial release and detention is explored. Second, the resultant progression of a criminal case from charging to arraignment to dismissal or conviction is reviewed. The various legal and extra-legal factors that are used to determine bond are discussed. Third, the history and function of jail is described as it relates to the pretrial period. As you will see, jail is distinct from prison despite their common usage as similes. Moreover, jail confinement is an interesting example of the use of confinement as a penalty both before and after conviction. As always, the crime control and due process rationales for these criminal justice processes are highlighted.

BAIL/BOND

Definitions

Bail is a form of pretrial release in which a defendant enters a legal agreement or promise that requires his or her appearance in court. The bail amount is statutory which means that legislatures establish monetary bails based on the legal seriousness of the charge. For example, class A or class I felonies may be "no bond" offenses. Magistrates or judges may increase or decrease the statutory bail amount based on aggravating and mitigating factors of the case. Pretrial service officers do not set bail amounts; they simply follow the statutory schedule of bail amounts. Even though defendants are released from jail custody, they are still under the supervision of the courts. If defendants do not comply with the conditions of their bail, such as abstaining from alcohol use or having no contact with the alleged victim in the case, the court can withdraw the defendant's previously granted release. This is known as bail revocation.

Bond is a pledge of money or some other assets offered as bail by an accused person or his or her surety (bail bondsman) to secure temporary release from custody. Bond is forfeited if the conditions of bail are not fulfilled. The best way to understand how the bail/bond process works is with an example. A person is arrested for felony theft and assigned a bail of $1,000. The defendant can pay $1,000 to the court in exchange for release from jail. The $1,000 is essentially collateral to entice the defendant to appear in court. If the defendant misses any court dates, he or she could lose the $1,000. However, if the defendant complies with all court appearances, he or she will receive the money back net any fees or fines that are imposed. What if the defendant cannot afford $1,000? The defendant can utilize the services of a bonding agent or bondsperson. A bondsperson is a social service professional who is contractually responsible for a criminal defendant once they are released from custody. Bondspersons typically charge a 15 percent fee for their services. Thus, the defendant would pay the bondsperson $150 to be released in turn the bondsperson is potentially liable for the entire $1,000 bond if the defendant misses any court dates or absconds. Bondspersons often have close working relationships with the criminal justice system and utilize many of the same criteria that are used to set bond, such as employment, residency, and criminal history. If defendants indeed abscond while on bond, bondspersons sometimes hire a third party, known as a bounty hunter, to find the escapee. Defendants, bondspersons, and bounty agents are bound by financial relationships. Of course, bondspersons and bounty hunters employ quasilaw enforcement tactics to facilitate their financial arrangements with criminal defendants. However, they are not law enforcement agents per se, thus constitutional safeguards that apply to police officers do not apply to them.

Strictly speaking, the term "bail" usually refers to the monetary value needed for release and the term "bond" refers to the type of release that the defendant was awarded. However, once released defendants are synonymously referred to as "being on bond" or "released on bail." Bail and bond are often used interchangeably even by criminal justice professionals. No great distinction is made here either. Whichever term is used, bail/bond attempts to ensure an accused person's appearance in court. Depending on the risks that they pose and the circumstances of the current charges, a promise, property, money, or some other assets are posted for release. If the defendant misses court appearances, the posted security (or liability in the event of a recognizance release) is forfeited.

Types of Bond

The "best" type of bond that a defendant can hope for is to be released on his or her own recognizance. A recognize bond is a written promise to appear in court in which the criminal defendant is released from jail custody without paying or posting cash or property. Variously referred to as personal recognizance (PR), own recognizance (OR), or release on recognizance (ROR), these bonds are reserved for arrestees with minimal or no prior criminal record, strong community ties, such as employment and long-term residency, and relatively non-serious charges. Persons who are released on recognizance bonds are considered to be low risk in terms of re-offending, dangerousness, and failing to appear in court.

Sometimes the defendant does not have the extensive community ties or minimal prior record to justify a recognizance release, but otherwise poses little risk to the community. In these types of cases, defendants are commonly released on cosigned recognizance bond where a family member, close friend, or business associate signs their name on the bond to guarantee the defendant's appearance in court. Other jurisdictions employ a third-party custody bond that works the same way. Sometimes, attorneys are granted third-party custody of their clients to ensure their appearance in court.

Other criminal defendants pose greater risks of missing court appearances and recidivating. Still others are too dangerous to release because they might be actively homicidal or suicidal. For "riskier" defendants, a variety of secured bonds are used (for example, see Box 7-1). Secured bonds require the payment of cash or other assets to the courts in exchange for release from custody. In the event that the defendant misses court dates or absconds, the cash or other assets are forfeited to the court. Various jurisdictions across the country employ various forms of secured bonds. Cash-only bonds mean that the defendant must post 100% of the bond in cash to be released. Property bonds are houses, real estate, or vehicles that may be cosigned to the court as collateral against pretrial flight. Absconding on a property bond could result in losing your home! Many criminal defendants pay 10 to 15% of their bond to professional bondspersons for release. In these cases, bondspersons act as sureties and are responsible for the total bond if the defendant absconds. Other jurisdictions use a deposit bail system where the court acts as bondsperson and the defendant posts a percentage of their total bond. Court-run deposit bail systems return the bond money to the defendant, net minor administrative fees, unlike bondspersons. Researchers have found that deposit bail systems produce comparable failure to appear rates as commercial bondspersons.[8]

History and Reform

The concept of bail has a long and interesting history. Processes resembling modern day bail practices appeared as early as 2500 B.C.E. and in Roman law as early as 700 B.C.E. For example, the concept known as "hostageship" involved a person who volunteered to be prosecuted and punished in the place of the actual suspect in the event that the suspect failed to appear for court proceedings.[9] In medieval Germany and England, *wergeld* was the assessed value of a person's life and considered their bail value. Trials by compurgation whereby criminal defendants established their innocence by taking an oath and having various witnesses swear or testify to the veracity of their oath also used *wergeld*. Both practices apply the concept of real or human assets to use as collateral for court proceedings.

Under English common law, sheriffs appointed their acquaintances that were often prominent members of the community called sureties. Sureties promised to pay money or land in the event that released defendants absconded. In this way, a surety is a guarantor that defendants will appear in court. Over time, sureties became de facto sheriffs because of their power of revocation. It is because of their financial investment that sureties, and modern-day bondspersons, employ enforcement-like methods to guarantee that defendants appear in court. There is an important distinction. Bondspersons have contractual power, not law enforcement power, thus they are not bound by the same constraints of police officers.

The English common law surety system was difficult to replicate in the burgeoning United States because of its sheer geographic size and the newness

CRIME SCENE   DO NOT CROSS

BOX 7-1

CRIMINAL JUSTICE WORKS

THE HOMELESS PRETRIAL RELEASE PROJECT

Community ties are an essential part of pretrial release, thus homeless persons should always receive punitive bonds. Perhaps this is not the case. Officials in San Francisco developed the Homeless Release Project (HRP), a pretrial release program that sought to reduce jail crowding caused by homeless nuisance offenders while monitoring these offenders to provide supervision and individualized care. Alissa Riker and Ursula Castellano found that a variety of innovative pretrial projects have been developed in the Bay Area. For example, a prior project included homeless offenders in a citation release program and produced a compliance rate, of homeless offenders, of 76%. The HRP serves a high-risk population, as over 85% of HRP clients have substance abuse problems and 50% have a co-occurring mental illness. The HRP screens homeless arrestees to determine their needs, their service history, establish temporary housing, and assign the client to a case manager for release. After release, the HRP client is monitored to ensure treatment and appearances in court. Ultimately, HRP can facilitate the relationships between the homeless population, social service providers, and the criminal justice system. Pilot data indicated that HRP participants were 50% less likely to be re-arrested than offenders not in the program.

Source: Riker, A., & Castellano, U. (2001). The Homeless Pretrial Release Project: An innovative pretrial release option. *Federal Probation, 65*, 9–13. Photo © 2011, Lou Oates, Shutterstock, Inc.

---

of community ties. Instead, pretrial release relied on the use of bondspersons. The concept of bail appears sporadically in colonial America. For example, the Eighth Amendment of the United States Constitution proscribes the requirement of excessive bail. The Judiciary Act of 1789 established bail as an absolute right in detainable criminal charges with the exception of capital offenses, or those potentially punishable by death.[10] The bail business grew with increasing numbers of bondspersons, bail recovery or enforcement agents, and bounty hunters operating at the periphery of American justice.

Due to concern about the constitutionality of pretrial release and supervision and bail enforcement, the courts addressed the issue. In New York State, *Nicolls v. Ingersoll* (1810) established that bounty hunters have the same rights of capture as bonding agents when authorized by those bonding agents.[11] The United States Supreme Court weighed in on *Reese v. United States* (1869), which established that bounty hunters were proxy pretrial officers that had complete control of returning absconders to the court.[12] *Taylor v. Taintor* (1873) clarified that bounty hunter behavior must conform to law, but was not bound by Fourth Amendment as are the police.[13]

The for-profit bondsperson business steamed along throughout the Nineteenth and Twentieth Centuries. Criminal defendants who had the monetary resources to post bail were released. Otherwise, criminal defendants waited in jail until their court appearances. However, many criminal cases are dismissed meaning that many jail detainees are confined for criminal charges for which they are never convicted. Increasingly, the plight of persons detained prior to trial became publicized and a strictly monetary bail system came under attack.

Six decades into the Twentieth Century, criminal defendants who were unable to pay their bail remained in jail custody. For all intents and purposes, ability to pay was the sole criterion for pretrial release from jail. This changed dramatically in 1961 when the Vera Institute of Justice became a driving force in the area of pretrial supervision of criminal defendants. The Vera Institute of Justice initiated the Manhattan Bail Project in New York City. For the project, Vera staff interviewed defendants to ascertain their community ties including their family connections in the city and employment history. After third party verification of the information, the defendants were assigned a numerical score that represented their likelihood of absconding. Persons with weak community ties were considered high risk and persons with strong community ties were considered low risk. Judges were presented with these recommendations and released criminal defendants accordingly. The results were compelling. Releasing defendants on promise to appear in court with attendant strong community ties was more effective than requiring money bail to assure court appearances. In fact, the experimental group that was released merely on their promise to appear had twice the appearance rate of those released on bail. The project saved more than $1 million in correctional costs for defendants who otherwise would have languished behind bars.[14]

In 1965, Ronald Goldfarb published *Ransom*, a scathing critique of the due process problems inherent in the American bail system. Goldfarb argued that defendants who remain in custody face a variety of risks for further criminal punishment compared to arrestees who are released on bond. For example, detained persons are more likely to be indicted, more likely to plead guilty, have greater trial conviction rates, and receive more punitive sentences.[15] Goldfarb's work and the Manhattan Bail Project prompted institutional change in pretrial services across the country and culminated in the Bail Reform Act of 1966. The Bail Reform Act authorized the use of releasing defendants on their own recognizance in non-capital federal cases when appearance in court can be shown to be likely. This effectively ended the de facto discrimination against indigent defendants. The Bail Reform Act of 1984 reinforced community ties clause of 1966 Act, but also provided for the preventive detention of defendants deemed dangerous or likely to abscond.

In 1967, the Vera Institute of Justice launched the Manhattan Bowery Project that aimed to remove alcoholic defendants in jail on nuisance offenses, such as public drunkenness, disorderly conduct, and vagrancy, and place

them in detoxification centers. Proactive police patrols identified visibly intoxicated individuals and encouraged them to enter treatment facilities. The
Project resulted in an 80 percent decline in the arrests of transient alcoholics,
which saved inordinate monies for jail detention and court costs. Since its
development, the program is today called Project Renewal and serves more
than 20,000 alcoholic and homeless persons annually.[16]

Another innovative Vera project was its Nonprofit Bail Bond Agencies
in Bronx, New York, Nassau County, Long Island, and Essex County,
New Jersey (Newark) launched in 1987. Vera paid defendants bail if they
agreed to submit to supervision and treatment that included a 24-hour observational period, drug testing, curfews, home visits, and employment monitoring. Defendants entered into agreement with Vera that they could be returned
to jail for failing to comply with any conditions of their release. Vera encoun-
tered severe problems with its Bronx operations because defendants tended
to have overlapping problems such as weak community ties and family support and crippling drug addiction. Many released defendants absconded and
Vera closed the operation in 1994. The operations in Nassau County and
Essex County were far more successful. Defendants were highly compliant
with conditions of their release and recidivism and absconding rates were
low. Both were incorporated into independent non-profit organization with
county contracts at the conclusion of the Vera Project.[17]

The bail reform movement also sparked federal initiatives to modernize
American bail practices. In 1978, the United States Department of Justice
awarded grants to the National Association of Pretrial Services Agencies
(NAPSA) to develop national professional standards and the Pretrial Services Resource Center (PSRC) to assess the status of the pretrial field. The
Bureau of Justice Assistance program then conducted national surveys of
pretrial services programs in 1979, 1989, and 2001. The results from the most
recent survey are discussed later in this chapter.

Bail Recovery/Enforcement and Bounty Hunters

Sensationalistic criminal justice lore, bounty hunters are persons hired by
bondspersons to enforce the conditions of bail and to recover the investment
asset of the bondsperson. In other words, bounty hunters track down bail
absconders and return them to jail. Afterward, bail agents will commonly revoke their bonds and pay the bounty hunter a fee for returning the absconder.
Bounty hunters serve a variety of important purposes. They help prevent insurance companies from raising premiums that they charge to insure bonds.
They also preserve the bonding agents' reputation, power, and influence as a
de facto member of the criminal justice system by keeping absconding rates
down. Bounty hunters are often stigmatized because of their direct contact
with criminal offenders and the enforcement aspects of their work. To some,
bounty hunters are rogues operating on the fringes of due process.

Brian Johnson and Greg Warchol have studied contemporary bounty hunters and found that these bail recovery/enforcement agents strive to mirror the professionalism, education, and experience of the courtroom workgroup. Johnson and Warchol found that bounty hunters have uneven working relationships with local police that have been characterized as (1) accepting and motivated, (2) cautious but accommodating, and (3) cold and rejecting. The working relationships between law enforcement and bounty hunters is influenced by ideological worldviews of the officers, their level of understanding of bounty hunter function, and acknowledgement of the legitimacy of the bounty hunter's role in the criminal justice system.[18]

Ronald Burns, Patrick Kinkade, and Matthew Leone conducted interviews with bounty hunters and examined their backgrounds and demographic characteristics, training and skills, professional motivation, perceptions of the profession, and bail enforcement practices. The modal bounty hunter was a 51-year-old, conservative, white male. Nearly 90% of the bounty hunters they interviewed were male and more than 80% were white. Nearly 30% had bachelor's degrees and nearly 10% had master's or law degrees. In terms of training and skills, bounty hunters frequently had military, private detection, security, and law enforcement backgrounds. About 92% had training in bail law, 63% had a formal bail certification, and 75% had formal bail training. Money and autonomy were the primary motivations for bounty hunter careers and most reported that bounty hunters were underappreciated and misunderstood by the criminal justice system. Bounty hunters use a variety of resources to locate absconders, including informants, paid information, local police, and the Internet. Most bounty hunters carried an array of sub-lethal weapons, such as mace and handcuffs. Less than 20% carried firearms or used weapons to affect an arrest, although the lethal of risk and physical danger was perceived to be high.[19]

PRETRIAL SERVICES TODAY

Bureau of Justice Assistance researches John Clark and Alan Henry analyzed data based on the national survey of more than 200 pretrial services programs across the United States. Their report is a comprehensive look at contemporary pretrial services nationwide. Important findings include:

Staffing, Operations, and Authority
The average pretrial service unit is staffed by 18 persons, receives funding from county and state sources, and interviews more than 5,000 defendants annually. About 40 percent of agencies have between two and five staff members. Programs serving large metropolitan areas, about 2% of all programs, interview more than 50,000 defendants annually. More than half of pretrial service programs operate during normal business hours, however some offer 24-hour, 7-day operations.

About 21 percent of programs have delegated release authority. Of those units with release authority, officers can release some felonies and most misdemeanor offenses. The administrative locus of pretrial service units varies greatly. Probation controls 31%, courts operate 29%, sheriff's departments operate 19%, and private, non-profit firms control 8%.[20]

Bond Interviews and Assessments

About 75% of agencies interview arrestees prior to their first appearance in court. They gather an array of information from the defendant on the social and criminal history. Self-reported criminal history is validated using a variety of data sources such as local police records, local judicial records, jail records, and the National Crime Information Center computer, which can access a database with over 25 million criminal histories.

Bond recommendations are based on objective risk scales, more than half of which have been validated, on subjective or expert judgments of pretrial service staff, or on a combination of objective and subjective approaches. About 42% of pretrial service units employ both, 35% use subjective criteria only, and 23% rely exclusively on a risk assessment instrument.

Special Populations and Monitoring

Nearly 75% of pretrial service programs ask questions about mental health and psychiatric history and many of these refer clients with mental health needs to appropriate agencies. About 25% have developed specialized protocols for dealing with clients arrested for domestic violence. Other special programs have been devised to assist homeless arrestees. Nearly 70% of agencies administer drug testing while defendants are on bond and 50% conduct alcohol testing. Often, substance abuse monitoring is done in conjunction with general counseling services. Approximately 54% of pretrial service units are servicing jails that operate at greater than 100% capacity. Given the problem of jail crowding, pretrial service units are viewed as both a valuable service for the courts and correctional systems, but also an important release valve for the jail population.[21]

Pretrial Release of Felony Defendants

How many criminal defendants are released on bond and what happens to them after their release? The National Pretrial Reporting Program is a national initiative sponsored by the Bureau of Justice Statistics. The National Pretrial Reporting Program collects detailed information about the criminal history, pretrial processing, adjudication, and sentencing of felony defendants in state courts in the 75 largest counties in the United States. A sample of more than 13,000 cases was representative of the more than 55,000 felony cases filed in these jurisdictions per month. Importantly, the 75 largest counties in the country accounted for 50% of the total crime occurring in the United States. Based on these data, Bureau of Justice statisticians Brian Reaves and Jacob

Perez produced a number of important findings about felony defendants during the pretrial period of the criminal justice system. For example:

- 63% of felony defendants are released from jail prior to the resolution of their case. This includes 24% of murder defendants, 48% of rape defendants, 50% of robbery defendants, and 68% of assault defendants.
- The most common form of release was personal recognizance, which 38% of all felony defendants received.
- 25% of persons released on felony bond fail to appear in court and have warrants issued for their arrest.
- Overall, 33% of felons released on bond are either re-arrested for a new offense, fail to appear in court, or commit some other violation that results in revocation of their bond.
- Among defendants already on pretrial release when arrested for their current felony, 56% were released again, 32% of these were released while on parole and 44% were on probation.
- 52% of all felony releases occurred the day of arrest.
- 55% of persons released from jail on felony charges had no prior convictions, 45% did have prior convictions. Moreover, 53% had prior arrests, 27% had prior felony convictions, and 9% had a prior violent felony conviction.
- Among those who were released and rearrested, about 8% were arrested within 1 week, 37% within 1 month, 71% within 3 months, and 91% within 6 months.[22]

Federal Pretrial Release and Detention

Pretrial services are not just a state function, but also occur in the federal criminal justice system. Recall that the landmark Bail Reform Act of 1966 was the federal initiative that de-emphasized monetary bail and required the courts to release any defendant charged with non-capital crimes on his or her recognizance or an unsecured appearance bond unless the court determined that the defendant posed significant risks to the community. Importantly, pretrial release facilitated due process in three ways. First, it furthered the presumption of innocence by avoiding unjust or undue jail detention. Second, it enabled criminal defendants to better participate in their defense. Third, it reduced the possibility that defendants would be detained longer than otherwise appropriate for the offense committed. In other words, they would not serve weeks or months for trivial charges, such as shoplifting.

The Federal Pretrial Services Act of 1982 established pretrial services for defendants in the United States district courts. Forty-two Federal districts are served by a federal pretrial service agency. United States Probation serves the remaining 52 districts. Federal pretrial services officers conduct investigations and supervise clients released into their custody. Like state pretrial service staff, federal officers conduct extensive criminal history checks and assess community ties. Together this information is used to assess risks of flight, recidivism, and danger.[23]

Like criminal defendants facing state charges, the preponderance of federal defendants are released from custody on some type of bond. John Scalia found that about 53% of the 56,982 defendants charged with a felony offense were released from custody. Nearly 60% of these were released on their own recognizance on an unsecured bond. More than 34% of federal defendants were detained pending adjudication of their charges, including roughly half of persons charged with violent crimes, immigration violations, and drug trafficking. Non-citizen and homeless defendants were also significantly less likely to be released due to their weaker ties to the community.[24]

Compared to state pretrial service units, federal authorities are more stringent in detaining defendants. In accordance with the Bail Reform Act of 1984, federal authorities conduct a detention hearing within three to five days of the defendant's arrest. At the detention hearing, federal authorities must present clear and convincing evidence that detention is the sole way to ensure not only the defendant's appearance in court, but also to reduce the risks of danger and recidivism that he or she posed. Certain conditions, such as if the defendant's current charges involve firearms, they are already on a criminal justice status, or are a violent recidivist automatically mandate pretrial detention.[25]

BOND DECISION-MAKING AND DETERMINANTS OF RELEASE/DETENTION

Types of Risk

Whether or not a criminal defendant is released from custody constitutes two sides of the same discretionary coin. Essentially, pretrial service personnel assess three basic types of risk when deciding whether to release a defendant from custody and how they should release the defendant, such as via recognizance or a more restrictive secured bond. The three risks for consideration are (1) danger risk, (2) recidivism risk, and (3) flight or failure to appear (FTA) risk.

Danger risk is the level of danger that the defendant poses toward himself or herself, the specific victim in the current case, or society at large. Danger risk is comprised of several factors, such as the level of injury that the current victim sustained, the seriousness of the current charges, whether the victim is actively homicidal, suicidal, or expresses homicidal or suicidal ideation, and the extent of the defendant's criminal history. Defendants that meet a variety of criteria related to the seriousness of their current charges or the magnitude of their criminal record can be statutorily prohibited from recognizance release. In the event that defendants are charged with capital crimes, criminal suspects can be denied bail altogether.

Recidivism risk refers to the likelihood, assessed by diagnostic instrument, pretrial officer expertise, or both, that the criminal defendant, if released, would immediately engage in criminal behavior. Obviously, pretrial staff cannot see the future and predict future behavior. However, one's criminal history is a relatively reliable predictor of one's future conduct. Thus, defendants with lengthy prior records containing numerous arrests, convictions, and previous involvements with the criminal justice system are viewed as high risk for re-offending. Conversely, persons with no prior record or great intervals of time between arrests, for example, a defendant who was arrested once, twenty years ago, are viewed as low risks for recidivism. Another important indicator of recidivism is current legal status. Many criminal defendants are already on parole, probation, bond, or summons for other charges in other or the same jurisdictions. Since these defendants are "already in legal trouble," the current charges, even if minor, are seen as illustrative that the defendant is a recidivist.

Flight risk is assessed primarily by three factors. First, prior history of missing court appearances, bond revocations, and failing to comply with conditions of probation are viewed as indicators that the defendant would likely miss immediate court dates. Since criminal records contain arrests for failing to appear in court (FTA), a defendant's flight risk is a function of their criminal record. Second, in addition to their current charges, criminal defendants are also found to have active warrants for their arrest because of previous incidents of failing to appear in court. Thus, defendants with one or more current FTA warrants are considered high risk for future missed court appearances. Third, flight risk is related to the community ties of a criminal defendant. Persons with long-term residency in the area, homeowners, currently employed, and persons with extensive family and friendship networks are low risks to miss court dates, flee the jurisdiction, or flee. Conversely, persons who are transient, have little to no financial investment in the community, are unemployed, and have little to no social support have little binding them to the community. As such, there is little incentive to "remain in town" and handle legal responsibilities. Those with weak community ties are viewed as high risks to leave the area, or at minimum, miss court.

Protective and Risk Factors

In determining the risks of recidivism, danger, and flight, pretrial service personnel weigh an assortment of characteristics of the defendant. Some of these factors present the defendant in a positive light and indicate that he or she poses little risk to the community. These are known as protective factors. Alternately, risk factors are damaging or aggravating circumstances that indicate that the defendant will pose some risk if released from custody. Derived from the United States Code Title 18, a partial list of protective and risk factors as well as conditions of pretrial release appears in Criminal Justice Spotlight Box 7-2.

CRIME SCENE   DO NOT CROSS   BOX 7-2

CRIMINAL JUSTICE SPOTLIGHT

DETERMINANTS OF PRETRIAL RELEASE OR DETENTION

PROTECTIVE FACTORS

Current charges are benign or relatively non-serious
Strong employment record
Homeowner
Entrenched community ties
Strong local family and friendship networks
Minimal or no prior criminal record
Persons' character
Financial resources

RISK FACTORS

Already on parole
Already on probation
Already on bond
Awaiting sentencing in other criminal matter
Not a resident of United States or local community
Homeless or transient
Unemployed
Substance abuse problem
Current charges involve crimes of violence
Lengthy criminal history
Multiple convictions, incarcerations, or imprisonments
History of FTA, absconding, or escape

BOND CONDITIONS

Abide by specified restrictions on personal associations, palace of abode, or travel
No contact with alleged victim or witnesses in case
Maintain employment
Actively seek employment
Maintain or commence an educational program
Daily reporting to designated criminal justice agency
Comply with specified curfew
Refrain from use of alcohol
Substance abuse monitoring, including urinalysis
No possession of weapons
Psychiatric, psychological counseling

Source: United States Code Title 18, Sections 3141–3150. Photo © 2011, joingate, Shutterstock, Inc.

For decades, criminologists have studied the protective and risk factors that influence the assignment of bail and the types of release accorded to criminal defendants, especially because of the traditionally discriminatory bail practices in American criminal justice.[26] Fortunately, the balance of research on pretrial decision-making and bail outcomes indicates that legal factors that influence flight, recidivism, and dangerousness risks are the strongest determinants of pretrial release and detention. By and large, pretrial detention and financially punitive bails are applied to defendants with lengthy criminal records, the most serious current charges, and poor community ties. On the other hand, pretrial release, recognizance bonds, and unsecured bonds are the norm for arrestees with little prior record and with strong community ties.[27]

Conceptually, protective and risk factors should inversely predict release on recognizance and mandatory detention. However, this is not always the case. For example, Sheila Royo Maxwell examined the congruence between predictors of release on recognizance (ROR) and failure to appear (FTA) violations. Expectedly, Maxwell found that defendants with lengthier records, prior crimes of violence, and current serious charges were both less likely to receive an ROR release and more likely to FTA. But, certain demographic characteristics also influenced the decision-making of pretrial officers. Women, persons with prior misdemeanor convictions, and property offenders were more likely to be released on recognizance although they had higher rates of missing court. White defendants were more likely than African Americans to be denied ROR even though race was not a significant predictor of absconding.[28] At the federal level, researchers have found that non-legal considerations also influence pretrial release and bail outcomes. Based on data from 5,660 defendants in ten Federal courts, Celesta Albonetti and her colleagues found that those with lengthy prior records, current or past crimes of violence, and weak community ties were less likely to be released before trial. Albonetti and associates also found that offense seriousness and dangerousness risks negatively affected white, not minority, defendants.[29]

That defendant demographic factors influence pretrial decision making is a troubling threat to due process; prior to the Manhattan Bail Project bail was explicitly detrimental to lower-income persons. Unfortunately, criminologists continue to unearth different pretrial treatment for different types of people.[30] Because of real or perceived weaker community ties, Hispanic arrestees are especially likely to receive more punitive bonds and remain in custody. Importantly, there is a silver lining. Even in studies that found significant differences in the types of bond afforded to various racial and ethnic groups, the size of these effects was negligible compared to the influence of legal factors. For example, Stephen Demuth and Darrell Steffensmeier analyzed the pretrial release process of nearly 40,000 felony defendants from the 75 largest counties in the United States and found that African American and Hispanic defendants were more likely to be detained and held on bail net the effect of legal factors. Yet, offense seriousness, for crimes like murder, rape, and robbery, ranged from 200 to 2000% more powerful of a predictor than race/ethnicity. Several criminal history indicators, such as multiple charges, FTA history, active criminal justice status, prior felony convictions, prior jail detention, and prior imprisonment were as important or usually more significant predictors than demographics.[31]

Conditional release on bond does not necessarily ensure that criminal defendants will either appear in court or desist from criminal offending. John Goldkamp and Peter Jones evaluated pretrial drug testing projects in Wisconsin and Maryland in 1983 and 1989. Goldkamp and Jones tested the assumption that intensive monitoring of drug use during pretrial release would reduce FTA and recidivism rates. The results were negative and counterintuitive. Although fewer than 10% of defendants produced positive drug tests, between 50 to 70% of clients recorded more than five violations of the drug program. Moreover, substance abuse monitoring did not improve the rates by which defendants appeared in court or re-offended. In short, they found substantial non-compliance and continued criminal behavior among drug-using defendants released on bond.[32] Subsequent replications of this approach in Florida and Arizona yielded similarly dismal results of continued non-compliance and criminal offending while on bond.[33]

To summarize, a defendant's risks of flight, recidivism, and danger are the primary determinants of whether he or she is released on bond and how punitive or lenient the bail process is. Strong community ties entail long-term residency, stable employment, and strong familial networks. Weak community ties entail transience, unemployment, and little social and personal connection to the local community. Although researchers still find that demographic characteristics, such as gender and race, significantly affect pretrial outcomes, the effects are negligible compared to legal considerations like offense seriousness and criminal record.

THE EFFECTS OF PRETRIAL DETENTION

Administrative Issues

Despite the advances in the bail process in American justice, there remain unresolved issues about the ultimate due process of pretrial detention. John Goldkamp, Michael Gottfredson, Peter Jones, and Doris Weiland conducted a national assessment of the pretrial process. Their observations were based on analyses of three very different approaches to pretrial service. In Dade County Florida, the department of corrections supervised the pretrial staff; however, an individual judge made the preponderance of bond decisions. In Boston, rotating judges determined bail without the assistance of a pretrial staff. In Arizona, a modern pretrial service unit handled the pretrial release duties as officers of the court.

Goldkamp and his colleagues offered this somewhat grim five-point conclusion. First, there is a continued reliance on financial bail as a major emphasis on release decisions. Of course, protective and risk factors influence the assignment of bail, however cold hard cash or other fiscal resources are still needed for release. Similarly, the presence of profiteering bondspersons remains a visible and dubious part of the pretrial process. Second, the judiciary must assume a leadership role in bringing consistency to the organization, administration, and release policies of bail. Third, it is incumbent that pretrial services move to the adoption of guidelines-based decision-making. Fourth, the judiciary must appropriately staff pretrial service units to meet the pressing problems of jail crowding and unfair or unjust pretrial detention. Fifth, pretrial supervision agencies must serve as the gatekeepers of information for the criminal process as well as for pretrial-release and detention.[34]

Procedural Justice Issues

Unquestionably, the masterwork in this area is Malcolm Feeley's aptly titled *The process is the punishment: Handling cases in a lower criminal court.* Based on his observations of the pretrial court processes in New Haven, Connecticut, Feeley argued that the real punishment for many people is the pretrial process itself, which is burdensome, uncomfortable, bewildering, and seemingly based on the subjective judgments of various criminal justice practitioners. For example, upon arrest defendants must interact with police officers, sheriff's officers and booking deputies, detention officers at the police station, pretrial service officers, bonding agents, defense counsel, private counsel, and the like. These interactions must be accomplished while the defendants are detained and without many of the resources that they need. Court appearances are set in accordance with the court schedule, not a defendant's personal calendar. Thus, the contingencies of being arrested and being released on bond can and often do interfere with work and family obligations. By and large, these officials or "supportive figures" have conflicting responsibilities and duties, and their lack of coordination creates logistical problems for defendants.

Upon intake to the criminal justice system, these "supportive figures" define issues and label defendants for all those who subsequently handle them. Although they may possess limited discretion, their decision-making can have significant consequences at later stages of the process. Because the process is so informal and depends so heavily on oral communications, decisions made by the courtroom workgroup are based heavily on the impressions, information, and recommendations passed on by these supportive figures. The sanctions imposed on defendants are heavily influenced by these people's initial impressions.

According to Feeley, due process concerns are subordinated to the profound short-term impressions of arrest and pretrial behavior and demeanor, arrest record (regardless of conviction record), and professional assessments of whether an individual is worthy or prosecution or dismissal, intervention or given a break, entered into the system or thrown back. Crime control is also not achieved because the courts are structured to offer rapid, informal justice that invites carelessness and error. Because the pretrial period is such a disorganized mess, the majority of criminal defendants prefer to accept plea bargains simply to end their involvement in the process. Since the "punishment is in the process," defendants invoke few adversarial options available to them. The defendant's goal is to end the case as quickly as possible. In return, the state produces perfunctory convictions for reduced criminal charges and justifies the troubling practices of the pretrial period.[35]

Substantive Justice Issues

Enduring the pretrial punishment process carries several legal implications. By and large, two classes of criminal defendants emerge at the pretrial period, those who are released from custody and those who remain in custody. The latter group are purported to suffer deleterious legal outcomes as a function of their remaining in jail prior to court. These negative outcomes can include a greater likelihood of imprisonment, longer sentences, and more punitive sentencing recommendations from the prosecution.[36] Unfortunately, some early research did not adequately control for legally relevant factors that explained pretrial detention. As such, the effects of pretrial detention on subsequent legal outcomes were somewhat cloudy.

Recently, Marian Williams conducted a methodologically more sophisticated examination of the effects of pretrial detention on legal outcomes. Using data from 412 Florida cases, Williams explored the effects of detention on likelihood of incarceration and length of sentence while controlling for a host of important variables, such as offense seriousness, number of felony charges, prior felony convictions, whether the defendant had a private attorney, length of disposition, age, race, and gender. Williams found that defendants who were held in jail prior to court were six times more likely than released arrestees to be sentenced to incarceration and for lengthier terms. Importantly, Williams noted that pretrial detention can be viewed as either a legal variable (or proxy for criminal history), or as an extra-legal variable that relates to social class and therefore ability to pay bond.[37] Irrespective of how it is framed, pretrial detention had meaningfully negative impacts on subsequent criminal justice system outcomes.

BOX 7-3

CRIME SCENE   DO NOT CROSS

CRIMINAL JUSTICE SNAPSHOT

WHO IS IN JAIL?

- Persons pending arraignment and held awaiting trial, conviction, or sentencing
- Probation, parole, and bail-bond violators and absconders
- Temporarily detained juveniles pending transfer to juvenile authorities
- Mentally ill persons pending transfer to juvenile authorities
- Hold individuals for the United States military, for protective custody, for contempt of court, and for the courts as witnesses
- Inmates awaiting transfer to state or federal prisons
- Persons wanted by other criminal justice/law enforcement agencies, known as courtesy holds
- Persons housed because of overcrowding at other facilities
- Persons serving various community-based sentences
- Persons convicted of misdemeanors and serving short terms generally less than one year
- Persons convicted of felonies and serving short terms less than two years

Source: Sabol, W. J., Minton, T. D., & Harrison, P. M. (2007). *Prison and jail inmates at midyear 2006*. Washington, DC: U. S. Department of Justice, Office of Justice Programs, Bureau of Justice Statistics. *Photo © 2011, Serg64, Shutterstock, Inc.*

JAILS

Definition and Purpose

Being detained in jail is the flip side to being released on bond. Jail is a local correctional or confinement facility that is typically administered by a county-level sheriff's department or a municipal-level law enforcement agency. Jails are utilized to control two general populations of offenders, defendants awaiting trial and persons who have already been convicted and sentenced for their crimes. In addition, jails house a multitude of individuals and are frequently used as waiting stations until persons can be transported to a more appropriate venue or social service provider (see Box 7-3). At any moment, a jail population might contain persons who have absconded from military service; persons wanted by probation or parole; persons awaiting placement in a psychiatric facility; persons awaiting transport to the hospital or some other medical facility; and juveniles who are being held (in isolation from adult inmates) until their age is ascertained for appropriate placement. Jails are also used by law enforcement as a last resort to detain transients, non-citizens or illegal aliens, people who are highly intoxicated on drugs or alcohol, and anyone else who poses risks to their own and public safety.

Jail Population

Nationally, more than 3,300 American jails supervise more than 767,000 persons. Of these, more than 90% are actually detained and the remaining are supervised in alternative programs outside the jail facility. These programs include weekender programs whereby offenders report for detention only when not working, by electronic monitoring, home detention, day reporting, community service, treatment and therapy, and other work release programs. Overall, the jail population constitutes more than one-third of the nation's correctional population. The jail population has increased fairly steadily since 1990 and reflects sharp demographic differences in rate of confinement. According to Bureau of Justice statisticians Paige Harrison and Allen Beck, males comprise nearly 90% of the jail population and men are seven times more likely than women to be detained in jail on a per capita basis. About 45% of the jail population is comprised of Caucasians, 39% African American, 15% Hispanic, and 2% other racial or ethnic identification. Per capita, blacks are five times more likely than whites, nearly three times more likely than Hispanics, and over eight times more likely than other races to have been in jail.[38]

Approximately 60% of the nation's jail inmates were awaiting court action on their current charge. Thus, more than half of the American jail population *had not yet been convicted for what they were currently charged.* The remaining 40% were post-adjudication defendants serving time for various convictions, probation violations, and parole violations pending transfer to a state department of corrections. Jail confinement is usually a temporary experience. When considering pre- and post-adjudication inmates, the average length of stay is a mere three days. Many defendants are detained for less than 24 hours, remaining in custody until they are able to mobilize resources for release. Ninety-four percent of jail capacity is occupied. Jail facilities vary tremendously in their size and capacity. The fifty largest jails in the United States house more than 30% of all jail detainees nationwide. For example, jail complexes in New York and Los Angeles, which are among the largest penal colonies in the world, house 5% of the American jail population.[39]

Social and Criminal Histories of Jail Inmates

Jail and prison are often used interchangeably in the mainstream media; however, there are vital differences between these facilities. Jails are local, administered usually by the sheriff's department, and entail brief lengths of stay. More than half of the jail population has not yet been convicted. Prisons, explored in Section Four of the textbook, are remote, state-administered correctional facilities used to confine convicted felons. Many people who are in jail will never be in prison, such as persons arrested for DWI; however, almost all prisoners have at some point been detained in jail.

Because jails detain both those who will not be convicted and those who already have been convicted, the population is heterogeneous in terms of the social and criminal history of the inmates. To be sure, many jail inmates have chronic criminal careers.[40] Using data from the national Survey of Inmates in Local Jails, Doris James discovered extensive criminality among some jail detainees. About 46% of all jail inmates were already on probation or parole at the time of their most recent arrest. Nearly 40% had served three or more separate commitments to state or federal prison. Seventy percent of jail inmates had some sort of prior criminal record and 41% of jail inmates had a current or past arrest for violent crimes, such as murder, rape, robbery, or aggravated assault.[41]

Nearly 60% of jail inmates were raised in single-parent households and one in nine was raised in a foster home or institution. Forty six percent of jail inmates had an immediate family member who had been incarcerated. More than 50% of female and 10% of male jail inmates reported that they had suffered from past sexual or physical abuse.[42] Sixty-seven percent of jail inmates were actively involved with drug use prior to their admission to jail, and 16% of jail inmates indicated that they committed their most recent crimes for the explicit purpose of obtaining money to purchase drugs.[43]

History, Reform, and Programs

American criminal justice owes an enormous debt to English common law, and the jail tradition is no exception. Unfortunately, jail history in the United States is overwhelmingly negative and these facilities have been referred to as the sewers and ghettos of the criminal justice system. In the colonial era, jails served no correctional function but instead were used to detain persons who were wanted in the interests of justice and debtors who could not meet their financial obligations. In lieu of jail confinement, those convicted of crimes were banished, branded, pilloried, executed, or maimed. Just as today, jails were then used as last-resort holding bins for groups of people considered outside the mainstream society, namely the mentally ill, alcoholics, and the poor. As the United States expanded and became more modernized, jails also increased in number so that nearly every county and/or municipality had one. However, for most of the Twentieth Century, jails were not appreciably different in their fundamental form and function from those of the Eighteenth Century. Indeed, substantive reform of jail and bail practices was not achieved until the 1960s to 1980s. Otherwise, until very recently, American jails were catchall asylums for the poor and disaffected.[44]

Recently, however, there has been progress. As this chapter has detailed, federal legislation and state and federal criminal justice initiatives have tremendously improved the pretrial phase of the criminal justice system. Professional and efficient pretrial service units utilize community ties and criminal history, not just financial resources, as the determinants of pretrial release.

Jail facilities themselves have been redesigned in terms of their physical environment and approach to inmate supervision. "New Generation" jails were first instituted in 1974 and featured podular or direct supervision whereby inmates were housed in single-occupancy cells that adjoined a larger communal area (see Box 7-4). Inmates interacted in the self-contained living unit or pod for most of the day.

Unlike the traditional jail structure that employed linear supervision or simply a corridor of separate cells, direct supervision facilities allowed correctional staff to constantly observe all aspects of the inmate's living space. The living space itself contained modern amenities, such as carpeting and basic features that one might find in a dormitory. New generation jails served two important interrelated purposes. First, they were more humane facilities compared to the traditional jail in which inmates lived in small cells for most of their detention. Since a jail stint is itself very brief, it makes sense to create a correctional atmosphere that promotes rehabilitation and facilities the offender's reintegration into the community. Second, the increased amenities offered jail inmates an incentive to obey jail regulations. Inmates that did not obey could lose their status in podular modules and go back to traditional cells. Thus, serving inmate needs and ensuring inmate and staff safety were symbiotic. New generation jails have produced a variety of positive outcomes, including reduced inmate violence and misconduct, reduced recidivism after inmates were released, longer delay until re-arrest, and increased inmate and staff satisfaction with the jail environment.[45]

Nevertheless, some continue to assert that jails are a glaring example of injustice and impediment to due process. In his provocative work, *The Jail: Managing the Underclass in American Society* (1985), criminologist John Irwin argued that the function and purpose of jails is to confine disreputable persons not because they have committed crimes but because they are offensive and disreputable. Irwin's thesis is that "rabble," various marginalized groups such as transients, drug abusers, alcoholics, and the like, must be controlled by the criminal justice system to justify and perpetuate the stratification system of American society. Irwin's thesis is radical and sparked subsequent research that largely disconfirmed his hypothesis. For instance, John Backstrand, Don Gibbons, and Joseph Jones empirically found no evidence that persons are arrested for their "offensiveness" or degree of disrepute, instead their actual criminal behavior and the seriousness of their charges influenced their status as jail inmate.[46]

Unquestionably, jail confinement is laden with implicit and explicit types of punishment that affect the social and legal standing of jail inmates.[47] Pure jail confinement is reserved primarily for the most serious criminal offenders with the most extensive criminal records. For the remaining majority of criminal defendants, the contemporary jail offers a variety of programs, treatments, and non-incarceration penalties that aim to serve the interests of

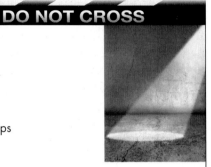

CRIME SCENE   DO NOT CROSS

BOX 7–4

CRIMINAL JUSTICE SPOTLIGHT

PRINCIPLES OF NEW GENERATION JAILS

- Effective control and supervision
- Total control
- Sound perimeter security
- Population divided into controllable groups
- Easily surveillable areas
- Maximize inmates' inner controls
- Staff-to-inmate ratio
- Officer in control of unit
- Competent and professional staff
- Facility safety for staff and inmates
- Manageable and cost-effective operations
- Effective staff-inmate communication
- Inmate classification, screening, and orientation
- Knowing with whom you are dealing
- Orientation
- Assumption of rational behavior
- Maximum supervision during initial hours of confinement
- Just and fair treatment of inmates

Source: Nelson, W. R., O'Toole, M., Krauth, B., & Whitemore, C. G. (1983). *New generation jails*. Longmont, CO: National Institute of Corrections, Jails Division. *Photo © 2011, joingate, Shutterstock, Inc.*

community safety (crime control), defendants' rights (due process), and a less damaging, more human pretrial period. Some of these programs are reviewed next.

Due to the prevalence of substance abuse, mental illness, and the co-occurrence of these problems among the jail population, some jurisdictions have devised programs to divert drug-using, mentally ill offenders from jails to more appropriate treatment facilities. Some jurisdictions divert clients prior to booking; others place defendants with appropriate agencies after they have been booked into a county jail (but will be released). A variety of positive outcomes have emerged. Persons who participated in the mental health, substance abuse diversion programs tended to gain independent living skills, reduce substance use, and have lower recidivism rates than persons who did not participate in the program and were simply jailed. Moreover, this saved significant jail space and provided more appropriate, problem-specific treatment.[48]

Henry Steadman and Michelle Naples recently evaluated six jail diversion programs (three pre-booking and three post-booking) in Memphis, Tennessee;

Montgomery County, Pennsylvania; Multnomah County, Oregon; Phoenix/ Tucson, Arizona; Hartford, New Haven, and Bridgeport, Connecticut; and Lane County, Oregon. Defendants who participated in the diversion programs were primarily female offenders with mental health problems, such as schizophrenia or mood disorders with psychotic traits. Across the six sites, diverted offenders experienced lower recidivism, two months more time spent in the community (and thus not in jail), and greater participation in mental health treatment and counseling, and taking prescribed medication. Diverted individuals did incur higher treatment costs, but these were offset by cost-savings in criminal justice, such as jail. Overall, Steadman and Naples concluded that jail diversion programs that reached out to offenders with mental health needs produced positive outcomes for individuals, criminal justice systems, and communities.[49]

Another programming option is to "outsource" the jail function to the defendant's home. Home incarceration programs, also known as house arrest, home detention, or home detention with electronic monitoring, allow criminal defendants to remain in the community so that they can continue working, fulfilling family responsibilities, and participating in treatment. However, court officials limit the movements and freedom of criminal defendants so that defendants can leave their house only for work, treatment, or other court-approved reasons. All other freedoms are restricted. Offenders are monitored with electronic devices (e.g., ankle bracelets), daily reporting to jail authorities, and other methods. Home incarceration programs are used during both pretrial and post-conviction periods and have met with modest success.[50] For instance, Robert Stanz and Richard Tewksbury examined the programs compliance and subsequent recidivism of nearly 2,500 defendants who participated in a house arrest program. They found that 85% of clients successfully completed the program, and that older defendants from "good" neighborhoods who were charged with DUI-related charges were the most likely to successfully complete the program. Home incarceration costs were 13 times less expensive than jail costs. Stanz and Tewksbury also found that recidivism rates were high, unfortunately. Nearly 70% of clients were re-arrested within five years. More than half of the study group was re-arrested within one year and the most common crime was another DUI.[51] Still, the dramatically reduced costs mean that jail programs that include non-detention components will continue to define the modern jail.

Federal Jails

Do federal jails exist? Actually, they do. The Federal Bureau of Prisons spends nearly $170 million to operate seven federal jails that house less than 6,000 inmates. Federal jails combined have a rate capacity of 3,810, thus federal jails operate at 155 percent of their rated capacity. In this way, they are more crowded facilities than local jails. Interestingly, most jail inmates who are under federal jurisdiction do not reside in federal jails. Instead, more than 12,000 persons wanted by federal authorities are held in local jails to await transfer to a federal facility.[52]

Chapter Summary: Balancing Crime Control and Due Process

- The pretrial phase is among the least studied but most important periods of the criminal justice system and contains the transition of police to court power.
- Bail/bond traditionally was limited to wealth, thus indigent persons remained in jail custody regardless of the risks they posed to society.
- Risks of recidivism, flight, and danger posed to victims and community are the primary determinants of bond and pretrial outcomes.
- More than half of the jail population awaits resolution in their criminal case. That so many un-convicted persons reside in jail is a troubling feature of American criminal justice.
- Most criminal defendants, even those charged with serious felonies, are released from jail custody prior to trial.
- A substantial segment of the jail population contains habitual and serious criminals.
- Law enforcement, judicial, and correctional agencies control the pretrial services function depending on jurisdiction.
- Pretrial confinement denotes several negative consequences for subsequent criminal justice decisions, such as sentencing.
- To alleviate crowding and deprivations of liberty, New Generation jails offer a multitude of programs, release options, and alternative sanctions.

Key Terms

Abscond	Flight risk
Bail	FTA
Bail Reform Act of 1966	Home detention, house arrest, home
Bail Reform Act of 1984	incarceration
Bond	Jail
Bondsperson	Jail diversion program
Bounty hunter	Linear supervision
Cash bond	Manhattan Bail Project
Dangerousness risk	New Generation jail
Deposit bail system	Post-adjudication
Detention	Pre-adjudication
Direct or podular supervision	Pretrial

Pretrial release units or bond commissioners
Pretrial Services Act of 1982
Protective factor
Recidivism risk

Recognizance
Risk factor
Secured bond
Surety
Vera Institute of Justice

TALKING POINTS

1. Does pretrial release lean more toward crime control or due process ideals? Use data from the chapter to support your position that too many or too few criminal defendants are released from jail?

2. Bail/bond has been criticized for social class bias. Are protective factors simply proxies for social class? Why or why not?

3. Is it improper or unethical for pretrial service personnel to make assessments of predictions of risk? What factors are and should be the strongest determinant of whether a criminal defendant is "dangerous?"

4. Despite the proliferation of jail programs, why has the jail population continued to increase? Would more programs help reduce the jail population further?

WEB LINKS

American Jail Association
(http://www.corrections.com/aja/index.shtml)

Bureau of Justice Statistics Pretrial Release of Felony Defendants
(http://www.ojp.usdoj.gov/bjs/pub/pdf/nprp92.pdf)

Los Angeles County Sheriff's Department (Jail Division)
(http://www.lasd.org/divisions/custody/twintowers/index.html)

National Institute of Corrections
(http://www.nicic.org/)

National Institute of Corrections Jails Division
(www.nicic.org/Jails)

New York City Department of Correction
(http://www.ci.nyc.ny.us/html/doc/home.html)

United States Probation and Pretrial Services
(http://www.uscourts.gov/fedprob/introduction.htm)

Vera Institute of Justice
(www.vera.org)

FURTHER READING

Feeley, M. M. (1992). *The process is the punishment: Handling cases in a lower criminal court*, revised edition. New York: Russell Sage Foundation. This look at the disorganization and subjectivity of the pretrial process is a criminological classic. The book can be viewed as a supplement to Herbert Packer's *The Limits of the Criminal Sanction.*

Goldfarb, R. (1976). *Jails: The ultimate ghetto of the criminal justice system.* New York: Doubleday. This book is an expose that motivated jail reform that resulted in New Generation Jails. The work contains excellent historical accounts of jail conditions and the types of offenders and social types that reside in jails.

Goldkamp, J. S., Gottfredson, M. R., Jones, P. R., & Weiland, D. (1995). *Personal liberty and community safety: Pretrial release in the criminal court.* New York: Plenum. Authored by some of the main researchers in the area, this text is a study of pretrial release procedures in Dade County Florida, Boston, Massachusetts, and Maricopa County Arizona. It is a must-read for students interested in pretrial services and contains a wealth of empirical data about how authorities arrive at determinations of flight, recidivism, and danger risks.

Irwin, J. (1985). *The jail: Managing the underclass in American society.* Berkeley, CA: University of California Press. Irwin, a prominent criminologist and ex-convict, offers a polemical look at the place of jail in managing those at the margins of society. Rooted in conflict theory, this is an interesting and thought-provoking look at the function of the criminal justice system.

Kerle, K. E. (1998). *American jails: Looking to the future.* Woburn, MA: Butterworth-Heinemann. This book is a veritable encyclopedia of jails. The author is the editor of *American Jails* magazine, a longtime consultant to jails and corrections, and has personally visited nearly 1,000 American jails. That experience is evident in this book.

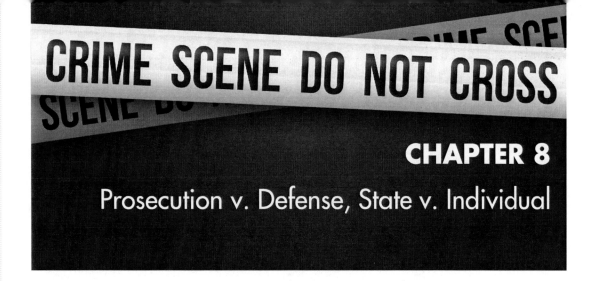

CHAPTER 8

Prosecution v. Defense, State v. Individual

CHAPTER OUTLINE

QUOTATIONS

"The first thing we do, let's kill all the lawyers."—*William Shakespeare*[1]

"The judge, the lawyers, even the witnesses appear to be playing roles, acting their parts in the unfolding story. And, most important, the play has a plot. The plot is always the same, justice. Justice done or justice denied. But it is a great plot."—*Richard Uviller*[2]

"Most prosecutors argue that while justice, crime control, and speedy case-processing are all worthy goals, each case is unique. Whether to accept a case, what charges to file, how much time to spend preparing it for a court proceeding, what charge or charges to allow the defendant to plead to in return for dropping other charges (or what sentence to recommend to the judge if the defendant pleads guilty to a particular charge) in any given case cannot be determined by pondering over abstract goals."—*Brian Forst*[3]

"An adversary presentation counters the natural human tendency to judge too swiftly in terms of the familiar that which is not yet fully known; the advocate, by his zealous preparation of facts and law, enables the tribunal to come to the hearing with an open and neutral mind and to render impartial judgments. The duty of a lawyer to his client and his duty to the legal system are the same: To represent his client zealously within the boundaries of the law."—*American Bar Association*[4]

INTRODUCTION

In his brilliant work, *The Tilted Playing Field: Is Criminal Justice Unfair?*, Richard Uviller argues that the prosecution and defense do not and should not have equal resources and powers given their prescriptively different roles in the criminal justice system. The prosecutor has unmatched and virtually unreviewable discretion to choose which cases to prosecute, which to drop, which to push for trial, and which to develop strategies for a plea agreement. Furthermore, the prosecutor is empowered to compel testimony and even offer immunity upon which testimonial cooperation is not only compelled but also explicitly mandated. The prosecution also carries the heavy burden of proving guilt beyond a reasonable doubt, a burden that justifies their resource advantage. Comparatively, the defense can broadly obtain evidence and information from the prosecutor during discovery. Even more fundamentally, the defense has virtual carte blanche to argue the innocence of their client regardless of whether the attorney believes it. Indeed, the preponderance of defense counsel is keenly aware they are representing mostly guilty people. Law and criminal justice can be accurately thought of as a great drama.

In the criminal justice system, the opposing functions of the prosecution and defense are the clearest and most obvious example of the desire for due process in American law. The prosecution is the advocate for the "people" that is the public interest or state. The defense is the advocate for the lone individual facing criminal charges. The judge is simply the arbiter of the courtroom who in a sense referees the interactions, plea agreements, trials, and sentencing procedures. Yet the prosecution and defense, the symbols of state interest versus individual liberty, are the real symbolic foils of due process.

Keeping with Uviller's thesis, the prosecution and defense are not on equal ground in terms of their resources, discretion, and threshold for victory. Our adversarial system places the burden on the prosecutor to demonstrate and prove beyond a reasonable doubt that the accused indeed committed the crime and deserves legal punishment. The defense merely complicates or challenges the prosecutor's ability to prove guilt beyond a reasonable doubt. (By comparison, an inquisitorial or accusatory system assumes that criminal charges are themselves indicators of guilt that the accused must actively disprove). This chapter describes the various duties and responsibilities of the prosecution and the defense as they relate process cases through the criminal courts.

THE PROSECUTION

Statistical Snapshot of American Prosecutors

Known in various jurisdictions as the district attorney or DA, county attorney, commonwealth attorney, or solicitor, the prosecutor is the lawyer or attorney that conducts criminal proceedings within a specific jurisdiction. An elected official who serves usually four-year terms, the prosecutor represents the state and therefore public interests in criminal justice and works to convict and sentence persons charged with violations of the criminal law.

According to the National Survey of Prosecutors, there are 2,344 prosecutors' offices in the United States.[5] These offices employed over 78,000 attorneys, investigators, victim advocates, and support staff with a median annual budget of $355,000. Nearly one in four prosecutors' offices participated in a homeland security task force as part of counterterrorism protocols. Over 60% have prosecuted computer-related crimes and nearly 95% used DNA evidence during plea negotiations or felony trials. On average, prosecutors have served for nearly eight years in office and have annual salaries of nearly $85,000.

Prosecutors serve many functions, including criminal investigations, child support enforcement, interpreter services, social services, community liaison, and partnering with local law enforcement agencies. Nearly all prosecutor offices have specialized bureaus or assistant district attorneys that handle special categories of crimes to enforce and prosecute. These include hate crime, domestic violence, elder abuse, stalking, child abuse, health care fraud, bank fraud, telemarketing fraud, firearms trafficking, and police use of excessive force. Prosecutors' offices rely almost entirely on negotiated plea agreements or plea bargains to secure convictions. As such, 88% of all cases and 90 percent of felony cases that are closed result in conviction. The median number of felony jury trial verdicts is a mere two annually! Finally, prosecutors are very active in community effects and regularly meet with school, advocacy, youth service, business, neighborhood association, religious, and tenant association groups.[6]

The Greatest Power in the Court Room?

It is common knowledge that the judge is the most powerful entity or presiding force in American justice. However, the typical disposition of felony cases in the United States provides compelling evidence that the prosecution is far more powerful than the judge. Consider these data. If the magnitude of all felony crimes in the United States were reduced to a scale of 100 arrests, the following is the typical outcome of those 100 cases. Of 100 felony arrests, about 70 are brought to the attention of the district or county attorney. Of these 70 cases, the prosecutor rejects 20 cases and accepts 50 cases. Already, 50 percent of the felony arrests have been removed from the system. Of those 50, the judge dismisses 5 cases due to insufficient evidence, procedural difficulty, triviality, or some other rationale and another 5 cases are dismissed because the defendant absconded while on bond. Of the remaining 40 cases, defendants plead guilty in 35 cases and go to trial in 5 cases, half of which will result in acquittal. Of 38 remaining cases, 24 defendants are sentenced to incarceration and 14 to probation. Among the incarcerated convicted felons, 14 are imprisoned for more than one year and 10 are jailed for less than one year. What do these estimates mean? For every felony case that a judge presides over in trial, the prosecution decides the fate of 14 adult felony cases brought by the police![7]

Functions and Responsibilities

With their considerable legal power, the prosecutor is expected to handle important and sometimes competing criminal justice responsibilities. Ultimately, the prosecutor attempts to ensure that both crime control and due process goals are achieved within a jurisdiction. This creates the difficult task of protecting the public and minding the rights of criminal defendants. Moreover, prosecutors must strike the balance between crime control and due process within the constraints of their budget, staff, and resources. These pragmatic factors sometimes supersede philosophical ideas about effective crime control. In other words, the prosecutor has to pick and choose which cases to pursue because of limiting time and resources. Complicating their job further, the prosecutor's decision making is evaluated from various entities within the criminal justice system and from the unofficial but sometimes influential court of public opinion.

There are several important functions and responsibilities of the prosecution (see Box 8-1). First, the prosecutor serves as a check-and-balance on the police and monitors the arrests that are made. For a variety of reasons, the prosecution can reject the charges that appear on an arrest report and decline to continue the prosecutorial process, known as *nolle prosequi*. These reasons include insufficient evidence or procedural problems relating to the arrest. The prosecution and police are not necessarily adversarial in their working relationship, however. Indeed, many jurisdictions enhance the effectiveness of their criminal justice operations with police-prosecutorial partnerships whereby both groups work with a common goal of producing arrests that are most likely to result in not only prosecution but also conviction.

Second, the prosecutor protects the constitutional rights of all community residents and criminal defendants by ensuring that his or her office operates in strict accordance with the law. In this sense, the prosecutor is not only a watchdog of the criminal justice system but also of other governmental organizations and private corporations.

Third, the prosecutor must focus on the community's interest of justice. The collective interest of justice means that serious crimes are dealt with in a serious manner and trivial crimes are dismissed or diverted from the system. In other words, a prosecutor who fails to prosecute persons charged with murder or kidnapping but does prosecute persons charged with disorderly conduct is not meeting the public expectations or interest in justice.

Fourth, and perhaps most importantly, the prosecutor must perform the duties of the office. This entails conducting investigations with and beyond those performed by law enforcement, making recommendations for bond and pretrial release, filing charges, conducing plea agreements, securing convictions, making sentencing recommendations, conducting trials, and responding to appeals of criminal defendants who have already been sentenced.

Prosecutorial Discretion

In the course of performing their duties, the prosecutor is influenced by many factors. For instance, in his seminal research on prosecutorial discretion, George Cole noted that the prosecution's office is a player in multiple arenas of local life, such as criminal justice, politics, and community relations. As such, the police, the dynamics of the local judicial culture (or courtroom workgroup), the congestion or backlog of cases awaiting adjudication, and community pressures, such as the frenzied publicity that often surrounds high-profile cases, influence what the prosecutor decides to do. Moreover, these factors influence prosecutorial discretion at multiple points along the criminal justice process from bond to arraignment and from trial to sentencing.[8]

BOX 8-1

CRIME SCENE   DO NOT CROSS

CRIMINAL JUSTICE RESEARCH

THE PROSECUTORIAL WAIVER

One of the most controversial choices that a prosecutor can make is the decision to punish a juvenile offender as an adult. The process of charging a juvenile delinquent in adult criminal court is known as transfer or waiver. When the prosecutor has the discretion to charge juveniles as adults, the process is referred to variously as prosecutorial waiver, concurrent jurisdiction, or a direct filing. The controversy surrounding the prosecutorial waiver stems from the somewhat aggressive stance that some prosecutors take against serious juvenile offenders. Some believe that because prosecutors are in effect local politicians, they are overly susceptible to public outcry to get tough on young offenders, even to prosecute them as adults. Indeed, states that employ prosecutorial waivers permit criminal court judges to "send back" the case to the juvenile court. This process is known as a reverse waiver or decertification.

In practice, prosecutorial waivers might not be the crime control panacea that they appear to be in dealing with the most violent, recalcitrant juvenile offenders. Donna Bishop, Charles Frazier, and John Henretta interviewed prosecutors in Florida, a state that allows the waiver, and found that very few of the juvenile delinquents who were waived to adult court were the type of dangerous, felonious offenders that the policy was created to target. Indeed, nearly one in four youths was first time offenders with no antisocial history.

Sources: Sanborn, J. B. (2003). Hard choices or obvious ones: Developing policy for excluding youth from juvenile court. *Youth Violence and Juvenile Justice, 1*, 198–214; Myers, D. L. (2003). Waiver to adult court. In M. D. McShane & F. P. Williams (Eds.), *Encyclopedia of juvenile justice* (Pp. 387–394). Thousand Oaks, CA: Sage; Bishop, D. M., Frazier, C. E., & Henretta, J. C. (1989). Prosecutorial waiver: Case study of a questionable reform. *Crime & Delinquency, 35*, 179–201. *Photo © JupiterImages, Corp.*

These organizational, sociological, and societal factors can exert formidable pressures on the application of law. Recall a fundamental empirical point from Part One of this textbook that the sheer volume of crime far exceeds the capacity of the criminal justice system to process every case. Nowhere is this more so than at the point of prosecution. Using data from highly populated jurisdictions with high crime rates, Barbara Boland and Brian Forst found that the volume of crime and organizational focus on trials or plea-bargains influenced how felony cases were screened. Prosecutors in high-trial jurisdictions had high rates of *nolle prosequi* and diversion as only the most "convictable" arrests were pushed for trial. Due to the quality of the arrests, such as the amount of evidence obtained, very few plea bargains are offered. Defendants face two difficult choices, plead guilty or face an almost certain conviction at trial. Other jurisdictions accepted high rates of arrests and used plea bargains to achieve conviction.[9] Boland and Forst's research illustrated that both prosecutorial approaches entail substantial filtering of arrest charges by either pursuing only those arrests with a high likelihood of conviction or liberally employing plea agreements to strike deals with criminal defendants and achieve trial-free convictions.

Just as police officers weigh legal and extra-legal factors in their decision making, prosecutors take both variables into account when deciding whether to pursue a case. As is the case with police discretion, prosecutorial discretion is significantly contingent on legal factors, such as evidence, offense seriousness, and the criminal history of the offender, than on extra-legal factors, such as race, gender, or demeanor. Not only do legal factors influence the decision to prosecute, but also the decision not to prosecute. For instance, Kenneth Adams and Charles Cutshall found that the *nolle prosequi* decision for minor offenses was overwhelmingly determined by legal factors not the demographics of the offender.[10]

Criminologists have also found that prosecutorial decision making is influenced by the dynamics surrounding specific types of cases and groups of defendants. For example, Joseph Sanborn found that juvenile court outcomes were based on the character and family support of adjudicated delinquents. Prosecutors considered a youth's family situation, his or her character and perceived amenability to treatment and rehabilitation, current charges, and prior delinquent record in the course of their professional duties.[11] Sanborn also observed that more affluent parents in suburban areas tended to appear more regularly in court to support their children and showed active participation in their children's delinquent cases. Parental support can convey the idea that the juvenile is potentially worthy of leniency and that the juvenile court should operate as a genuine family court. Conversely, youths who appear in court with no parental support can be viewed as throwaways that will receive more punitive dispositions.[12]

In domestic violence cases, the prosecution focuses on relationships-specific factors between the suspect and victim who are usually spouses. Defendants who use weapons during domestic disputes, were intoxicated during the altercation, and have previously abused the same victim are most likely to face prosecution. Domestic violence cases in which the arrest appeared to be an isolated mistake on the part of perpetrator were less likely to be prosecuted.[13] A similar situation characterizes drug offenders. Persons arrested for drug crimes that had extensive criminal records, were male, older, and involved with narcotics were more likely to face prosecution. Comparatively, younger offenders, females, persons with minimal prior record, and those arrested for marijuana related offenses were more often screened for diversion.[14]

Beyond these factors, a multitude of individual-level characteristics of the criminal defendant, the victim, and the specific criminal case also influence how it is processed through the criminal justice system. Gerard Rainville recently summarized the defendant and case-specific variables that affect prosecutorial decision making. Prosecutors are most likely to act punitively in cases that (1) include strong evidence, (2) are based on a lawful, quality police investigation, (3) involve a serious felony, (4) have a defendant with an extensive criminal history, (5) the perpetrator and victim were strangers, and (6) there are aggravating circumstances related to the crime. Prosecutors are more likely to screen, divert, or *nolle prosequi* cases with (1) weak evidence, and that are (2) based on shoddy police investigations. Cases involving (3) family members or intimates as combatants, (4) defendants with little criminal record, (5) unsympathetic victims, and (6) other mitigating circumstances.[15]

Unlike most areas of criminal justice, crime victims actually play a major role in the prosecutorial process. Regrettably, victims are often treated negatively by the criminal courts especially in domestic violence and sexual assault cases. Prosecutors have traditionally viewed domestic violence cases as unattractive ones to prosecute because family intimates are often unwilling to testify against their spouses, parents, or siblings. At times, witnesses and even victims in family violence cases can be uncooperative. Indeed, family assault cases are 300% less likely to be prosecuted than similar assault cases involving strangers.[16] Similarly, prosecutors focus on the perceived sympathetic character and culpability of rape victims. For example, Jeffrey Spears and Cassia Spohn found that victim characteristics were the only significant predictors of whether a prosecutor filed charges in a rape case. Evidentiary and other case specific factors had no significant effects. Instead, prosecutors screened cases that they viewed were unlikely to result in conviction based on factors such as whether the victim abused drugs, had multiple sexual partners, was dressed provocatively, and the like.[17] Subsequent research found that the credibility of the sexual assault victim was also the focal concern of prosecutors within a specialized unit that exclusively handled sexual assault cases.[18]

To summarize, the prosecutor ensures the public interest in crime control and due process and is the chief judicial enforcer. Because of the reliance on plea-bargaining (which is explored in Chapter 9), the prosecutor decides the fate of many more cases than judges. Like the police, the prosecution has wide latitude of discretion to determine which cases deserve prosecution or dismissal. The prosecutor is also a political entity that balances the interests and influences of citizens, civic groups, businesses, and other components of the criminal justice system (for an example, see Box 8-2).

CRIME SCENE   DO NOT CROSS

BOX 8-2

CRIMINAL JUSTICE SNAPSHOT

COMMUNITY PROSECUTION

A relatively new criminal justice innovation is community prosecution. Similar in philosophy to community policing, community prosecution is a partnership between the local district attorney's office and community residents who together seek to reduce crime, identify and solve social problems, engage in crime prevention, and improve their quality of life. Elaine Nugent and Gerard Rainville conducted a national survey of over 300 prosecutors to examine the status of community prosecution in the United States. They found that community prosecution was generally the outgrowth of greater coordination between organizations within the criminal justice system and various community constituencies. Community prosecution often developed hand-in-hand with community policing initiatives and increased the opportunities for civic groups, schools, and citizens to play a part in crime control and crime prevention.

A common focus of community prosecution has been the targeted improvement of areas known for vice or nuisance-oriented crimes, such as drug sales, prostitution, and vagrancy. Many residents view "skid row" areas as reducing the quality of life in their community. Neighborhood district attorneys, police, and citizen groups have been generally effective in controlling nuisance crime and reducing community disorder by using nuisance abatement, civil sanctions, improved lighting, and increased police patrols. However, others found no significant differences between traditional and community prosecution offices in terms of community outreach and coordination with police. Thus, although the specific term community prosecution is a relatively recent phenomenon, it is important to note that the courts have traditionally interacted with their various criminal justice peers and civilian constituents.

Sources: Nugent, E., & Rainville, G. A. (2001). The state of community prosecution: Results of a national survey. *The Prosecutor, 35,* 26–28, 30–33; Weinstein, S. P. (1998). Community prosecution. *FBI Law Enforcement Bulletin, 67,* 19–24; Boland, B. (1996). What is community prosecution? *National Institute of Justice Journal, 231,* 35–40; Rainville, G., & Nugent, M. E. (2002). Community prosecution tenets and practices: The relative mix of 'community and prosecution.' *American Journal of Criminal Justice, 26,* 149–164. Photo © 2011, Serg64, Shutterstock, Inc.

THE DEFENSE

Constitutional Bases and Responsibilities

Whereas the prosecution derives its power from its resource base, discretion, and political and public support, the power of the defense attorney is rooted in the United States Constitution. Examine the Fifth and Sixth Amendments:

> *No person shall be held to answer for a capital, or otherwise infamous crime, unless on a presentment or indictment of a Grand Jury, except in cases arising in the land or naval forces, or in the Militia, when in actual*

service in time of War or public danger; nor shall any person be subject for the same offence to be twice put in jeopardy of life or limb; nor shall be compelled in any criminal case to be a witness against himself, nor be deprived of life, liberty, or property, without due process of law; nor shall private property be taken for public use, without just compensation.

In all criminal prosecutions, the accused shall enjoy the right to a speedy and public trial, by an impartial jury of the State and district wherein the crime shall have been committed, which district shall have been previously ascertained by law, and to be informed of the nature and cause of the accusation; to be confronted with the witnesses against him; to have compulsory process for obtaining witnesses in his favor, and to have the Assistance of Counsel for his defense.

Based on these Amendments, the defense has a variety of important responsibilities. First and foremost, defense counsel are the guardians of due process in the sense that they must ensure that all Constitutional safeguards were protected and affirmed as they relate to the defense's client. Defense counsel monitor the arrest report to ensure that law enforcement officials did not breach the Fourth Amendment protection against unlawful searches and seizures. If their client participated in a custodial interrogation, defense counsel ascertain that the interrogation was lawful, that it did not violate the right against self-incrimination, and ultimately that Fifth Amendment protections were ensured. In accordance with the Sixth Amendment, the defense ensures that criminal defendants have a right to a speedy and public trial with an impartial jury in their venue or vicinage. Defendants must be informed of the nature of the charges against them, be able to confront opposing or prosecutorial witnesses, be able to secure or obtain favorable or defense witnesses, and retain the advisement of counsel in a variety of legal settings and circumstances.

Former Supreme Court Justice Byron White eloquently described the mission, responsibility, and duty of the defense. "The defense counsel has no obligation to ascertain or present the truth. Our system assigns him a different mission. Defense counsel need present nothing even if he knows what the truth is. He need not furnish witnesses to the police, or reveal any confidence in his client, or furnish any other information to help the prosecution's case. If he can confuse a witness, even a truthful one, or make him appear at a disadvantage, unsure or indecisive, that will be his normal course. Our interest in not convicting the innocent permits counsel to put the State to its proof, to put the State's case in the worst possible light, regardless of what he thinks or knows to be the truth."

The Development of Rights to Counsel

Of all the expressed entitlements in the Bill of Rights, the right to counsel in criminal court is arguable the most important. Unfortunately, the language "assistance of counsel for his defense" in the Sixth Amendment is ambiguous.

As a result, the rights to counsel for court proceedings have developed sporadically throughout American history. For example, the Judiciary Act of 1789 provided that defendants in federal courts could manage and plead their own cases personally or by the assistance of counsel as provided by the rules of court. The bourgeoning state courts offered various entitlements to counsel, and many appointed counsel for indigent defendants for non-capital crimes. In this sense, rights to counsel were afforded informally based on the customary practices of English common law. Importantly, this meant that rights to counsel were not officially established by the Supreme Court. This changed in 1932 with the landmark ruling in *Powell v. Alabama.*

Powell v. Alabama (1932) was a decision that has been popularly referred to as the Scottsboro Boys case. On March 25, 1931, a group of nine African American youths aged 13 to 21 years and were riding on a train crossing Alabama. During the ride, the youths engaged in a fight with a group of white boys and threw them from the train. After this, a message was relayed to the next station to apprehend the black youths. Meanwhile, two white females claimed that several of the black youths raped them on the train. After reaching the train station, eight of the Scottsboro Boys (as the defendants became known) were arraigned and entered pleas of not guilty. The 13-year-old boy was not indicted because of his age. The eight were summarily tried, convicted, and sentenced to death.

The case generated national outrage and the United States Supreme Court ordered two re-trials and established the legal guarantee of counsel for defendants facing capital charges. Specifically, the Court held that "the necessity of counsel was so vital and imperative that the failure of the trial court to make an effective appointment of counsel was likewise a denial of due process....[I]n a capital case, where the defendant is unable to employ counsel, and is incapable adequately of making his own defense because of ignorance, feeble mindedness, illiteracy, or the like, it is the duty of the court, whether requested or not, to assign counsel for him as a necessary requisite of due process of law."[19] Continued appeals in 1938 determined that the boys could not be retried. Ultimately, four of the youths were released from custody during the appeals, three eventually were paroled, and one escaped.[20]

Over the next several decades, the rights to counsel were expanded beyond the rather narrow purview of capital cases (see Box 8-3). *Johnson v. Zerbst* (1938) established an absolute rule requiring appointment of counsel for indigent criminal defendants in all federal cases.[21] *Griffin v. Illinois* (1956) held that the due process and equal protection clauses of the Fourteenth Amendment required that all indigent defendants be furnished a transcript or legal record of their case to be used for an appeal.[22] Two important ruling were established in 1963. *Douglas v. California* held that there is an absolute right to the assistance of counsel during the first appeal of a conviction. The more famous ruling was *Gideon v. Wainwright,* which held that persons charged

BOX 8-3

CRIME SCENE   DO NOT CROSS

CRIMINAL JUSTICE INTEREST

When Does the Sixth Amendment "Kick In"?

Recall that the landmark Miranda rights do not apply until the police initiate a custodial interrogation of a criminal suspect. In the
same way, the various Sixth Amendment rights to counsel are not immediately activated. Instead, they are attached or activated once the government has committed
itself to the prosecution of the case by the initiation of adversarial judicial proceedings, such as formal charges, preliminary hearing, indictment, or arraignment. Prior
to this, law enforcement officials conducting an investigation may continue their
efforts unrestrained by the Sixth Amendment right to counsel. Kimberly Crawford,
a legal instructor at the FBI Academy, advised that two aspects of law enforcement
investigations, lineups and deliberate elicitation, are critical functions that require
Sixth Amendment protections. Once criminal defendants indicate a desire to have
legal counsel, any subsequent police lineup must be conducted with defense counsel present or an intelligent waiver from the defendant. Also, any attempt to elicit
information from accused individuals regarding their criminal charges must be done
with defense counsel present. The definition of "deliberate elicitation" is broad and
encompasses any adversarial context where incriminating evidence is sought.[34] In
short, Sixth Amendment rights to counsel "kick in" once it is clear, at least in the
minds of legal authorities, that the person in custody is the perpetrator in question.

Source: Crawford, K. A. (2001). The Sixth Amendment right to counsel: Application and
limitations. *FBI Law Enforcement Bulletin, 70,* 27–33. *Kirby v. Illinois,* 406 U.S. 682 (1972)
established that Sixth Amendment protections are not invoked until adversarial court action is
taken by the state. *Photo © 2011, Lo, Shutterstock, Inc.*

with felonies in state court, including indigent defendants, had the right to be
represented by counsel.[23] *Argesinger v. Hamlin* (1972) expanded the right to
adequate legal representation for anyone facing detention or imprisonment as
a possible penalty.[24] Rights to counsel and general due process were applied
to juveniles via the rulings in *In re Gault* (1967) and *In re Winshop* 1970).[25]

Statistical Snapshot and Types of Defense Counsel

The Bureau of Justice Statistics conducts the National Survey of Indigent
Defense Systems to collect, analyze, and disseminate information about the
defense counsel in the American criminal justice system. According to Carol
DeFrances and Marika Litras, more than $1.2 billion was spent annually on
indigent criminal defense for more than 4.2 million cases in the 100 most
populous counties in the United States. Indigent defense comprised 3% of all
local criminal justice expenditures and 16% of judicial expenditures. County
governments provide about 60% and state governments provide 25% of the
funding for indigent defense.[26]

Indigent defense services are provided in three general ways, public defender, assigned counsel, and contract. A public defender is a salaried staff of full- or part-time attorneys that render criminal defense services through a public or private non-profit organization or as direct government paid employees. In many jurisdictions, the public defender's office is located proximally to the district attorney's office and both entities comprise the local courtroom workgroup and culture. Public defenders are the most common form of indigent defense and handle more than 80% of the 4 million cases and account for 73% of the total expenditures on indigent defense. Public defender programs employ nearly 13,000 attorneys. Because of their funding advantage, public defenders are able to furnish resources, such as hiring expert witnesses, conducting investigations, and offering translator and transcript services. The average annual criminal caseload for a public defender's office is 23,242 cases.

Assigned counsel is the appointment from a list of private bar members who accept cases on a judge-by-judge, court-by-court, or case-by-case basis. This may include an administrative component and set of guidelines governing the appointment and processing of cases handled by the private bar members. Assigned counsel handled 15% of all indigent defense cases and accounted for 21% of the total expenditures. Nearly 31,000 attorneys participated in an assigned counsel program. The average annual criminal caseload for an assigned counsel office is 4,151 cases.

The contract system is the least common form of indigent defense whereby non-salaried individual private attorneys, bar associations, law firms, or non-profits contract with a funding source to provide court-appointed representation in a specific jurisdiction. This does not include public defender offices. Contract attorneys handle about 3% of all indigent defense cases and account for 6% of total expenditures. Forty-two percent of the most populous counties utilize contract services. The average annual criminal caseload for contract programs is 1,412 cases.[27]

The Criminal Justice Act of 1964 established the Defender Services Division of the Administrative Office of the U. S. Courts to provide indigent representation in federal cases. Two programs are used. Panel attorneys are appointed by the court from a list of private attorneys on a case-by-case basis. All 94 United States district courts use panel attorneys, twenty districts use them exclusively. Federal defender organizations (FDOs) take one of two forms. Federal public defender organizations are staffed with federal employees and headed by a public defender appointed by the court of appeals. Community defender organizations are incorporated nonprofit legal service organizations that receive grant funding from the Administrative Office of the United States Courts. Sixty-three federal or community defender organizations served 74 U. S. districts.

Public or Private Counsel: Does It Make a Difference?

Conventional wisdom and the entertainment media convey that to receive a court-appointed attorney is to surely face defeat. Defense counselors that are not paid for by the defendant are presumed to be overburdened legal novices that lack the financial clout to adequately represent their clients. In reality, many types of indigent defense counsel are outstanding attorneys who not only have a great deal of experience and expertise of the criminal law, but also are themselves members of a local courtroom workgroup. In other words, indigent defense counsel are "insiders" of the local judicial culture, this is often not the case for privately financed lawyers.

Regarding court dispositions, there is virtually no difference between type of legal representation and conviction rates. According to Bureau of Justice Statistics researcher Caroline Wolf Harlow, three in four defendants with either court-appointed or private counsel were convicted. In federal courts, nine in ten felony defendants with public or private attorneys were found guilty. However, higher percentages of defendants with publicly financed counsel were sentenced to incarceration. For instance, 88% of publicly represented felons received a federal prison sentence compared to 77% of federal felons with private counsel. Among persons facing state-level felony charges, private counsel actually disadvantaged criminal defendants. The average length of prison sentence for state drug offenders was 97 months with public counsel and 140 months with private counsel. For public-order offenders, the respective average sentence lengths were 80 and 98 months.[28]

Because most criminal cases in the United States result in a conviction via a plea agreement, one could conclude that the type of legal representation one has determines his or her quality of justice. Indeed, criminal defendants with private counsel have more frequent, immediate, and continuous contact with their attorneys. Comparatively, 33% of defendants with publicly appointed counsel in state courts do not talk with their attorney until more than one week before their trial. In this sense, the perceptions of justice among criminal defendants who received publicly appointed counsel can often be negative compared to clients who secured their own attorney. For more information on rights to counsel, see Boxes 8-4 and 8-5.

ADVERSARIAL JUSTICE, CRIME CONTROL, AND DUE PROCESS

The Sixth Amendment accords important legal entitlements that were designed to guarantee the due process rights of the accused and enable the due process mission of American justice. In the course of our adversarial justice system, however, the goals of due process and crime control can be compromised. Using the right to a speedy trial to illustrate, this section describes common legal scenarios that variously advantage the prosecution or the defense.

CRIME SCENE　　DO NOT CROSS

CRIMINAL JUSTICE CASES

6ᵗʰ AMENDMENT RIGHTS AND PROTECTION FOR VARIOUS CRIMINAL JUSTICE FUNCTIONS

- Police lineup for identification purposes that occurs after charging and before trial.[35]
- Police "deliberate elicitation" of any incriminating evidence.[36]
- Arraignment is a critical stage of prosecution and requires counsel.[37]
- Preliminary hearing is a critical stage of prosecution and requires counsel.[38]
- Plea bargaining.[39]
- Trial.[40]
- Sentencing.[41]
- Appeal.[42]
- Probation revocation hearings where sentence had been deferred.[43]
- Probation and parole revocation hearings.[44]
- Systemic due process provisions of 6ᵗʰ Amendment pertain to juveniles.[45]

Photo © Condor 36, 2008.

BOX 8-4

CRIME SCENE　　DO NOT CROSS

CRIMINAL JUSTICE INTEREST

PRO SE: A FOOL FOR A CLIENT?

It is often said that he who represents himself has a fool for a client. Nevertheless, *Faretta v. California* (1975) held that even if it works to the detriment of the defendant, the Constitution ordinarily guarantees people the opportunity to do so. A defendant who represents himself, known as pro se defense, cannot thereafter complain that the quality of his defense denied him effective assistance of counsel. It is a right the defendant must adopt knowingly and intelligently. For example, under some circumstances the trial judge may deny the authority to exercise it if the defendant simply lacks the competence to make a knowing or intelligent waiver of counsel. *McKaskle v. Wiggins* (1984) held that a defendant's pro se right preserves control over the case he or she chooses to present to the jury and that appointed standby counsel are not allowed to "destroy the jury's perception that the defendant is representing himself." Participation of standby counsel even in the jury's presence and over the defendant's objection does not violate the defendant's 6ᵗʰ Amendment rights when serving the basic purpose of aiding the defendant in complying with routine courtroom procedures and protocols.

Sources: *Faretta v. California*, 422 U. S. 806 (1975); *McKaskle v. Wiggins*, 465 U. S. 168 (1984). Photo © 2011, Lo, Shutterstock, Inc.

BOX 8-5

Both prosecution and defense can have a vested interest in the right to a speedy trial. For the defense, the speedy trial provision safeguards against lengthy and undue pretrial detention and helps to expedite the ability of the defendant to mobilize his or her defense. For the prosecution who carries the burden of proof beyond a reasonable doubt, the speedy trial provision allows them to "strike while the iron is hot." In other words, the prosecutor can expeditiously call witnesses and mobilize evidence for the case. Excessive delays disadvantage the state because witnesses can move, die, or otherwise lose their interest in and zeal for the case. This is particularly true in cases where victims are the primary or sole witness. Court delays simply "drag on" an already negative experience and many victims and witnesses to crime wish to move onward.

The case *Dickey v. Florida* (1970) is illustrative. For more than seven years while in federal custody, petitioner Dickey made repeated but unsuccessful efforts to secure a prompt trial in state court where he also faced charges. During this time, three witnesses either died or became unavailable and police records were lost or destroyed. Thereafter the Florida court filed against him and quashed the motion that he had been denied his right to a speedy trial. On appeal, the Supreme Court held that Dickey was at all times available to the State and there was no valid excuse for the prejudicial delay, the judgment against petitioner must be vacated by the trial court.[29]

Another incentive for the state to move quickly is to reduce the costs of pretrial detention and attendant jail space. Thus, the speedy trial provision offers a mixed opportunity for crime control and due process. The longer a case is delayed, the more difficult it becomes to secure a conviction. Whether justice is expedited or delayed also impacts recidivism, such as a defendant absconding or re-offending while awaiting trial on bond. Similarly, prosecutors might be enticed to offer plea agreements because they will not be ready for trial in time, thus reducing crime control and the ability to provide justice to the community. In short, court delays retard the deterrent and rehabilitative effects of the criminal law.

Klopfer v. North Carolina (1967) established the right to a speedy trial in federal prosecutions. In the case, Klopfer criminal trespass indictment ended with a declaration of a mistrial when the jury failed to reach a verdict. After the case had been postponed for two terms, Klopfer filed a motion with the trial court to determine when his trial would occur. In the meantime, the prosecutor moved for permission to take a "*nolle prosequi* with leave," a procedural device whereby Klopfer was discharged from custody but was subject to future prosecution. On appeal, the North Carolina Supreme Court affirmed the trial court's action holding that while a defendant has a right to a speedy trial if there is to be a trial, that right does not require the State to prosecute if the prosecutor, in his discretion and with the court's approval, elects to use a *nolle prosequi*. The indefinite delay or postponement violated Klopfer's right to a speedy trial resolution.[30]

However, a defendant's constitutional right to a speedy trial cannot be established by any inflexible rule but instead on an ad hoc basis whereby the conduct of the prosecution and the defendant are weighed. In *Barker v. Wingo* (1972), the Supreme Court held that factors such as the length of and reason for the delay, the defendant's assertion of his right, and prejudice to the defendant must be determined when assessing delays to a speedy trial. In this case, the lack of any serious prejudice to the petitioner and that he did not want a speedy trial outweighed opposing considerations and compelled the conclusion that petitioner was not deprived of his due process right to a speedy trial.[31]

The "Barker factors" of delay were replaced by the Speedy Trial Act of 1974 which was amended in 1979. The Speedy Trial Act established time limits for completing the various stages of a federal criminal prosecution. The information or indictment must be filed within 30 days from the date of arrest or service of the summons. Trial must commence within 70 days from the date the information or indictment was filed, or from the date the defendant appears before an officer of the court in which the charge is pending, whichever is later. To ensure that defendants were not rushed to trial without an adequate opportunity to prepare, the Act provided that trials could not begin less than 30 days from the date the defendant first appears in court, unless the defendant agrees in writing to an earlier date. Delays caused by various pretrial motions were automatically excluded from the time limits of the Speedy Trial Act.[32]

THE JUDGE: REFEREE FOR THE ADVERSARIES OF JUSTICE

It seems that the judge is often left out of the cataclysmic battle between the prosecution and defense, the state and the individual. In a sense, it is true. The prosecutor has the burden, responsibility, and clout of proving that the accused violated the criminal law. The defense has the responsibility and duty to monitor that due process is always preserved during the course of crime control. Thus, the mandates of the prosecution and defense are formidable. Still, the judge is immensely important to the judicial process in several ways. First, the judge can dictate the philosophy and normative operated procedures of the court. This does not mean that the judge can rewrite the Constitution. Instead, the judge's idiosyncratic views of justice, crime control, and due process meaningfully affect how the prosecution and defense counsel conduct themselves in court.[33] As such, the judge influences court operations and procedures, the degree of professionalism, the degree of coordination with other criminal justice agencies and social service providers, and the amount of latitude granted to criminal defendants by the prosecution and defense.

Second, the judge's influence extends outside the courtroom to other arenas of the criminal justice system, especially the police. For example, a stridently pro-law enforcement judge might be strongly supportive of police tactics and view officer testimony as unable to be impugned. Conversely, a judge who is a former public defender might be especially compassionate toward criminal defendants and rule in ways that reflect this advocacy.

Third, judges have a number of responsibilities to advise and, in effect, supervise other parties in court. These activities include formally advising defendants of their rights at their first appearance or arraignment, settling questions of evidence and procedure raised by prosecutors and defense, considering bond recommendations from pretrial service staff and counsel, advising jury members on the considerations they must weigh to arrive at a verdict, deciding cases when jury trial is waived, and imposing sentences (to the degree that their discretion is not legislatively limited). The roles and responsibilities of the judge are explored in detail in Chapter 9.

CHAPTER SUMMARY: BALANCING CRIME CONTROL AND DUE PROCESS

- The prosecution is arguably the most powerful entity in the legal system and is responsible for prosecuting criminals, protecting the public, and ensuring the interests of justice within the resource, logistical, and political restraints of their office.
- The prosecution must prove guilt with the burden beyond a reasonable doubt.
- The defense primarily intends to complicate the ability of the state to prove guilt in the American system of adversarial justice.
- The defense counsel evaluates cases to catch potential procedural violations, primarily pertaining to the Fourth, Fifth, Sixth, and Eighth Amendments.
- Most criminal defendants are indigent and receive counsel via public defender, assigned counsel, or contract defense systems.
- Legal outcomes are very similar regardless of whether defendants had public counsel or had privately retained counsel.
- The rights to counsel in the Sixth Amendment have been developed and broadened over time.
- Legal factors, such as evidence, offense seriousness, number of charges, and criminal history, are the strongest influences on the decision to prosecute.
- Other factors include the offender and victim characteristics, publicity surrounding the case, political culture of the prosecutor's office, and resource availability.
- In many respects, the judge serves as the referee in the epic struggle between the powers of the state and the individual.

KEY TERMS

Adversarial justice
Argesinger v. Hamlin
Assigned counsel
Burden of proof (beyond a
reasonable doubt)
Community prosecution
Contract defense system
Courtroom workgroup
District attorney
Double jeopardy
Fifth Amendment
Gideon v. Wainwright
In re Gault

In re Winshop
Indigent
Johnson v. Zerbst
Nolle prosequi
Powell v. Alabama
Pro se
Prosecutorial discretion
Prosecutorial waiver
Public defender
Scottsboro Boys
Sixth Amendment
Speedy Trial Act of 1974
Victim credibility

TALKING POINTS

1. Should the prosecution and defense have equal resources or should one be advantaged over the other given their different missions?

2. Why does conventional wisdom hold that publicly appointed counsel are much less effective than privately retained counsel? How does type of counsel affect various legal outcomes?

3. Should prosecutors have more or less discretion given the amount of crime that goes un-prosecuted and un-punished? Provide details to support your answer.

4. Is it ethical for defense counsel to represent clients that they know are guilty? Should similar burdens be placed on defense counsel to help ensure more convictions?

5. Would such a scenario contribute to more justice or more injustice?

WEB LINKS

The Prosecutor
(http://www.ndaa-apri.org/publications/ndaa/toc_prosecutor.html)

American Prosecutors Research Institute
(http://www.ndaa-apri.org/)

American Judicature Society
(http://www.ajs.org/)

International Association of Prosecutors
(http://www.iap.nl.com/)

National Association of Prosecutor Coordinators
(http://www.napcsite.org/)

National Commission on the Future of DNA Evidence
(http://www.ojp.usdoj.gov/nij/topics/forensics/dna/commission/welcome.html)

National Legal Aid and Defender Association
(http://www.nlada.org/)

National Center for State Courts
(http://www.ncsconline.org/)

FURTHER READING

Lewis, A. (1989). *Gideon's trumpet*. New York: Vintage. This legal classic chronicles the case of Clarence Earl Gideon and its landmark effects on rights to counsel.

McIntyre, L. J. (1987). *The public defender: The practice of law in the shadows of repute*. Chicago: University of Chicago Press. This is a fascinating inside-look at the public defender's office in Cook County, Illinois.

The Spangenberg Group. (2001). *Keeping defender workloads manageable*. Washington, DC: U. S. Department of Justice, Office of Justice Programs, Bureau of Justice Assistance. The Spangenberg Group is a nationally recognized criminal justice research and consulting firm that specializes in research on criminal defense. This final report examines the workloads and caseloads of indigent defense counsel and explores strategies to improve indigent defense and thus due process.

Uviller, H. R. (1999). *The tiled playing field: Is criminal justice unfair?* New Haven, CT: Yale University Press. This is a thought-provoking look at the fundamental differences between the prosecution and the defense written with the flair and brilliance of a novelist. This book truly captures the great drama inherent in criminal justice and the timeless struggle between the state and the individual.

CHAPTER 9

Trials, Plea Bargains, and the Philosophy of Punishment

CHAPTER OUTLINE

QUOTATIONS

"Plea bargaining rests on the constitutional fiction that our government does not retaliate against individuals who wish to exercise their right to trial by jury."—*Timothy Lynch*[1]

"The criminal trial overshadows all other ceremonies as a dramatization of the values of our spiritual government, representing the dignity of the State as an enforcer of law, and at the same time the dignity of the individual when he is an avowed opponent of the State, a dissenter, a radical, or even a criminal."—*Thurman Arnold*[2]

"Secrecy creates possibilities and opportunities fraught with the danger of venal and dishonest release of defendants on the pretext of 'bargaining.' And there is the distinct possibility that dangerous individuals may receive inadequate punishment because of the bargaining system."—*Abraham Blumberg*[3]

"Facts are stubborn things; and whatever may be our wishes, our inclinations, or the dictates of our passions, they cannot alter the state of facts and evidence."—*John Adams*[4]

"Through the local legal culture informal rules and practices arise within particular settings, and the 'way things are done' differs from place to place. The customs and traditions of each jurisdiction seem to vary because local practices are affected by such factors as size, politics, and population characteristics."—*George Cole*[5]

INTRODUCTION

Figure 9-1 illustrates the magnitude of serious violent crime, murder, rape, robbery, and aggravated assault, in the United States. The figure clearly shows the gulfs between (1) the actual amount of crime and victimization that occurs annually, (2) the amount of these crimes that are reported to the police, (3) the amount of crimes that are actually recorded by police, and (4) the crimes that result in arrest. In a different way, the figure graphically represents the funnel-like effect of the criminal justice system that has been a recurrent theme in this book. Simply put: There is too much crime for the criminal justice system to handle.

Nowhere does this fact manifest more prominently than in the criminal courts. It is because there are so many cases that the prosecutor exercises great discretion in choosing which ones to dismiss, *nolle prosequi*, or pursue. Cases that are pursued face two fates: plea-bargain or trial. Between 95 and 100 of cases are disposed of via guilty plea, meaning that fewer than 5% of

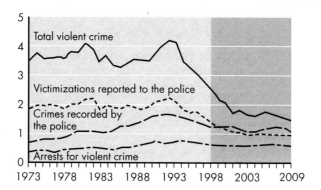

FIGURE 9-1   The Magnitude of Violent Crime in the United States

Source: Rand, M. R., & Truman, J. (2010). *Criminal victimization, 2009*. Washington, DC:
U. S. Department of Justice, Office of Justice Programs, Bureau of Justice Statistics.

criminal cases are resolved via trial. In this sense, the somewhat informal
practice of plea-bargaining has easily overtaken formalized trial procedures.

Marjorie Zatz and Alan Lizotte offered the following heuristic about pleas
and trials:

> The system allows first-time offenders to move quickly under four
> general conditions. First, if defendants are not seen as 'hardened
> criminals,' they move quickly through the system.... Second, when cases
> are seen as typical or 'normal crimes,' they are processed in a routine
> way and this increases processing speed.... Where they are not 'normal,'
> they move slowly to conclusion at trial. Third, the less serious the case
> the more willing the prosecutor is to bargain and the faster the rate of
> pleading. Fourth, in 'dead-bang' cases which involve hard physical
> evidence pleading is swift.... Conversely, serious cases move slowly,
> especially when first-time offenders' rights or society's well-being are of
> elevated concern.[6]

Finally, resources are conserved for repeat criminals who are processed
quickly when possible or slowly to trial if needed. Zatz and Lizotte's characterization of the legal process is accurate and this chapter explores why
plea-bargaining figures so prominently in the judicial process in addition to
assorted aspects of pleas and trials.

Could the criminal justice system survive without plea-bargaining? No.
For example, William Rhodes examined the crime savings and losses that
are the result of plea-bargains, trials, and dismissals. Using data from defendants in Washington, DC, Rhodes found that if defendants who pled guilty
had gone to trial, 34% of assault defendants, 16% of robbery defendants,
31% of larceny defendants, and 32% of burglary defendants would have
been acquitted! Furthermore, Rhodes found that among dismissed cases,
59% of assaults, 78% of robberies, 67% of larcenies, and 64% of burglaries

would have resulted in conviction.[7] What is clear is that the judicial process is an imperfect system of evaluating criminal cases. What you will have to decide is whether justice is served by the judicial system and its plea and trial functions. More importantly, does it serve crime control and due process functions?

COURT APPEARANCES AND PROCEDURES

Recall from Chapter 7 that bail is assigned to most criminal defendants via pretrial court personnel. Local administrative orders preclude the setting of bond for some criminal defendants, such as those charges with serious violent felonies, until the defendant appears formally in court. For defendants who were unable to post bond and remained in custody, they must appear in court within 48 hours of their arrest otherwise they must be released on their own recognizance. This prevents unnecessary delays in due process and guards against prolonged pretrial detention.[8] Importantly, if criminal defendants are not brought to court in time, the judge must release the defendant on his or her recognizance regardless of the underlying charge, even the most serious felonies. Because of this, the courts work swiftly and efficiently to ensure that recently arrested defendants appear in court in due time. For defendants who posted bond and were released, their first appearance occurs within two weeks of their arrest.

Arraignment

The first appearance that a criminal defendant makes in court is known as arraignment. Arraignment is the hearing before a court having original jurisdiction in a criminal case, in which the identity of the defendant is established, the defendant is informed of the charges and penalties potentially faced, the defendant is advised of his or her legal rights, and the defendant is required to enter a plea (if the charges are for misdemeanors). The preponderance of defendants are (1) represented by public defenders or some other publicly assigned counsel and (2) seek to plead guilty to some form of their criminal charges to expedite the case. Often, defendants who wish to talk with an assistant district attorney for plea negotiations will seek a pretrial conference. A pretrial conference is a meeting between the defendant, defense counsel, and the prosecutor to arrange a plea agreement or plea-bargain for misdemeanor, petty, and traffic offenses. (Plea-bargaining is examined extensively in this chapter). Plea negotiations for misdemeanor, petty, and traffic offenses are incredibly brief, provide immediate convictions (favoring the prosecution) for reduced charges (favoring the defense) and result in often-meager penalties. For example, defendants facing non-serious charges often plead guilty to the charges in exchange for a jail sentence equivalent to the time they have already been in custody. "Time served" in the county jail is frequently the sentence for and outcome of plea negotiations for low-level crimes. Finally, nearly all defendants charged with misdemeanor charges admit guilt (guilty plea) or accept guilt without directly admitting it (no contest or *nolo contendere*). For those who plead not guilty, a trial date is set at the arraignment.

For felony cases, the first appearance is more complex to reflect the greater seriousness and penalties implied in felony crimes. As is the case with misdemeanor charges, felony arraignments involve the judge reading the charges and penalties against the defendant, advising the defendant of his or her rights to a preliminary hearing, jury trial, and rights to counsel. The judge can also re-evaluate the setting of bail if requested by defense counsel or the defendant. However, defendants do not enter pleas to felony charges at arraignment. Instead, the matter is set for a preliminary hearing, which is a court appearance to establish if a crime has been committed and if there is probable cause to believe that the defendant committed the offenses alleged in the complaint. At the preliminary hearing, three general outcomes (some jurisdictions refer to products of the preliminary hearing as information) can occur. First, the judge can find that the prosecution lacks probable cause that the suspect committed the crime for which he or she is charged. In this event, the charges are dismissed and the defendant is released. Second, the judge can find that probable cause does exist and the matter is transferred or bound over to district court for trial. Third, criminal defendants frequently waive their right to a preliminary hearing in which the case is automatically bound over to district court. Defendants waive their right for a variety of reasons such as they want to expedite the process or believe that they will plead guilty prior to the initiation of the trial.

Indictment

Some states employ the preliminary hearing to determine the formal filing of charges and whether probable cause exists for trial worthiness. Other states use a grand jury to deliver an indictment (as is explicitly mentioned in the Fifth Amendment). The grand jury is a body of persons who have been selected according to law and sworn to hear the evidence against accused persons and determine whether there is sufficient evidence to bring those persons to trial. Grand juries also investigate criminal activity generally as well as the conduct of public officials and agencies. Grand juries are referred to as investigatory grand juries when they are themselves investigating crimes and charging grand juries when they are deciding to ratify the prosecutor's request for a formal charge. After the grand jury completes an investigation, they prepare a report called a presentment.

The grand jury meets at the request of the prosecution. Unlike preliminary hearings, which are open court proceedings, grand jury hearings are closed and secret. The grand jury hears the testimony of witnesses who had been subpoenaed to testify and evaluates the evidence gathered by the prosecution, a process known as presentment. Unless they need to actually hear testimony from the accused, the defendant is not present at the grand jury hearing. If the grand jury finds that probable cause exists, they issue an indictment, or true bill, which is the formal accusation of charges. If probable cause is not found, the grand jury outcome is a no bill.

The roots of the grand jury extend to 1166 when King Henry II of England required knights and other freemen to file criminal accusations with the criminal court. Historically, the grand jury has served as a counterbalance or buffer between the state (especially the prosecution) and individuals (persons who could be charged with crimes). Trial juries or petit juries have 12 members whereas grand juries have between 12 and 23 members (23 is the conventional number of grand jury members). Although the federal justice system and most states have grand jury systems, most states opt to use the direct filing/preliminary hearing system.

Pleas

The majority of defendants whose case results in conviction plead guilty. According to Bureau of Justice Statistics researchers, 94% of the more than 1.1 million felons sentenced in state courts pleaded guilty. Comparatively, juries found guilt in only 2% of cases and judges found 3% guilty.[9] In pleading guilty, criminal defendants not only acknowledge their guilt and the commensurate punishment, but also waive their constitutional rights implied or expressed in the Fifth and Sixth Amendments. Because of the gravity of these consequences, judges ensure that guilty pleas are made voluntarily, that the defendant understands what he or she is doing, that counsel be provided during plea negotiations, and that the defendant is aware of the maximum punishments for their crimes. Defendants can rescind or withdraw their guilty plea up until sentencing under some circumstances.

A plea of no contest or *nolo contendere* produces the same consequence as a guilty plea, but the defendant does not formally admit guilt. Rather, the defendant has not contested the charges against them. A no contest plea is simply a legal way to secure conviction while the defendant presumably saves face. Similarly, an Alford plea occurs when a defendant does not admit guilt but acknowledges that he or she will be found guilty and thus does not contest the charges. A not guilty plea is entered when a defendant does not accept responsibility for the charges by claiming that he or she did not commit the offense. Defendants that are unresponsive during court proceedings, also technically plead not guilty. Once a not guilty plea is entered, a trial date is set. Although rarely used, defendants can also plead not guilty by reason of insanity in which they assert that they cannot be held legally responsible or accountable for the alleged criminal conduct.

Sentencing Hearing

For defendants who either plead guilty or were found guilty, the adjudication proceeding occurs separately from sentencing. The court appearance where convicted defendants formally receive their punishment or sentence is known as a sentencing hearing, or variously referred to as the sentencing phase or penalty phase. Sometimes, trials are referred to as bifurcated trials with the adjudication and sentencing components held separate.

Pleas have become integral to American justice. Indeed, more than nine of ten cases that result in conviction are achieved via plea bargains, not trials. Plea-bargaining, arguably the most dominant practice in criminal justice is explored next.

PLEA-BARGAINING

Definition and Purposes

Plea-bargaining, also known as a plea agreement, is the practice involving negotiation between prosecutor, the defendant, and his or her defense attorney that results in the defendant entering a guilty plea in exchange for the state's reduction of charges or the prosecutor's promise to recommend a more lenient sentence than the offender would have ordinarily received.[10] There are three general types of plea-bargains that occur in the criminal courts. First, reduced charge plea bargains are characterized by the reduction of the original charge that automatically reduces the penalty that could be imposed. For example, a youngster arrested for auto theft may agree to plead guilty to unauthorized use of a vehicle, which is usually a misdemeanor. Second, reduced count plea bargains occur when the district attorney dismisses or significantly reduces the number of charges in the complaint to induce the defendant to plead guilty. For instance, an offender charged with four counts of robbery would plead guilty to a single count with the remaining three being dismissed. Third, reduced sentence plea bargains occur when the prosecutor agrees to recommend a reduced sentence in exchange for the guilty plea. For example, although felony convictions denote a prison sentence, prosecutors will commonly recommend that convicted felons receive probation or some other intermediate sanction instead of confinement.

Plea-bargaining produces a legal resolution that satisfies all parties involved. Two truisms explain why plea-bargaining is so frequently used. First, the preponderance of criminal defendants who reach the point of entering a plea is, in fact, guilty! Everyone knows that the defendant is guilty, including the prosecutor, the defense counsel, and the defendant. Recall that the criminal justice system filters cases constantly. Had the defendant not been guilty, he or she would have not only avoided arrest but also had their charges dismissed at arraignment. Second, the power and resources differentials

CRIME SCENE   DO NOT CROSS

CRIMINAL JUSTICE AND THE LAW

PLEA-BARGAINING AND THE UNITED STATES SUPREME COURT

United States v. Ruiz, 536 U.S. 622 (2002): the Constitution does not require prosecutors to inform defendants during plea-bargaining negotiations of evidence that would lead to the impeachment of the state's witnesses.

Godinez v. Moran, 509 U.S. 389 (1993): the competency standard for pleading guilty and for waiver of right to counsel is the same as the competency standard for standing trial.

United States v. Broce, 488 U.S. 563 (1989): the entry of a guilty plea foreclosed the defendant's right to challenge those pleas by collateral attack on double jeopardy grounds.

Ricketts v. Adamson, 483 U.S. 1 (1987): double jeopardy was not violated by prosecution of the defendant for first-degree murder following his breach of a plea agreement under which he had pled guilty to a lesser offense, been sentenced, and begun serving a prison term.

Hill v. Lockhart, 474 U.S. 52 (1985): to prove ineffectiveness of defense counsel, a defendant must show a reasonable probability that except for counsel's errors, the defendant would not have pled guilty.

Mabry v. Johnson, 467 U.S. 504 (1984): defendant's acceptance of a proposed plea bargain that the prosecutor erroneously made does not create a constitutional right to have the bargain enforced by the trial court.

Bordenkircher v. Hayes, 434 U.S. 357 (1978): due process was not violated when a prosecutor carried out a threat made during plea-bargaining to re-indict the defendant on more serious charges if the defendant refused to plead guilty to the offense originally charged.

Corbitt v. New Jersey, 439 U.S. 212 (1978): upheld a New Jersey law that made a sentence of life imprisonment mandatory upon jury conviction for first-degree murder, but allowed lesser sentences if the defendant entered a plea of *nolo contendere.*

Hutto v. Ross, 429 U.S. 28 (1976): a confession was not per se inadmissible in a trial merely because it was made as the result of a plea-bargain agreement.

Henderson v. Morgan, 426 U.S. 637 (1976): defendant's guilty plea was involuntary because he had not received adequate notice of the charges and the elements of the crimes charged.

Santobello v. New York, 404 U.S. 257 (1971): the promise of a prosecutor that rests on a guilty plea must be kept in a plea-bargaining agreement.

North Carolina v. Alford, 400 U.S. 25 (1970): accepting a guilty plea from a defendant who maintains his innocence is valid. The Alford plea means that the defendant does not admit guilt but acknowledges that the state has a strong enough case to convict.

Brady v. United States, 397 U.S. 742 (1970): attempts to avoid a possible death sentence are not grounds to invalidate a guilty plea.

Boykin v. Alabama, 395 U.S. 238 (1969): a defendant must make an affirmative statement that the plea is voluntary before the judge can accept it.

Photo © 2011, Le Loft 1911, Shutterstock, Inc.

between the prosecution and defense (recall Chapter 8) make it very easy to balance the goals of crime control and due process. In terms of crime control, plea-bargaining guarantees a conviction and some form of punishment albeit in reduced form. Moreover, plea-bargaining permits an inexpensive way to punish criminals because of the time and resource savings of avoiding trials. In terms of due process, plea-bargaining only occurs if there are no procedural errors or violations against the defendant. Moreover, prosecutors are ethically bound to pursue pleas or any prosecution against criminal defendants that they believe are in fact guilty. Finally, the leniency inherent to plea-bargaining gives criminal defendant's a glimpse or mercy that could be viewed as a second chance for the offender to correct his or her behavior. Thus, plea bargains efficiently and expeditiously serve the interests of crime control and due process, prosecution and defense.

The Roles of the Courtroom Workgroup

Legal scholar Albert Alschuler conducted some of the seminal analyses of the roles of court officials in plea-bargaining. Alschuler described the prosecutor as an administrator, advocate, judge, and legislator during plea negotiations. The administrator role pertains to the need to secure convictions in the most efficient and fast way possible. As advocate, the prosecutor is serving the public interest in justice by ensuring that criminal offenders pay a legal price for their crimes. As a judge, the prosecutor uses his or her discretion to mete out the deserved or just plea and sentence for each offender based on the defendant's criminal record, culpability, and other characteristics. As a legislator, the prosecutor can water-down or weaken statutes that appear to be too strict or punitive.[11] On balance, these multiple roles help to serve the multiple agendas of the prosecution. However, it has been argued that the structure of plea-bargaining is calamitous for defense counsel since they are coerced to assist their clients to plead guilty by the court system that almost entirely depends on pleas to operate. Some have asserted that the defense counsel role is so compromised by plea bargains that the practice should be abolished.[12] For more on the controversial aspects of plea-bargaining refer to Box 9-1.

Concerns about the powerlessness of defense attorneys during plea negotiations may have been overstated in early research. Criminologists have found that defense attorneys are an integral part of the plea negotiating process, professionals that are viewed as indispensable colleagues that facilitate court operations. For example, David Lynch and David Evans found that expert defense attorneys tended to be emotionally stable legal experts who exercised charm, creativity, and likeability during plea negotiations. Indeed, the personality characteristics and expertise of defense counsel guarantee that plea-bargaining is conducted professionally and fairly.[13]

Others have also noted the variable roles that the prosecutor, defense attorney, defendant, and judge play in plea-bargaining (see Box 9-2).

BOX 9–2

CRIME SCENE   DO NOT CROSS

CRIMINAL JUSTICE CONTROVERSY

Plea-Bargaining: Necessary Evil or Simply Evil?

Because the magnitude of crime dwarfs the resources and capabilities of the criminal justice system, the system exerts great discretion in choosing the cases to prosecute. Without the speedy practice of plea-bargaining, the criminal courts would grind to a halt if all defendants actually went to trial. Since the judicial system already costs about $40 billion annually, how expensive would it become if plea-bargaining were discontinued? Due to these concerns, many legal scholars view plea-bargaining as a necessary evil.

For others, plea-bargaining is a dubious practice that accomplishes neither crime control nor due process goals. There are several important criticisms. First, plea-bargains are fundamentally acts of legal leniency since the most serious charges and penalties are reduced. In effect, this excuses and mitigates the actual criminal harm that offenders commit because the system is more interested in resolving the case quickly and inexpensively. A second and related point is that plea-bargains are an affront to crime victims for the reasons stated in point one. For example, a sexual assault arrest that results in a guilty plea to simple assault completed changes the dynamic of the case in the eyes of the victim. Reducing a sexual assault to a minor assault or harassment is legally tantamount to implying that the original crime never occurred. Third, since plea bargains are virtually inevitable, the rights to a criminal trial specifically and judicial due process generally are coerced by the legal system. Fourth, this coercion could result in innocent criminal defendants accepting guilty pleas. Fifth, defendants who insist on taking their cases to trial sometimes receive harsher legal penalties, a phenomenon that has been referred to as the "trial tariff."

Both crime control and due process proponents have important concerns about the practice of plea-bargaining. What do you think?

Sources: Alschuler, A. (1975). The defense attorney's role in plea-bargaining. *Yale Law Journal, 84,* 1179–1313; Barbara, J., Morrison, J., & Cunningham, H. (1976). Plea-bargaining: Bargain justice? *Criminology, 14,* 55–64; McCoy, C. (1993). *Politics and plea-bargaining: Victims' rights in California.* Philadelphia: University of Pennsylvania Press; Schulhofer, S. (1984). Is plea-bargaining inevitable? *Harvard Law Review, 97,* 1037–1107. Photo © JupiterImages, Corp.

John Padgett discovered that due to the highly discretionary practice of plea-bargaining, court personnel worked together to arrive at the most appropriate legal resolution. Which legal actor took the lead in plea bargains depending on the character, prior record, and apparent criminality of the defendant and the strength of the prosecutor's criminal case. For example, Padgett described:

- *Implicit plea-bargaining* is when the defendant threw himself to the mercy of the court.
- *Charge reduction plea-bargaining* is where the prosecutor eliminated or reduced charges in exchange for a guilty plea.

- *Judicial plea-bargaining* is when the judge, after conferring with the prosecution and defense, offered the defendant a specific guilty plea sentence. Padgett noted that career criminals and other serious offenders were most likely to face judicial pleas, the most severe form of plea-bargaining.
- *Sentence recommendation plea-bargaining* is when the prosecutor, who had already secured a guilty plea, made a sentencing recommendation to the judge who often complied with the recommendation.[14]

Judges have been found to be somewhat passively involved in plea negotiations. When they do exert influence, judges tend to exercise great uniformity in their acceptance of pleas and subsequent sentencing.[15] For instance, Alissa Worden found that judges tend to go along with the sentencing recommendations made by prosecutors and that judicial attitudes are not importantly related to their behavior during plea bargains.[16] Overall, judges rely almost exclusively on legal factors when making assessments of risk to be used in their sentencing decision. For example, Michael Vigorita analyzed more than 1,000 judicial assessments of criminal offenders and found that variables such as, length of criminal careers, prior arrests, convictions, and incarcerations, and whether the defendant had a noted drug problem were the greatest determinants of sentencing.[17]

Criminal defendants actually exert considerable control and discretion when deciding whether to enter a plea agreement. It should be noted that both agreeing to plead guilty and refusing to do so carries various legal costs. Jodi Viljoen, Jessica Klaver, and Ronald Roesch found that young criminal defendants were significantly likely to plead guilty in the first place because they were likely to perceive that the prosecution has a strong case against them. Furthermore, criminal defendants with a poor understanding of their legal rights and court processes were less likely to agree to plea bargains.[18] It is important to recognize that all criminal defendant know with absolute certainty whether they are truly guilty or not. Whether they believe that they should be found guilty or admit their guilt is another matter entirely. Nevertheless, plea-bargaining is so widespread because criminal defendants are able to calculate the degree of justice that is produced with a guilty plea. Oftentimes, this amount of justice is far more palatable than the justice that could be administered upon conviction at trial. It is a gamble that most defendants are not willing to take. Indeed, defendants who opt for trials instead of plea bargains often face more serious legal penalties.[19]

Finally, does the victim play any part in plea-bargaining? Most states provide crime victims with some level of prosecutorial consultation about plea negotiation; however, in no state does the victim have veto power over the plea agreement. The victim can provide input but has no real power.[20] Indeed, one of the most compelling arguments against plea-bargaining is the "bargained" justice that the defendant receives at the expense of the victimization and suffering of the crime victim.

Legal and Extra-Legal Factors

A recurrent theme in American criminal justice is the salience and primacy of legal factors, such as evidence, offense seriousness, prior record, and criminality, compared to extra-legal factors, such as gender, race, and social class, to official discretion, decision-making, and criminal justice outcomes. This is also the case for plea-bargaining.[21] Gary LaFree conducted one of the most authoritative comparative studies of plea-bargaining and trial using data from 3,269 male robbery and burglary defendants in El Paso, Texas; New Orleans, Louisiana; Seattle, Washington; Tucson, Arizona; Norfolk, Virginia; and Delaware County, Pennsylvania. Three of the jurisdictions had few restrictions on plea-bargaining whereas the others had recently attempted to eliminate or greatly reduce the practice. LaFree produced two important findings. First, although defendants who "pushed" for trial received greater penalties than defendants who plead, the effects disappeared when trial acquittals were included. In other words, this contradicts the assertion made by critics of plea-bargaining who maintain that defendants face a "trial tariff" or penalty for exercising their Sixth Amendment rights. Second, legal factors such as criminal record and offense seriousness were the greatest predictors of adjudication for both trials and pleas. Again, this indicates that the legal system relies on legal criteria, not discriminatory variables such as gender.

Reform and Future Prospects

Plea-bargaining has been one of the most controversial legal topics in criminological and legal discourse. For some, it is a disaster that precludes both crime control and due process. To others, plea-bargaining is a perfectly lawful practice that involves legal experts (the prosecutor and defense attorney) conscientiously and appropriately weighing the costs and benefits of the plea and producing justice.[22] Calls to abolish plea-bargaining were mostly academic, but one jurisdiction did just that. The Memphis Tennessee District Attorney's Office implemented a no plea-bargain policy for murder, aggravated rape, and aggravated robbery. Defendants either pleaded guilty to the maximum (non-reduced) charge or faced trial on the charge. In the first year, 164 cases of first-degree murder and nearly 2,000 cases of aggravated robbery were processed. The result was a 90% combined conviction rate. Thus, the most violent criminals were convicted and received longer sentences; moreover, the policy did not result in a predicted backlog of cases. In fact, community support of the criminal justice system increased after the policy's implementation.[23] In the end, plea-bargaining is an imperfect but effective way of efficiently processing the massive volume of cases in the criminal courts. For creative ways that criminal courts have attempted to address specific crimes, see Boxes 9-3 and 9-4.

CRIME SCENE   DO NOT CROSS

BOX 9-3

CRIMINAL JUSTICE SPOTLIGHT

DRUG COURTS

The criminal courts process the broad spectrum of criminal behavior, from traffic violations to felonies, nuisance offenses to violent crimes. However, some criminal behaviors are viewed as specialized problems that may require different types of adjudication than the traditional courts can offer. One example is drug court that combines intensive drug rehabilitation services for addicted offenders with legal requirements to complete treatment. Unlike traditional criminal courts that simply impose a legal punishment for drug violations of the criminal law, drug courts have a different mission. Drug courts provide longer treatment, address overlapping drug and mental health problems, provide intensive supervision and monitoring, and help children with various social services.

Federally funded drug courts have been established in California, Florida, Maryland, Oklahoma, Nevada, Kentucky, Oregon, and Hawaii, mostly as a response to local cocaine or methamphetamine problems. Professionals have identified several key components of effective drug courts.

- Drug courts integrate alcohol and other drug treatment services with justice system case processing.
- Using a non-adversarial approach, prosecution and defense counsel promote public safety while protecting offender due process rights.
- Eligible participants are identified early and promptly placed in the drug court program.
- Drug courts provide access to a continuum of treatment and rehabilitation services.
- Abstinence is monitored via frequent drug testing.
- A coordinated strategy governs drug court responses to participant compliance.
- Ongoing judicial interaction with each drug court participant is essential.
- Monitoring and evaluation measure the achievement of program goals and assess effectiveness.
- Continuing interdisciplinary education promotes effective drug court operations.
- Forging partnerships among drug courts, public agencies, and community-based organizations generates local support and enhances drug court effectiveness.

Drug courts appear to be working. Across several locations, about 15% of drug court participants are re-arrested and retention and graduation rates are high (especially compared to normal recidivism statistics that hover around 70% or higher). Sustained abstinence from drugs also resulted in 40 to 80% reductions in crime. In addition to reductions in recidivism, drug courts also help address some of the collateral problems associated with drugs and crime.

Sources: Goldkamp, J. S. (2003). The impact of drug courts. *Criminology & Public Policy, 2,* 197–206; Gottfredson, D. C., Najaka, S. S., Kearley, B. (2003). Effectiveness of drug treatment courts: Evidence from a randomized trial. *Criminology & Public Policy, 2,* 171–196; Harrell, A. (2003). Judging drug courts: Balancing the evidence. *Criminology & Public Policy, 2,* 207–212; Harrell, A., & Roman, J. (2001). Reducing drug use among offenders: The impact of graduated sanctions. *Journal of Drug Issues, 31,* 207–232; Huddleston, III, C. W. (2005). *Drug courts: An effective strategy for communities facing methamphetamine.* Washington, DC: U. S. Department of Justice, Office of Justice Programs, Bureau of Justice Assistance; Senjo, S. R., & Leip, L. A. (2001). Testing and developing theory in drug court: A four-part logit model to predict program completion. *Criminal Justice Policy Review, 12,* 66–87. Photo © 2011, joingate, Shutterstock, Inc.

BOX 9-4

CRIME SCENE   DO NOT CROSS

CRIMINAL JUSTICE SPOTLIGHT

DOMESTIC VIOLENCE COURTS AND BATTERER INTERVENTION PROGRAMS

Another "specialized" criminal problem is domestic violence. The prevalence of domestic violence or spousal violence is relatively high; however, domestic violence, like drunk driving, is also frequently committed by persons who otherwise are not involved in criminal behavior. As such, a number of jurisdictions have devised programs specifically for persons charged with domestic violence. Instead of being sentenced to jail, batterers are sentencing to a domestic violence or batterer education program that contains months of group therapy that seek to reduce not only violent behavior but also antisocial attitudes that the defendant may harbor against women and about domestic violence (the modal offender is the male husband who abused his female spouse). Batterer courts offer the promise of reducing recidivism and the circumstances and attitudes that give rise to domestic violence.

Unfortunately, recent studies indicate that domestic violence courts and batterer intervention programs are ineffective. The National Institute of Justice sponsored two evaluation studies of batterer intervention programs in Broward County, Florida and Brooklyn, New York. The Broward study found no significant difference between the treatment and control groups in attitudes toward women, whether wife beating should be a crime, and whether the state has the right to intervene in domestic violence situations. It also found no differences in whether victims expected their partners to beat them again. Furthermore, no significant differences were found in probation violations or re-arrests except that men who were assigned to the treatment program but did not attend all of the sessions were *more likely* to be re-arrested than the control group. Attending the batterer program had no effect on the incidence of violence. Like Lawrence Sherman found in studies of mandatory arrest for domestic violence, offenders who had a greater stake in conformity (e.g., employed, married, homeowners) were less likely to commit violence.

In Brooklyn, batterers assigned to 26 weeks of treatment were less likely to re-cidivate than a control group and batterers ordered to eight weeks of treatment. The former group has fewer subsequent criminal complaints but no differences existed in terms of attitudes toward domestic violence.

These early results indicate that specialized courts for the treatment of domestic violence are not overwhelmingly better than traditional courts that sentence batterers to jail or non-conditional probation. Fortunately, criminologists are devising ways to improve batterer intervention programs so that domestic violence courts meet with some of the successes of specialized drug courts.

Sources: Davis, R. C., Taylor, B. G., & Maxwell, C. D. (2000). *Does batterer treatment reduce violence? A randomized experiment in Brooklyn.* Washington, DC: U.S. Department of Justice, Office of Justice Programs, National Institute of Justice; Feder, L., & Forde, D. R. (2000). *A test of the efficacy of court-mandated counseling for domestic violence offenders: The Broward Experiment.* Washington, DC: U.S. Department of Justice, Office of Justice Programs, National Institute of Justice; Jackson, S., Feder, L., Forde, D. R., David, R. C., Maxwell, C. D., & Taylor, B. G. (2003). *Batterer intervention programs: Where do we go from here?* Washington, DC: U.S. Department of Justice, Office of Justice Programs, National Institute of Justice. Photo © 2011, joingate, Shutterstock, Inc.

TRIALS AND TRIAL PROCEDURES

Trial Initiation

Pursuant to the 1974 Speedy Trial Act, cases must be brought to trial within two months of arrest unless motions have caused delays. Prior to trial initiation, a pretrial conference is held whereby the prosecution, defense, and judge stipulate those things that are agreed upon and thus narrow the scope of the trial to the things that are in dispute. Other activities include the disclosure of required information about witnesses and evidence, making motions, and organizing the presentation of motions, witnesses, and evidence. The process whereby the prosecution presents his or her case to the defense is known as discovery.

Jury Selection

Being called for "jury duty" is a part of Americana. The list of potential jurors, called the jury array or venire, is produced from voter registration lists, motor vehicle lists, or property tax assessments. The list of potential jurors is meant to encompass the local citizenry to ultimately produce a jury of peers to decide the legal fate of criminal defendants. A variety of persons are automatically excluded from serving on juries, such as convicted felons (in most states), public officials, attorneys, and the like. Those deemed unqualified or ineligible under state law are removed from the list. Otherwise, the court clerk randomly produces 12 jurors and two alternates. Interestingly, the use of 12 jurors is not mandated in the Constitution, but is more a reflection of common law custom. Indeed, the Supreme Court held in *Williams v. Florida* (1970) that the traditional 12-person jury was the result of "historical accident" and smaller juries are permissible under the Sixth Amendment.[24] Nevertheless, a 12-person jury remains the normal standard at least for felony trials.

Voir Dire

Voir dire, meaning to speak the truth, is the actual process of selecting a jury from the list of potential jurors. Both the prosecution and defense play a role in determining the appropriateness of an individual to sit on the jury in an unbiased and objective manner. The background, work and residency history, interest in, and knowledge of the current case are evaluated. During *voir dire*, potential jurors can be removed from consideration because they are deemed to be potentially biased and subjective. A challenge for cause occurs when either the prosecution or defense removes a juror because specific circumstances imply that the juror would be unable to impartially evaluate the evidence and render a verdict in the case. For example, jurors who are relatives, friends, or acquaintances of the defendant would be removed for cause. Additionally, persons who indicate that they have already arrived at a verdict in the case can be removed for cause. Because the jury must be fair and impartial, the prosecution and defense are not limited in the number of jurors they can challenge for cause, thus *voir dire* can be a prolonged process.

The United States Supreme Court has evaluated some interesting legal scenarios that have arisen from challenges for cause. For instance, *Witherspoon v. Illinois* (1968) held that a sentence of death cannot be carried out if the jury that imposed or recommended it was chosen by excluding prospective jurors for cause simply because they voice general objections to the death penalty, or expressed conscientious or religious scruples against its infliction.[25] On the other hand, the Court held in *Wainwright v. Witt* (1985) that a juror may be excluded in a death penalty case if his or her personal views on capital punishment would prevent or substantially impair the performance of his or her duties as a juror in accordance with the instructions and his or her oath to serve on the jury.[26] Similarly, *Lockhart v. McCree* (1986) held that the Constitution did not prohibit the removal for cause, prior to the guilt phase of a bifurcated capital trial, of prospective jurors whose opposition to the death penalty was so strong that it would prevent or substantially impair the performance of their duties as jurors at the sentencing phase of the trial.[27] In *Mu' Min v. Virginia* (1991), the Court held that questioning during *voir dire* in a capital murder case, which asked jurors if they had heard something about the case and formed an opinion, but did not ask specifics regarding what prospective jurors had heard did not violate the Sixth and Fourteenth Amendments.[28] As is always the case, the application of the law is open to interpretation especially when attempting to remove prospective jurors for substantive reasons.

More controversial is the peremptory challenge, which is the dismissal of a potential juror by either the prosecution or defense for unexplained, discretionary reasons. With peremptory challenge, attorneys need not provide justification as to why a particular individual should be removed. Given the competing goals of the prosecution and defense, it is east to imagine that the composition of the jury differently meets the needs of counsel. Prosecutors want jurors whose demeanor and responses to questions indicate that they are conservative, tough-on-crime, punitive, and perhaps prone to side with the state. Conversely, defense counsel might want jurors who appear to be more liberal, sympathetic to characteristics of the accused, and more due process oriented. Predictably, court officers often used demographic characteristics like age, race, and gender as proxies for criminal justice orientation or group-based behavior. For instance, the state might prefer a predominantly female jury when prosecuting a male defendant for multiple counts of rape.[29]

The Supreme Court has established a variety of rulings on the use of peremptory challenges as they relate to gender, race, and viewpoints about gender and race. *Ristaino v. Ross* (1976) held that the defendant had the right to have prospective jurors questioned regarding their racial prejudices only if the facts of the case suggested a significant likelihood that racial prejudice might infect the black defendant's trial.[30] *Turner v. Murray* (1986) held that a defendant in a capital case who was accused of an interracial crime was entitled to have prospective jurors informed of the race of the victim and questioned on the issue of racial bias. A defendant could not complain that the trial judge did not question prospective jurors on racial prejudice unless the defendant specifically requested such an inquiry during jury selection.[31]

In *Batson v. Kentucky* (1986), the Court held that the equal protection clause of the Fourteenth Amendment forbid prosecutorial use of peremptory challenges to exclude potential jurors solely on the account of their race or on the assumption that black jurors as a group would be unable to impartially consider the state's case against a black defendant. To establish a case the defendant must show that he or she is a member of a cognizable racial group and that the prosecutor had exercised peremptory challenges to remove members of the defendant's race from the jury. After the defense makes this initial showing the burden shifts to the prosecution to use a neutral explanation for challenging jurors.[32] *Powers v. Ohio* (1991) held that a white defendant had standing to have a conviction reversed due to violation of the equal protection clause of the Fourteenth Amendment if the prosecutor used peremptory challenges to exclude prospective black jurors.[33] This doctrine was affirmed in *Purkett v. Elem* (1995), which held that peremptory challenges could not be used for racially discriminatory reasons.[34] Finally, *J. E. B. ex rel. T. B.* (1994) held that the Fourteenth Amendment equal protection clause prohibited the use of peremptory challenges by state actors on the basis of gender. The case arose from a civil paternity suit filed by the State of Alabama. The equal protection clause prohibited discrimination in jury selection on the basis of gender, or on the assumption that an individual would be biased in a particular case for no reason other than the fact that the person happens to be a woman.[35] This case basically applied the logic of *Batson* to gender.

Opening Statements

Once the jury is officially selected or impaneled, the trial adversaries make their opening statements to the court and jury. Because the prosecution carries the burden of proof beyond a reasonable doubt, they make the initial opening statement. Here, the prosecutor concisely tells a story as to the evidence that the state has assembled that proves that the accused committed the crimes for which they are charged. The opening statement contains an overview of the evidence, witnesses, motives, and expert witnesses that will prove that the accused is guilty. The opening statement is confined to facts and cannot be made in an argumentative fashion. In kind, defense counsel presents their story that the state's case cannot or does not prove that the client is guilty. Since defense counsel has already reviewed the state's case during discovery, the purpose is simply to show how the state cannot prove guilt beyond a reasonable doubt. Opening statements are very important because they provide a summation of the facts of the case to the jury. If the defendant waives his or her right to a jury trial and instead opts for the judge to serve as jury, known as a bench trial, opening statements are often not made.

By this point, it should be clear that the prosecution and state are the offense and the defense is, obviously, the defense. The subsequent stages in the criminal trial, such as presentation of evidence, direct and cross examination of witnesses, and closing statements, are presented first by the prosecution then by the defense. These adversarial positions are the hallmark of American justice and are intended to best meet the twin goals of crime control and due process.

Rules of Evidence

Recall that the Bill of Rights is the procedural rulebook for the police, courts, and correctional systems. The Federal Rules of Evidence are the "rulebook" that governs proceedings in American courts. Although the Federal Rules of Evidence do not apply directly to state courts, the states have modeled their judicial rules of evidence on the federal model. The Federal Rules of Evidence contain eleven articles that encompass 67 judicial rules pertaining to:

- general provisions
- judicial notice
- presumptions in civil actions and proceedings
- evidence relevancy and its limits
- privileges
- witnesses
- opinions and expert testimony
- hearsay
- authentication and identification
- contents of writings, recordings, and photographs, and
- miscellaneous rules.

Whether at the federal or state level, the purpose of the rules of evidence is to secure fairness in judicial administration, the elimination of unjustifiable expense and delay, and the promotion of growth and development of the law of evidence to the end that the truth may be ascertained and proceedings justly determined.[36]

Presentation and Types of Evidence

Evidence is information provided to the courts during trials and includes testimony, documents, and physical objects that are intended to resolve the factual dispute that exists between the prosecution and defense. Several types of evidence may be presented at trial. Direct evidence establishes a fact without the need for inferences or presumptions. The majority of direct evidence that is presented in trials is eyewitness testimony and videotaped documentation. Circumstantial evidence proves facts that may support an inference or presumption of the disputed facts. Prima facie evidence suffices to prove a fact until there is evidence presented that could be used for rebuttal. Real evidence consists of physical material or traces of physical activity, such as fingerprints. Once the trial judge approves the admission of real evidence, it is presented in the form of an exhibit. With real evidence, prosecutors attempt to establish associative evidence defined as the link between the accused and the crime scene by information obtained from physical evidence found at the crime scene and physical evidence found on the accused or in places traceable to the accused. Again, evidence is primarily used as "proof" or data to support the presentation of the prosecution or the defense. The totality of the evidence presented often means the difference between conviction and acquittal.

Direct Examination

The prosecuting attorneys begin the presentation of evidence by calling their witnesses. The questions they ask of the witnesses are direct examination that may produce both direct and circumstantial evidence. Witnesses may testify to matters of fact or be called to identify documents, pictures, or other items that are introduced into evidence. Generally witnesses cannot state opinions or give conclusions unless they are experts or are especially qualified to do so. Witnesses qualified in a particular field as expert witnesses may give their opinion based on the facts in evidence and may give the reason for that opinion. Attorneys generally may not ask leading questions of their own witnesses. Leading questions are questions that suggest the answers desired, in effect prompting the witness. Objections may be made by the opposing counsel for many reasons under the rules of evidence, such as to leading questions, questions that call for an opinion or conclusion by a witness, or questions that require an answer based on hearsay. Most courts require a specific legal reason be given for an objection. Usually, the judge will immediately either sustain or overrule the objection. If the objection is sustained, the lawyer must re-phrase the question in a proper form or ask another question. If the objection is overruled and the witness answers the question, the lawyer who raised the objection may appeal the judge's ruling after the trial is over.

Cross-Examination

Once the prosecution completes direct examination, the defense attorneys may then cross-examine the witness. Cross-examination is generally limited to questioning only on matters that were raised during direct examination; however, leading questions may be asked during cross-examination since the purpose of cross-examination is to test the credibility of statements made during direct examination. Moreover, when a lawyer calls an adverse or hostile witness (one whose testimony is likely to be prejudicial) on direct examination, the lawyer can ask leading questions as on cross-examination. Essentially, defense counsel are attempted to impeach the witness or the evidence in the sense that they want to reduce the credibility of the witness or evidence. For example, witnesses may be asked if they have been convicted of a felony or a crime involving moral turpitude (dishonesty), since this is relevant to their credibility. Opposing counsel may object to certain questions asked on cross-examination if the questions violate the state's laws on evidence or if they relate to matters not discussed during direct examination. In short, cross-examination is the pure arena of adversarial justice.

The same process then occurs with the legal adversaries switching roles. The defense will offer evidence that indicates that their client was not guilty of the charges. In turn, the prosecutor can cross-examine the defense witnesses. However, the defense does not have to present evidence particularly if they are confident that the state/prosecutor did not prove its case. In a criminal case, the witnesses presented by the defense may or may not include the defendant. Because the Fifth Amendment to the U.S. Constitution protects against self-incrimination, the prosecution cannot require the defendant to take the stand and explain what happened, nor can it comment or speculate on the reasons the defendant has chosen not to testify. The jury will be instructed not to take into account the fact that the defendant did not testify. Once the defense has completed its presentation, the prosecution can present rebuttal witnesses or evidence to refute evidence presented by the defendant. This may include only evidence not presented in the case initially or a new witness who contradicts defense witnesses.

Directed Verdict and Closing Arguments

After the presentation of evidence, either the prosecution or defense can move for a direct verdict that, if granted, means that the trial is over. In closing arguments, first the prosecutor, then the defense attorney discuss the evidence and properly drawn inferences in their summation of the case. They cannot discuss issues or evidence that was not presented at trial. Before closing, the judge indicates to the lawyers which instructions he or she intends to give the jury. In turn, in their closing arguments the lawyers can comment on the jury instructions and relate them to the evidence. The closing argument is the opportunity for each side to "tell their story" about why they won, or should win, the case. The defense is not obligated to make a closing argument.

The Judge Instructs the Jury

The judge instructs the jury about the relevant laws that should guide its deliberations. The judge reads the instructions to the jury in what is often referred to as the judge's charge to the jury. In giving the instructions, the judge will state the issues in the case and define any terms that may not be familiar to the jurors. The judge must discuss the standard of proof, which in all criminal cases is beyond a reasonable doubt. Indeed, the Supreme Court held in *Sullivan v. Louisiana* (1993) that failure to give the jury an adequate instruction on "proof beyond a reasonable doubt" violates the defendant's right to a jury trial and is a fundamental error requiring reversal.[37]

Fundamentally, the judge instructs the jury to objectively as possible arrive at a verdict. In doing so, the judge may (1) read sections of applicable laws, (2) advise the jury that it is the sole judge of the facts and of the credibility of witnesses, (3) acknowledge that the jurors are to base their conclusions on the evidence as presented in the trial, and that the opening and closing arguments of the lawyers are not evidence, (4) explain what basic facts are in dispute, and what facts do not matter to the case, (5) note the relevant laws that govern the case and that jurors are required to adhere to these laws in making their decision, regardless of what the jurors believe the law is or ought to be. In short, the jurors determine the facts and reach a verdict within the guidelines of the law as determined by the judge. Many states allow the lawyers to request that certain instructions be given, but the judge makes the final decisions about them. To increase fairness and uniformity, some states created standardized instructions or give the jurors' copies or a recording of the instructions.

Jury Deliberation, Verdict, and Judgment

After receiving the instructions, the jury begins the process of deliberation. The jury elects a presiding juror or foreperson that will lead discussions, handle the voting process, and deliver the verdict to the court. The jury works with the court bailiff who ensures that no one communicates with the jury during deliberations and obtains needed information or exhibits from the court at the request of the jury. If jurors have questions about the evidence or the judge's instructions, they give a note to the bailiff to take to the judge. The judge may respond to the note, or may call the jury back into the courtroom for further instructions or to have portions of the transcript read to them. Of course, any communication between the judge and jury should be in the presence of lawyers for each side or with their knowledge. The court provides the jury with written forms of all possible verdicts so that when a decision is reached, it only has to choose the proper verdict form. In most but not all instances, the verdict in a criminal case must be unanimous (12-0).

Sometimes juries are unable to arrive at a decision or appear to be deadlocked because of one or two obstinate jurors.[38] In this event, the judge will bring the jury to the court and advise them of their duties. Known as an Allen Charge, this judicial warning is a subtle form of judicial coercion to keep the jury on course.[39] Additionally, the jurors may be sequestered where they are housed in a hotel and secluded from all contact with other people and news media. Unless the jury was sequestered because of concerns about their physical safety, jury members are permitted to go home at night but instructed not to consider or discuss the case with anyone outside of the jury room.

When jurors cannot agree on a verdict, the result is a hung jury and mistrial. A variety of factors can increase the likelihood of a hung jury. Case complexity was a major determinant of hung juries, as cases with multiple counts of criminal offenses, complex or sophisticated types of evidence, and complex, difficult-to-interpret legal instructions increased the likelihood of juries being unable to reach a verdict. Other important concerns among hung juries were concerns about a weakly presented case, questions about police credibility, and overall concerns about fairness of the law.[40] Since the case is not adjudicated or decided, it may be tried again at a later date before a new jury. The prosecution may also decline to pursue the case further.

After reaching a decision, the jury notifies the bailiff, who notifies the judge. All of the participants reconvene in the courtroom and the jury foreperson or court clerk announces the verdict, guilty or not guilty. Sometimes the losing side requests that the jury be polled whereby each juror is asked whether they agree with the decision. Afterward, the decision is read, accepted by the court, the jury is dismissed, and the trial is over. The decision of the jury does not legally take effect until the judge enters a judgment on the decision or files it in the public record.

Sentencing

Upon conviction, the judge sets a separate court proceeding to formally sentence the defendant. Judges rely on a formal report called a pre-sentence investigation (PSI), which is a legal dossier that includes information about the defendant's criminal history, family, work, and residency history, diagnostic information, and other relevant legal information. Depending on the jurisdiction, the PSI is prepared by pretrial services officers, judicial officers, or even probation officers. The PSI guides the judge's decision to determine the appropriate sentence from the range of possible sentences established by the legislature in the state statutes. However, the judge receives input from several sources, including the prosecutor, defense attorney, victims who deliver a victim-impact statement, the defendant, and occasionally family members of the defendant and victim. With the exception of death sentences, only the judge determines the sentence to be imposed.

Although the judge ultimately decides the sentence, his or her discretion is overwhelmingly guided by legislative sentencing guidelines that are primarily a function of two factors, the legal seriousness of the offense and the criminal history of the defendant. Within sentencing guidelines is room for flexibility for the judge to impose a minimum (leniency) or maximum (punitive) sentence. Factors that lead a judge to sentence in a lenient manner are mitigating factors or circumstances or characteristics that seem to reduce the seriousness of the charge. Age can be a mitigating factor since very young and very old defendants are often viewed as less deserving of harsh punishment. Factors that worsen sentences are aggravating factors or circumstances or characteristics that seem to exacerbate the seriousness of the charge. For example, violent crimes that are committed in an especially cruel, depraved, or heinous manner will often result in the most severe sentence.

Finally, implicit in the sentencing of a criminal defendant is a punishment philosophy or rationale. Five general punishment philosophies are utilized in the criminal courts. Retribution implies the payment of a debt to society and the expiation or atonement of one's offense. From this perspective, punishment is deserved and appropriate based on the seriousness and harm of the criminal offense. Criminals must be administered their "just desserts," almost as a form of societal revenge. Deterrence is the idea that swift, certain, and severe punishment will generally discourage or deter future criminal acts. General deterrence refers to the "general message" that is sent to potential criminals that they will be punished for their crimes. Specific deterrence pertains to the individual offender who is being punished. Deterrence rests on the theory that humans are rational actors empowered with free will who choose whether to commit crime. If the legal consequences are grave enough, theoretically people are discouraged from criminal behavior. Incapacitation, the modal punishment rationale in the contemporary United States, is the removal of criminals from society that precludes their ability to commit crimes against the citizenry. Incapacitation is achieved by incarceration. Rehabilitation seeks to restore, repair, or correct an offender's behavior so that he or she can become a non-criminal, productive member of society. The rationale is that punishment shows the offender a needed lesson or provides some type of treatment that can help the offender overcome the inclination or motivation to commit crime. Restoration, the newest of the rationales, seeks to respond to the needs of crime victims by building a coalition of sorts between the offender, victim, and community. The restoration philosophy has spawned a different paradigm of justice known as restorative justice that places exceedingly less emphasis on crime control and more on making efforts to rehabilitate ad reintegrate offenders into the community.[41]

Appeal

An appeal is the legal right of the defendant to contest a material error of law that occurred in his or her trial, such as a procedural violation. A substantive basis for appeal is also known as a potentially reversible error. A trivial error that did not substantively impair the case is known as a harmless error and cannot be appealed. Of course, the defendant cannot appeal merely because they were convicted. The prosecution cannot appeal a case because of the Fifth Amendment prohibition of double jeopardy. A "catchall" tactic for appeal for defendants in state courts is to file a writ of habeas corpus in federal court to show a constitutional rights violation. Importantly, an appeal is *not* a retrial. Instead, appellate courts review the trial's procedure or examine errors in the judge's interpretation of the law.

The appeals process goes as follows. First, the appeal is initiated by the filing of a formal document in the court having appellate (as opposed to original) jurisdiction. Second, a record of the original proceedings of the trial court is obtained from the court reporter's official transcript. Third, the opposing parties file briefs and if there will be oral arguments, a hearing is scheduled and the arguments are heard. Finally, after presentation of briefs and/or oral arguments, the appellate court deliberates by considering the original trial and the arguments made by both sides. The ultimate ruling of the appellate court is referred to as the majority opinion. Appellate judges who agree with the outcome but have a different rationale often write a concurring opinion whereas the minority that disagrees with the majority will write a dissenting opinion. An opinion of the entire appellate court is known as *per curiam*.

MOTIONS

A motion is an oral or written request made to a court at any time before, during, or after court proceedings that asks the court to make a specified finding, decision, order, or ruling. Written motions are referred to as petitions. Both the prosecution and defense can and often do make formal motions before, during, and after criminal trials. The most common trial motions appear below. As you will see, defense counselors are more likely to file motions in an effort to equalize their chances against the prosecution.

Discovery
The motion of discovery is functionally the most important motion. It is filed by the defense and allows the defendant's lawyers to view the prosecution's evidence that will be presented at trial. The defense is provided physical evidence, witness lists, documents, and any other evidence that the state will use against the accused. During discovery, the defense counsel ascertains the strength or weakness of the case that the state is brings against their client.

Bill of Particulars
A motion for a bill of particulars asks the prosecutor to provide detailed information about the charges that are being filed. Defendants facing multiple charges or multiple counts of the same offense commonly make the motion.

Dismissal
The motion to dismiss the charges is the criminal defendant's dream because if the motion is accepted, the case is terminated. A variety of circumstances can result in the dismissal of charges. For example, procedural violations that breach the due process rights of the defendant taint the government's case and must result in dismissal. Other times, cases are dismissed because the prosecutor's case is simply too weak to proceed to trial (let alone result in a

conviction). Defendants who agree to testify for the state against co-defendants often have their charges dismissed as part of the agreement. Finally, the motion to dismiss is sometimes prompted by a different motion. For instance, the motion to suppress evidence (discussed below) can greatly weaken the prosecutor's case and necessitate a dismissal.

Suppress Evidence

The motion to suppress evidence occurs when defense counsel moves to exclude evidence that the prosecution obtained unlawfully. Consider this scenario. A defendant is arrested upon suspicion for murder. During a lengthy interrogation, the defendant confesses to the killing. However, not only did the police ignore the defendant's repeated requests for an attorney, but also the police did not advise the defendant of his Miranda rights. Such a scenario is doubly crippling for the prosecution. First, the confession itself is tainted and worthless. Second, if it is the sole evidence of guilt and is suppressed, the prosecution's case dissolves.

Change of Venue

Cases involving famous persons as defendants or victims and cases characterized by extreme violence, such as multiple homicides, generate enormous public interest and media frenzy. Because of this, it may be difficult or nearly impossible to assemble a jury that can objectively deliver a verdict. Often, the defense will file a motion of change of venue to transport a case to another jurisdiction within the state where presumably the pretrial publicity is markedly lower and the likelihood of selecting unbiased jurors is greater.

Severance of Offenses and Severance of Defendants

Frequently, a single criminal episode contains numerous charges and multiple co-defendants. In an effort to save time and money, the prosecution often files a single criminal case that encompasses all of the charges and pertains to the co-defendants. To some, the consolidation of charges gives the appearance of obvious guilt. For example, the prosecutor may present a case against two defendants that includes 80 counts of burglary, 35 counts of felony theft, and 30 counts of receiving and selling stolen property. A motion for severance of offenses requests that defendants be tried separately for the charges. A motion for severance of defendants is requested when the defense believes that one defendant is clearly more responsible than the other (usually the defense counsel's client), and trying the individuals separately might reduce the likelihood of conviction.

Continuance

The motion for a continuance seeks to delay a criminal trial for some substantive reason, such as change in counsel. The judge must walk a fine line when considering motions for continuance. On one hand, the defense must be provided enough time to locate witnesses and adequately defend the accused. On the other hand, frequent delays in a trial tend to favor the defense and could be used as a tactic to prolong and thus weaken the state's case. Even when granted for substantively important reasons, continuances can significantly increase trial length.

Arrest of Judgment

A motion for arrest of judgment is requested after the jury returns a guilty verdict but prior to sentencing whereby the defendant believes there is a legally substantive reason why he or she should not be sentenced at that particular time. Physical illness, mental illness, and insanity are some reasons that may prompt a defendant to request an arrest of judgment.

Present Sanity

Similarly, a motion to determine present sanity occurs when the defense asserts that the defendant has become insane during the course of a trial. Importantly, defendants cannot be tried, sentenced, or punished if they are currently insane. A motion to determine present sanity seeks to delay court proceedings until the defendant can be stabilized. It is different from a plea of non guilty be reason by insanity.

Mistrial and New Trial

A motion for a mistrial is commonly filed when either the prosecution or defense makes highly inflammatory remarks that would seem to irreparably alter the case. Other reasons for a mistrial are the death of a juror or attorney, impropriety in the drawing of the jury that was discovered during trial, a fundamentally prejudicial error against the defendant, jury misconduct, or the inability of the jury to reach a verdict. Such a motion suggests that the current trial is broken and court proceedings must start over. If the defense moves for a mistrial, they cannot subsequently claim that a new trial is a violation of the double jeopardy clause of the 5th Amendment. Upon discovery of important evidence that will incontrovertibly show that their client is not guilty, the defense may file a motion for a new trial that will set aside or invalidate a prior conviction.

CHAPTER SUMMARY: BALANCING CRIME CONTROL AND DUE PROCESS

- Although the criminal trial is the symbolic battle of the state versus the individual, virtually all convictions are secured via plea-bargaining.
- Plea-bargaining has its pros and cons in terms of the achievement of crime control and due process goals. However, the judicial system likely would not work with the reliance on guilty pleas.
- The adversarial system of justice is less pronounced with plea-bargaining.
- Legal factors, such as quality and quantity of evidence, number of charges, offense severity, and the defendant's prior criminal history, are the strongest determinants of judicial outcomes.

- Challenges for cause and peremptory challenges are legal maneuvers used by the prosecution and defense to produce a jury that will be most amenable to their version of events.
- Despite public hype, hung juries and jury nullification are rare and caused mostly by case complexity.
- A variety of specialized courts addressing offenders/offenses such as domestic violation and drug violations have been devised to increase the treatment and rehabilitative potential of the criminal justice system.
- Criminal sentences are laden with philosophical rationales for punishing the criminal offenders. These include retribution, deterrence, incapacitation, rehabilitation, and restoration.

KEY TERMS

Acquittal	Jury selection
Alford plea	Mistrial
Allan charge	Motion
Appeal	No bill
Arraignment	*Nolo contendere*
Arrest of judgment	Opening statements
Bifurcated trial	*Per curiam*
Bill of Particulars	Peremptory challenge
Challenge for cause	Plea-bargain
Change of venue	Present sanity
Circumstantial evidence	Presentment
Closing argument	Real evidence
Continuance	Rehabilitation
Cross-examination	Restoration or restorative justice
Deliberation	Retribution
Deterrence	Rules of evidence
Direct evidence	Sentencing
Direct examination	Sentencing guidelines
Directed verdict	Sentencing hearing
Discovery	Severance of charges
Dismissal	Severance of defendants
Grand jury	Suppress evidence
Hung jury	Trial
Incapacitation	Trial initiation
Indictment or true bill	Trial tariff
Judgment	Verdict
Jury nullification	*Voir dire*

TALKING POINTS

1. Is jury nullification ever justifiable? Under what circumstances would jury nullification serve the interests of a pure crime control agenda?

2. Most states require unanimous verdicts. Is the 12–0 standard too high of a threshold to achieve justice? Would the judicial system be improved or damaged by verdicts of 11–1, 10–2, or even 7–5?

3. Nearly 100 percent of convictions are secured via plea-bargaining. Does this lend support to the belief of crime control enthusiasts and their presumption of guilt? Conversely, does the reliance on plea-bargains mean that due process is systemically compromised?

4. Are specialized courts a good innovation? Do they serve the needs of specific offenders with specific treatment and criminogenic needs? Should each type of criminal behavior be administered through specialized courts? What are the theoretical implications of drug court, batterer court, etc?

WEB LINKS

The Federal Judiciary
(www.uscourts.gov)

Community Justice Initiatives
(www.cjiwr.com)

Federal Judicial Center
(www.fjc.gov)

Federal Rules of Evidence
(www.law.cornell.edu/rules/fre/#article_vii)

United States Code
(www.uscode.house.gov/usc.htm)

National Drug Court Institute
(www.ndci.org/home.htm)

United States Sentencing Commission
(www.ussc.gov)

FURTHER READING

American Bar Association. (1999). *Facts about the American judicial system.* This 35-page booklet contains valuable answers to many questions that students may have about the judicial process, the federal judiciary, the state judiciary, and other legal information. Other important sourcebooks are also available on the American Bar Association website.

Frankel, M. E. (1973). *Criminal sentences: Law without order.* New York: Hill and Wang. This landmark book argued for uniform standards in the judicial process that Frankel argued were plagued by the personal instincts and subjective biases of judges.

Hickey, T. (2007). *Taking sides: Clashing views on criminal justice.* New York: McGraw-Hill. Part of the best-selling series, this concise book provides point-counterpoint arguments on a host of criminal justice issues ranging from arrest to execution. The book is especially helpful in identifying crime control and due process perspectives on legal and criminological issues.

Wilson, J. Q. (1983). *Thinking about crime*, revised edition. New York: Vintage. This classic work contains important chapters on the criminal courts, sentencing, and the philosophical and ideological bases of criminal justice. It could be viewed as the counterpoint to Frankel's book.

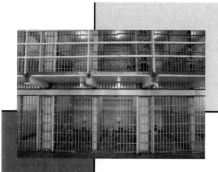

PART FOUR

CORRECTIONS AND PUNISHMENT

CHAPTER 10

Intermediate Sanctions, Probation, and Offender-Community Integration

CHAPTER OUTLINE

QUOTATIONS

"Under current conditions, probation and parole are probably best thought of as legal statuses allowing swifter incarceration or re-incarceration when fresh offenses are detected rather than as programs with independent incapacitative or rehabilitative effects."—*Mark Kleiman*[1]

"Currently, the social work function has given way to the law enforcement function, and probation and parole officers are less interested today in treating clients than in controlling their behavior."—*Joan Petersilia*[2]

"Judges choosing between confinement and intermediate sanctions, or among intermediate sanctions, are to be guided by a series of presumptions about purposes relevant to individual cases."—*Michael Tonry*[3]

"In our district we see the clients more often to hold them more accountable. It is better to err by giving too much supervision than to give too little and get burned by it later. This protects the officer and community. We have to over-supervise in this district."—*Anonymous probation officer*[4]

"The less extreme the post-parole environment in accepting or rejecting the prisoner norms, the greater will be the motivations to achieve success on parole."—*Jerome Skolnick*[5]

"The risk principle, which simply states that the level of supervision and treatment should be commensurate with the offender's level of risk, has been confirmed by research in corrections for more than a decade."—*Christopher Lowenkamp, Edward Latessa, and Alexander Holsinger*[6]

INTRODUCTION

Earlier in this textbook, criminal behavior and its resultant victimization were likened to raw materials of the criminal justice system. Due to the enormous magnitude of crime in the United States and the simultaneous limitations of time, jail space, and financial resources, a fraction of known criminal offenses actually enters the criminal justice system. The remaining crimes and the criminal defendants that commit them are diverted, dismissed, or otherwise funneled away from the system.

Several factors are used to determine which criminal cases enter the system. Generally, criminologists have investigated two types of variables that influence officer discretion, practitioner decision making, and criminal justice outcomes. These are legal variables, such as offense severity, prior criminal record, and number of charges, and extra-legal variables, such as demographic characteristics. Overwhelmingly (and fortunately), legal variables explain much more variation in criminal justice than extra-legal variables. Yet there is another important variable that is a combination of the legal and extra-legal classifications: criminality. Criminality is the propensity toward antisocial behavior that a defendant embodies. Often, criminologists use assorted risk and protective factors as proxies of criminality. In this way, characteristics such as age, onset of criminal behavior, employment status, family structure, and intelligence score on diagnostic tests such as psychopathy or antisocial personality disorder.

Criminality has an important practical value because it is one of the factors used by practitioners to decide the most appropriate type of sanction to fit the treatment and punishment needs of the offender. When the criminality and crime are exceedingly low, such as most traffic violations, the punishment is a fine and no treatment is needed. When the criminality and crime are exceedingly high, such as capital murder, the punishment can be death and the treatment moot. Of course, most crimes fall between these two extremes and so criminal punishment attempts to offer some balance of treatment and punishment. Commensurately, community corrections reflect a continuum of sanctions, a range of criminal penalties whose treatment and punishment modalities seek to match the varying criminality of correctional clients.[7]

Alex Holsinger and Edward Latessa studied the application of the sanction continuum to juvenile offenders and found that criminal justice practitioners appeared to be striking the appropriate balance between treatment and punishment of clients with varying degrees of criminality. Their study contained 544 delinquents who were sentenced to diversion, probation, special/intensive probation, a residential rehabilitation center, or the department of youth services. Sharp differences in criminality existed across the five placements. Those who received diversion were the lowest risks and had the lowest criminality and those sentenced to confinement were the highest risks and demonstrated the most criminality. For instance, Holsinger and Latessa found that delinquents who were sent to prison had an average criminal risk index score that was 400% greater than youths who were diverted. In terms of average behavioral risk score, youths who were placed in a residential center and department of youth services were 236% and 220% respectively more of a behavioral risk than youths were diverted![8]

Thus, the criminality of the criminal defendant, of course in conjunction with the crime for which he or she was convicted and other factors, are the potential for rehabilitation that criminal justice system agents are evaluating. How these discretionary agents evaluate whether someone is a "good risk," "a lost cause," or "a bad seed" can mean the difference in determining where on the continuum of punishment an offender should be placed.

INTERMEDIATE SANCTIONS/COMMUNITY CORRECTIONS

General Information

Interchangeably referred to as intermediate sanctions, community corrections, or community-based corrections, intermediate sanctions is any form of correctional treatment that deals with the offender within as opposed to outside of society. Community corrections are a lenient alternative to incarceration that accords criminal offenders the opportunity to rehabilitate themselves and become functioning, non-criminal members of society while still integrated in the society. That community-correctional clients remain at large, embedded in the community, symbolically represents the opportunity that they are given. In fact, all community corrections strike a balance between protecting the community and rehabilitating the offender. This blended practice of law enforcement and social work functions can create tension because of the competing purposes of these goals. Finally, community corrections are significantly less expensive than prison in terms of the fiscal costs of administering the sanction and the punishment severity inflicting on the offender. For these reasons, criminal offenders and criminal justice practitioner alike often view any criminal punishment short of prison as a "last resort" or "final opportunity" for the criminal offender to reform his or her antisocial behavior.

Norval Morris argues that intermediate sanctions must serve legitimate treatment and correctional needs otherwise they will not alleviate prison crowding. Morris articulated three principles to guide the placement of offenders on community corrections. First, the sentence should be parsimonious and provide the least restrictive punishment should apply. Second, offenders should receive their just desserts, in that no sanction should be imposed that is greater than what is deserved. In other words, the punishment and the crime need to match. Finally, Morris was apprehensive about whether policy makers could accurately make predictions of future dangerousness. Instead, sentencing should follow from observed legal characteristics like offense severity.[9] Following these principles should result in defendants being placed on the most appropriate and just intermediate sanction.

Strengths and Weaknesses of Intermediate Sanctions

Against the traditional punishments of confinement and probation, intermediate sanctions are versatile criminal punishments that can fit multiple purposes. According to Michael Tonry, intermediate sanctions are punitive in the sense that they are more intrusive and burdensome than standard probation. Because of the "burdensome" conditions that are a part of most intermediate sanctions, violations and non-compliance rates tend to be high. Second, intermediate sanctions can be viewed as rehabilitative because programs with well-designed treatment protocols can reduce recidivism among offenders. Third, intermediate sanctions reduce money and prison-bed costs without sacrificing public safety.[10] For instance, probation and parole receive about 15% of state expenditures for corrections yet they supervise more than 70% of correctional clients.

Despite these positives, the primary criticism of intermediate sanctions is that they are responsible for the dramatic growth in the American correctional population. According to Lauren Glaze of the Bureau of Justice Statistics, the total correctional population in the United States is more than 7.2 million. Of these, approximately 70%, or more than 5 million people, received community supervision, such as probation or parole. Approximately one in 32 adults was under the supervision of the correctional system. Interestingly, the correctional population declined by nearly 49,000 offenders in 2009 which was the first time ever since the Bureau of Justice Statistics began gathering data in 1980.[11] The growing of the correctional population via the proliferation of community corrections or intermediate sanctions is referred to as "net widening." Although intermediate sanctions provide the opportunity for offenders to avoid prison and taxpayers to avoid paying for them to go to prison, the offenders must go somewhere. That somewhere is the community. Joan Petersilia summarized the situation nicely: "Probation and parole, systems developed in the United States more by accident than by design, now threaten to become the tail that wagged the corrections' dog."[12] The dramatic growth of both the correctional population and correctional spending is shown in Figure 10-1 and 10-2.

Finally, some criminologists view net widening as significantly worse than a mere fiscal or policy issue. For example, Malcolm Feeley and Jonathan Simon used the term "the new penology" to describe how the criminal justice system has increasingly utilized surveillance and punishment as a means to manage or supervise large aggregates of people that are described as dangerous or criminal. John Irwin, James Austin, and their colleagues have argued that the growth of the correctional population and its increasingly widening net pander to concerns among the general public about crime and safety. Critics of net widening view the growth of the criminal justice system as an extension of the power of conservative policy makers.[13] Overall, an overly large correctional population is viewed as threatening to due process and civil liberty. From a crime control perspective, net widening is an inevitable and inexpensive way to punish criminal offenders while granted them an opportunity for rehabilitation. Given the magnitude of criminal offending and the finite resource of prison space, it is impossible to incarcerate every convicted felon who deserves it. In this way, net widening is a pragmatic, realistic way to facilitate the criminal justice process.[14]

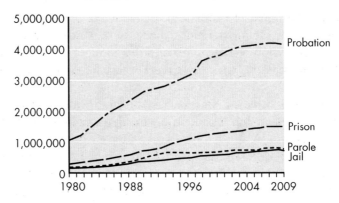

FIGURE 10-1 Correctional Population Growth

Source: Retrieved February 25, 2011, from **http://bjs.ojp.usdoj.gov/content/glance/ corr2.cfm**.

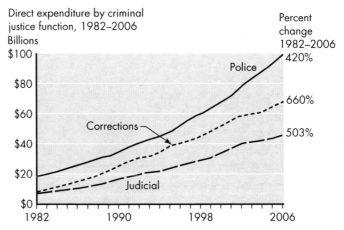

FIGURE 10-2 Corrections Spending Explodes 660%

Source: Retrieved February 25, 2011, from **http://bjs.ojp.usdoj.gov/content/glance/ exptyp.cfm**.

Types of Intermediate Sanctions

Fines and Restitution

Fines are monetary payments imposed on criminal offenders as a way to "repay" society for their violation of the law. Fines are the oldest form of intermediate sanction, and arguably the oldest form of criminal punishment along with death. Before the formalization of criminal justice systems, fines were paid to the specific victim, his or her family, and the community. Today, fines are the universal penalty because virtually all statutes denote some financial penalty often to supplement another sanction. For example, persons convicted of drunk driving may receive one year of probation and a $500 fine.

Fines are collected in a variety of ways. Particularly for petty, traffic, and misdemeanor offenses, fines are imposed upon conviction and the defendant pays upon release from custody. More frequently, community corrections personnel monitor the payment of fines in the course of supervising their client. For example, the correctional officer interviews the defendant to ascertain his or her financial situation, income, and ability to pay to arrange the schedule for repayment. Failure to pay the fine within the time span specified by the court or administrating agency could result in a warrant for non-compliance (technically, failure to pay). Other jurisdictions employ day fines that are geared to the average daily income of the offender. Day fines help to ensure payment because of the daily responsibility placed on the offender. Other jurisdictions garnish a defendant's wages to ensure payment of fines and restitution. Finally, jail inmates and prisoners often work while incarcerated. That income can similarly be garnished to pay fines, court costs, restitution, and outstanding child support.

The monetary amount of fines varies greatly to match the legal seriousness of the crime. For instance, fines for petty and misdemeanor crimes are often less than $100 whereas fines for individuals or corporations convicted of securities, fraud, or other white-collar crimes can be hundreds of millions of dollars. Indeed, it has been argued that affluent, white-collar offenders should be forced to pay exorbitant fines that would impose the same level of hardship as prison.[15] Another positive consequence would be increased local, state, or federal revenue depending on the jurisdiction that imposed the fine. Whatever the fiscal potential of fines, they do not generally affect recidivism. Criminologists have found that fines were not helpful in reducing recidivism among offenders forced to pay them primarily because fines were viewed as such an indirect, almost incidental, form of punishment.[16]

Whereas fines are paid to the state, restitution is paid to the crime victim to recoup some of the harm caused by the offender's wrongful acts. All criminal courts have the authority to order convicted offenders to pay restitution to victims as part of their sentences. In many states, courts are required to order restitution to victims in cases involving certain types of crimes, typically violent felony offenses.

Restitution can cover any out-of-pocket losses directly relating to the crime, including medical expenses, therapy costs, prescription charges, counseling costs, lost wages, expenses related to participating in the criminal justice process, lost or damaged property, insurance deductibles, crime-scene clean up, or any other expense that resulted directly from the crime.[17]

When courts order restitution, they look not only at the victim's losses, but also at the offender's ability to pay. In some states, the court may reduce the total amount of restitution ordered if the offender is unlikely to be able to pay that amount. In other states, courts will order the offender to pay for the full amount of the loss, but then set a payment schedule based on the offender's finances, which may only be a minimal amount per month. Offenders who have greater resources, more protective factors, and minimal criminal record are most likely to pay restitution on time.[18] Unfortunately, many victims wait years before they receive any restitution because of the assorted deficits of the modal criminal offender. To help ensure the payment of restitution, it is often an explicit condition of probation or parole such that failure to pay restitution will result in revocation of the sentence.

Forfeiture

Another financial-based intermediate sanction is forfeiture. Forfeiture is the loss of ownership for the illegal use of some property or asset. Criminal forfeiture is *in personam*, which means that the criminal defendant is the target of the forfeiture that can only occur after criminal conviction. Civil forfeiture is *in rem*, which means that it targets property. Moreover, civil forfeiture does not require formal adversarial proceedings and adjudication of guilt is not needed. Criminal forfeiture became part of contemporary criminal justice in 1970 with the enactment of the Racketeer Influenced and Corrupt Organization (RICO) statutes that targeted the operations of organized crime activities, such as racketeering, extortion, drug trafficking, or money laundering. The RICO statutes provided the legal justification to seize any assets associated with or produced by criminal enterprises. Many states have similarly developed RICO statutes based on the federal model.

Although developed to tackle organized crime, forfeiture has increasingly been used to target drug violators. Criminal justice system agents employed both criminal and civil forfeiture as a way to cripple the resources of drug offenders (that were comparable to organized crime networks) and utilize proceeds from the seized assets. Because civil forfeiture did not depend on adversarial criminal prosecution, it was viewed as a violation of the due process rights of criminal defendants. The passage of the Civil Asset Forfeiture Reform Act (CAFRA) of 2000 rectified this by providing the procedural protections available to criminal defendants to those whose assets were seized. Moreover, the prosecutor was charged with the burden of proving that particular crimes had occurred and that the seized assets were the fruits of criminal activity, had facilitated criminal activity, or was contraband in itself.[19]

Criminologists have produced mixed findings regarding the prevalence of forfeiture and the reliance of the criminal justice system on the sanction. John Worrall surveyed 1,400 municipal and county law enforcement agencies to examine their use of civil forfeiture against drug violators. Worrall found that law enforcement agencies commonly used civil forfeiture and that 40% of agencies reported that forfeiture was a necessary way to supplement the departmental budget.[20] James Clingermayer, Jason Hecker, and Sue Madsen surveyed 70 law enforcement agencies in Ohio and Kentucky and found a much different situation regarding forfeiture. Although they found that virtually all jurisdictions used forfeitures, the forfeitures were overwhelmingly

CRIME SCENE   DO NOT CROSS

BOX 10-1

CRIMINAL JUSTICE PRACTICE

THE FEDERAL ASSET FORFEITURE PROGRAM

The United States Marshals Service administers the Department of Justice's Asset Forfeiture Program by managing and disposing of properties seized and forfeited by federal law enforcement agencies and U.S. attorneys nationwide. The three goals of the Asset Forfeiture Program are enforcing the law; improving law enforcement cooperation; and enhancing law enforcement through revenue.

In 1984, Congress enacted the Comprehensive Crime Control Act, which gave federal prosecutors new forfeiture provisions to combat crime. Also created by this legislation was the Department of Justice Assets Forfeiture Fund (AFF). The proceeds from the sale of forfeited assets such as real property, vehicles, businesses, financial instruments, vessels, aircraft, and jewelry are deposited into the AFF and are subsequently used to further law enforcement initiatives. Under the Equitable Sharing Program, the proceeds from sales are often shared with the state and local enforcement agencies that participated in the investigation that led to the seizure of the assets. This important program enhances law enforcement cooperation between state/local agencies and federal agencies.

The asset forfeiture community consists of The Marshals Service; U.S. Attorney's Offices; Federal Bureau of Investigation; Drug Enforcement Administration; Department of Homeland Security, and the Bureau of Alcohol, Tobacco, Firearms and Explosives. The Marshals Service, U.S. Attorneys Offices, and the investigative agencies in pre-seizure planning which is the first critical step to ensuring that sound, well-informed forfeiture decisions are made.

The role of the Marshals Service is to not only serve as custodian of seized and forfeited property but also to provide information and assist prosecutors in making informed decisions about property that is targeted for forfeiture. The Marshals Service manages and disposes of all assets seized for forfeiture by utilizing successful procedures employed by the private sector. The Marshals Service contracts with qualified vendors who minimize the amount of time an asset remains in inventory and maximize the net return to the government.

Source: Retrieved February 25, 2011, from www.usmarshals.gov/assets/index.html.
Photo © 2011, J. Helgason, Shutterstock, Inc.

of the criminal variety following a criminal prosecution. Most agencies did not ever use civil forfeiture. Moreover, agencies received a very small part of their budgets from seizures and the sanction had little impact on police procedures and policies.[21] Nevertheless, forfeiture is a useful and potentially lucrative intermediate sanction used to cost-effectively punish criminal offenders (see Box 10-1).

Day Reporting

Day reporting is a multifaceted intermediate sanction that serves both pretrial and post-conviction criminal defendants. The sanction requires that defendants report to an official criminal justice facility on a daily basis to "check-in" and demonstrate to correctional staff that they are complying with the conditions of their current legal status. For pretrial defendants who have been released on bond, day reporting usually occurs at the county jail or a community corrections facility. Depending on the conditions of their bond, defendants may submit to Breathalyzer tests or provide proof that they worked or attending counseling. Because clients must daily interact with correctional staff, they theoretically reduce the incentives to engage in criminal behavior that would violate the conditions of bond. Concomitantly, day reporting allows defendants to remain in the community to work toward their own rehabilitation. Pretrial day reporting also saves on jail space and costs and is one of the most widely used alternatives to incarceration.

Day reporting is also used for post-conviction groups, especially probationers and parolees. Day reporting centers provide an assortment of services, such as substance abuse treatment, cognitive restructuring, anger management classes, batterer education classes, parenting skills education, mental health treatment, and others, that are designed to reduce antisocial attitudes and behaviors that lead to crime. Day reporting is an explicit condition of their supervision and provides greater supervision than traditional probation because of the frequency of contact. Day reporting centers also refer correctional clients to services in the community not provided by the center.

Several evaluations of day reporting indicated that the sanction is a promising way to reduce recidivism and increase the prosocial functioning of criminal offenders. D. J. Williams and Tiffany Turnage conducted a one-year follow-up study of 92 day reporting clients in Utah and found that 67% had no post-discharge problems. Moreover, 78% of the offenders remained out of jail or prison.[22] Based on data from offenders in Indiana, Sudipto Roy and Jennifer Grimes found that 69% of clients successfully completed the day reporting program compared to 31% who did not.[23] An evaluation of nearly 1,400 day reporting clients in Illinois found that clients who utilized more services offered by the day reporting center had lower recidivism rates than clients who did not take advantage of the resources provided.[24]

In sum, who succeeds and fails in a day reporting program depends primarily on the criminality and risk factors that the individual offender poses. Indeed, habitual criminals have been found to be 400% more likely to violate the conditions of day reporting than first-time offenders.[25] Nevertheless, day reporting has proven to be a viable, cost-effective intermediate sanction that can serve the needs of all but the most recalcitrant offenders.[26]

Community Service
Community service is a form of restitution that involves civic participation toward the improvement of the community. Examples of community service are volunteering with social service providing agencies, such as the Red Cross or the Boys and Girls Club, cleaning public parks or roadways, and

any activity that constitutes a non-paid donation of time to the public good. Community service is usually ordered in conjunction with other intermediate sanctions. For example, a defendant is sentenced to one year of probation in which he or she must pay $500 in fines, court costs, and restitution, and perform 100 hours of community service. Depending on the sentence, community service is monitored by a probation officer or community corrections specialist. In most jurisdictions, a network of social service providers are approved by the courts and defendants select the agencies that they want to collaborate with. Sometimes, defendants are ordered to donate their time to a specific social service agency especially if the agency is related to the crime. For instance, a person convicted of domestic violence may be ordered to work with practitioners in a domestic violence shelter.

Unlike other intermediate sanctions, the criminal justice system does not expect significant reductions in recidivism because of community service. Because it is usually ordered in conjunction with other penalties, it is somewhat difficult to separate the potential independent effects of performing a public good on reducing crime rates. Depending on their criminal history and other social characteristics, offenders view community service as an annoying, even onerous time commitment; a welcome opportunity in lieu of jail; or an empowering experience that will likely deter future crime. Irrespective of what offenders feel about it, community service allows the criminal justice system to mandate civic activity that improves the community. Moreover, many courts permit indigent defendants to perform community service to work off fines.[27]

Deferred Prosecution, Judgment, or Sentence
Variously referred to as a deferred prosecution, judgment, or sentence, deferring a defendant's sentence is one of the most widespread and cost-effective ways to control the correctional population by diverting offenders from it. Here is how the sanction works. Suppose a defendant, with minimal criminal history, is arrested for theft. He or she pleads guilty to the crime in exchange for a deferred judgment period usually ranging from six months to two years. Unlike probation, deferred sentences entail no conditions and do not require the defendant to check in with correctional personnel. Instead, clients who received a deferred sentence must simply not get arrested during the specified time period (and theoretically abstain from committing crime). If the defendant remains crime-free for the specified period, the guilty plea is voided and the entire event expunged from the defendant's record.

Deferred sentences are used for both misdemeanor and felony crimes. Because of the possibility of expungement, deferred sentences offer one of the best incentives for offenders to reform their criminal ways. If defendants are re-arrested during the deferred sentence, two courses of action are pursued. First, the deferred period is extended, for example from six months to one year, and the defendant is provided another opportunity on the deferred sentence. Second, the deferred sentence is revoked and the client is placed on probation. Importantly, a guilty plea that results in probation will not be dismissed and expunged regardless of how well the client complies while under supervision.

Conrad Printzlien, the first probation officer in the Eastern District of New York, originally devised deferred prosecution. Printzlien noted the differences in criminality among juvenile offenders and hoped to divert non-serious offenders from the criminal justice system and reserve punishment resources for the most serious offenders. Printzlien conducted a background investigation on his clients. Those with stable community ties and minimal prior record had their criminal charges held in abeyance for a specific time frame contingent on the defendant's good behavior. If the juvenile delinquent did well on the deferred sentence, the case was closed and expunged. Youths who did not comply faced the original complaint or prosecution. This early form of deferred sentencing was known as the Brooklyn Plan.[28]

Halfway Houses/Residential Treatment

The term "halfway house" describes the status of a criminal defendant that is partially confined and partially integrated into the community. Traditionally, halfway houses served post-conviction offenders as they transitioned from prison confinement to a period of aftercare or parole. However, for a variety of reasons, such as alcohol or drug treatment, mental health counseling, or some other risk factor, halfway house clients were viewed as too risky to be entirely released to the community. Unlike prisons which are absolutely secured, halfway houses are correctional facilities from which residents are regularly permitted to leave, unaccompanied by a correctional official, to attend treatment, use community resources (pertaining to their rehabilitation), attend school or some educational program, work, or seek employment. Halfway house residents generally sleep at the facility and are free to participate in their structured activities during specified times, usually during normal business hours.

Today, halfway houses are often referred to as residential communities, residential community corrections, or residential treatment facilities. Halfway houses are advantageous as an intermediate sanction for two reasons. First, they are more cost-effective than prison and many jurisdictions utilize private halfway houses that offer even greater cost-savings. For example, Travis Pratt and Melissa Winston analyzed a nationwide census of public and private correctional facilities and found that private halfway houses were among the most cost-efficient forms of community supervision.[29]

Similarly to most intermediate sanctions, halfway houses now serve both pretrial and post-conviction offenders. Depending on the jurisdiction, parolees or probations can reside in halfway houses. In some places, high-risk defendants on bond can reside in halfway houses or even county jails in special work release or "work-ender" units in which offenders reside in the facility when not working or attending treatment. Using various data sources and types of offenders, residential treatment has been found to be fairly effective at reducing recidivism and violence among criminal offenders.[30] Even more importantly from an administrative perspective, halfway houses provide another inexpensive opportunity to supervise criminal offenders for whom prison would be too expensive and perhaps too severe a sanction.[31]

Boot Camps/Shock Incarceration
Correctional boot camps, sometimes referred to as shock incarceration or intensive incarceration, are short-term incarceration programs that incorporate the strict discipline, hard labor, and physical training of military basic training followed by an aftercare program, parole, or probation depending on the state and the legal classification of the offender, that contains conditions and treatment. A major advantage of boot camps is that they are significantly less expensive than placing felons in traditional prison.[32]

Boot camp participants are young convicted felons without extensive criminal histories for whom boot camp is an opportunity for rehabilitation in lieu of prison confinement. Boot camps were first introduced in 1983 in Georgia and Oklahoma to tremendous public and political fanfare. Citizens appreciated the harsh discipline, physical coercion, and "tough love" approach to simultaneously treating and punishing youthful criminals. Some academic criminologists detested boot camps for these same reasons.[33]

Evaluations of boot camps in many states have produced conflicting findings about the overall effectiveness of boot camps as an intermediate sanction depending on the study outcome. For example, Faith Lutze found that boot camps were successful in providing an environment of safety and discipline, which offenders felt was more conducive to rehabilitation than what a minimum-security prison could offer.[34] Even if boot camps offer an environment that seems conducive to rehabilitation, offenders do not always take advantage. For instance, a variety of criminologists have found that offenders who attended boot camp were no better than traditional prisoners in terms of reducing their antisocial attitudes, delinquent cognitions, or recidivism.[35] The effectiveness of boot camps is also contingent on the legal classification and even criminality of the participants. Boot camps were designed for offenders with little to no criminal history and tend to be most effective for such clients. When offenders with more extensive criminal records are placed in boot camp, the results are less impressive.[36]

After twenty years of research on boot camps, three important conclusions should be drawn. First, the ultimate effectiveness of boot camps (and any sanction for that matter) depends greatly on the criminality of the clients. To illustrate, Brent Benda and his colleagues have consistently found that boot camp graduates who have low self-control, deficits in social skills, and frequent associations with criminal peers are significantly more likely to recidivate when followed for five years. Moreover, boot camp alumni with gang, drug, and weapons histories were also more problematic than clients who did not have this criminal baggage.[37]

Second, the overall effects of boot camps on recidivism and related outcomes are modestly positive. Doris Layton MacKenzie, David Wilson, and Susanne Kider conducted an exhaustive meta-analysis of 29 studies that used 44 samples of boot camp offenders. In nine studies, boot camp participants had lower recidivism than comparison groups who either did not participate in the boot camp or were simply sentenced to prison. In eight studies, boot camp clients were worse than their counterparts. In 12 studies, no significant differences emerged.[38] Boot camps that were most effective offered more rehabilitation components, such as drug treatment and education programs, and targeted prison-bound offenders.[39] Third and finally, even if boot camps modestly affect recidivism, they are important intermediate sanctions because they cost significantly less money than sending the same offenders to prison. These short-term costs savings will likely continue to justify the use of boot camps.

Home Detention, House Arrest, and Electronic Monitoring
Home detention, variously referred to as house arrest or home confinement, and electronic monitoring are distinct intermediate sanctions that are routinely combined for use in the same sentence. House arrest is a sanction where the offender must not leave his or her home with the exception of court-approved times for work and treatment. For example, a person may be permitted to leave the house between the hours or 8AM and 5PM Monday through Friday. When not working or traveling to work, the client must remain in the home. Offenders can be monitored by telephone, work visits, or, more commonly, via electronic surveillance devices that are attached to the body of the offender. The electronic monitoring device, known in popular culture as an "ankle bracelet," sends a signal that notifies correctional personnel if the client leaves the house and thus, violates the sentence.

Home detention and electronic monitoring are appealing intermediate sanctions for a variety of reasons. First, they permit convicted offenders to remain in the community and continue to be contributing members of society. Since their freedom is curtailed to work and treatment, the sanctions force offenders into a concentrated commitment to conventional behavior. In the same way, offenders are not permitted to go to bars or other places with criminal opportunities. Indeed, Randy Gainey and Brian Payne interviewed offenders who had been placed on home detention with electronic monitoring and found that most offenders viewed the intermediate sanction as a positive experience that was certainly better than jail.[40]

Second, house arrest and electronic monitoring address offenders who ordinarily would have been sentenced to jail. Consequently, the sanctions offer significant savings in terms of jail-space, jail operating costs, and jail crowding.[41] Third, evaluation studies from several states, including California, Georgia, and Virginia, found evidence that offenders on house arrest/electronic monitoring had lower recidivism rates than comparable offenders.[42]

Of course, home detention and electronic monitoring also has its deficiencies. First and foremost is that the sanctions cannot address criminal behaviors that occur within the home. Offenders may successfully comply with their sentence while engaging in domestic violence, child abuse, or using drugs within their home. Second, the crime-saving effects of house arrest and electronic monitoring are equivocal. For example, Kevin Courtright, Bruce Berg, and Robert Mutchnick studied offenders in Pennsylvania and found that these offenders were as likely as jail inmates to get re-arrested or have their probation revoked.[43] Similarly, James Bonta and his colleagues found that electronic monitoring was ineffective at reducing recidivism, added little value as an intermediate sanction, and only served to widen the net of the correctional apparatus.[44]

PROBATION

Definitions and General Information

Probation is a sanction for criminal offenders who have been sentenced to a period of correctional supervision in the community in lieu of incarceration. Probation offers conditional freedom to offenders who must abide by a variety of conditions that are imposed to facilitate their rehabilitation. Common probation conditions are substance abuse counseling and urinalysis, no contact with victims in the case, psychiatric counseling, restitution, community service, maintain employment, and communicate regularly with one's probation officer. Standard conditions refer to universal mandates that apply to all probationers, such as regularly reporting to their probation officer. Treatment conditions address a problem or issue that if resolved will help the offender remain crime-free. Punitive conditions are burdens placed on probationers convicted of the most serious crimes.

A probation officer is the practitioner who oversees and monitors a probationer's case to determine that the defendant is complying with all conditions of probation. When probationers do not comply with their sentence, their probation officer can pursue two courses of action. Unless there is a grievous violation, such as an arrest for a new violent felony, the probation officer will warn the probationer and potentially seek to impose new conditions or extend the period of probation. Both of these actions must be court-approved before the probation department may act. Other times, the probation officer arrests the probationer for violating the terms of his or her sentence. At court, the probation sentence can be terminated, usually resulting in a prison sentence, or made more restrictive. Importantly, probationers who are performing exceptionally well can also have their probation terminated early. Violations of probation that are based on relatively minor conditional violations are oftentimes referred to as technical violations.

Probation is the "jack of all trades" sanction because it touches virtually all aspects of criminal justice. Upon arrest, it is usually the department of probation that conducts a pre-sentence investigation (PSI) that is the primary source of information that the court uses to determine which cases will be deferred from formal prosecution. The criminal and social history information in the PSI can affect bond and pretrial release, adjudication, sentencing, correctional placement, and supervision (see Box 10-2). As described by Joan Petersilia, "No other justice agency is as extensively involved with the offender and his case as is the probation department."[45]

Probation also plays a major part in deflecting or diverting crimes from the criminal justice system and thus provides great savings on court and correctional expenditures. Aside from nominal criminal offenders, recidivism rates are relatively high. This means that offenders already on probation commit many new crimes. Once this happens, the courts have a decision to make. They can either initiate prosecution for the new crimes or simply use the new arrest as the basis for a violation or revocation of probation. Prosecutors favor the latter approach. Rodney Kingsnorth, Randall MacIntosh, and Sandra Sutherland found that prosecutors believed that case disposition by means of a probation violation hearing and revocation was preferable to filing new charges. Because probation violations could readily result in jail or prison sentences, new charges were often rejected or dismissed to streamline the case against the offender.[46] In this way, probation and its violation can serve a para-judicial function.

Types of Probation
Jurisdictions offer a variety of forms of probation depending on the risk, criminality, and treatment needs of the probationer. Unsupervised (or summary) probation is reserved for first-time or low-level offenders with little to no probation conditions. Unsupervised probation is comparable to a deferred sentence in that probationers do not need to meet with a probation officer instead they must simply abstain from crime and avoid re-arrest during the specified period of supervision. However, a conviction and probation sentence will remain on one's permanent criminal record.

Automated (or banked) probation is a form of unsupervised probation that entails no supervision, services, or personal contacts. Automated probation is used primarily in large urban centers with massive probation caseloads. For example, Joan Petersilia reported that 70% of probationers in Los Angeles

CRIME SCENE   DO NOT CROSS

BOX 10-2

CRIMINAL JUSTICE SPOTLIGHT

THE PSI

Elements of an Offense-Based Presentence Report

1. The offense
   Charge(s) and conviction(s)
   Related cases
   The offense conduct
   Adjustment for obstruction of justice
   Adjustment for acceptance of responsibility
   Offense level computation
2. The defendant's criminal history
   Juvenile Adjudications
   Criminal convictions
   Criminal history computation
   Other criminal conduct
   Pending charges (include if pertinent)
3. Sentencing options
   Custody
   Supervised release
   Probation
4. Offender characteristics
   Family ties, family responsibilities, and community ties Mental and emotional health
   Physical condition, including drug dependence and alcohol abuse
   Education and vocational skills
   Employment record
5. Fines and restitution
   Statutory provisions
   Guidelines provisions for fines
   Defendant's ability to pay
6. Factors that may warrant departure (from sentence guidelines
7. The impact of plea agreement (if pertinent)
8. Sentencing recommendations
   Offender characteristics
   Fines and restitution
   Factors that may warrant departure
   Impact of the plea agreement
   Sentencing recommendations

Source: Adapted from Center on Juvenile and Criminal Justice, www.cjcj.org.
Photo © 2011, joingate, Shutterstock, Inc.

County (nearly 100,000 clients) received automated probation; this included 5,000 offenders convicted of violent Index crimes.[47]

Intensive supervised probation (ISP) is the most highly restrictive form of punishment that is designed to supervise criminal offenders that embody the most risk factors for continued involvement in crime. Clients on ISP must abide by a multitude of conditions and are subject to the most intense supervision and surveillance by probation officers. Usually, probation officers that supervise ISP clients have reduced caseloads because of the added supervision needed for their clients. Intensive supervised probation is viewed as the last resort form of community corrections before an offender is sentenced to prison.

Statistical Snapshot

More criminal offenders are on probation than any other form of criminal punishment. With a population of more than 4.2 million, probation accounts for 84% of the entire community supervision population. The growth in probation has far outpaced other forms of criminal punishment and resulted in tremendous increases in expenditures. Since 1995, the adult probation population increased at a rate of 3.4% per year. Forty-nine percent of all probationers are serving a sentence upon conviction for a misdemeanor, 49% for a felony, and 1% for other infractions. Drug violators and persons convicted of drunk driving comprised 41% of the probation population.

About 57 percent of probationers successfully complete the terms of their sentence and 18 percent of clients are discharged from probation because they are incarcerated due to a rule violation of new criminal offense. Ten percent of probationers have their probation revoked without incarceration and 4 percent are revoked for absconding. Nationally, one in eleven probationers failed to report to their probation officer and cannot be located.[48]

History

Probation, Latin for "a period of proving or trial," began in 1841 and is credited as the invention of John Augustus, a Bostonian shoemaker of financial means who secured the release of a confirmed alcoholic arrested for being a "common drunk" by acting as surety for him. At sentencing, Augustus asked the judge to defer sentencing for three weeks and release the defendant to his custody. After three weeks, the offender convinced the judge of his rehabilitation and received a fine. The period of community correction alleviated the need for jail and probation was born. Until his death in 1859, Augustus bailed out 1,800 persons and was liable for nearly $250,000.

Augustus was selective as to who could be on his probationary caseload. The ideal candidate was a first-time offender for a non-serious charge who had moral character and demonstrated potential for reforming his or her criminal behavior. Augustus also developed the basic operating procedure of the modern probation system: conducting a pre-sentence investigation, mandating probation conditions, developing a caseload, reporting to the court, and revoking the sentence. In 1878, Massachusetts would become the first state to formally adopt probation for juveniles. All states would follow between 1878 and 1938. By 1956, all states and the federal system had adult probation.[49]

As described above, probation is today arguably the most important component, certainly the most versatile, of the criminal justice system. Similar to the way that recognizance release transformed the pretrial period, probation allowed for the offender of varying degrees of criminality to remain in the community and work toward their rehabilitation. Prior to the advent of probation, confinement was the de facto way to punish in the United States.

Administration and Caseloads

Unlike parole that is a state function administered by a single agency, probation is a local or state activity and is administered by 2,000 separate probationary agencies in the United States. Mark Cunniff and Ilene Bergsmann conducted a national assessment of probation in the United States. More than 30% of probation agencies provide both pretrial and post-adjudication services for both juvenile and adult offenders. Half of probation agencies are conjoined with parole services. Probation is a labor-intensive function. The preponderance of a probation officer's time is spent conducting a PSI and writing a report for the courts. Supervision of clients is also a central responsibility. Most probationers receive conditions of their sentence indeed nearly half have five or more conditions.[50] Usually probationers report to the office of their probation officer. Another important component of probation is the home visit in which the probation officer visits the domicile of the offender to ensure that the client is leading a crime-free life. According to a survey conducted by the American Probation and Parole Association, probation officers in 38 states or territories carry firearms primarily when conducting home visits.

The ways that probation services are administered varies greatly, especially considering the caseload of probation officers. A caseload is the roster of probationary clients that a single probation officer supervises. Douglas Thomas conducted a nationally representative survey of 1,197 probation administrators and found that caseloads ranged from less than ten to more than 400. The median caseload was 41 and the national average ranged from 100 to 175.[51] To put this into perspective, the Los Angeles County Probation Department has 900 line officers that supervise more than 90,000 adult and juvenile clients (it is the largest probation department in the world).

Immense caseloads are problematic in the sense that probation officers simply do not have the resources to adequately supervise, monitor, and provide treatment to their clients. Nationally, probation is woefully funded.

Although community correction service more than 70 percent of correctional clients, the services receive just 15 percent of state budgetary allocations. Interestingly, the research community has produced mixed findings about the effects of probation officer caseload on probationer recidivism. Robert Carter and Leslie Wilkins conducted the seminal San Francisco Project that compared the recidivism of four groups of probationers that varied between 20 and several hundred. After two years, all four groups had violation rates of about 25%, but offenders for officers with the highest caseload had dramatically higher violation rates. In other words, increased supervision increased the likelihood of detecting violations. Subsequent research has been mixed; however, the most current study found that as probation caseloads increased so did the crime rates of probationers.[52]

The Criminality of Probationers, Recidivism, and Noncompliance

Does probation work? This question is the central concern of criminal justice officials who rely on community corrections to balance the goals of public safety, rehabilitation, and a cost-effective managing government. The primary measure of success for probation is recidivism, or the rate that probationers re-offend within some specific time period, such as during their probationary sentence or one year after discharge. The success of probation is largely contingent on the criminality of the study group. For example, between 75 to 80% of offenders placed on probation successfully complete their sentence. This seems remarkable. However, the overwhelming majority of these successes are those who were convicted of misdemeanor offenses. Generally, misdemeanant probationers are persons for whom an isolated conviction for drunk driving constitutes their criminal record. As such, it is relatively easy for them to complete a probationary sentence. To the extent that there are some risk factors for further crime, probation can serve as an effective deterrent.

Unfortunately, the same story does not typify more serious offenders. By almost any measure, felony probationers are a group with pronounced criminal history, continued criminal involvement, and several overlapping problems that limit their likelihood of social adjustment. Based on data from a national survey of state prison inmates, Robyn Cohen of the Bureau of Justice Statistics found that 45% of state prisoners were on probation at the time of their most recent offense. Nationally, the 162,000 probation violators committed 6,400 murders, 7,400 rapes, 10,400 aggravated assaults, and 17,000 robberies while on probation. Nearly half were using drugs on a daily basis and about 20% were convicted of new firearms charges even though felons are proscribed from possessing weapons.[53]

Patrick Langan and Mark Cunniff analyzed the offending patterns of 79,000 probationers from 17 states. They found that within three years, 62% of probationers were either re-arrested for another felony or had a disciplinary hearing for violating the terms of their probation. Moreover, 46% were re-turned to jail or prison or absconded. Langan and Cunniff found that the modal felony probationer had multiple conditions to address his or her sub-stance abuse and mental health needs, and was responsible for restitution, supervision fees, and court costs. Less than half of probationers actually met these financial responsibilities.[54]

Many of the same risk factors emerged from studies based on more local-ized samples of probationers. Using data from Texas offenders, Patricia Har-ris, Rebecca Petersen, and Samantha Rapoza compared probation violators and probationers who were arrested for new offenses. Overall, they found that 60% violated the conditions of their probation and 40% were re-arrested (one third of which for a felony offense). Perhaps more troubling was the behavioral history of these probationers. For instance, 41% had a history of armed or assaultive crimes, 63% had criminal companions, 63% had employ-ment problems, 74% had educational deficits, and nearly 40% had previously been confined or placed on community supervision.[55] Using data on proba-tioners from Michigan, Roni Mayzer, Kevin Gray, and Sheila Royo Maxwell found that probation absconders and violators were noteworthy for their poor "stake in conformity" evidenced by unstable employment history, frequent changes in residency, and lower educational attainment.[56] Using the criminal records of 1,672 felony probationers in southern California, Joan Petersilia and her colleagues found that 65% were re-arrested, 51% were reconvicted, and 34% were re-incarcerated within a three-year follow-up period.[57]

To summarize, how well probation "works" depends largely on the crimi-nality of the study group. Low-level offenders such as those on misdemeanor probation tend to perform well on probation, indeed upwards of 80% suc-cessfully complete their sentence. Among felony probations, between 30 to 40% remain crime free in follow-up periods after their discharge from proba-tion. Probation success stories are offenders who reintegrate and reattach, or commit for the first time, to conventional social institutions, such as employ-ment, marriage and family, and sobriety. For those who fail on probation, there is little to no attachment to these conventional institutions and instead a reverting to what is habitual criminal behavior.[58]

The Future of Probation

The costs of supervising a felon on probation are ten to fifteen times less expensive than prison. The costs of ISP are approximately 150% higher than standard probation but still dramatically cheaper than prison. For no other reason than these sheer differences in costs, probation will continue to grow the correctional population.[59] Because probation is such a "break" compared to incarceration, many defendants willingly accept plea-bargains with pro-bationary sentences. Without the availability of probation, many offenders would opt for trials, which would secure far fewer convictions than pleas.

Consequently, probation is a vital cog in the criminal justice system because it is a middle-ground sanction for minimum-, medium-, and high-risk criminals.[60] In their overview of ISP Edward Latessa and his colleagues acknowledged that although ISP has neither greatly alleviated prison crowding nor greatly reduced recidivism, it is a more effective form of punishment than prison in the sense that it delivers more treatment and reduces system costs.[61]

Beyond the cost-savings, probation does work for some offenders, even high-risk felons with multiple problems. A recurrent theme in the criminological literature is that probationary systems that combine a law enforcement and treatment function tend to work better than probation policies that serve as a proxy for the police. Paul Gendreau, Frank Cullen, and James Bonta have argued that the next generation of probation and intermediate sanctions generally could be described as "intensive rehabilitation supervision" since the blending of treatment/social work and punishment yields the most fruit when supervising offenders in the community.[62]

PAROLE

General Information and Definitions

Parole is a method of completing a prison sentence in the community rather than in confinement. A paroled offender can legally be recalled to prison to serve the remainder of the sentence if he or she does not comply with the conditions of parole. Parole conditions are similar to probation conditions as parolees are expected to seek or maintain employment, attend mental health counseling or therapy, participate in substance abuse treatment, be subject to drug tests, avoid contact with victims in their case, and avoid contact with other negative influences such as felons or fellow gang members (if applicable). More than 80% of parolees have various conditions by which they must abide. Two types of parole exist. Discretionary parole occurs where parole boards have the discretionary authority to conditionally released prisoners based on a statutory or administrative determination of eligibility. Mandatory parole occurs in jurisdictions using determinate sentencing statutes (e.g., conviction for Class B felony is 25 years) where inmates are conditionally released from prison after serving a portion of their original sentences minus any good time earned.[63]

Parole plays three critical roles in the criminal justice system. First, parole boards determine the actual length of prison sentences once an offender has served the minimum term of his or her sentence. On a case-by-case basis, the parole board determines whether a prisoner is ready to be released into the community. In this sense, the parole board, an executive branch agency, has considerable oversight on the judiciary. Second, parole agencies supervise probationers and therefore oversee the reintegration of returning prisoners. Third, parole boards and parole officers are authorized to revoke parolee sentences if they are not in compliance. In this sense, parole serves an important crime control function by removing high-risk criminal offenders from the community once it is clear that they are recidivistic and non-compliant.[64]

The primary distinction between parole and all of the other forms of community corrections is that parolees are placed in the community after serving time in prison. Conversely, other intermediate sanctions place offenders in the community in lieu of prison.[65] Parole shares the same nomenclature as probation. For instance, parole officers supervise parolees, monitor them for parole violations, and have the authority to revoke parole. There is one important difference. Parole is always a state function that is administered by one executive department per state.

To many, parole is the most serious form of community corrections because of the criminality of the population. Unlike probationers, half of whom were simply convicted of misdemeanors, parolees are all convicted felons who have served time in prison. Parolees are the most high-risk group of correctional clients. Because of this, the parole board, the administrative board that is empowered to grant parole, must be mindful of crime control when deciding which inmates to grant another opportunity for redemption.

Historical Background

The history of parole in the United States can be understood by following the penal history of New York State. In the early Nineteenth Century, judges sentenced inmates to flat, determinate sentences, such as 30 years. Due to the inflexibility of these sentences, governors were forced to grant mass pardons to alleviate prison crowding. In 1817, New York introduced the nation's first "good time" law that rewarded prison inmates with time off their period of imprisonment for good behavior. In 1876, Zebulon Brockway, a penologist and superintendent of the Elmira Reformatory created parole and the indeterminate sentence whereby judges set a minimum and maximum term and permitted parole release of those who had served the minimum. Both of Brockway's innovations were predicated on the belief that criminals could be reformed and that their punishment and correction should be individualized to fit the diversity of the criminal population. In 1930, the Division of Parole was established in the Executive Department and a Board of Parole was created within the Division and given the responsibility, formerly held by the Department of Corrections, for decisions on parole releases from prisons.[66] From the late Nineteenth Century through the first decades of the Twentieth Century, the other states followed the lead of New York and revamped their own sentencing structure and correctional approach to include indeterminate sentencing and parole.

CRIME SCENE   DO NOT CROSS

CRIMINAL JUSTICE QUESTION

DOES FEDERAL PAROLE EXIST?

Parole in the federal criminal justice system has a convoluted history. Federal parole was enacted in 1910, and three parole boards consisting of the warden of the federal institution (three federal penitentiaries exited in 1910), the physician in the institution, and the Superintendent of Prisons of the Department of Justice. A single federal Board of Parole was created in 1930. In 1976, the United States Parole Commission was established after the passage of the Parole Commission and Reorganization Act. The Comprehensive Crime Control Act of 1984 created the United States Sentencing Commission to establish sentencing guidelines for the federal courts and a regime of determinate sentences. These sentencing guidelines took effect on November 1, 1987, thus defendants sentenced on or after that date served determinate terms and were not eligible for parole consideration. For all intents and purposes, federal parole was abolished in 1987 and federal correctional clients who were not in a Bureau of Prison facility were dubbed "supervised releases."

Due to federal offenders who were sentenced prior to November 1, 1987, the United States Parole Commission has been unable to be legally phased out. Federal parole has been extended via the Judicial Improvements Act of 1990, the Parole Commission Phase-out Act of 1996, and the Twenty-first Century Department of Justice Appropriations Authorization Act of 2002. Once the final federal offender sentenced before 11/01/87 terminates his or her case, federal parole will end. Ultimately, the United States Probation and Pretrial Services System monitors all federal supervised release clients.

Photo © 2011, bouzou, Shutterstock, Inc.

Perhaps more than any other form of criminal punishment, parole has been the most susceptible to fluctuations in public opinion regarding the twin goals of crime control and due process. From its inception, parole was hailed as a mechanism to both permit criminal offenders an opportunity for reform and cost-effectively reduce the prison population. Over time, however, both crime control and due process enthusiasts grew tired of parole because the sanction was neither providing the necessary treatment or correction to reform criminals nor were criminals serving meaningful terms behind bars. Due to indeterminate sentencing and parole, there was little truth-in-sentencing. Indeed, the recent changes in how parole is administered demonstrate how susceptible it is to political pressure. For instance, between 1980 and 2000, the discretionary parole release rate remained relatively constant. During the same period, mandatory parole releases increased 500%.[67] In other words, the discretionary freedom of parole boards has been severely curtailed, and these tensions continue to surround parole to the present day.

Statistical Snapshot

There are nearly 820,000 persons on parole in the United States. Since 1995, the parole population has increased by 1 to 2% annually. About 52% of parolees were released as a result of mandatory parole or via good-time provisions and 35% were released by discretionary parole. One out of every 284 adults is on parole. Fifty-one percent of adults successfully completed parole in 2009, meaning that nearly half failed. Among the parole failures, 34% were returned to prison, 9% absconded, and 1% of parolees died.[68]

As shown in Figure 10-3, there has been a pronounced shift in state parole policies away from discretionary release by parole boards in favor of determinate sentences and mandatory supervised release. Timothy Hughes, Doris Wilson, and Allen Beck reported that by 2000, sixteen states (Arizona, California, Delaware, Florida, Illinois, Indiana, Kansas, Maine, Minnesota, Mississippi, North Carolina, Ohio, Oregon, Virginia, Washington, and Wisconsin) had abolished discretionary parole for all offenders. Certain violent offenders were denied discretionary parole in Alaska, Louisiana, New York, and Tennessee. Also by 2000, 35 states and the District of Columbia had adopted the federal truth-in-sentencing standard that requires Part I violent offenders to serve at least 85 percent of their sentence before they are eligible for parole. By adopting this standard, states received federal funds under the Violent Offender Incarceration and Truth-in-Sentencing (VOITIS) incentive grant program established by the 1994 Crime Act.[69]

Criminal History of Parolees

In their national assessment of parole for the Bureau of Justice Statistics, Timothy Wilson and his colleagues documented that parolees often have extensive criminal histories. Fifty-six percent had previously served time in prison before their most recent parole release. Among these recidivists, 10% had two prior incarcerations, 15% had three to five priors, and more than 10% of parolees had been imprisoned six or more times. About 55% of parolees were already being supervised by the criminal justice system, mostly parole and probation, when they were most recently convicted and imprisoned. Parolees demonstrate additional serious risk factors: nearly 85% of parolees had drugs and alcohol involved at the time of their most recent offense, 14% were mentally ill, nearly 12% were homeless, and 51% had less than a high school education. Finally, more than 45% of parolees were classified as re-releases, which means that they were most recently imprisoned for parole violation or a new offense committed while on parole.[70] Obviously, the average profile of a parolee contains several risk factors, which suggest that rehabilitation will be difficult if unlikely. By the same token, these risk factors indicate that recidivism will be expected, if not a certainty.

Parole Success and Failure

Parole is successful for an offender who manages to abide by the conditions of his or her sentence for the specified parole period and does not get re-arrested. Overall, only 51% of parolees successfully complete their sentence. Success rates are largely contingent on type and method of release. Among inmates facing their first release on parole, 64% succeed; among inmates facing re-release on parole, just 21% succeed. Inmates who received discretionary release by parole boards had a success rate of 54%; those released via mandatory parole had a 33% success rate. The lowest success rate, 17%, was found among offenders that had received mandatory re-release.[71]

Offender reintegration, the successful commitment and reattachment to conventional (non-criminal) life by a former offender, is the operating principle that determines whether a parolee succeeds or fails after release from prison. In many respects, an offender's rehabilitation and ultimate re-integration begins in prison, evidenced by the significantly higher success rates among parolees who were released at the discretion of the parole board. Parole boards consider a variety of factors, such as the inmate's involvement in work, educational, and other correctional programming, infraction history, substance abuse history, gang involvement, criminal and incarceration history, social support, and the inmate's parole plan, when deciding to grant conditional release. Inmates who appear ready to reconnect to conventional society and repudiate their criminal past are likely those who will be given the opportunity.

The flipside of reintegration is parole failure evidenced by absconding, failure to abide by parole conditions, or resumed criminal activity and re-arrest. The predictors of parole failure are largely the opposite of the predictors of success. Offenders who recidivate and are returned to prison are those who have no stake in conformity, meaning they are unemployed, do not participate in treatment, have no social support, and, of course, continue to run afoul of the law.[72]

Collateral Problems of Parole

All intermediate sanctions entail the uphill challenge of criminal offenders working toward their rehabilitation. The preponderance of felons has a multitude of problems that make their treatment very difficult for them to improve their life chances. Offenders themselves readily admit this. The same applies to parole; however, only parole contains offenders who were recently incarcerated. In addition to the stigma of prison, parolees must maneuver the difficult transition from an environment characterized by violence, malaise, and disease to life on the outside. For others, prison and correctional statuses are badges of honor in lives that reflect pronounced and habitual antisocial behavior. For the most intractable and dangerous criminal offenders, prison and death are the ultimate punishments. These two penalties are explored next in Chapters 11 and 12.

CHAPTER SUMMARY: BALANCING CRIME CONTROL AND DUE PROCESS

- Intermediate sanctions or community corrections are cost-effective ways to supervise and provide treatment for criminal offenders in lieu of jail or prison confinement.
- Prior criminal history, offense seriousness, number of criminal charges/convictions, and an offender's stake in conformity are the primary variables that explain placement in community corrections, sentence revocation, and parole.
- Differences in community corrections largely reflect variations in the criminality of the offender population, for example unsupervised through intensive supervised probation.
- Upwards of 70% of the correctional population is supervised in the community.
- All community corrections must balance law enforcement and social work functions to achieve crime control and due process goals.
- Even if intermediate sanctions do not meaningfully reduce recidivism, they are beneficial because of their low costs compared to incarceration.
- Sanctions that "work" tend to provide treatment and punishment that promote offenders' conventional attitudes and behaviors while reducing antisocial attitudes and behaviors.
- Probation impacts all aspects of the criminal justice process, including investigation, adjudication, and corrections.
- Parole is the most severe form of community supervision because of the criminality of the offenders and because clients were recently imprisoned.

KEY TERMS

Abscond	Halfway Houses/Residential
Automated probation	Treatment
Boot Camps/Shock Incarceration	Home Detention/House Arrest
Caseload	Intermediate sanctions
Community corrections	ISP
Community Service	Mandatory parole
Conditions	Net widening
Criminality	Parole
Day Reporting	Parole board
Deferred Prosecution, Judgment, or	Probation
Sentence	PSI
Discretionary parole	Reintegration
Electronic Monitoring	Restitution
Expiration of sentence	Revocation
Fines	Technical violation
Forfeiture	Unsupervised probation

TALKING POINTS

1. The placement of offenders on community corrections could be likened to fishing: small fish are sent back and only big fish are kept. Using risk and protective factors as evidence, what types of offenders are perceived by the criminal justice system as small and big fish?

2. Should parole be abolished? What would be the effects of such a policy? In terms of crime control, how could the abolishment of parole reduce crime rates?

3. Fines, restitution, and forfeiture are monetary forms of punishment. Should wealthy criminal defendants be forced to pay greater fines and restitution in lieu of punishment? Would this be discriminatory against the non-poor?

4. Is forfeiture an appropriate sanction or a slippery slope toward governmental exploitation? How might crime control and due process advocates debate this?

5. What is criminality? Which factors have deterrent or punishment value for persons with low criminality? High criminality? Should the criminal justice system exclusively focus on offenders with the highest criminality? Discuss.

WEB LINKS

American Correctional Association
(www.aca.org)

American Probation and Parole Association
(www.appa-net.org)

Bureau of Justice Statistics Homepage
(www.ojp.usdoj.gov/bjs/welcome.html)

National Criminal Justice Reference Service
(www.ncjrs.gov)

The Official Home of Corrections
(www.probation.com)

FURTHER READING

Bureau of Justice Statistics. (Various years). *National Corrections Reporting Program (NCRP); Annual Parole Survey; National Prisoners Statistics (NPS-1); Survey of Inmates in State and Federal Correctional Facilities, 1991 and 1997.* These assorted projects provide the data for correctional clients and statisticians in the BJS produce many concise and informative reports. BJS publications are must-read material for any criminologist, expert, or student.

Carter, R. M., & Wilkins, L. T. (1970). *Probation and parole: Selected readings.* New York: John Wiley & Sons. This anthology of studies contains some of the earliest criminological investigations of probation and parole. The editors are legends in the field of penology.

Glaser, D. (1964). *The effectiveness of a prison and parole system.* Indianapolis: Bobs-Merrill. This classic work was one of the first to study prisoner characteristics as they related to recidivism and parole success/failure. Glaser's work helped motivate the use of actuarial parole decisions and is still cited today.

Travis, J., & Visher, C. (2005). *Prisoner reentry and crime in America.* New York: Cambridge University Press. This excellent anthology contains a series of chapters that explore the difficulties of rehabilitation, the interchange between confinement and community supervision, and collateral issues relating to prisoners returning to society.

CHAPTER 11

Prison

CHAPTER OUTLINE

QUOTATIONS

"While society in the United States gives the example of the most extended liberty, the prisons of the same country offer the spectacle of the most complete despotism."—*Gustave de Beaumont and Alexis de Tocqueville*[1]

"With few and isolated exceptions, the rehabilitative efforts that have been reported so far have had no appreciable effect on recidivism."—*Robert Martinson*[2]

"The nation has invested billions of dollars into locking up offenders. The policies around reentry have become increasingly an avoidance of risk. As a result, we have created a revolving door of offenders who will be committed to prison time and again as they fail in the community."—*Richard Seiter and Karen Kadela*[3]

"The general public has begun to realize that many adult offenders lack the social skills necessary to become successful, contributing members of their communities."—*David Allender*[4]

"The prison experience has historically been meant to be unpleasant, and prisoners have been expected to suffer to some degree."—*Craig Hemmens and James Marquart*[5]

"Most of the racial disproportionality in prison admissions results from differential involvement in crimes by Blacks and Whites."—*Jon Sorensen, Robert Hope, and Don Stemen*[6]

"There is little reason to believe that habitual criminals with extensive arrest and incarceration experience will suddenly 'behave' while imprisoned." —*Matt DeLisi*[7]

INTRODUCTION

With the possible exception of the police, no other area of the criminal justice system has inspired as much public interest, political wrangling, and academic study as prisons. Indeed, prisons and the state of the prisoner population have meaningful implications for both crime control and due process. To crime control advocates, prisons are good because the most serious criminal offenders, or at least persons convicted of the most serious criminal offenses, are removed from conventional society. As such, prisons literally incapacitate the most serious criminals' (unless, of course, the offender escapes) opportunity to victimize others. Moreover, roughly 30% of prisoners seem to "learn their lesson" and do not recidivate after release from custody. Prisoners who are able to reform their behavior tend to reattach and re-commitment themselves to conventional social institutions, such as family, work, church, or military. Many former prisoners receive substantive counseling and treatment for substance abuse problems, mental illness, and other personal problems. Prison treatment amenities facilitate their rehabilitation.

Crime control proponents also have at least three reasons to be dissatisfied with prisons. First and foremost, the recidivism rates among ex-prisoners (discussed later in this chapter) are approximately 70%. Although prisons effectively incapacitate offenders, most do not commit themselves to rehabilitation. In this sense, the crime control capacity of prison confinement is short-lived. Second, prison is the most expensive form of social control and, as described above, does little to reduce offending patterns among most prisoners.

Third, there is evidence that incarceration and mere exposure to incarceration actually exacerbates inmates' antisocial attitudes and behaviors, which results in higher rates of recidivism after release. Consider the example of Scared Straight programs. Created in 1979 at the Rahway State Prison in New Jersey, Scared Straight programs feature an aggressive presentation of prison life by inmates serving life sentences to at-risk and adjudicated juvenile delinquents. The inmates harangue the youthful offenders, use shocking street language and profanity, and intimidate the youths in hopes that the deterrence program will literally "scare" the youths into renouncing their delinquency and leading productive lives. Scared Straight programs remain very popular among the general public.

Unfortunately, the programs do not work. In fact, instead of controlling crime, they tend to increase it. Anthony Petrosino, Carolyn Turpin-Petrosino, and John Buehler conducted a systematic review of Scared Straight programs and found that youths who went through the program had higher rates of offenders than youths who did not. In their words, "on average these programs result in an increase in criminality in the experimental group when compared to a no-treatment control. According to these experiments, doing nothing would have been better than exposing juveniles to the program."[8]

Due process-oriented persons often have more cause for alarm when considering prisons. However, the majority of this concern does not deal with fundamental due process rights that have been discussed throughout this text. Instead, the due process concern is more an overtly liberal concern about the salience of prisons in American life, particularly as prisons have impacted the poor and racial minorities. As shown in Figure 11-1, there has been a 400% increase in the imprisonment rate since 1980. To many, the dramatic increase in the use of imprisonment, and the inequalities or disparities of imprisonment by race, suggest a fundamentally unfair American society. To others, disparities in imprison reflect real differences in criminal offending. This controversy is explored in Box 11-1.

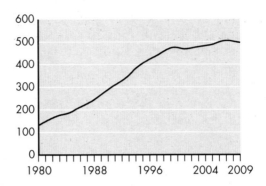

FIGURE 11-1 Imprisonment Rate, 1980–2009

Source: Bureau of Justice Statistics. (2011). Key facts at a glance. Accessed March 1, 2011, from http://bjs.ojp.usdoj.gov/content/glance/incrt.cfm.

Finally, another criminal justice controversy pertains to the *types* of offenders that are subjected to incarceration. A popular viewpoint is that many drug offenders should not be incarcerated because they are benign criminals who require treatment, not punishment, to overcome their substance abuse problem. The assorted myths, rhetoric, and evidence about incarcerated drug offenders are explored in Box 11-2. In the end, crime control and due process advocates can agree about one thing: Prisons are an exciting and controversial subject matter in criminal justice.

HISTORY OF AMERICAN PRISONS

Overview and Major Themes
Although confinement has existed in Western societies for centuries, prisons as they are understood today are considered an American invention. At their inception, prisons, then symbolically known as penitentiaries, were hailed as an outgrowth of the Enlightenment in which criminal offenders were confined and expected to contemplate their criminal behavior and work toward their rehabilitation and ultimate redemption. Indeed, inmates were expected to be penitent, defined as feeling or expressing remorse for one's misdeeds or sins. As such, the penitentiary was designed as a place for criminals to repent. Throughout American history, prisons have reflected the social conditions of the day. Early prisons reflected the intense religiosity of the colonial era. Modern prisons reflect the pragmatic goals of incapacitation, crime control, and due process. Prisons have always been controversial and, like the history of the police, been marked by periods of reform. This section briefly highlights the social history of American prisons.

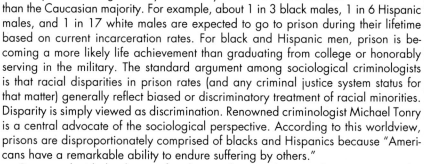

CRIME SCENE   DO NOT CROSS

BOX 11-1

CRIMINAL JUSTICE CONTROVERSY

RACE, DISPROPORTIONATE MINORITY CONFINEMENT, AND PRISON

A major controversy in criminal justice centers on the racial and ethnic composition of the prisoner population. African Americans and Hispanics are significantly more likely to ever be incarcerated than the Caucasian majority. For example, about 1 in 3 black males, 1 in 6 Hispanic males, and 1 in 17 white males are expected to go to prison during their lifetime based on current incarceration rates. For black and Hispanic men, prison is becoming a more likely life achievement than graduating from college or honorably serving in the military. The standard argument among sociological criminologists is that racial disparities in prison rates (and any criminal justice system status for that matter) generally reflect biased or discriminatory treatment of racial minorities. Disparity is simply viewed as discrimination. Renowned criminologist Michael Tonry is a central advocate of the sociological perspective. According to this worldview, prisons are disproportionately comprised of blacks and Hispanics because "Americans have a remarkable ability to endure suffering by others."

Contrasted with the theory of widespread criminal justice discrimination is the argument that racial differences in imprisonment reflect actual differences in criminal offending by various racial groups. Criminologists have produced compelling evidence to support this view using methodologically rigorous methods and nationally representative data. Alfred Blumstein found that 80 percent of the prison racial gap was directly explained by the greater black involvement in crimes such as murder and robbery. Blumstein found zero evidence of discrimination. Patrick Langan found that 85% of the prison racial gap was accounted for by higher offending levels among blacks. Scholars at the Vera Institute of Justice found that violent crime by blacks explained 110% of murder, 84% of rape, and 88% of robbery prison admissions. Finally, Robert Crutchfield, George Bridges, and Susan Pitchford found that 90% of the prison racial gap was accounted for by higher crimes rates by blacks.

Sources: Bonczar, T. P. (2003). *Prevalence of imprisonment in the U. S. population, 1974–2001*. Washington, DC: U. S. Department of Justice; Pettit, B., & Western, B. (2004). Mass imprisonment and the life course: Race and class inequality in United States incarceration. *American Sociological Review, 69,* 151–169; Huebner, B. M. (2005). The effect of incarceration on marriage and work over the life course. *Justice Quarterly, 22,* 281–303; Tonry, M. (1994). Racial disproportion in US prisons. *British Journal of Criminology, 34,* 97–115, p. 113; Pratt, T. C. (1998). Race and sentencing: A meta-analysis of conflicting empirical research results. *Journal of Criminal Justice, 26,* 513–523; Blumstein, A. (1982). On the racial disproportionality of United States' prison populations. *Journal of Criminal Law & Criminology, 73,* 1259–1281; Langan, P. A. (1985). Racism on trial: New evidence to explain the racial composition of prisons in the United States. *Journal of Criminal Law & Criminology, 76,* 666–683; Sorensen, J., Hope, R., & Stemen, D. (2003). Racial disproportionality in state prison admissions: Can regional variation be explained by differential arrest rates? *Journal of Criminal Justice, 31,* 73–84; Crutchfield, R. D., Bridges, G. S., & Pitchford, S. R. (1994). Analytical and aggregation biases in analyses of imprisonment: Reconciling discrepancies in studies of racial disparity. *Journal of Research in Crime and Delinquency, 31,* 166–182. Photo © JupiterImages, Corp.

BOX 11-2

CRIME SCENE   DO NOT CROSS

CRIMINAL JUSTICE CONTROVERSY

WHO'S REALLY IN PRISON FOR DRUGS?

It is widely argued, even among criminologists, that the criminal justice system has devoted far too many resources to supervise and punish non-violent drug offenders. To the degree that drug offenders, who are purported to be neither dangerous nor recidivistic, displace violent offenders and habitual criminals, punishing drug offenders is bad policy. How many drug offenders are in prison, and what do they look like?

The available evidence indicates that the idea of the benign drug offenders is largely a myth. The vast majority of drug prisoners are violent criminals, chronic offenders, traffickers, or all of these. According to a recent report by the Office of National Drug Control Policy, less than one percent of state prisoners were confined with marijuana possession as their only charge. Moreover, few (0.3%) of these criminals were first time offenders. Among federal inmates, only 63 persons actually served time behind bars for marijuana possession.

Among those convicted of selling drugs, the average amount of marijuana among federal inmates was 6,000 pounds. Matt DeLisi found that non-violent drug offenders were significantly likely to also be arrested for violent Index, property Index, and public-order crimes. This profile is in direct opposition to the popular view that drug violators are non-criminals who are unfairly embroiled in the criminal justice system. Matthew Durose and Christopher Mumola studied the criminal histories of nonviolent offenders, mostly persons convicted of drug crimes, existing state prisons. They found that these "benign" offenders averaged more than nine arrests and four prior convictions. More than 30% had prior arrests for violent crimes and 20% reported that they had previously been convicted of a violent crime.

Finally, the criminal justice system does two rather extraordinary things to *remove* drug offenders from the prison system. First, federal district courts can grant reductions in federal prison sentences for offenders who provide "substantial assistance" to the government. Nearly 70% of these reductions were for drug offenders and the average amount of the reduction in sentence was about 40%. Second, inmates in the BOP can be released via "extraordinary release," such as having their sentence commuted or their conviction vacated. However, 60% of extraordinary releases were for federal offenders who successfully completed a drug treatment program. Based on the evidence, it appears that the criminal justice system goes to considerable lengths to exclude drug offenders from prison.

Sources: Robinson, J. (2005). *Who's really in prison for marijuana?* Washington, DC: Office of National Drug Control Policy; DeLisi, M. (2003). The imprisoned nonviolent drug offender: Specialized martyr or versatile career criminal? *American Journal of Criminal Justice, 27,* 167–182; Durose, M. R., & Mumola, C. J. (2004). *Profile of nonviolent offenders existing state prisons.* Washington, DC: U. S. Department of Justice, Office of Justice Programs, Bureau of Justice Statistics; Sabol, W. J., & McGready, J. (1999). *Time served in prison by federal offenders, 1986–1997.* Washington, DC: U. S. Department of Justice, Office of Justice Programs, Bureau of Justice Statistics. *Photo © JupiterImages, Corp.*

The Colonial Era, Pennsylvania System, and Auburn System

The colonial American criminal justice system was rooted in the English common law tradition in which most criminal offenses were punishable by death and corporal punishment, including torture and mutilation, were considered appropriate punishments of criminals. When criminals were detained, they were kept in municipal jails that were characterized by squalor, the inappropriate mixing of men, women, children, and criminals of diverse criminality, and brutal administrative control.[9]

Led by William Penn, the Pennsylvania Quakers were dissatisfied with the abuses of these early forms of confinement and initiated reforms of the colonial approach to correction in which physical punishment would be replaced by isolation. In 1787, Benjamin Franklin and Dr. Benjamin Rush (among other distinguished citizens) organized The Philadelphia Society for Alleviating the Miseries of Public Prisons, which mobilized the Commonwealth of Pennsylvania to set the international standard in prison design. It took decades to convince state leaders of the superiority of such an approach, but would culminate in the Eastern State Penitentiary that opened in 1829.

Eastern State Penitentiary was the most expensive American building of its day (it had running water and central heat before the White House), one of the most famous buildings in the world, and a major tourist attraction. As described earlier, the function of the Penitentiary was not simply to punish, but to move the criminal toward spiritual reflection and change. The Quaker-inspired system involved total isolation from other prisoners, labor in solitary confinement, and strictly enforced silence. The social control was extraordinarily strict, for instance inmates were hooded whenever they were outside their cells. Theoretically, the forced silence and extreme isolation would cause criminals to think about the wrongfulness of their crimes and become genuinely penitent.[10]

As a punishment philosophy, the Pennsylvania System was developed in the Eighteenth Century. However, the Auburn System began in 1816 with the opening of the Auburn Prison in New York—13 years before the opening of Eastern State Penitentiary. Although heavily influenced and similar to the Pennsylvania System, the Auburn System was a congregate system in which inmates ate and worked together during the day and were kept in solitary confinement at night with enforced silence at all times. The Auburn System was viewed as more humanistic in the sense that it replaced the systemic use of solitary confinement. But the Auburn System also employed the lockstep (inmates marching in single file, placing the right hand on the shoulder of the man ahead, and facing toward the guard), the striped suit, two-foot extensions of the walls between cells, and special seating arrangements at meals to insure strict silence. Auburn also introduced the tier system with several floors or wings that have stacked cells over another and classified (and punished) inmates by their level of compliance. By the 1830s, the Auburn System generally replaced the Pennsylvania System, which was discontinued as a prison approach by 1913.

The Reformatory Movement

During the Jacksonian Era spanning the first several decades of the Nineteenth Century, there was dissatisfaction with American prisons that essentially revolved around the perennial goals of crime control and due process. Upon visiting Eastern State Penitentiary in 1842, Charles Dickens wrote, "I hold this slow and daily tampering with the mysteries of the brain to be immeasurably worse than any torture of the body." In other words, the methods of correction inherent in the Pennsylvania and Auburn Systems were viewed as cruel, counterproductive, and flagrantly in violation of basic tenets of human, civil, and due process rights.

There was also the widespread public belief that crime threatened the stability and order of society, and prisons appeared to be doing little to reduce the crime rate. Even in the middle Nineteenth Century, the general public considered prisons as mere holding stations, regardless of how innovative their design, until criminals were released to offend again. Edgardo Rotman described the state of American prisons as follows:

> The elements of the original penitentiary designed, based on regimentation, isolation, religious conversion, and stead labor, had been subverted by a pervasive over-crowding, corruption, and cruelty. Prisoners were often living three and four to a cell designed for one, and prison discipline was medieval-like in character, with bizarre and brutal punishments commonplace in state institutions. Wardens did not so much deny this awful reality as explain it away, attributing most of the blame not to those who administered the system but to those who experienced it. Because the prisons were filled with immigrants who were ostensibly hardened to a life of crime and impervious to American traditions, those in charge had no choice but to rule over inmates with an iron hand.[11]

These concerns did not go unnoticed. The New York Prison Association commissioned Enoch Cobb Wines and Theodore Dwight to conduct a national survey of prisons and correctional methods. Inspired by their report, the National Congress on Penitentiary and Reformatory Discipline met in October 1870 in Cincinnati, Ohio and established principles of modern, humanistic correctional theory and practice (see Box 11-3). One of the most famous practitioners who placed the reformatory theory into practice was Zebulon Brockway (you may recall Brockway as the innovator of parole and indeterminate sentencing from Chapter 10). Brockway, who was warden of the Elmira (New York) Reformatory, infused educational programs, vocational training, an administrative and operating system based on military discipline, and a humanistic orientation to American corrections.[12]

BOX 11-3

CRIME SCENE   DO NOT CROSS

CRIMINAL JUSTICE HISTORY

PRINCIPLES FROM THE 1870 NATIONAL CONGRESS ON PENITENTIARY AND REFORMATORY DISCIPLINE

WANTED
DEAD OR ALIVE

REWARD 1.000.000$

   I. Punishment is inflicted on the criminal in expiation of the wrong done, and especially with a view to prevent his relapse by reformation.

   II. Treatment is directed at the criminal and his new birth to respect for the laws.

   III. Practice shall conform to theory and the process of public punishment be made in fact, as well as pretense, a process of reformation.

   IV. A progressive classification should be established and include at least three stages: a penal stage, a reformatory stage, and a probationary stage worked on some mark system where they earn promotion, gaining at each successive step, increased comfort and privilege.

   V. Since hope is a more potent agent than fear, rewards more than punishments are essential to every good prison system.

   VI. The prisoner's destiny during his incarceration should be put in his own hands.

   VII. The two master forces opposed to the reform of the prison systems are political appointments and instability of administration.

  VIII. Prison officers need a special education for their work, special training schools should be instituted for them and prison administration should be raised to the dignity of a profession.

   IX. Sentences limited only by satisfactory proof of reformation should be substituted for those measured by mere lapse of time.

   X. Of all the reformatory agencies religion is the first in importance.

   XI. Education is a matter of primary importance in prisons.

   XII. No prison can be made a school of reform until there is, on the part of officers, a hearty desire and intention to accomplish this effect.

  XIII. There must be a serious conviction in the minds of prison officers that the imprisoned criminals are capable of being reformed.

  XIV. A system of prison reform must gain the will of the convict.

  XV. The interest of society and the interest of the convicted criminal are really identical. Society is best served by saving its criminal members.

  XVI. The prisoner's self-respect should be cultivated.

 XVII. In prison administration moral forces should be relied upon with as little mixture of physical force as possible.

XVIII. Steady honorable labor is the basis of all reformatory discipline. It not only aids information, it is essential to it.

  XIX. It is important that criminals be trained while in prison to the practice and love of labor.

  XX. We regard the contract system of prison labor as prejudicial—alike to discipline, finance and reformation.

  XXI. The stage of conditional leave is problematic to administer but we believe Yankee ingenuity is competent to devise some method of practical application among separate jurisdictions and the vast reach of our territory.

Photo © Yanta, 2011, Shutterstock, Inc.

BOX 11–3 (Continued)

CRIME SCENE   DO NOT CROSS

XXII. Prisons, as well as prisoners, should be classified or graded. There shall be prisons for the untried; prisons for young criminals; prisons for women; for misdemeanants; male felons; and the incorrigible.

XXIII. It is believed that repeated short sentences are worse than useless.

XXIV. Greater use should be made of the social principal in prison discipline than is now. The criminal must be prepared for society in society.

XXV. Public preventative institutions for the treatment of children constitute a true field of promise in which to labor for the repression of crime.

XXVI. More systematic and comprehensive methods should be adopted to serve discharged prisoners. Having raised him up, it has the further duty to aid in holding him up.

XXVII. The successful prosecution of crime requires the combined action of capital and labor.

XXVIII. It is plainly the duty of society to indemnify the citizen who has been unjustly imprisoned.

XXIX. Our laws regarding insanity and its relationship to crime need revision.

XXX. Does society take all the steps it easily might to change, or at least improve, the circumstances in our social state that thus lead to crime?

XXXI. The exercise of executive clemency is one of grave importance, and at the same time of great delicacy and difficulty.

XXXII. The proper duration for imprisonment for a violation of the laws of society is one of the most perplexing questions in criminal jurisprudence.

XXXIII. The establishment of a National Prison Bureau or a National Prison Discipline Society is recommended.

XXXIV. We declare our belief that the education and self-respect of the convict would be served by the establishment of a weekly newspaper to enable him to keep pace with passing events.

XXXV. Prison architecture is a matter of grave importance. The proper size of prisons is a point of much interest. In our judgment 300 inmates are enough to form the population of a single prison; and, in no case, would we have the number exceed five or six hundred.

XXXVI. The organization and construction of prisons should be by the state.

XXXVII. As a general rule, the maintenance of all penal institutions, above the county jail, should be from the earnings of their inmates, and without cost to the state.

XXXVIII. A right application of the principles of sanitary science in the construction and arrangements of prisons is another point of vital importance.

XXXVIX. The principle of the pecuniary responsibility of parents for the full or partial support of their criminal children in reformatory institutions, extensively applied in Europe, has been found to work well in practice.

XL. It is our intimate convictions that one of the most effective agencies in the repression of crime would be the enactment of laws, by which the education of all the children of the state should be made obligatory.

XLI. It is our conviction that no prison system can be perfect or successful to the most desirable extent, without some central and supreme authority to sit at the helm, guiding, controlling, unifying, and vitalizing the whole.

Bureau of Prisons (BOP)

Another important correctional innovation was the development of a formalized federal prison system. In 1930, the Bureau of Prisons was established within the Department of Justice and charged with the management and regulation of all Federal penal and correctional institutions. This responsibility covered the administration of the 11 Federal prisons in operation at the time. At the end of 1930, the agency operated 14 facilities and over 13,000 inmates. By 1940, the BOP had grown to 24 facilities with 24,360 inmates. Except for a few fluctuations, the number of inmates did not change significantly between 1940 and 1980 when the population was 24,252. However, the number of facilities almost doubled (from 24 to 44) as the BOP gradually moved from operating large facilities confining inmates of many security levels to operating smaller facilities that each confined inmates with similar security needs. As a result of Federal law enforcement efforts and new legislation that dramatically altered sentencing in the Federal criminal justice system, the 1980s brought a significant increase in the number of Federal inmates. The Sentencing Reform Act of 1984 established determinate sentencing, abolished parole, and reduced good time; additionally, several mandatory minimum sentencing provisions were enacted in 1986, 1988, and 1990. From 1980 to 1989, the inmate population more than doubled, from just over 24,000 to almost 58,000. During the 1990s, the population more than doubled again. Today, the BOP inmate population is more than 210,000 and the staff population is nearly 40,000.[13]

The Hands-Off Doctrine, Prisonization, and Deprivation

The reforms initiated by Brockway and others proliferated across the country as correctional systems attempted to strike a balance between punishing offenders to assuage concerns about public safety and providing the opportunities for rehabilitation. For many decades, the prison rate was low and remained relatively constant.[14] A "hands-off" doctrine characterized American prisons whereby prison administrators enjoyed unfettered discretion to run their facilities without outside influence or pressure from the government, press, or academics.

By 1940, academic criminologists began to gain entrée into American prisons. What they described was unsettling. Donald Clemmer's *The Prison Community* published in 1940 showed that prisons were wholly separate micro-societies that contained their own language or argot, values, beliefs, and norms, and expectations of behavior. Clemmer developed the idea of prisonization defined as the socialization process whereby inmates embrace the oppositional and antisocial culture of the prisoner. A variety of circumstances made prisonization more likely, such as serving a lengthy sentence, having an unstable personality and associating with similarly disturbed inmates, having few positive relations with those on the outside, readily integrating into prison culture, blindly accepting prison dogma, associating with hardened offenders or career criminals, and continuing to engage in antisocial behavior while imprisoned.[15] Indeed, Norman Hayner and Ellis Ash, two contemporaries of Clemmer, depicted prison conditions in the following way, "a clear realization of the degenerating influence of our present prison system should encourage more experiments aiming to devise a community for offenders that will actually rehabilitate."[16]

In 1958, Gresham Sykes' *The Society of Captives: A Study of a Maximum Security Prison* portrayed the prison as a despotic, punitive, inhumane social organization designed purely for punishment, retribution, and retaliation—not rehabilitation. This became known as the deprivation model of inmate behavior in which guards created a regime or social order that forced inmates to conform. The regime was totalitarian, not because guards felt this was the best way to proceed, but rather because of society's desire to prevent escape and disorder. Sykes highlighted the deficiencies of this approach, including the lack of a sense of duty among those who were held captive, the obvious fallacies of coercion, the pathetic collection of rewards and punishments to induce compliance, and the strong pressures toward the corruption of the guard in the form of friendship, reciprocity, and the transfer of duties into the hands of trusted inmates. The deprivation resulted in five pains of imprisonment: 1) deprivation of liberty, 2) deprivation of goods and services, 3) deprivation of heterosexual relationships, 4) deprivation of autonomy, 5) deprivation of security.

To adjust to this new environment, Sykes developed archetypal inmate roles, such as rats, center men (those who aligned with guards), gorillas, merchants, wolves, punks, real men, toughs, etc.[17] Over time, criminologists have found that the deprivation model of inmate behavior is still relevant to the present day and that correctional facilities characterized by regimes of rigid social control tended to experience more inmate-related problems than facilities with a treatment or less repressive form of administrative control.[18]

Importation and the Crime Boom, Circa 1965–1993

For all of the strengths of the deprivation model as an explanation of inmate behavior, there is a glaring weakness. Prisoners are inarguably among the most violent and lawless of citizens, thus it should be expected that prisons are dangerous, bad places given the concentration of antisocial people. Academic penology ushered in a subtle but important change in our national view of prisons, one that persists today. The point is this. Early critiques of prison centered on the deplorable conditions of confinement and the unjust and unconstitutional treatment of inmates. These were righteous concerns about due process violations. But, academic penologists usually attributed blame for the appalling state of American prisons toward the criminal justice system (e.g., wardens, prison administrators, correctional officers), not the inmates.

Indeed, whether one blames the criminal justice system or criminals for various crime-related problems often informs whether one is crime control or due process oriented.

Ironically, it was a former prisoner turned academic named John Irwin who along with Donald Cressey advanced a new explanation of prisoner behavior in 1962.[19] The importation model argued that prisoner behavior and the conditions of prisons were mostly a function of the characteristics, values, beliefs, and behaviors that criminals employed on the outside of prison. In other words, inmates of varying degrees of criminality imported their behavioral repertoire and behaved accordingly. To connect to the earlier point, prison conditions were often horrendous because of the commensurate behavior that offenders brought to the facility. The importation model has received substantial empirical support evidenced by the continuity in criminal behavior among the most hardened offenders.

It was during the late 1960s where the link between prisons and conventional society achieved its greatest synergy since the initial design of the penitentiary in the early Eighteenth Century. The 1960s and 1970s were decades of great turmoil, malaise, and revolution that centered on civil rights, minority rights, women's rights, worker's rights, and overall a broadening liberalization of society. Also occurring between 1965 and 1993 was an unprecedented increase in the crime rate.[20] Rising crime rates, particularly for violent crimes such as murder, rape, and robbery, became a primary concern of the general public and an increasingly important political item. To appear "soft" on crime was to virtually guarantee a loss at election polls. American society generally shifted to the political right during the 1980s and 1990s, and correctional policy followed suit.

The New Penology and Beyond

As shown in Figure 11-1, the imprisonment rate increased approximately 400% since 1980. Imprisonment became the standard method of punishing criminal offenders and incapacitation was the assumed rationale for confinement. Malcolm Feeley and Jonathan Simon dubbed this approach "the new penology," defined as the management of groups or sub-populations of offenders based on their actuarial risk to society. The new penology emphasized control and surveillance of offenders, considered rehabilitation to be largely idealistic, and de-emphasized the likelihood of offender reintegration.[21] For ideological reasons discussed in the introduction of this chapter, the increased reliance on imprisonment was portrayed as unjust and discriminatory. Moreover, many criminologists disliked and were apparently confused by the excessive use of prison during an era of falling crime rates that occurred from about 1993 to the present.

Just as prisons were the policy response to the proliferation of crime during the latter part of the Twentieth Century, the exponential growth in imprisonment was also the chief reason for the rather amazing decline in crime that occurred and continues to occur from approximately 1991 to the present. During this era, two correctional factors contributed to the crime decline. First, the likelihood that criminal offender were sentenced to prison increased. Second, the amount of time served behind bars increased dramatically as most states adopted the 85% federal truth-in-sentencing standard. The impact of these policies and practices was that more active and chronic offenders were being sentenced to prison and they were staying there for longer periods of time. Criminologists have feverishly studied the effects of prison expansion on crime, and the bottom line is that the prison boom explained between 13 to 54% of the recent crime decline.[22] Based on official and victimization data, the violent crime rate dropped between 34 to 50% from 1991 to 2001 and many of the largest American cities experienced reductions in the homicide rates upward of 80%.[23]

Compared to penitentiaries, reformatories, and prisons from any other era in American history, the contemporary prison is the safest, provides the most humane treatment, provides the most treatment and programming, and is the most transparent in terms of its openness to outside scrutiny. Today's correctional systems use scientifically influenced actuarial methods to appropriately classify, supervise, treat, and manage prisoners based on their level of risk. Unfortunately, there are currently and always have been a cadre of criminal offenders who are thoroughly opposed to quitting crime and for whom there is no realistic chance of rehabilitation. Many of the most serious criminals are intractably antisocial and are increasingly punished via an extreme form of solitary confinement.[24] In this sense, the American prison has regressed to the methods of the Pennsylvania System to punish the most non-compliant prisoners.

STATISTICAL PROFILE OF PRISONERS AND PRISONS

Prisoner Population

Overall, the United States imprisoned more than 1.6 million persons as of December 2010, the most recent point of data collection. The rate of imprisonment was 502 per 100,000 residents. When taking into account those who have been imprisoned, more than 5.6 million Americans, or one in every 37 adults, have prison experience. The prisoner population is 93% male and 7% female. Thus, the male imprisonment rate is 14 times higher than the female imprisonment rate. By race and ethnicity, the prisoner population is 38% African American, 34% Caucasian, 21% Hispanic, and 7% multi-racial or other. In the federal Bureau of Prisons (BOP), 30% of inmates were foreign citizens the majority of whom were Mexican Nationals. Blacks have an imprisonment rate that is six times higher than the rate for whites and three times higher than the rate for Hispanics. Differential involvement in criminal activity accounts for these racial and ethnic disparities.[25]

Offense Type

The American prisoner population is increasingly comprised of violent offenders. From 1980 to 2000, the proportion of state prisoners who were confined for a violent crime increased by more than 200%. Today, about 52% of state prisoners were incarcerated for a violent offense. The most common offense types were robbery and murder/manslaughter. Roughly 18% of state prisoners were confined for property offenses, the most common of which was burglary. Drug offenders comprised 18% of offenders and those convicted of public-order crimes comprised 9% of prison admissions. By comparison, drug offenders comprised 51% of the federal inmate population. However, the number of federal offenders incarcerated for violent offenses has increased dramatically. In the past decade and a half, the amount inmates in federal custody increased nearly 150% for homicide and nearly 100% for other serious violent crimes.[26]

Time Served and Truth-in-Sentencing

Recall from Chapter 10 that the criminal justice system goes to rather extraordinary efforts to utilize community corrections before sending felons to prison. In terms of its costs, prison is the last resort. Curiously, once an offender is sentenced to prison, the criminal justice system again goes to great lengths to release him or her from custody. Since the 1970s, many state legislatures have sought to reduce judicial discretion in sentencing and the determination of when the conditions of a sentence have been satisfied. Determinate sentences, mandatory minimum sentences, and guidelines-based sentencing have increased the predictability of release. Today, 90% of state prisoners can estimate their probable release date and more than 95% of inmates will be released from prison (very few are sentenced to death or meaningful life-imprisonment). For these reasons, there tends to be very little truth-in-sentencing, defined as the correspondence between the prison sentence and the time actually served prior to prison release.[27]

Indeed, the statistics on how little time felons actually serve in prison are alarming. Lawrence Greenfeld analyzed the time served in prison for violent offenders in 31 states. These persons had been convicted of murder, kidnapping, rape, sexual assault, robbery, assault, extortion, intimidation, reckless endangerment, hit-and-run driving with injury, or child abuse. Overall, violent offenders were sentenced to 89 months in prison but served just 43 months on average. In other words, the most violent criminals in the United States served about 48 percent of their actual sentences. The average sentence, average time served, and percent of sentence served followed this trend even for the most serious offenses. For example:

- Homicide   149 months   71 months   48%
- Rape   117 months   65 months   56%
- Kidnapping   104 months   52 months   50%
- Robbery   95 months   44 months   46%
- Sexual assault   72 months   35 months   49%
- Assault   61 months   29 months   48%

The Violent Crime Control and Law Enforcement Act of 1994 rectified the truth-in-sentencing problem by assuring that offenders served a larger portion of their sentences. By 1998, incentive grants were awarded to 27 states and the District of Columbia to require that violent offenders serve at least 85% of their sentence. Eleven additional states adopted truth-in-sentencing laws in 1995. Immediately prior to the 1994 legislation, violent offenders were sentenced to 85 months and served 45 months on average. After, the average sentence for a violent offender was 104 months and the average time served was 88 months. Nationally, about 70% of state prison admissions for a violent offense were required to serve at least 85% of their sentence. Nearly one in five inmates (18%) served their entire prison sentence.[28]

State prison systems have been following the lead of the federal system for some time. William Sabol and John McGready of The Urban Institute examined time served in prison by federal offenders between 1986 and 1997. The results were comparable to the trends produced from data from state prisoners. Between 1986 and 1997, federal prison sentences increased from 39 months, on average, to 54 months and the average time served of a BOP inmate increased from 21 months to 47 months. In terms of proportion of time served, this increased from 58 to 87%.

From the mid 1980s to mid 1990s, the number of BOP inmates increased 65%of this increase was attributable to an increase in the time served. During this time frame, the time served until first release nearly doubled from 15 months to 29 months on average. The number of federal inmates serving life sentences increased 872%![29]

Prison Facilities

The Bureau of Justice Statistics has conducted a census of correctional facilities in 1974, 1979, 1984, 1990, 1995, 2000, and 2005 to produce a national snapshot of prison systems in the United States. Based on data from the most recent census, James Stephan found that there were 1,821 federal, state, and private correctional facilities. About 71% are confinement facilities and the remaining 29% are community-based facilities. About 53% of all facilities were rated as minimum-security, 26% as medium-security, and 20% as maximum-security. Commensurately, 40% of inmates were classified as minimum-security, 40% as medium-security, and 20% as maximum-security.[30] Private prisons house slightly more than 5% of the total prisoner population,[31] are generally no more cost-effective than public prisons,[32] and produce equivalent recidivism outcomes as public prisons.[33]

The overall safety of correctional facilities depends on the classification of the inmates and the facility. For instance, assaults on inmates and staff were overwhelmingly concentrated in state prison facilities and significantly less common in federal and private facilities. Moreover, the rate of inmate assaults against staff was dramatically higher in maximum-security facilities compared to medium- and ultimately minimum-security facilities. In state correctional facilities, the rate of assault on staff was *61 times* greater in maximum-security than minimum-security facilities. The respective differences in assault rates were eight times in private facilities and four times in federal facilities.

Correctional facilities serve a variety of functions to address the punishment and treatment needs of the inmates. The primary purpose is general confinement evidenced that nearly all correctional purposes are simply geared toward general confinement or incapacitation. Correctional facilities are also used for boot camp/shock incarceration; reception, diagnosis, and classification; medical treatment or hospitalization; substance abuse treatment; youthful offender placement; and work-release programs. The second most common facility type is described as "other." These facilities house very specific sub-populations of offenders, such as geriatric inmates, sex offenders, inmates in protective custody, inmates with profound psychiatric problems, and condemned offenders.

As a rule, prisons are crowded places with limited capacity to house inmates. The rated capacity is the number of beds or inmates assigned by a rating official to institutions within a jurisdiction. The operational capacity is the number of inmates that can be accommodated based on the facility's staff, programs, and services. The design capacity is the number of inmates that planners intended for the facility. One in five correctional facilities operated under a court order or consent decree to limit its population. The BOP and 24 state prison systems operated above capacity, indeed the BOP operated at nearly 150% of rated capacity. Servicing these facilities is a correctional work staff of 445,000.[34]

Correctional Programs and Treatment

Chapters 10 and 11 have documented the assortment of risk factors and individual-level deficiencies that present so many difficulties for serious criminal offenders. Data on educational attainment by criminal justice status are illustrative. State and federal prisoners were 200 to 300% more likely than the general population to have dropped out of completed high school. The prevalence of college graduation is 1,100% higher among the general population than the state prisoner population. Nearly 50% of prisoners reported that behavioral problems, academic difficulties, disinterest, or criminal activity as the reasons why they dropped out of high school. Depending on the inmate's level of education, the unemployment rate among prisoners was between 400 to 800% higher than the general population. Approximately 30% of prisoners derived their income from illegal sources in the month before their most recent arrest. Finally, the prevalence of homelessness and welfare dependency among prisoners is several times the rate of these social problems among the general population.[35]

To surmount these deficiencies, correctional facilities offer an array of educational and treatment programs to facilitate the rehabilitation of prisoners. Caroline Wolf Harlow of the Bureau of Justice Statistics reviewed educational programs and other treatment amenities among federal, state, and private prisons. Federal prisons have the greatest resources and offer the most educational programs. All facilities within the Bureau of Prisons (BOP) have an education program that provides basic adult education and secondary education, 94% provide vocational training, 60% provide special education, and more than 80% provide college courses. More than 90% of state prisons provide educational programs, 56% provide vocational training, 40% provide special education, and 27% provide college courses. In private prisons, 88% offer educational programs, 44% provide vocational training, 22% provide special education, and 27% offer college courses. Despite the availability of these programs, inmates only modestly take advantage. About 52% of state prisoners and 57% of federal prisoners have participated in an educational program during their current incarceration. Vocational programs are the most popular among inmates because they are an opportunity to learn a particular trade to use after release.[36]

Prisons also offer an array of work, treatment, and counseling services to inmates. Across federal, state, and private facilities, approximately 97% of confinement facilities and 75% of community-based facilities provide work programs. The most common forms of prisoner work were facility support services and public works programs. About 46% of prisons had prison industries, 29% operated farms or other agricultural activities, and 60% performed road and parks maintenance.

More correctional facilities provided counseling programs than either educational or work programs. Indeed, 97% of state confinement facilities, 93% of state community-based facilities, and 92% of BOP facilities offered counseling or other special programs to inmates. Drug and alcohol dependency counseling or awareness was the most common. Among facilities providing counseling programs, all BOP facilities, 66% of state, and 46% of private facilities offered psychological and psychiatric counseling. Counseling services for employment and job skills, life skills and community adjustment, HIV/AIDS awareness and education, parenting classes, sex offender treatment, and others are also provided.[37]

Correctional treatment is certainly difficult given the multitude of problems (attitudinal, behavioral, mental health, substance abuse, etc.) that the average prisoner has. Moreover, many criminals have absolutely no intentions of reducing their antisocial behavior upon release from custody. Fortunately, there are a variety of correctional programs that seek to rehabilitate criminal offenders. For instance, Moral Reconation Therapy (MRT) increases the moral reasoning ability of offenders. Reasoning and Rehabilitation (RR) programs seek to change antisocial or criminogenic thinking patterns and attitudes. Both MRT and RR are cognitive treatments designed to correct maladaptive/criminal thoughts, beliefs, and attitudes into conventional and pro-social ones. To date, they have produced modestly positive treatment outcomes.[38]

Similarly, evaluations of correctional substance abuse treatment programs and therapeutic communities have shown favorable results particularly when there is continuity in care from prison to the community. Vocational and work programs have been shown to reduce recidivism and improve job readiness skills for ex-offenders. Educational programs do not reduce recidivism but increase the educational achievement scores of offenders. In sum, assorted correctional programming has proven to be helpful in the sense that offenders who participate in treatment programs tend to reintegrate into society better and desist from crime sooner than prisoners who do not.[39]

Suicide, Homicide, and Sources of Mortality among Prisoners

The assorted risk factors posed by prisoners are not simply sociological, but are literal matters of life and death. As shown in Figure 11-2, suicide and homicide rates have dropped dramatically in jails and prisons since 1980. Suicide is more common among jail inmates than prisoners. The suicide rate among jail inmates is 427% higher than the general population. Christopher Mumola of the Bureau of Justice Statistics standardized the United States resident population to match the demographic composition of the prisoner population and found that the homicide rate would be 500 to 600% greater if the general population matched the prisoner population. Across the nation, approximately 1000 inmates die behind bars per year. The most frequent causes of death were illness, including AIDS, suicide, and intoxication/overdose. About 2% of inmate deaths are the result of homicide perpetrated by another inmate.[40]

The overall rate of confirmed AIDS cases in the prisoner population was 350% higher than the general population, and one in 11 deaths of state prisoners were due to AIDS-related illnesses.[41] A similar trend exists for other forms of disease. For example, Jacques Baillargeon and his colleagues studied more than 170,000 prisoners who were incarcerated in the Texas Department of Criminal Justice to create a "disease profile" of the prisoner population. Their findings were alarming. More than 20% of Texas prisoners

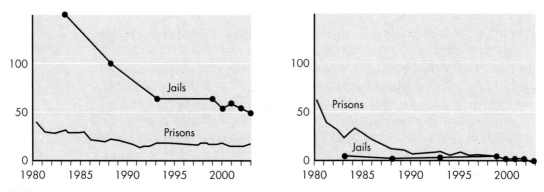

FIGURE 11-2 Suicide and Homicide Rates Per 100,000 Inmates 1980–2003

Source: Mumola, C. J. (2005). *Suicide and homicide in state prisons and local jails.* Washington, DC: U. S. Department of Justice, Office of Justice Programs, Bureau of Justice Statistics.

had tuberculosis, 10% suffered from hypertension, and 5% had hepatitis. For a number of serious medical conditions, the prison population exhibited prevalence rates that were substantially higher than those reported for the general population.[42]

Collateral Costs of Imprisonment

The American correctional population creates a variety of collateral costs that likely have wide-reaching impact on society. The majority of men and women behind bars are parents meaning that nearly 1.5 million children under the age of 18, more than 2% of the national child population, have one or more parents currently in prison. Approximately 80% of prisoners see their children less than once per month.[43] Due to parental incarceration, these children are shunted into various living conditions with various caregivers, such as grandparents, other relatives, foster homes, and other social service agencies. Given the exceedingly high rates of substance abuse, unemployment, mental illness, and abusive criminal behavior, many children of prisoners are exposed to some of the most deleterious social environments.

The collateral costs of imprisonment also extend to the communities from which prisoners originate. John Hagan and Ronet Dinovitzer identified several ways that incarceration damages communities, social institutions, and prisoners' likelihood of reintegration. For instance, prisoners have lackluster work histories that are further damaged by ex-convict status. Thus, they are less able to contribute to their families and communities. Additionally, many prisoners have no intentions of "going straight" and instead return to their neighborhoods and immediately engage in damaging criminal behavior. To the most impoverished communities, a large increase in paroled offenders can result in a substantial short-term crime wave. In sum, the large correctional population has serious implications for the prosperity and sustainability of social institutions, such as family and work.[44]

PRISONER CRIMINALITY

Criminal History

Since prison is the punishment of last resort, the criminality of prisoners is significantly higher than the criminality of offenders who are placed on intermediate sanctions. Generally speaking, one has to earn their way to prison via their pronounced and recurrent antisocial behavior. This applies to the most violent and notorious criminals and even the seemingly non-serious offenders. Matthew Durose and Christopher Mumola of the Bureau of Justice Statistics recently created a profile of nonviolent prisoners released from prisons in 15 states. Nonviolent offenders were defined as persons convicted of drug violations, theft, or burglary. In other words, these were not offenders who were convicted of murder or rape, but instead those convicted of what are commonly considered "garden variety" crimes. The following are highlights of what the average criminal history of a nonviolent (non-serious) prisoner:

- Over 40% had less than a high school education.
- Nearly 70% were using drugs in the month preceding the commitment offense.
- About 40% were using drugs during their commitment offense.
- About 95% had a prior arrest history.
- Over 84% had previously been convicted of a crime.
- The average number of prior arrests was 9.3.
- The average number of prior convictions was 4.1
- Over 50% had three or more prior prison or probation sentences.
- About 64% were on parole, probation, or escape at the time of their commitment offense.
- Over 88% had any "serious offender" indicator on their rap sheet.[45]

Extensive criminal history was also found in an investigation of drug offenders charged in federal district courts. John Scalia examined the offending patterns of nearly 40,000 drug suspects referred to United States attorneys in 1999. Over 65% of those charged had previously been arrested and 505 had previously been convicted of a crime, 33% for a felony. About 44% of federal drug offenders had 5 or more prior arrests, which is the standard criminological measure for career or habitual criminality. One in three federal drug offenders in the sample were already under criminal justice supervision upon their arrest.[46]

This extreme risk profile not only applies to adult prisoners, but also to juvenile delinquents. For example, Brent Benda and Connie Tollett analyzed the criminal histories of 244 adolescents who had been in a serious offender programs operated by the Arkansas Division of Youth Services (DYS). The criminal history of these adolescents indicated an array of serious risk factors.

On average, these offenders first committed crime at age 12, first used drugs at age 12, first carried a deadly weapon at age 13, and had previously been confined to a juvenile detention center. Maternal and paternal drug abuse, neglect and abuse, family strife, and other family members who had also been imprisoned characterized their family backgrounds. Benda and Tollett also found that criminal history was itself the greatest predictor of subsequent recidivism and return to confinement. For example, youths who had prior commitments to DYS were nearly 14 times more likely to be returned to confinement than youths without prior incarcerations. Similarly, youths with prior weapons offenses were 335% and gang members 203% more likely to be returned to DYS.[47]

Institutional Misconduct

Given the pronounced criminality of most prisoners and the stressful conditions of prison life, inmate violence and misconduct behind bars are fairly commonplace. In their census of federal and state correctional facilities, James Stephan and Jennifer Karberg found that more than 34,000 inmate-on-inmate assaults occurred annually, an average of 94 per day. Inmates murdered 51 fellow inmates in 2000, an average of nearly one murder per week. Additionally, inmates totaled nearly 18,000 assaults against staff members, an average of nearly 50 per day. In 2000, five of these assaults resulted in the death of prison officials. While in custody, inmates also caused 606 major disturbances defined as incidents involving five or more inmates and resulting in serious injury or significant property damage, set 343 fires, and caused 639 other disturbances.[48] The projected rate of crime per 100,000 persons is much higher in prisons than in American society. For instance, Matt DeLisi found that the prison murder rate was nearly twice the national murder rate and the incidence of male-on-male sexual assault in prison was higher than forcible rape rates in conventional society. Rates for arson, aggravated assault, and theft were dramatically higher behind bars than in conventional society.

Most inmate violence and misconduct can be attributable to the most habitual and recalcitrant criminals. For example, about 30% of inmates are never contacted for prison violations and more than 70% are never contacted for a serious or violent violation. On the other hand, 40% of inmates continued to be chronic criminal offenders even while incarcerated. A small cadre of inmates accounted for 100% of the murders, 75% of the rapes, and 80% of the arson incidents occurring in one state's prison system.[49] Indeed, a variety of studies have found that individual-level characteristics of prisoners, such as their criminal propensity, criminal record, number of prior prison sentences, psychopathology, and antisocial attitudes are the strongest predictors of continued misconduct, non-compliance, and violence behind bars.[50]

Post-Release Recidivism

The staggeringly high recidivism rates among released prisoners are arguably the main reason that many citizens, social commentators, and academics are critical of prisons. Indeed, the norm among parolees or ex-convicts who served their entire prison term to expiration is to rather quickly engage in criminal behavior. Patrick Langan and David Levin of the Bureau of Justice Statistics conducted the most impressive study of recidivism in terms of the scope, magnitude, and representativeness of their sample. Langan and Levin tracked more than 27,000 former inmates for three years after their release from prison in 1994. The study group represented two-thirds of all prisoners released during that year and contained released offenders from Arizona, California, Delaware, Florida, Illinois, Maryland, Michigan, Minnesota, New Jersey, New York, North Carolina, Ohio, Oregon, Texas, and Virginia. Four measures of recidivism were used: re-arrest, re-conviction, re-sentence to prison, and return to prison with or without a new sentence.[51]

Within three years from their release from prison, the following are highlights from Langan and Levin's study:

- 68% of prisoners were re-arrested for a new offense (almost exclusively a felony or serious misdemeanor).
- 47% were re-convicted for a new crime.
- 25% were re-sentenced to prison for a new crime.
- 52% were back in prison for new crimes or parole violations.
- 30% of the recidivism occurred within 6 months of release and 44% occurred by the end of the first year.
- Prisoners committed an average of four new crimes after release.
- Offenders averaged 18 arrest charges over their criminal career.
- About 6% of prisoners totaled 45 or more career arrests.
- Among prisoners with the lengthiest criminal records, 82% recidivated.
- Prisoners were arrested for homicide at a rate 53 times higher than the homicide arrest rate for the adult population.
- No evidence was found that spending more time in prison raised the recidivism rate. The evidence was mixed regarding whether serving more time reduced recidivism.[52]

The same theme is found using different classifications or types of offenders. Patrick Langan, Erica Schmitt, and Matthew Durose studied nearly 10,000 sex offenders from the same 15-state-sample described before. The sex offender sub-sample contained 3,115 rapists; 6,576 sexual assaulters; 4,295 child molesters, and 443 statutory rapists. The sex offenders comprised less than 4% of all offenders and had an average prison sentence of 8 years of which they served over three years (45 percent of total sentence).

Compared to non-sex offenders, sex offenders were 400% more likely to be re-arrested for a new sex crime. About 40% of the recidivism occurred within one year of release. Sex offenders were 200% more likely than non-sex offenders to be re-arrested for child molestation. Overall, the more prior arrests that a sex offender has, the greater recidivism for all types of crimes. Within three years of release, 43% of sex offenders were re-arrested, 24% were re-convicted, and nearly 40% were returned to prison.

Like other criminals, sex offenders tended to have extensive criminal histories for a multitude of crimes. Nearly 80% had previously been arrested, 58% had prior convictions, 25% had previously been imprisoned, and 14% had prior convictions for a violent sex offense.[53] The average number of prior arrests among sex offenders was nearly five, again the standard threshold for habitual criminality.[54]

CHAPTER SUMMARY: BALANCING CRIME CONTROL AND DUE PROCESS

- Prisons are among the most controversial of criminal justice topics and are critiqued from both crime control and due process perspectives.
- The Pennsylvania System viewed prison as an opportunity for the offender to be redeemed through isolation, work, prayer, and strict social control.
- The Auburn System employed the same general philosophy but allowed inmates to congregate for work during the day.
- Solitary confinement was historically not a punishment but the means to be penitent.
- Prisons generally reflect the social conditions of the era, reflecting the degree of public leniency and punitiveness, and can be used to reduce crime.
- Deprivation theorists assert that prison conditions cause inmate behavior; importation theorists assert that inmate characteristics do.
- More than 2.4 million people are held in a variety of correctional facilities in the United States.
- Racial and ethnic minorities, such as African Americans and Hispanics, commit crime and are imprisoned at levels that are disproportionate to their numbers in the general population.
- Because so few offenders served even half of their sentence, the federal and many state correctional systems mandated that the most serious criminals serve at least 85% of their sentence to reflect truth-in-sentencing.
- The average prison provides educational and vocational training as well as several types of treatment.
- Prison creates collateral costs, such as damaging family and work networks in communities from which inmate originate.
- The criminality of prisoners is extremely high based on their criminal histories, institutional misconduct, and post-release recidivism rates.
- The extreme criminality of prisoners lends support to the notion that prison is the punishment of last resort in the corrections continuum.

KEY TERMS

Auburn System
Bureau of Prisons
Collateral costs
Correctional programs
Deprivation model
Disproportionate minority
   confinement
Eastern State Penitentiary
Expiration of sentence
Extraordinary release
Importation model
Misconduct
Moral Reconation Therapy
National Congress on Penitentiary
   and Reformatory Discipline

Pains of imprisonment
Penitentiary
Pennsylvania System
Prison
Prisonization
Private prison
Reasoning and Rehabilitation
Recidivism
Reformatory
Scared Straight
Solitary confinement
Substantial assistance
Time served
Truth-in-sentencing
Zebulon Brockway

TALKING POINTS

1. Does disproportionate minority confinement reflect racial differences in offending, system differences in responding to racial groups, or some combination? If the criminal justice system was systematically discriminating against persons of color, why are white males more involved in crime than all minority females combined?

2. How would strict crime control and due process advocates discuss the talking point above? Are criminal justice controversies reflective of different evidence or different ideological lenses through which evidence is viewed?

3. Why is it so difficult for many prisoners to stop committing crime? Using theories of crime from other classes, which criminological theories best explain the difficulty of successful offender reintegration?

4. What is criminality? What are some of the best measures of criminality? Can one make predictions about recidivism or reintegration based on measures of criminality?

5. If the 500 percent increase in the prison rate between 1980 and 2004 has so reduced the crime rate, why do criminologists still disagree about the effectiveness of prison as a means of crime control?

WEB LINKS

American Correctional Association
(www.aca.org)

Association of State Correctional Administrators
(www.asca.net)

Bureau of Justice Statistics: Corrections Statistics
(www.ojp.usdoj.gov/bjs/correct.htm)

Federal Bureau of Prisons
(www.bop.gov/)

National GAINS Center
(www.gainscenter.samhsa.gov/html/default.asp)

National Institute of Corrections
(www.nicic.org/)

National Law Enforcement and Corrections Technology Center
(www.nlectc.org/)

State Departments of Corrections
(www.corrections.com/links/state.html)

The Center for Community Corrections
(www.communitycorrectionsworks.org)

FURTHER READING

Clemmer, D. (1940). *The prison community*. New York: Holt, Rinehart and Winston. Clemmer's classic work introduced the ideas of prisonization defined as the antisocial socialization process that inmates undergo during their imprisonment and the deprivation model, which argued that the structural conditions and culture of the prison largely mold inmate behavior.

DiIulio, J. (1987). *Governing prisons: A comparative study of correctional management*. New York: The Free Press. This comparative analysis of the Texas, Michigan, and California prison systems provided compelling evidence that prison administration is the ultimate determinant of how well or poorly a prison facility is run. Wardens that balance tight, authoritative control and respectful treatment of inmates are often the best types of facilities.

Jacobs, J. B. (1977). *Stateville: The penitentiary in mass society.* Chicago: University of Chicago Press. This work provides an analysis of Stateville Prison from 1925 to 1975 and shows the decline in deprivation models of inmate behavior and the rise of the importation model of inmate behavior, especially as it is explained by the increased imprisonment of minority street gangs.

Sykes, G. (1958). *The society of captives.* Princeton, NJ: Princeton University Press. Sykes' classic is the definitive argument for the deprivation model of inmate behavior based on the five deprivations (liberty, goods and services, heterosexual relations, autonomy, and security) that the prison environment imposes.

Useem, B., & Kimball, P. (1989). *States of siege: U. S. prison riots, 1971–1986.* New York: Oxford University Press. This is the definitive text on prison rioting. Although rare, prison riots, like the ones that occurred at Attica and Santa Fe, usually spark correctional reform and place prisons into the national conscientiousness.

CHAPTER 12
Capital Punishment

CHAPTER OUTLINE

QUOTATIONS

"Only a fraction of even the most vicious killers ever get executed. Neither deterrence nor justice can possibly be achieved in this way."—*Thomas Sowell*[1]

"An eye for an eye leaves everybody blind."—*Mohandas Gandhi and Martin Luther King, Jr.*[2]

"If we execute murderers and there is in fact no deterrent effect, we have killed a bunch of murderers. If we fail to execute murderers, and doing so would in fact have deterred other murders, we have allowed the killing of a bunch of innocent victims. I would much rather risk the former. This, to me, is not a tough call."—*John McAdams*[3]

"Nothing is simpler than the governments of some petty barbarian kings, yet no governments are more absolute in character."—*Emile Durkheim*[4]

"A court of law should certainly be a place of judgment, vindication, and even retribution."—*Thane Rosenbaum*[5]

"Origins of the death penalty rested primarily upon the effort to placate the gods, lest their beneficent solicitude for the group be diverted as a result of apparent group indifference to the violation of the social codes supposedly revealed by the gods of the people. The complete blotting out of the culprit was looked upon as a peculiarly forceful demonstration of groups' disapproval of the particular type of antisocial conduct involved in the case."—*Harry Elmer Barnes*[6]

"The respect for the law is the obverse side of our hatred for the criminal transgressor."—*George Herbert Mead*[7]

INTRODUCTION

"Murderer removed from death row:

Indiana governor makes decision on eve of term's end."[8]

"Connecticut execution puts the spotlight on 'death row syndrome.'"[9]

"High court: Juvenile death penalty unconstitutional"[10]

"Texas executes killer of mom, 3 others"[11]

"New hearings sought for Mexicans on death row:

Bush administration filing response to international criticism"[12]

"Murderer upbeat, joking in seconds before execution: 'Put some headphones on my head and rock 'n' roll me when I'm dead'"[13]

"Nabbed killer back in Texas: Death row inmate extradited from Louisiana[14]

There is nothing quite like capital punishment in the world of criminal justice. Statistically, an execution is a rare event only 46 persons were executed in 2010. Moreover, there were 3,173 state and federal death row inmates.[15] Put another way, the death row population is more than *500 times* smaller than the non-death row prisoner population. Many states that have the death penalty either do not use it or administer it with great infrequency.

Despite the rarity of a condemned offender actually being executed, the death penalty galvanizes the general public, policy makers, news commentators, and criminologists and is among the most politicized of talking points. The news headlines that began this section touch on just a few of these. For example, outgoing governors sometimes grant reprieves to death row inmates or in the case of the former governor of Illinois, commute the sentences of the entire condemned population, and commute their sentences to life imprisonment. The timing of these reprieves is crucial. The general public is overwhelmingly supportive of the death penalty, and politicians who appear weak on crime (evidenced by non-support of the death penalty) face risks at the polls. Indeed, the death penalty is the most visceral symbol of a society's commitment to crime control and revulsion toward the worst criminals.

Capital punishment embodies important social, moral, and legal debates. For instance, since condemned offenders wait for prolonged periods of time, some have speculated that "death row syndrome" is an unconstitutional form of psychological torture in which inmates never know when they will be actually put to death. The status of the death penalty itself hinges on the social, moral, and legal debates that give it life. For instance, the Supreme Court held in 2005 that the execution of persons who were under the age of 18 when they committed their capital crimes was unconstitutional.[16] Similarly, the United States is an exception among westernized nations in that it has retained the death penalty. Furthermore, several foreign nationals, most of whom are Mexican Nationals, have been sentenced to death in the United States. Thus, the international debate whether the United States can lawfully execute a foreign national, particularly if that defendant's country of origin does not use the death penalty, remains unresolved.

Finally, the headline "Texas executes killer of mom, 3 others" describes the February 2005 execution of Dennis Bagwell. Bagwell was condemned for the 1995 murder of his own mother, his half-sister, and two child relatives (ages 4 and 14). Bagwell had also raped the 14-year-victim. Curiously, the news articles did not provide any information about Bagwell's criminal history. Alternately, records maintained by the Texas Department of Criminal Justice indicated that Bagwell had been on parole for a mere four months before committing the quadruple homicide. He was paroled after serving 13 years in prison for a prior conviction for attempted capital murder![17]

That the article neglected to show the entire story of the condemned offender's criminal past was neither unintentional nor isolated. The simple truth is this: The academic literature on the death penalty is the most unbalanced, one-sided area of research in criminology. Although the general public is perennially for the death penalty, academics are overwhelmingly against it. In fact, the American Society of Criminology and American Bar Association have officially taken an organizational stance against capital punishment. Often, death penalty "scholarship" is written in an explicit and unapologetically activist tone whereas the abolition of the death penalty is portrayed as righteous and arguments in favor of the death penalty are portrayed as benighted. Importantly, it is irrelevant whether one is for or against the ultimate punishment. However, the empirical support for arguments for and against the death penalty should be presented on equal terms. As such, the various justifications or rationales for capital punishment are presented below with attention to arguments against the punishment (often called the abolitionist perspective) and for it (often called the retentionist perspective).

CAPITAL PUNISHMENT IN THE UNITED STATES

Statistical Snapshot
At year end 2010, 36 states and the federal prison system held 3,173 prisoners under sentences of death. About half of the death row population was comprised of inmates from California, Texas, Florida, and Pennsylvania. The preponderance of death penalty activity occurs at the state level. For instance, only 55 persons currently reside on federal death row and the United States government has executed only three persons since 1977. Last year, 112 inmates received death sentences and 46 persons were executed. Of those under the sentence of death, 56% were White, 42% were African American, and 14% were Hispanic. Less than 2% of the death row population is constituted by females, thus males comprised over 98% of condemned offenders.[18]

Death Penalty Statute
Only the most serious forms of criminal conduct can potentially qualify for a death sentence. Essentially, the criterion is to be convicted of a "felony murder," defined as the commission of a homicide in conjunction with some other serious felony offense, such as kidnapping, rape, armed robbery, child molestation, or additional homicides. Rape was excluded as a capital crime in the landmark case *Coker v. Georgia* (1977).[19] Capital offenses for the states and federal government appear in Table 12-1 and Table 12-2. The following jurisdictions do not have the death penalty: Alaska, District of Columbia, Hawaii, Iowa, Maine, Massachusetts, Michigan, Minnesota, New Jersey, New Mexico, North Dakota, Rhode Island, Vermont, West Virginia, and Wisconsin.

TABLE 12-1 Criminal Justice and The Law Table: Capital Offenses by State

Alabama. International murder with 18 aggravating factors (Ala. Stat. Ann. 13A-5-40(a)(1)-(18)).

Arizona. First-degree murder accompanied by at least 1 of 14 aggravating factors (A.R.S. § 13-703(F)).

Arkansas. Capital murder (Ark. Code Ann. 5-10-101) with a finding of at least 1 of 10 aggravating circumstances; treason.

California. First-degree murder with special circumstances; sabotage; train wrecking causing death; treason; perjury causing execution of an innocent person; fatal assault by a prisoner serving a life sentence.

Colorado. First-degree murder with at least 1 of 17 aggravating factors; first-degree kidnapping resulting in death; treason.

Connecticut. Capital felony with 8 forms of aggravated homicide (C.G.S. § 53a-54b).

Delaware. First-degree murder with at least 1 statutory aggravating circumstance (11 Del. C. § 4209).

Florida. First-degree murder; felony murder; capital drug trafficking; capital sexual battery.

Georgia. Murder; kidnapping with bodily injury or ransom when the victim dies; aircraft hijacking; treason.

Idaho. First-degree murder with aggravating factors; first-degree kidnapping; perjury resulting in death.

Illinois. First-degree murder with 1 of 21 aggravating circumstances (720 Ill. Comp. Stat. 5/9-1).

Indiana. Murder with 16 aggravating circumstances (IC 35-50-2-9).

Kansas. Capital murder with 8 aggravating circumstances (KSA 21-3439, KSA 21-4625, KSA 21-4636).

Kentucky. Murder with aggravating factors; kidnapping with aggravating factors (KRS 532.025).

Louisiana. First-degree murder; treason (La. R.S. 14:30 and 14:113).

Maryland. First-degree murder, either premeditated or during the commission of felony, provided that certain death eligibility requirements are satisfied.

Mississippi. Capital murder (Miss. Code Ann. § 97-3-19(2)); aircraft piracy (Miss. Code Ann. § 97-25-55(1)).

Missouri. First-degree murder (565.020 RSMO 2000).

Montana. Capital murder with 1 of 9 aggravating circumstances (Mont Code Ann. § 46-18-303); aggravated sexual intercourse without consent (Mount. Code Ann. § 45-5-503).

Nebraska. First-degree murder with a finding of at least 1 statutorily-defined aggravating circumstance.

Nevada. First-degree murder with at least 1 of 15 aggravating circumstances (NRS 200.030, 200.033, 200.035).

New Hampshire. Murder committed in the course of rape, kidnapping, or drug crimes; killing of a law enforcement officer; murder for hire; murder by an inmate while serving a sentence of life without parole (RSA 630:1, RSA 630:5).

New York*. First-degree murder with 1 of 13 aggravating factors (NY Penal Law § 125.27).

North Carolina. First-degree murder (NCGS § 14–17).

Ohio. Aggravated murder with at least 1 of 10 aggravating circumstances(O.R.C. secs. 2903.01, 2929.02, and 2929.04).

Oklahoma. First-degree murder in conjunction with a finding of at least 1 of 8 statutorily-defined aggravating circumstances; sex crimes against a child under 14 years of age.

Continued

TABLE 12-1 Continued

Oregon. Aggravated murder (ORS 163.095-150).
Pennsylvania. First-degree murder with 18 aggravating circumstance.
South Carolina. Murder with 1 of 12 aggravating circumstances (§ 16-3-20(C)(a)).
South Dakota. First-degree murder with 1 of 10 aggravating circumstances.
Tennessee. First-degree murder with 1 of 15 aggravating circumstances (Tenn. Code Ann. § 39-13-204).
Texas. Criminal homicide with 1 of 9 aggravating circumstances (Tex. Penal Code § 19.03).

Utah. Aggravated murder (76-5-202, Utah Code Annotated).
Virginia. First-degree murder with 1 of 15 aggravating circumstances (VA Code § 18.2-31).
Washington. Aggravated first-degree murder.
Wyoming. First-degree murder; murder during the commission of sexual assault, sexual abuse of a minor, arson, robbery, escape, resisting arrest, kidnapping, or abuse of a minor under 16 (W.S.A. § 6-2-101(a)).

*The New York Court of Appeals has held that a portion of New York's death penalty sentencing statute (CPL 400.27) was unconstitutional (People v. Taylor, 9 N Y.3d 129 (2007)). As a result, no defendants can be sentenced to death until the legislature corrects the errors in this statute.

TABLE 12-2 Criminal Justice and The Law: Federal Death Penalty Laws

Statute	Description
8 U.S.C. 1342	Murder related to the smuggling of aliens.
18 U.S.C. 32–34	Destruction of aircraft, motor vehicles, or related facilities resulting in death.
18 U.S.C. 36	Murder committed during a drug-related drive-by shooting.
18 U.S.C. 37	Murder committed at an airport serving international civil aviation.
18 U.S.C. 115(b)(3) [by cross-reference to 18 U.S.C. 1111]	Retaliatory murder of a member of the immediate family of law enforcement officials.
18 U.S.C. 241, 242, 245, 247	Civil rights offenses resulting in death.
18 U.S.C. 351 [by cross-reference to 18 U.S.C. 1111]	Murder of a member of Congress, an important executive official, or a Supreme Court Justice.
18 U.S.C. 794	Espionage.
18 U.S.C. 844(d), (f), (i)	Death resulting from offenses involving transportation of explosives, destruction of government property, or destruction of property related to foreign or interstate commerce.

Continued

TABLE 12-2 Continued

18 U.S.C. 924(i)	Murder committed by the use of a firearm during a crime of violence or a drug-trafficking crime.
18 U.S.C. 930	Murder committed in a Federal Government facility.
18 U.S.C. 1091	Genocide.
18 U.S.C. 1111	First-degree murder.
18 U.S.C. 1114	Murder of a federal judge of law enforcement official.
18 U.S.C. 1116	Murder of a foreign official.
18 U.S.C. 1118	Murder by a federal prisoner.
18 U.S.C. 1119	Murder of a U.S. national in a foreign country.
18 U.S.C. 1120	Murder by an escaped federal prisoner already sentenced to life imprisonment.
18 U.S.C. 1121	Murder of a state or local law enforcement official or other person aiding in a federal investigation; murder of a state correctional officer.
18 U.S.C. 1201	Murder during a kidnapping.
18 U.S.C. 1203	Murder during a hostage taking.
18 U.S.C. 1503	Murder of a court officer or juror.
18 U.S.C. 1512	Murder with the intent of preventing testimony by a witness, victim, or informant.
18 U.S.C. 1513	Retaliatory murder of a witness, victim, or informant.
18 U.S.C. 1716	Mailing of injurious articles with intent to kill or resulting in death.
18 U.S.C. 1751 [by cross-reference to 18 U.S.C. 1111]	Assassination or kidnapping resulting in the death of the President or Vice President.
18 U.S.C. 1958	Murder for hire.
18 U.S.C. 1959	Murder involved in a racketeering offense.
18 U.S.C. 1992	Willful wrecking of a train resulting in death.
18 U.S.C. 2113	Bank-robbery-related murder or kidnapping.
18 U.S.C. 2119	Murder related to a carjacking.
18 U.S.C. 2245	Murder related to rape or child molestation
18 U.S.C. 2251	Murder related to sexual exploitation of children.
18 U.S.C. 2280	Murder committed during an offense against maritime navigation.
18 U.S.C. 2281	Murder committed during an offense against a maritime fixed platform.

Continued

TABLE 12-2 Continued

18 U.S.C. 2332	Terrorist murder of a U.S. national in another country.
18 U.S.C. 2332a	Murder by the use of a weapon of mass destruction.
18 U.S.C. 2340	Murder involving torture.
18 U.S.C. 2381	Treason.
21 U.S.C. 848(e)	Murder related to a continuing criminal enterprise or related murder of a federal, state, or local law enforcement officer.
49 U.S.C. 1472-1473	Death resulting from aircraft hijacking.

Aggravating and Mitigating Circumstances

Death penalty statutes essentially describe the conditions under which a homicide is escalated into a capital crime. Two types of circumstances are considered. Aggravating circumstances, such as serial murder or hate/bias-motivated murder, are characteristics that make the crime seem worse in totality and thus deserving of death as the only appropriate punishment. Mitigating circumstances, such as youth, mental retardation, or victimization, render a crime less serious or add context that seems to reduce the overall viciousness of the behavior.

Aggravating and mitigating circumstances resuscitated the death penalty after its ban from 1972–1976 because they allowed states to limit discretion by providing sentencing guidelines for the judge and jury when deciding whether to impose death. These guided discretion statutes were approved by the Supreme Court in five cases (*Gregg v. Georgia, Jurek v. Texas, Roberts v. Louisiana, Woodson v. North Carolina*, and *Proffitt v. Florida*) collectively referred to as the *Gregg* decision. This landmark decision held that the new death penalty statutes in Florida, Georgia, and Texas were constitutional, and that the death penalty itself was constitutional under the Eighth Amendment.

The *Gregg* decision resulted in three other procedural reforms: 1) bifurcated trials in which there are separate deliberations for the guilt and penalty phases of the trial. Only after the jury has determined that the defendant is guilty of capital murder does it decide in a second trial whether the defendant should be sentenced to death or given a lesser sentence of prison time, 2) automatic appellate review of convictions and sentence, and 3) proportionality review which helps the state to identify and eliminate sentencing disparities by comparing the sentence in the case with other cases within the state.[20]

Case Procedure and Automatic Review/Appeal

The legal road that a capital case follows is extremely convoluted. The American Bar Association highlighted 40 steps that occur from the homicide event to execution. After the homicide, the police conduct an investigation and make an arrest. The courts seek an indictment through the grand jury or the prosecutor directly files the case (depending on the jurisdiction). The courts must determine the defendant's competency, hold a trial with separate guilty and penalty phases, and ultimately impose a death sentence. After conviction, the general scenario is as follows: motion for new trial, motion denied, appeal to state supreme court, conviction and sentence upheld, motion for rehearing filed, motion denied, decision affirmed, petition United States Supreme Court, petition denied, state post-conviction petition filed, petition denied, appeal to state court of appeals, decision affirmed, appeal to state supreme court, decision affirmed, petition Supreme Court for review (writ of certiorari), petition granted, decision re-affirmed, federal post-conviction petition filed, petition denied in federal district court, appeal to United States Court of Appeals, decision affirmed, petition Supreme Court for another review, petition granted, decision affirmed, request post-conviction loop, petition for clemency filed, and petition denied. If all of these steps fail, the defendant is executed.[21]

A little known fact is that the criminal justice system automatically appeals its own conviction once an offender is sentenced to death—a move that blends crime control and due process interests of the state. Of the 36 states with capital statutes, all but one had automatic appeal procedures regardless of the wishes or interests of the defendant! In each jurisdiction, the state's highest appellate court usually conducted the review. If either the conviction or sentence was vacated, the case could be remanded to the trial court for additional proceedings or retrial. As a result of retrial or re-sentencing, a death sentence could be re-imposed. The only exception was South Carolina where defendants had the right to wave sentence review if deemed competent by the courts. The federal system does not have an automatic appeal.[22]

Method of Execution

The predominant method of execution is legal injection, which is used in all death penalty states and in the federal system. Lethal injection involves the intravenous administering of three drugs. First, an anesthetic called sodium thiopental (the trademark name is sodium pentothal) puts the condemned offender into a deep sleep within 30 seconds. The anesthetic is about 50 times greater that given in normal surgical operations and is itself a lethal dose. Second, a lethal dose of a paralyzing agent called pancuronium bromide (Pavulon) is given which stops the inmate's breathing by paralyzing the diaphragm and lungs. Third, a toxic agent such as potassium chloride is given at a lethal dose to interrupt the electrical signaling essential to heart functioning and induce cardiac arrest.

Although each of the three drugs used in lethal injection is itself a fatal dose, the method has come under tremendous criticism beginning in 2007. On September 25, 2007, the U.S. Supreme Court agreed to hear a case challenging the use of lethal injection. In *Baze v. Rees* (No. 07-5439), the Supreme Court will consider whether lethal injection constitutes cruel and unusual punishment as it is currently implemented. No executions have been carried out since the Supreme Court agreed to consider this issue.[23]

Nine states use electrocution, four states use lethal gas, three states use hanging, and two states use firing squads. Seventeen states have authorized more than one method; lethal injection is the default and the condemned offender can elect the other method. Several states offer alternative methods of execution in the event that lethal injection is ruled unconstitutional.

Criminal History Background of Condemned Offenders

As shown in Table 12-3, death row inmates generally have extensive prior involvement in crime. About 66% of death row inmates had prior felony convictions before their death sentence. Nearly one in every ten death row inmates had previously been convicted of homicide *before* being sentenced to death for an additional homicide. Approximately 40% of death row inmates were already under criminal justice supervision or had pending legal status at the time of their capital crimes. Specifically, 15% were on parole, 11% were on probation, 8% had charges pending and were on bond, nearly 4% were incarcerated, and almost 2% were on escape status.[24]

Dorothy Van Soest and her colleagues studied the life histories of 37 death row inmates who had committed heinous crimes. All of these offenders demonstrated an early onset of antisocial behavior during childhood, including alcohol and drug abuse, school behavior problems, reports of conduct problems, and crime. Moreover, violence was a predominant theme in their lives across settings, contexts, and ages. Death row inmates who committed heinous crimes experienced sexual abuse, emotional abuse, and neglect and had significantly high rates as the perpetrator and victim of violence.[25]

Condemned offenders exemplify a criminological profile that matches the dire seriousness of their legal punishment. On average, their lives are startling histories of abuse, victimization, trauma, crime and criminal justice system involvement, substance abuse, and assorted psychiatric and psychopathological problems that are significantly greater than the average prisoner. In their review of the characteristics of death row inmates, Mark Cunningham and Mark Vigen advised that, "It is disturbing that so many inmates on death row are so obviously damaged developmentally, intellectually, educationally, neurologically, and psychologically."[26]

There seem to be two general groups of offenders among those ultimately sentenced to death. The first is a career criminal group for whom capital offenses are the culmination of a decades-long pattern of criminal versatility, violence, and recurrent arrest and incarceration. Matt DeLisi and Aaron Scherer studied criminals who committed multiple homicides (some of whom were sentenced to death) and found that 30 percent were serious, habitual

TABLE 12-3 Criminal Justice Data: Criminal History Profile of Prisoners under Sentence of Death

	Percent of prisoners under sentence of death[a]			
	All[b]	White[c]	Balck[c]	Hispanic
U.S. total	100%	100%	100%	100%
Prior felony convictions				
Yes	65.7%	62.1%	71.4%	61.8%
No	34.3	37.9	28.6	34.3
Number unknown	257			
Prior homicide convictions				
Yes	8.6%	8.8%	9.0%	6.7%
No	91.4	91.2	91.0	93.3
Number unknown	56			
Legal status at time of capital offense				
Charges pending	7.7%	8.6%	7.6%	5.0%
Probation	10.5	9.1	11.7	11.4
Parole	15.2	12.9	16.5	19.2
On escape	1.5	2.0	0.9	1.5
Incarcerated	4.1	4.5	3.9	3.5
Other status	0.5	0.4	0.5	0.6
None	60.6	62.5	58.9	58.9
Number unknown	347			

offenders with multiple violent convictions even before being condemned. The second group consists of offenders with minimal criminal records who commit some atrocious act of extreme violence, such as spree killing. In sum, a sustained, intensive, and lifelong involvement in antisocial behavior is typical of persons who reside on death row.[27]

Historical Trends

As explored in Chapter 11, capital punishment was widespread and in colonial America. Death was a normal punishment for upwards of 200 criminal offenses, nearly all of which today would not be considered serious enough to warrant prison let alone death. The birth of the penitentiary reflected a more tempered American criminal justice system, as confinement replaced corporal and capital punishment. The last century of death penalty activity has similarly been marked by wildly contrasting trends.

As shown in Figures 12-1 and 12-2, executions were once a frequent occurrence. During the 1930s, nearly 170 prisoners were executed annually. Approximately 130 executions were performed annually during the 1940s and around 80 per year during the 1950s. The broad due process reforms of the 1960s forever changed the course of American capital punishment

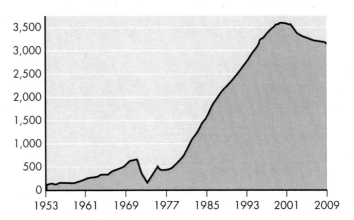

FIGURE 12-1 Death Row Population

Source: Snell, T. L. (2010). *Capital punishment, 2009—Statistical tables.* Washington, DC: U. S. Department of Justice, Office of Justice Programs, Bureau of Justice Statistics.

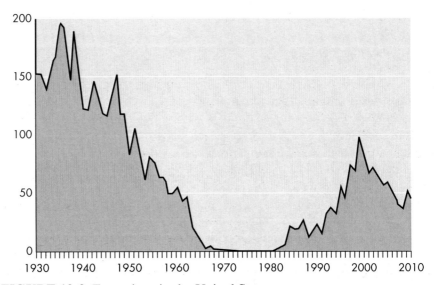

FIGURE 12-2 Executions in the United States

Source: Snell, T. L. (2010). *Capital punishment, 2009—Statistical tables.* Washington, DC: U. S. Department of Justice, Office of Justice Programs, Bureau of Justice Statistics.

as the general public, for the first time, began to express dissatisfaction with the ultimate punishment. Moreover, the criminal justice system was growing increasingly unnerved by the wide variability in which juries opted for capital punishment, as shown in Table 12-4. As such, the execution rate plummeted. Only three persons were executed in 1966 and 1967, and from 1968 to 1976 there was a de facto moratorium on the death penalty. From 1972 to 1976, the death penalty was officially held to be unconstitutional. In three cases (*Furman v. Georgia*, *Jackson v. Georgia*, and *Branch v. Texas*) collectively known as the *Furman* decision, the Supreme Court, in a 5-4 decision, held that the manner in which the death penalty was imposed and carried out under the laws of Georgia and Texas was cruel and unusual and overall in violation of the Eighth and Fourteenth Amendments.[28] The ruling voided death penalty statutes nationwide and commuted the sentences of more than 600 death row inmates.

The new death statutes with aggravating and mitigating factors to guide sentencing re-instituted the death penalty, but only 11 people were executed between 1977 and 1983. Over the past twenty years, approximately 40 executions have been conducted annually. Consequently, the death row population has increased nearly seven-fold between 1980 and today. Currently, the overwhelming majority of Americans support capital punishment and it is one of the few political issues on which Democrats and Republicans agree. Indeed, politicians who steadfastly maintain an anti-death penalty stance risk appearing soft on crime or unable to meet the crime control wishes of the public.[29] For instance, James Galliher and John Galliher conducted a study that illustrated the political capital and public opinion of the death penalty. Galliher and Galliher analyzed the death penalty debate that occurred in New York State from 1977, the time of the first execution after the reaffirmation of the constitutionality of the death penalty, and 1995, an era when the penalty was reintroduced in New York. They found that the enormous public support for the sanction and faith in its deterrent value was greater than the criminological findings about the death penalty's deterrent effects.[30] In other words, politicians often want to please the public by giving them what they want, and the death penalty is a preferred piece of public policy.

Twenty-First Century Trends

In the Twenty-first Century, the death penalty appears at an uncertain crossroads. The federal government and almost 80 percent of the states continue to execute the worst types of criminals. Among persons sentenced to death, the probability of execution is significantly increasing and the time until execution is declining. Virginia, one of the most active death penalty states, is unquestionably the most severe in terms of likelihood of execution and waiting time until execution. Recent federal law should only hasten the swiftness of the death penalty with the passage of the Antiterrorism and Effective Death

TABLE 12-4 Criminal Justice History: Number of Persons Executed, by Jurisdiction, 1930–2007

Jurisdiction	Number executed	
	Since 1930	Since 1977
U.S. total	5,047	1,188
Texas	744	447
Georgia	412	46
New York	329	0
North Carolina	306	43
California	305	13
Florida	238	68
Ohio	205	33
South Carolina	204	42
Virginia	197	105
Alabama	179	44
Mississippi	164	10
Louisiana	160	27
Pennsylvania	155	3
Oklahoma	151	91
Arkansas	145	27
Missouri	129	67
Kentucky	106	3
Illinois	102	12
Tennessee	99	6
New Jersey	74	0
Maryland	73	5
Arizona	61	23
Indiana	61	20
Washington	51	4
Colorado	48	1
Nevada	41	12
District of Columbia	40	0
West Virginia	40	0
Federal system	36	3

Continued

TABLE 12-4 Continued

Massachusetts	27	0
Delaware	26	14
Connecticut	22	1
Oregon	21	2
Utah	19	6
lowa	18	0
Kansas	15	0
Montana	9	3
New Mexico	9	1
Wyoming	8	1
Nebraska	7	3
Idaho	4	1
Vermont	4	0
South Dakota	2	1
New Hampshire	1	0

Source: Snell, T. L. (2010). *Capital punishment, 2009—Statistical tables.* Washington, DC: U. S. Department of Justice, Office of Justice Programs, Bureau of Justice Statistics.

Penalty Act of 1996.[31] Finally, some states that presently do not have the death penalty, such as Iowa, are considering the reinstatement of the ultimate penalty as the only appropriate punishment for persons who commit the most heinous crimes.

On the other hand, the death penalty is also currently facing perhaps its greatest legitimacy crisis in the name of wrongful convictions and miscarriages of justice. At the forefront of this initiative is The Innocence Project. The Innocence Project at Cardozo School of Law was created in 1992 by attorneys Barry Scheck and Peter Neufeld. It is a non-profit legal clinic that handles cases where post-conviction DNA testing of evidence can yield conclusive proof of innocence. At this writing, The Innocence Project has exonerated 266 persons many of whom had been erroneously sentenced to death (the importance of The Innocence Project is explored in Part One of this textbook). Several factors contributed to these miscarriages of justice, the most common are mistaken identification, false confessions, erroneous information/testimony from informants, and erroneous microscopic hair matches.[32] Criminologists, most notably Talia Roitberg Harmon, have also found that prosecutorial misconduct, the discovery of new exculpatory evidence, police misconduct, witness perjury, racial bias, ineffective attorneys, and evidence insufficiency also contributed to miscarriages of justice in capital cases.[33] The exoneration of factually innocent people, and the public outrage it engenders, is an important policy item and growing area of academic inquiry.[34]

Unfortunately, the criminological research on this important issue is often one-sided and specious.[35] It has been reported that more than 90% of the cases of "innocent" persons being condemned relied exclusively on the pleadings of the accused or declarations of innocence.[36] By this logic, any criminal defendant who insisted that he or she was innocent should simply be considered innocent. In addition to criminologists, some political leaders, religious leaders, and media figures also contend that innocent persons have been executed or are about to be executed often to fit their pre-existing agenda. For example, in 2006 DNA analysis confirmed the guilt of a Virginia man who was executed in 1992. The defendant had maintained his innocence, as did a growing support network. Indeed, no executed convict in the United States has ever been exonerated by scientific testing.[37]

Despite the contention, there are calls to make the death penalty the ultimate punishment that can serve both crime control and due process interests. For example, Matt DeLisi argued that federal and state governments should assume the responsibility for conducting post-conviction DNA analyses to ensure that condemned offenders are indeed guilty of their crimes.[38] It is the state's responsibility to ensure that capital punishment is administered without error, not due process organizations, such as The Innocence Project. Of course, such a policy would forensically affirm the guilt of most condemned offenders and should theoretically increase the speed with which executions are conducted. If DNA technology incontrovertibly confirms one's guilt, why continue endless appeals? Finally, criminologist Jon Sorensen has convincingly argued that the American death penalty was currently operating at its most efficient and professional level. In the lead article in the newsletter of the Academy of Criminal Justice Sciences, Sorensen assessed that there was not racial bias in the administration of the death penalty and that racial disparities stemmed from legitimate factors, such as actual offending differences by race. Moreover, the danger of executing truly innocent persons has been shown to be virtually zero and there was little chance that miscarriages of justice could occur due to factual innocence. Finally, "the process itself has become more efficient without sacrificing protection for defendants. Capital punishment in active death penalty jurisdictions is at least as efficient as life imprisonment, and perhaps more so."[39]

DETERRENCE

Evidence Against

Deterrence is the punishment philosophy that rests on the idea that people are rational thinkers endowed with freewill who weigh the costs and benefits of each course of action in their lives and then choose to act. Punishments that are swift, certain, severe (but proportionate to the crime) should theoretically dissuade potential criminals from choosing to commit crime. For most people deterrence works pretty well. Most Americans do not engage in felonious behavior for several reasons, one of which is that they are afraid of the prospect of going to prison. In terms of capital punishment, the severity of the sentence should dissuade prospective murderers from killing.

There is no question that most scholarly research has found that the death penalty does not deter murder. Indeed, the American Society of Criminology took an official stance against capital punishment because "social science research has found no consistent evidence of crime deterrence through execution." William Bailey and Ruth Peterson, two prominent criminologists who have studied the death penalty for decades, assessed that the criminological research literature has shown that the death penalty does not deter crime rates, murder rates, and even specific types of capital murder such as the murder of a police officer.[40] Michael Radelet, arguably one of the most accomplished death penalty scholars, has surveyed both academic and applied experts for their views on the deterrent effects of capital punishment. Over 85% of criminologists and nearly 70% of police chiefs and county sheriffs indicated that the death penalty offered no deterrent effect.[41]

Early deterrence research employed crude forms of data analysis and were methodologically weak. For instance, the murder rates of contiguous states, one with and one without the death penalty were compared and offered as evidence against deterrence. Recent research is much more sophisticated but tends to yield the same conclusion even when controlling for an assortment of variables that are known to affect the crime rate. Indeed, Derral Cheatwood even found that capital punishment increased violent crime rates net the effects of other important variables.[42]

Several other criminologists have also found that capital punishment can actually produce an increase in homicides. This unexpected anti-deterrent effect is known as brutalization defined as the increase in violent crime, specifically homicide, in the wake of an execution. Evidence for a brutalization effect has been found using data from South Carolina, Arizona, Oklahoma, and California.[43] John Cochran and Mitchell Chamlin, two of the prominent scholars on the brutalization thesis, have also found that the effects of the death penalty were contingent on the type of homicide. For instance, California executed Robert Harris in 1992 after a 25-year moratorium in that state. The execution resulted in a decrease in the level of non-stranger felony murders (evidence of deterrence) but an increase in argument-based murders of strangers (evidence of brutalization).[44] Finally, William Bailey reanalyzed their data and found no evidence for brutalization or deterrence and the death penalty.[45]

Supportive Evidence

Although the bulk of criminological research has found that the death penalty did not deter murder, much of that research was extraordinarily crude in its analysis. Moreover, sociologists conducted the preponderance of death penalty research and great speculation exists that sociological criminologists were either ideologically unwilling to produce evidence of deterrence, were unable to conduct more sophisticated data analysis, or both. Curiously, economists have produced considerable support for the idea that the death penalty deters murder. Isaac Ehrlich conducted the seminal study of death penalty deterrence using highly sophisticated quantitative models that were able to control for a variety of variables that influence crime. Ehrlich found that each execution would have saved between seven and eight murders from occurring.[46] Ehrlich was excoriated for the research finding and several criminologists hurried to disconfirm his findings. Although some of these re-analyses cast doubt on Ehrlich's work, more studied confirmed that the death penalty actually did deter murder.[47]

Contemporary research continues to suggest an important deterrent effect for the death penalty. Joanna Shepherd recently found that each execution resulted in three fewer murders; pertained to domestic violence murders and murders of passion, crimes that were previously thought to be beyond the reach of deterrence; and that one less murder was committed for every 33 month reduction in the wait on death row.[48] A related study found that each execution resulted in 18 fewer murders.[49]

Hashem Dezhbakhsh and Joanna Shepherd recently conducted the most impressive and methodologically sophisticated study of the potential deterrent effects of the death penalty using data from all 50 states and spanning 1960–2000. Dezhbakhsh and Shepherd used the 1972–1976 official moratorium period as a judicial experiment. By comparing the murder rates immediately before and after 1972 and 1976, they could assess the effects of imposing and then lifting the moratorium on the death penalty. They produced several important findings. First, the annual murder rate increased 9.3% when the Supreme Court ruled that the death penalty was unconstitutional. Second, the murder rate increased 16.3% after two years and 21% after three. Third, the annual murder rate dropped 8.3% after executions became lawful. Fourth, the murder rate dropped 8.2% after two years and 4% after three. Fifth, the murder rate increased 23% between 1972 and 1976. These results held regardless of the data's aggregation level, the time period used, the specific variable used to measure executions, and of controls for general trends in crime and specific offenses that often lead to murder. They concluded that, "we verify that the negative relationship between the death penalty and murder is not a spurious finding."[50]

A likely empirical reason for the dispute between the death penalty camps was the timing of the deterrent effect. Theoretically, the deterrent effects of an execution should be immediate and short-term, such as within a month. Studies that looked at homicides over a year period were missing the very truncated time period when deterrence should occur. Indeed, criminologists discovered this very point. David Phillips found that homicides decreased 36% immediately following a publicized execution and that cases with the greatest publicity resulted in the greatest reductions in killings. No long-term deterrent effect was found.[51] Steven Stack found that a publicized execution resulted in a drop of 30 homicides in the month of the story. Executions that received little to no publicity had no deterrent effect. Importantly, Stack also found that the importance of executions as a means of crime control was exaggerated. For instance, the percent of the population that was in the most homicide-prone age group was 21 times more closely associated with the monthly murder rate than publicized executions.[52]

Substantive Problems with the Deterrence Argument

Irrespective of evidence for or against a deterrent effect for the death penalty, there are major substantive problems to consider. First, executions simply are not conducted soon enough after conviction to adequately explore deterrent effects. Punishment must be swift, certain, and severe to achieve deterrence. From 1977–2004, the average length of stay on death row until execution was 124 months or more than 10 years. In 2010, offenders waited an average of 14 years before their execution. In other words, among persons who commit capital crimes *today* and are convicted and sentenced to death, they must wait more than a decade until their execution if it is one of the 1 to 2% of cases that actually result in execution. With this temporal order, it is impossible to adequately assess the degree to which prospective murders are deterred by capital punishment.

The second major substantive problem in the administration of the death penalty is the infrequency with which it is actually imposed. For instance, Derral Cheatwood studied more than 9,000 homicides from Chicago spanning the years 1879 to 1930 and found that 1.2% resulted in a death sentence and less than 1% of these cases actually resulted in an execution.[53] In other words, even among inmates sentenced to death, execution is rarely carried out. Similarly, Steven Levitt assessed that the likelihood of being executed conditional on committing murder was less than one in 200 and that even among those who were condemned the annual execution rate was 2%.[54] In the end, the evaluation of whether the death penalty deters murder will likely never be answered given the typical way the punishment is administered in the United States.

RETRIBUTION

Moral, Philosophical, and Religious Bases

Retribution is the philosophical rationale that implies the payment of a debt to society and the criminal offender's expiation or atonement for his or her crime. In simple terms, retribution is a form of revenge or retaliation in which the criminal justice system inflicts a proportionate level of suffering to the criminal offender. For capital punishment, the execution is the "payback" or revenge exacted from the criminal for committing murder. This philosophy was historically described as the *lex talionis* or law of the claw. The *lex talionis* is the law of retaliation such that punishment must be inflicted "an eye for an eye and a tooth for a tooth." One of main historical proponents of retribution was the philosopher Immanuel Kant. Kant believed that criminal punishment, even death, recognized the agency, autonomy, and free will of the actor or criminal. Since a criminal chooses to commit homicide, then the state must recognize their volition and autonomy and respond accordingly. Kant would argue that the deterrent capacity of the death penalty is irrelevant; the sole purpose of an execution is to give the criminal his due justice. Kant disposed of arguments calling for the abolishment of capital punishment as sentimentality or humanitarian posturing.[55]

Retribution entails reciprocity between the crime and its punishment. It is closely connected with the idea of dessert or just desserts. Just desserts is the philosophy of justice that assumes that individuals freely choose to violate criminal laws and therefore the state or criminal justice has the legal and moral right and duty to punish them according to the nature of their acts. Many people deeply believe in the idea of just desserts. For example, people who do good things for others are viewed as deserving of rewards or similarly positive treatment. On the other hand, serial killers who are put to death are often described as "getting what they deserved."

Capital punishment has been extensively used immemorially in Babylonian society, the Kingdoms of Judah and Israel, the Roman Empire, Ancient Greece, Ancient India, China, under English common law, and throughout the majority of American history. The death penalty has an important place among the world's three major religions, Judaism, Christianity, and Islam.[56] Then, as today, capital punishment was viewed as a righteous, retributive response to criminal offenders who violate the moral order, humanity, or God. But, then as today, there were mixed feelings about the appropriateness and application of the death penalty particularly in the Judeo-Christian ethic. In a magisterial review, Scott Johnson summarized that the Bible contained "several overt endorsements of capital punishment. Most of these explicit endorsements occur in the Old Testament. The Mosaic Law articulated in the Pentateuch prescribes death as the punishment for several offenses against God and humanity. The New Testament contains no similar overt endorsements. . . . Some New Testament statements appear to support capital punishment; however, these passages do not speak directly to the issue of the death penalty. They mention the death penalty and presume its correctness or these statements demand good citizenship from believers, meaning that believers should accept the death penalty provided it is the policy of a legitimate government."[57] Johnson also identified inconsistencies in the Bible in which murderers were variously executed, condemned but allowed to live, or treated in another manner. In this sense, the "arbitrary and capricious" application of the death penalty is not new. Curiously, many Americans derive their support or opposition to the death penalty from religious teachings. From one perspective, a retributive death penalty is not only viable policy, but also mandated from scripture. From another perspective, only God can stand in judgment of criminal offenders, thus the death penalty is an affront to God.

Contemporary Public Philosophy

The average citizen does not contemplate the arguments of Kant while forming their opinion about the death penalty. The overwhelming majority of Americans support the death penalty and arguably the primary basis for their support centers around retribution.[58] The contemporary public philosophy toward retribution is simple and unambiguous. Certain criminal behaviors are considered intrinsically wrong, even evil, and the punishment for these crimes must not only provide just desserts to the offender, but also "cleanse" the public by removing the person from society. These "evil" crimes are known as *mala in se* offenses and include murder, rape, abduction or kidnapping, and any sexual-based offense against a child. There is a universal revulsion against these forms of behavior and the persons who commit them. To many Americans, the death penalty is the symbolic vehicle by which evil wrongdoers are legally, lawfully, and morally extinguished from human society. As such, retribution can be viewed as a righteous, philosophically defensible justification for capital punishment.[59]

Harboring retributive views is also part of a larger constellation of ideological values and beliefs. Researchers have found that persons who favor the death penalty tend to hold more conservative political beliefs and invoke a highly moralistic, good versus evil worldview in which criminal offenders are considered to be reprehensible monsters that should be punished in the most severe way. For others, retributive death penalty attitudes are correlated with racial prejudice or the attribution of crime to persons of color. Finally, some citizens employ a retributive death penalty stance as a symbolic affirmation of their crime control beliefs.[60]

Modern retribution also is driven by the idea that many citizens are disgusted with the inability of the criminal justice system to adequately control crime. There is widespread public indignation that condemned offenders, many of which are serious repeat offenders, are seemingly allowed to recurrently commit crime and victimize others. It could be argued that modern retribution is influenced by overemphasis on the due process rights of criminal defendants and a de-emphasis on punishing criminals.[61] Walter Berns summarized the type of retribution that characterizes many Americans' views on the subject: "Anger is the passion that recognizes and cares about justice."[62]

Racial Elements, Capital Punishment, and Retribution

One of the major death penalty controversies centers on the disproportionate number of African Americans who have been executed or await execution on death row. There are comparable numbers of whites and blacks on death row despite the huge differences in these racial groups proportion of the population.[63] Indeed, the idea that the death penalty is discriminatory in its application is one of the primary reasons why the American Society of Criminology (ASC) took an official organizational stance against the death penalty. The ASC's decision was motivated by the pioneering research of David Baldus, Charles Pulanski, and George Woodworth who found that defendants charged with killing white persons were more than four times more likely to be sentenced to death than those charged with killing blacks.[64] Similarly, many Americans oppose the death penalty because of concerns that it is racially biased in its application.

Irrespective of one's thoughts on potential racial elements of the death penalty, the Supreme Court ruled on this issue in the landmark case *McClesky v. Kemp* (1987). In *McClesky*, the Court held that the Baldus study that indicated that black defendants received the death penalty more often than whites, especially when the victim was white, was not sufficient to demonstrate that racial considerations enter into capital sentencing determinations. The Court also found that the specific defendant did not show a violation of equal protection under the law (Fourteenth Amendment) because he had not shown that there was purposeful discrimination in his own case. Additionally, the Court found that the Baldus study was "flawed in many respects" and because of these deficiencies "failed to contribute anything of value."[65]

Two earlier studies shed further light on the putative racial biases of the death penalty. Michael Radelet examined 637 homicide indictments in 20 Florida counties in 1976 and 1977 and produced some vital findings. First, Radelet confirmed the widespread empirical point that crime was mostly intraracial, that is whites tended to offend against whites and blacks tended to victimize blacks. Second, when murder was interracial, it tended to be overwhelmingly black-on-white and involved strangers as offender and victim. For instance, homicides involving strangers were 700 percent more likely to be black-on-white than white-on-black. Third, those accused of murdering whites faced a higher probability of being indicted for first-degree murder and being sentenced to death. Fourth, once indicted for first-degree murder, neither race of the defendant, neither victim, nor the interaction between these two variables was significantly related to the probability of being sentenced to death.[66]

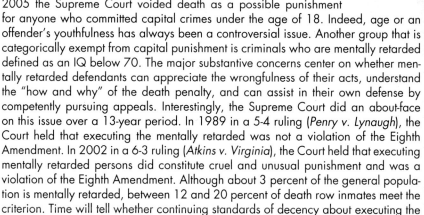

CRIME SCENE   DO NOT CROSS

CRIMINAL JUSTICE CONTROVERSY

CAPITAL PUNISHMENT AND THE MENTALLY RETARDED/DISABLED

Not all persons are eligible for certain criminal punishments because of the mitigating characteristics of specific groups. For instance, in 2005 the Supreme Court voided death as a possible punishment for anyone who committed capital crimes under the age of 18. Indeed, age or an offender's youthfulness has always been a controversial issue. Another group that is categorically exempt from capital punishment is criminals who are mentally retarded defined as an IQ below 70. The major substantive concerns center on whether mentally retarded defendants can appreciate the wrongfulness of their acts, understand the "how and why" of the death penalty, and can assist in their own defense by competently pursuing appeals. Interestingly, the Supreme Court did an about-face on this issue over a 13-year period. In 1989 in a 5-4 ruling (*Penry v. Lynaugh*), the Court held that executing the mentally retarded was not a violation of the Eighth Amendment. In 2002 in a 6-3 ruling (*Atkins v. Virginia*), the Court held that executing mentally retarded persons did constitute cruel and unusual punishment and was a violation of the Eighth Amendment. Although about 3 percent of the general population is mentally retarded, between 12 and 20 percent of death row inmates meet the criterion. Time will tell whether continuing standards of decency about executing the mentally retarded will motivate further change in current policy.

Sources: *Roper v. Simmons*, 543 U.S. 551 (2005); *Atkins v. Virginia*, 536 U S. 304 (2002); *Penry v. Lynaugh*, 492 U.S. 302 (1989); Acker, J. R., & Lanier, C. S. (1997). Unfit to live, unfit to die: Incompetency for execution under modern death penalty legislation. *Criminal Law Bulletin, 33*, 107–150; Tobolowsky, P. M. (2004). Capital punishment and the mentally retarded offender. *The Prison Journal, 84*, 340–360. Photo © JupiterImages, Corp.

BOX 12-1

A contemporaneous study by Gary Kleck examined race and the death penalty using data spanning 1930 to 1978. Kleck produced five findings that elucidated the role of race in the application of the death penalty. "First, the death penalty has not generally been imposed for murder in a fashion discriminatory toward blacks, except in the South. Elsewhere, black homicide offenders have been less likely to receive a death sentence or be executed than whites. Second, for the 11% of executions, which have been imposed for rape, discrimination against black defendants who had raped white victims was substantial. Such discrimination was limited to the South and has disappeared because death sentences are no longer imposed for rape. Third, regarding non-capital sentencing, the evidence is largely contrary to a hypothesis of general or widespread overt discrimination against black defendants, although there is evidence of discrimination for a minority of specific jurisdictions, judges, crime types, etc. Fourth, although black offender-white victim crimes are generally punished more severely than crimes involving other racial combinations, the evidence indicates that this is due to legally relevant factors related to such offenses, not the racial composition itself. Fifth, there appears to be a general pattern of less severe punishment of crimes with black victims than those with white victims, especially in connection with imposition of the death penalty."[67] Recent re-analyses of capital punishment data from Maryland further revealed that earlier showings of racial bias were the result of methodological errors and limitations and that there is no evidence of racial discrimination in the administration of the death penalty.[68]

In the end, the racial bias concern about the death penalty has empirically less to do with race and more to do with the circumstances of capital crimes. The most common scenario that leads to a death sentence is a first-degree murder committed during the course of an armed robbery. This scenario 1) usually involves strangers, 2) satisfies the aggravating circumstances of a felony murder, and 3) armed robbery is the offense that is most disproportionately committed by African American males. These characteristics, not the race of the specific offender and victim, lead to capital convictions.

CHAPTER SUMMARY: BALANCING CRIME CONTROL AND DUE PROCESS

- Capital punishment is the most punitive, sensationalistic, controversial, and infrequently used form of criminal punishment.
- Capital punishment is susceptible to political and public opinion and has been used extensively or sporadically depending on the political era.
- From 1972 to 1976, the death penalty was illegal in the United States because it was applied in a manner that was in violation of the Eighth Amendment's proscription of cruel and unusual punishment.
- Although deterrence is the explicit rationale for capital punishment, the evidence is very mixed about its actual deterrent effects.
- Death sentencing guidelines specify aggravating and mitigating circumstances to determine the appropriateness of capital punishment.
- Retribution is the philosophical rationale which states that the worst criminals deserve death as a means of repayment, retaliation, or deservedness for their crimes.
- Lethal injection, consisting of lethal doses of an anesthetic, a barbiturate to stop respiration, and a toxic agent to induce cardiac arrest, is the most common method of execution.
- Virtually all death sentences are automatically/legislatively reviewed and appealed by the state regardless of the wishes of the condemned defendant.
- Condemned offenders wait more than 10 years on death row primarily due to a convoluted appeals process.
- Despite claims to the contrary, the death penalty is not racially biased in its application and instead reflects legally relevant case variables.

KEY TERMS

Eighth Amendment
Abolitionist
Aggravating circumstances
Atkins v. Virginia
Bifurcated trial
Brutalization
Capital punishment or death
  penalty
Coker v. Georgia
Cruel and unusual punishment
Death row syndrome
Desert or just deserts
Deterrence
Expiation
Felony murder

Furman v. Georgia
Gregg v. Georgia
Kantian retribution
Lethal injection
Lex talionis
Mala in se
McClesky v. Kemp
Mitigating circumstances
Moratorium
Proportionality review
Retentionist
Retribution
Roper v. Simmons
The Innocence Project
Writ of certiorari

TALKING POINTS

1. Are you for or against the death penalty? Why? Which deterrence and retribution arguments do you use to defend your position?

2. Why is there a disjunction between public and elite/academic views toward the death penalty? With whom do political leaders tend to agree?

3. Is the death penalty administered in a racially discriminatory manner? Has this changed over time? What evidence can you marshal to support your answer?

4. Will the death penalty be voided anytime soon? On what bases could the Supreme Court invalidate the ultimate punishment?

5. Minors and the mentally retarded are categorically exempt from the death penalty? Is this appropriate? Should other groups, such as females, be similarly exempt? What does categorical exemption indicate about that social group?

WEB LINKS

Bureau of Justice Statistics: Capital Punishment Statistics
(www.ojp.usdoj.gov/bjs/cp.htm)

Center on Wrongful Convictions
(www.law.northwestern.edu/wrongfulconvictions/)

Death Penalty Information Center
(www.deathpenaltyinfo.org/)

Legal Information Institute: Death Penalty Resources
(www.law.cornell.edu/topics/death_penalty.html)

Pro-Death Penalty Information
(www.prodeathpenalty.com)

Texas Department of Criminal Justice Death Row
(www.tdcj.state.tx.us/stat/deathrow.htm)

The Innocence Project
(www.innocenceproject.org)

FURTHER READING

Bedau, H. A. (Ed.). (1997). *The death penalty in America: Current controversies*. New York: Oxford University Press. Bedau is one of the key figures in death penalty scholarship and this well-respected anthology contains chapters on the many issues pertaining to capital punishment. This is must reading for students interested in learning the death penalty literature.

Berns, W. (1979). *For capital punishment: Crime and the morality of the death penalty*. Lanham, MD: University Press of America. Simply the best and one of the only pro-death penalty works in the scholarly literature.

Mandery, E. J. (2011). *Capital punishment: A balanced examination*, second edition Sudbury, MA: Jones & Bartlett. This exhaustive, 700-page volume is the most comprehensive and balanced anthology devoted to the death penalty. Whereas most books have token contributions that favor the death penalty, Mandery's work is (as the title suggests) balanced.

Radelet, M. L., Bedau, H. A., & Putnam, C. E. (1992). *In spite of innocence: Erroneous convictions in capital cases.* Boston, MA: Northeastern University Press. This book recounts over 400 miscarriages of justice that occurred in the 20th Century and highlights the substantive, procedural, and criminal justice system errors that lead to wrongful capital convictions. The authors call for the abolishment of the death penalty.

Rosenbaum, T. (2005). *The myth of moral justice: Why our legal system fails to do what's right.* New York: Harper Collins. Written by a law professor who has "renounced" his law degree, this insightful book argues that the criminal justice system is so fixated on administrative and bureaucratic ideals, that the vital moral issues in crime and punishment are completely ignored. Although it does not focus specifically on the death penalty, the book touches on the feelings of indignation and dissatisfaction that most Americans (who are pro-death penalty) feel about the administration of justice.

ENDNOTES

CHAPTER 1

[1] Quotation taken from address delivered at the dedication of the new hall at the Boston University School of Law, Boston, Massachusetts, January 8, 1897.

[2] Quotation from Adam Smith, *The Theory of Moral Sentiments*, originally published 1759.

[3] American Civil Liberties Union, http://www.aclu .org/CriminalJustice/CriminalJusticeMain.cfm, Retrieved February 24, 2011.

[4] Quotation from Plato's Republic. Philosophy experts disagree over the attribution of the quotation. Some attribute it to Plato, others to Thrasymachus, and still others to a character named Thrasymachus who was created by Plato.

[5] United States Supreme Court Justice Hugo Black, *Griffin v. Illinois*, 351 U. S. 12 (1956).

[6] Uviller, H. R. (1996). *Virtual justice: The flawed prosecution of crime in America* (p. xii). New Haven, CT: Yale University Press.

[7] Bufkin, J. (2004). Criminology/criminal justice master's programs in the United States: Searching for commonalities. *Journal of Criminal Justice Education, 15,* 239–262.

[8] Hughes, K. A. (2006). *Justice expenditure and employment in the United States, 2003.* Washington, DC: U. S. Department of Justice, Office of Justice Programs, Bureau of Justice Statistics.

[9] For trade and academic perspectives on natural law and related topics, students may be interested in the following works: Black, D. (1983). Crime as social control. *American Sociological Review, 48,* 34–45; DiCristina, B. (2000). Compassion can be cruel: Durkheim on sympathy and punishment. *Justice Quarterly, 17,* 485–517; Pinker, S. (2002). *The blank slate: The modern denial of human nature.* New York: Viking; Rossi, P. H., Waite, E., Bose, C. E., & Berk, R. E. (1974). The seriousness of crimes: Normative structure and individual differences. *American Sociological Review, 39,* 224–237; Shermer, M. (2004). *The science of good and evil: Why people cheat, gossip, care, share, and follow the golden rule.* New York: Henry Holt; Wilson, J. Q. (1997). *The moral sense.* New York: The Free Press.

[10] Friedman, L. M. (1993). *Crime and punishment in American history* (p. 22). New York: Basic Books.

[11] Packer, H. L. (1968). *The limits of the criminal sanction* (pp.160–161). Stanford, CA: Stanford University Press.

[12] Packer, note 11, p. 165.

[13] Spangenberg, R. L., & Beeman, M. L. (1998). *Improving state and local criminal justice systems: A report on how public defenders, prosecutors, and other criminal justice system practitioners are collaborating across the country.* Washington, DC: U. S. Department of Justice, Office of Justice Programs, Bureau of Justice Assistance.

[14] Herraiz, D. S. (2004). *Project Safe Neighborhoods: America's network against gun violence.* Washington, DC: U.S. Department of Justice, Office of Justice Programs, Bureau of Justice Assistance.

[15] Gist, N. E. (2000). *Comprehensive Communities Program: A unique way to reduce crime and enhance public safety.* Washington, DC: U.S. Department of Justice, Office of Justice Programs, Bureau of Justice Assistance.

[16] Retrieved February 24, 2011, from www.innocenceproject.org.

[17] Scheck, B., Neufeld, P., & Dwyer, J. (2001). *Actual innocence: When justice goes wrong and how to make it right.* New York: Signet.

[18] Scheck, B. C., & Neufeld, P. J. (2002). Toward the formation of 'innocence commissions' in America. *Judicature, 86,* 98–105.

CHAPTER 2

[1] Doerner, W. G., & Lab, S. P. (2002). *Victimology* (p. 1), 3rd edition. Cincinnati, OH: Anderson.

[2] Harris, A. R. (1977). Sex and theories of deviance. *American Sociological Review, 42,* 3–16, p. 14.

[3] Hindelang, M. J. (1981). Variations in sex-race-age-specific incidence rates of offending. *American Sociological Review, 46,* 461–474, p. 473.

[4]Federal Bureau of Investigation. (2010). *Crime in the United States, 2009.* Washington, DC: U.S. Department of Justice, Government Printing Office.

[5]Vandiver, M., & Giacopassi, D. (1997). One million and counting: Students' estimates of the annual number of homicides in the U. S. *Journal of Criminal Justice Education, 8,* 135–144.

[6]Federal Bureau of Investigation. (2010). *Crime in the United States, 2009.* Washington, DC: U. S. Department of Justice, Government Printing Office; Federal Bureau of Investigation. (2005). *Uniform Crime Reporting Handbook, 2004.* Washington, DC: U. S. Department of Justice, Government Printing Office.

[7]Federal Bureau of Investigation. (2005). *Uniform Crime Reporting Handbook, 2004.* Washington, DC: U. S. Department of Justice, Government Printing Office.

[8]Federal Bureau of Investigation, note 4.

[9]Uniform Crime Reporting (UCR) Summary Reporting: Frequently Asked Questions, Retrieved February 24, 2011, from http://www.fbi.gov/ucr/ucrquest/htm.

[10]Federal Bureau of Investigation, note 4.

[11]Federal Bureau of Investigation. (2005). *Uniform Crime Reporting Handbook, 2004.* Washington, DC: U.S. Department of Justice, Government Printing Office. Definitions and other information about Part II offenses can be found in the UCR Handbook from pages 139 to 147.

[12]http://www.fbi.gov/ucr/ucrquest.htm, Retrieved February 24, 2011.

[13]For more summary information on NIBRS, readers can consult the following. Maxfield, M. G. (1999). The National Incident-Based Reporting System: Research and policy applications. *Journal of Quantitative Criminology, 15,* 119–149; Rantala, R. R., & Edwards, T. J. (2000). *Effects of NIBRS on crime statistics, Special Report.* Washington, DC: U.S. Department of Justice, Office of Justice Programs, Bureau of Justice Statistics.

[14]Hirschel, D. (2009). *Expanding police ability to report crime: The National Incident-Based Reporting System.* Washington, DC: U.S. Department of Justice, National Institute of Justice.

[15]Rantala & Edwards, note 13.

[16]Biderman, A. D., & Reiss, A. J. (1967). On exploring the 'dark figure' of crime. *The Annals of the American Academy of Political and Social Science, 374,* 1–15.

[17]Truman, J. L., & Rand, M. R. (2010). *Criminal victimization, 2009.* Washington, DC: U.S. Department of Justice, Office of Justice Programs, Bureau of Justice Statistics.

[18]For investigations of the strengths and weaknesses of victimization data, see Bachman, R. (1998). Factors related to rape reporting behavior and arrest: New evidence from the NCVS. *Criminal Justice and Behavior, 25,* 8–29; Bachman, R. (2000). A comparison of annual incidence rates and contextual characteristics of intimate-partner violence against women from the National Crime Victimization Survey (NCVS) and National Violence Against Women Survey (NVAWS). *Violence Against Women, 6,* 839–867; Gottfredson, M. R., & Hindelang, M. J. (1977). A consideration of telescoping and memory decay biases in victimization surveys. *Journal of Criminal Justice, 5,* 205–216; Lauritsen, J. L. (2001). The social ecology of violent victimization: Individual and contextual effects in the NCVS. *Journal of Quantitative Criminology, 17,* 3–32; Maltz, M. D., & Zawitz, M. W. (1996). *Displaying violent crime trends using estimates from the NCVS.* Washington, DC: U.S. Department of Justice, Office of Justice Programs, Bureau of Justice Statistics.

[19]Truman & Rand, note 17.

[20]Baum, K., & Klaus, P. (2005). Violent victimization of college students, 1995–2002. Washington, DC: U.S. Department of Justice, Office of Justice Programs, Bureau of Justice Statistics.

[21]Rennison, C. (2001). *Violent victimization and race, 1993–1998.* Washington, DC: U. S. Department of Justice, Office of Justice Programs, Bureau of Justice Statistics.

[22]Perkins, C. (2003). *Weapon use and violent crime, National Crime Victimization Survey, 1993-2001.* Washington, DC: U.S. Department of Justice, Office of Justice Programs, Bureau of Justice Statistics.

[23]Lauritsen, J. L. & Schaum, R. J. (2005). *Crime and victimization in the three largest metropolitan areas, 1980-1998.* Washington, DC: U.S. Department of Justice, Office of Justice Programs, Bureau of Justice Statistics.

[24]For studies that dispute the UCR-NCS or NCVS overlap, see, Menard, S. (1987). Short-term trends in crime and delinquency: A comparison of UCR, NCS, and self-report data. *Justice Quarterly, 4,* 455–474; Menard, S., & Covey, H. C. (1988). UCR and NCS: Comparisons over space and time. *Journal of Criminal Justice, 16,* 371–384. For studies that affirmed the overlap, see, Blumstein, A.,

Cohen, J., & Rosenfeld, R. (1991). Trend and deviation in crime rates: A comparison of UCR and NCS data for burglary and robbery. *Criminology, 29,* 237–264; Hindelang, M. J. (1974). The uniform crime reports revisited. *Journal of Criminal Justice, 2,* 1–17; MacDowall, D., & Loftin, C. (1992). Comparing the UCR and NCS over time. *Criminology, 30,* 125–132; Messner, S. F. (1984). The 'dark figure' and composite indexes of crime: Some empirical explorations of alternative data sources. *Journal of Criminal Justice, 12,* 435–444; O'Brien, R. M. (1991). Detrended UCR and NCS crime rates: Their utility and meaning. *Journal of Criminal Justice, 19,* 569–574.

[25]Although it is commonly understood that there is more crime than the criminal justice system can handle, few criminologists have explicitly commented on this. Indeed, there are scores of books and articles lamenting the size of the American criminal justice system, but none of these make the obvious point that criminal justice would be even more pronounced if more crimes were processed. An exception is a study by economist Richard Freeman who found that about 2% of the American GDP is allotted to crime control activities. Depending on your perspective, crime control or due process, this is part of the overhead of running a modern society or is pure waste. See, Freeman, R. B. (1996). Why do some many young American men commit crimes and what might we do about it? *Journal of Economic Perspectives, 10,* 25–42.

[26]Smith, S. K., & Motivans, M. (2005). *Federal criminal case processing, 2002: With trends 1982–2002.* Washington, DC: U.S. Department of Justice, Office of Justice Programs, Bureau of Justice Statistics.

[27]Cohen, T. H., & Kyckelhahn, T. (2010). *Felony defendants in large urban counties, 2006.* Washington, DC: U.S. Department of Justice, Office of Justice Programs, Bureau of Justice Statistics; Cohen, T. H., & Reaves, B. A. (2006). *Felony defendants in large urban counties, 2002.* Washington, DC: U.S. Department of Justice, Office of Justice Programs, Bureau of Justice Statistics.

[28]Federal Bureau of Investigation, note 4.

[29]Cohen & Kyckelhahn, note 27.

[30]Durose, M. R., & Langan, P. A. (2007). *Felony sentences in state courts, 2004.* Bulletin, June. Washington, DC: U.S. Department of Justice, Office of Justice Programs, Bureau of Justice Statistics; Greenfeld, L. A. (1995). *Prison sentences and time served for violence.* Washington, DC: U. S. Department of Justice, Office of Justice Programs, Bureau of Justice Statistics.

[31]Peterson, J. L., & Hickman, M. J. (2005). *Census of publicly funded forensic crime laboratories, 2002.* Washington, DC: U. S. Department of Justice, Office of Justice Programs, Bureau of Justice Statistics; Durose, M. R.(2008). *Census of publicly funded forensic crime laboratories, 2005.* Washington, DC: U.S. Department of Justice, Office of Justice Programs, Bureau of Justice Statistics.

[32]Steadman, G. W. (2002). Survey of DNA crime laboratories, 2001. Washington, DC: U. S. Department of Justice, Office of Justice Programs, Bureau of Justice Statistics.

[33]National Institute of Justice. (2004). *DNA in "minor" crimes yields major benefits in public safety.* Washington, DC: U.S. Department of Justice, Office of Justice Programs, National Institute of Justice.

[34]Pratt, T. C., Gaffney, M. J., Lovrich, N. P., & Johnson, C. L. (2006). This isn't "CSI": Estimating the national backlog of forensic DNA cases and the barriers associated with case processing. *Criminal Justice Policy Review, 17,* 32–47.

[35]Elliott, D. S. (1994). Serious violent offenders: Onset, developmental course, and termination—the American Society of Criminology 1993 Presidential address. *Criminology, 32,* 1–21; Farrington, D. P., Loeber, R., Stouthamer-Loeber, M., Van Kammen, W. B., & Schmidt, L. (1996). Self-reported delinquency and a combined delinquency seriousness scale based on boys, mothers, and teachers: Concurrent and predictive validity for African-Americans and Caucasians. *Criminology, 34,* 493–514; Jolliffe, D., Farrington, D. P., Hawkins, J. D., Catalano, R. F., Hill, K. G., & Kosterman, R. (2003). The predictive, concurrent, prospective and retrospective validity of self-reported delinquency. *Criminal Behavior and Mental Health, 13,* 179–197.

[36]Hindelang, M. J., Hirschi, T., & Weis, J. G. (1979). Correlates of delinquency: The illusion of discrepancy between self-report and official measures. *American Sociological Review, 44,* 995–1014; Thornberry, T. P., & Farnworth, M. (1982). Social correlates of criminal involvement: Further evidence on the relationship between social status and criminal behavior. *American Sociological Review, 47,* 505–518.

[37]Compare, Sampson, R. J. (1986). Effects of socioeconomic context on official reaction to juvenile

delinquency. *American Sociological Review, 51,* 876–885; Short, J. F. (1997). *Poverty, ethnicity, and violent crime.* Boulder, CO: Westview Press; Steffensmeier, D., Ulmer, J., & Kramer, J. (1998). The interaction of race, gender, and age in criminal sentencing: The punishment cost of being young, black, and male. *Criminology, 36,* 763–797 and Bastian, L. D., & Taylor, B. M. (1994). *Young black male victims.* Washington, DC: U. S. Department of Justice, Office of Justice Programs, Bureau of Justice Statistics; Harms, P. D., & Snyder, H. N. (2004). *Trends in the murder of juveniles: 1980–2000.* Washington, DC: U.S. Department of Justice, Office of Justice Programs, Office of Juvenile Justice and Delinquency Prevention.

[38] A cottage industry of works exists that examine the real and purported biases in the American criminal justice system. For a diverse sampling, see Cole, D. (1999). *No equal justice: Race and class in the American criminal justice system.* New York: The Free Press; Cole, G. F., Gertz, M. G., & Bunger, A. (2002). *The criminal justice system: Politics and policies,* 8th edition. Belmont, CA: Wadsworth; Gabbidon, S. L., & Greene, H. T. (2005). *Race, crime, and justice: A reader.* London: Routledge; Mac Donald, H. (2003). *Are cops racist? How the war against the police harms black Americans.* Chicago: Ivan R. Dee; Tracy, P. E. (2002). *Decision making and juvenile justice: An analysis of bias in case processing.* Westport, CT: Praeger; Wilbanks, W. (1987). *The myth of a racist criminal justice system.* Monterey, CA: Brooks/Cole.

[39] Hirschi, T., & Gottfredson, M. (1983). Age and the explanation of crime. *American Journal of Sociology, 89,* 552–584; Steffensmeier, D. J., Allan, E. A., Harer, M. D., & Streifel, C. (1989). Age and the distribution of crime. *American Journal of Sociology, 94,* 803–831.

[40] Harris, A. R. (1977). Sex and theories of deviance. *American Sociological Review, 42,* 3–16; Hindelang, M. J. (1979). Sex differences in criminal activity. *Social Problems, 27,* 143–156; Smith, D., & Visher, C. (1980). Sex and involvement in deviance/crime. *American Sociological Review, 45,* 691–701; Steffensmeier, D. J., & Allan, E. (1996). Gender and crime. *Annual Review of Sociology, 22,* 459–487; Steffensmeier, D. J., & Cobb, M. J. (1981). Sex differences in urban arrest patterns, 1934–1979. *Social Problems, 29,* 37–50.

[41] D'Alessio, S. J., & Stolzenberg, L. (2003). Race and the probability of arrest. *Social Forces, 81,* 1381–1397; DeLisi, M., & Regoli, B. (1999). Race, conventional crime, and criminal justice: The declining importance of skin color. *Journal of Criminal Justice, 27,* 549–557; Elliott, D. S., Ageton, S. S. (1980). Reconciling race and class differences in self-reported and official estimates of delinquency. *American Sociological Review, 45,* 95–110; Hindelang, M. J. (1978). Race and involvement in common law personal crimes. *American Sociological Review, 43,* 93–109; Hindelang, M. J. (1981). Variations in sex-race-age-specific incidence rates of offending. *American Sociological Review, 46,* 461–474; Weiter, R. (1996). Racial discrimination in the criminal justice system: Findings and problems in the literature. *Journal of Criminal Justice, 24,* 309–322.

[42] Braithwaite, J. (1981). The myth of social class and criminality reconsidered. *American Sociological Review, 46,* 36–57; Dunaway, R. G., Cullen, F. T., Burton, V. S., & Evans, T. D. (2000). The myth of social class and crime revisited: An examination of class and adult criminality. *Criminology, 38,* 589–632; Thornberry, T. P., & Farnworth, M. (1982). Social correlates of criminal involvement: Further evidence on the relationship between social status and criminal behavior. *American Sociological Review, 47,* 505–518; Tittle, C. R., & Meier, R. F. (1990). Specifying the SES/delinquency relationship. *Criminology, 28,* 271–299; Tittle, C. R., Villemez, W. J., & Smith, D. A. (1978). The myth of social class and criminality: An empirical assessment of the empirical evidence. *American Sociological Review, 43,* 643–656.

CHAPTER 3

[1] Alschuler, A. W. (2000). *Law without values: The life, work, and legacy of Justice Holmes* (p. 107). Chicago: University of Chicago Press.

[2] Montesquieu, B. (1989/1748). *The spirit of the laws* (p. 155). Cambridge: Cambridge University Press.

[3] Quotation was taken from speech given February 8, 1900 at a U.S. Senate hearing for women's suffrage.

[4] Attributed to Gandhi's comments on the ending of the First World War in 1918.

[5] Rousseau, J. (1762). *The social contract* (p. 697). Quotation selected from, Russell, B. (1972). A history of Western philosophy. New York: Simon and Schuster.

[6] McIlvanney, W. (1993). *Laidlaw* (p. 35). Orlando, FL: Harvest Books.

[7]Retrieved February 25, 2011, from http://www.ameri-canbar.org/aba.html.

[8]*Marbury v. Madison*, 5 U.S. 137 (1803).

[9]Neubauer, D. W. (2005). *America's courts and the criminal justice system,* 8th Edition. Belmont, CA: Thomson/Wadsworth (see p. 33).

[10]For a copy of the U. S. Constitution consult http://www.house.gov/Constitution/Constitution.html.

[11]The literature on the corpus delicti and its elements is immense and illustrates the interpretable nature of criminal law. For some diverse examples, see Denno, D. W. (2003). A mind to blame: New views on involuntary acts. *Behavioral Sciences and the Law, 21,* 601–618; Dershowitz, A. (1994). *The abuse excuse and other cop-outs, sob stories, and evasions of responsibility.* Boston: Little, Brown; McSherry, B. (2003). Voluntariness, intention, and the defense of mental disorder: Toward a rational approach. *Behavioral Sciences and the Law, 21,* 581–599; Morse, S. J. (1999). Craziness and criminal responsibility. *Behavioral Sciences and the Law, 17,* 147–164; Simon, R. J., & Aaronson, D. E. (1988). *The insanity defense: A critical assessment of law and policy in the post-Hinckley era.* New York: Praeger.

[12]For intriguing scholarship on these issues, see Gegan, B. E. (1990). More cases of depraved mind murder: The problem of mens rea. *St. John's Law Review, 64,* 429–469.

[13]Robinson, P. H., & Dubber, M. D. (2004). An introduction to the Model Penal Code of the American Law Institute, retrieved February 25, 2011, from http://ssrn.com/abstract=661165.

[14]For intriguing research on this issue, see Oleson, K. C., & Darley, J. M. (1999). Community perceptions of allowable counterforce in self-defense and defense of property. *Law and Human Behavior, 23,* 629–651.

[15]For intriguing research on the issue of somnambulism, see Broughton, R., Billings, R., Carwright, R., Douchette, D., Edmeads, J., Edwardh, M., Ervin, F., Orchard, B., Hill, R., & Turrell, G. (1994). Homicidal somnambulism: A case report. *Sleep, 17,* 253–264.

[16]Borum, R., & Fulero, S. M. (1999). Empirical research on the insanity defense and attempted reforms: Evidence toward informed policy. *Law and Human Behavior, 23,* 117–135.

[17]For a concise look at law in America, especially during the early stages of the United States, see Friedman, L. M. (2002). *Law in America: A short history.* New York: Random House.

[18]The citation for the *M'Naghten* case is 8 Eng. Rep. 718, 722–723 (1843), 10 Cl. & F. 200, 210–211 (1943).

[19]*Durham v. U. S.,* 214 F.2d 862 (D.C. Cir.) (1954).

[20]*U. S. v. Brawner*, 471 F.2d 969 (D.C. Cir.) (1972).

[21]Model Penal Code and Commentaries (Official Draft and Revised Comments) (1985). Philadelphia: The American Law Institute.

[22]Important case law pertaining to the insanity defense include: *Jones v. U.S.*, U.S. Sup. Ct., 33 CrL 3233 (1983); *Ake v. Oklahoma,* 470 U.S. 68, 105 S.Ct. 1087, 84 L.Ed.2d 53 (1985); *Ford v. Wainwright,* 477 U.S. 399, 106 S.Ct. 2595, 91 L.Ed.2d 335 (1986).

[23]18 U.S.C. § 401.

[24]Callahan, L. A., McGreevy, M. A., Cirincione, C., & Steadman, H. J. (1992). Measuring the effects of the guilty but mentally ill (GBMI) verdict. *Law and Human Behavior, 16,* 447–462; Bumby, K. M. (1993). Reviewing the guilty but mentally ill alternatives: A case of the blind pleading the blind. *Journal of Psychiatry and the Law, Summer 1993,* 191–220; Borum, R., & Fulero, S. M. (1999). Empirical research on the insanity defense and attempted reforms: Evidence toward informed policy. *Law and Human Behavior, 23,* 117–135.

[25]Pasewark, R. A., & McGinley, H. (1985). The insanity plea: National survey of frequency and success. *Journal of Psychiatry and Law, 13,* 101–108; Callahan, L. A., Steadman, H. J., McGreevy, M. A., & Robbins, P. C. (1991). The volume and characteristics of insanity defense pleas: An eight-state study. *Bulletin of the American Academy of Psychiatry and the Law, 19,* 331–338; Steadman, H. J., Keitner, L., Braff, J., & Arvanites, T. M. (1983). Factors associated with a successful insanity plea. *American Journal of Psychiatry, 140,* 401–405.

[26]Borum, R., & Fulero, S. M. (1999). Empirical research on the insanity defense and attempted reforms: Evidence toward informed policy. *Law and Human Behavior, 23,* 117–135.

[27]Borum, R., & Fulero, S. M. (1999). Empirical research on the insanity defense and attempted reforms: Evidence toward informed policy. *Law and Human Behavior, 23,* 117–135; Silver, E., Cirincione, C., & Steadman, H. J. (1994). Demythologizing inaccurate perceptions of the insanity defense. *Law and Human Behavior, 18,* 63–70.

[28]Boehnert, C. E. (1989). Characteristics of successful and unsuccessful insanity pleas. *Law and Human Behavior, 13,* 31–39.

[29]Pasewark, R. A., Parnell, B., & Rock, J. (1994). The insanity defense: Shifting the burden of proof. *Journal of Police and Criminal Psychology, 10,* 1–4.

[30]Pickel, K. L. (1998). The effects of motive information and crime unusualness on jurors' judgments in insanity cases. *Law and Human Behavior, 22,* 571–584.

[31]Porterfield, E. (1994). Still crazy after all these years. *Law Enforcement Quarterly, 4,* 19–22.

[32]Estrich, S. (1998). *Getting away with murder: How politics is destroying the criminal justice system* (pp. 119–130). Cambridge, MA: Harvard University Press.

CHAPTER 4

[1]Vollmer, A. (1936). *The police and modern society* (p.222). Berkeley, CA: University of California Press.

[2]Greene, J. R. (2000). Community policing in America: Changing the nature, structure, and function of the police. In K. Heimer (Ed.), *Criminal Justice 2000,* Volume 3 (pp. 299–370). Washington, DC: U. S. Department of Justice, National Institute of Justice (quotation from p. 353).

[3]Reiss, Jr., A. J. (1971). *The police and the public* (p. 145–147). New Haven, CT: Yale University Press.

[4] Wadman, R. C., & Allison, W. T. (2004). *To protect and to serve: A history of police in America.* Upper Saddle River, NJ: Pearson Prentice Hall.

[5]For variations on the macro sociological effects of modernity on social order, including policing and criminal justice, consult Friedman, L. M. (1993). *Crime and punishment in American history.* New York: Basic Books; Friedman, L. M. (2002). *Law in America: A short history.* New York: Random House; Monkkonen, E. H. (1981). *Police in urban America, 1860–1920.* Cambridge, UK: Cambridge University Press; Walker, S. (1998). *Popular justice: A history of American criminal justice.* New York: Oxford University Press.

[6]Kelling, G. L., & Moore, M. H. (2004). The evolving strategy of policing. In S. Brandl & D. Barlow (Eds.), *The police in America: Classic and contemporary readings* (pp. 5–25). Belmont, CA: Thomson/Wadsworth.

[7]Kelling & Moore, note 6, p. 7.

[8]Williams, H., & Murphy, P. V. (2004). The evolving strategy of policing: A minority view. In S. Brandl & D. Barlow (Eds.), *The police in America: Classic*

and contemporary readings (pp. 26–46). Belmont, CA: Thomson/Wadsworth.

[9]Kelling & Moore, note 6, p. 10.

[10]Rush, G. E. (2000). *The dictionary of criminal justice,* 5th edition. New York: Dushkin/McGraw-Hill.

[11]The best account of the crime boom of the late Twentieth Century and its related problems is James Q. Wilson's classic *Thinking about crime* (New York: Vintage Books, 1975).

[12]Goldstein, H. (1979). Improving policing: A problem-oriented approach. *Crime & Delinquency, 25,* 236–258; Goldstein, H. (1990). Problem-oriented policing. New York: McGraw-Hill; Trojanowicz, R., & Bucqueroux, B. (1990). *Community policing: A contemporary perspective.* Cincinnati, OH: Anderson.

[13]For more information about zero-tolerance policing and broken windows theory, consult the following works: Wilson, J. Q., & Kelling, G. L. (1982). Broken windows: The police and neighborhood safety. *Atlantic Monthly, 249,* 29–38; Kelling, G. L., & Coles, C. M. (1996). *Fixing broken windows: Restoring order and reducing crime in our communities.* New York: Free Press; Skogan, W. G. (1990). *Disorder and decline: Crime and the spiral of urban decay in American neighborhoods.* New York: Free Press. Despite and perhaps because of its populist appeal, some criminologists sharply disagree with the "get tough" approach of zero-tolerance policing and broken windows theory and dispute that it has led to the widespread reductions in crime. For example, see Harcourt, B. E. (2001). *Illusion of order: The false promise of broken-windows policing.* Cambridge, MA: Harvard University Press.

[14]DeLisi, M. (2010). The criminal justice system works! *Journal of Criminal Justice, 38,* 1097–1099.

[15]Koper, C. S., Maguire, E., Moore, G. E., & Huffer, D. E. (2001). *Hiring and retention issues in police agencies: Readings on the determinants of police strength, hiring and retention of officers, and thee federal COPS program.* Washington, DC: Urban Institute Justice Police Center; Koper, C. S., Moore, G. E., & Roth, J. A. (2002). *Putting 100,000 officers on the street: A survey-based assessment of the federal COPS program.* Washington, DC: Urban Institute Justice Policy Center.

[16]Zhao, J., Scheider, M. C., & Thurman, Q. (2002). Funding community policing to reduce crime: Have COPS grants made a difference? *Criminology & Public Policy, 2,* 7–32.

[17]Hickman, M., & Reaves, B. (2001). *Community policing in local police departments 1997 and 1999*. Washington, DC: U. S. Department of Justice, Office of Justice Programs, Bureau of Justice Statistics.

[18]Weisburd, D., Mastrofski, S. D., McNally, A. M., Greenspan, R., & Willis, J. J. (2003). Reforming to preserve: COMPSTAT and strategic problem solving American policing. *Criminology & Public Policy, 2,* 421–456.

[19]Cordner, G., & Perkins Biebel, E. (2005). Problem-oriented policing in practice. *Criminology & Public Policy, 4,* 155–180.

[20]Greene, J. R. (2000). Community policing in America: Changing the nature, structure, and function of the police. In K. Heimer (Ed.), *Criminal Justice 2000,* Volume 3 (pp. 299–370). Washington, DC: U. S. Department of Justice, National Institute of Justice.

[21]Bayley, D. H. (1998). Policing in America. *Society, 36,* 16–20.

[22]Wilson, J. Q. (1968). *Varieties of police behavior: The management of law and order in eight communities*. Cambridge, MA: Harvard University Press.

[23]Mazerolle, L., Rogan, D., Frank, J., Famega, C., & Eck, J. E. (2002). Managing citizen calls to the police: The impact of Baltimore's 3-1-1 call system. *Criminology & Public Policy, 2,* 97–124.

[24]Bittner, E. (1967). The police on skid-row: A study of peace keeping. *American Sociological Review, 32,* 699–715, pp. 710–711.

[25]Engel, R. S. (2001). Supervisory styles of patrol sergeants and lieutenants. *Journal of Criminal Justice, 29,* 341–355; Engel, R. S. (2000). The effects of supervisory styles on patrol officer behavior. *Police Quarterly, 3,* 262–293.

[26]Kelling, G. L., Pate, T., Dieckman, D., & Brown, C. E. (1974). *The Kansas City Preventive Patrol Experiment: A Summary Report*. Washington, DC: Police Foundation.

[27]Police Foundation Research Brief: *The Kansas City Preventive Patrol Experiment.* www.policefoundation.org.

[28]Police Foundation Research Brief: *The Newark Foot Patrol Experiment.* Retrieved February 25, 2011, from www.policefoundation.org.

[29]Police Foundation Research Brief: *The Minneapolis Domestic Violence Experiment.* Retrieved February 25, 2011, from www.policefoundation.org.

[30]Berk, R. A., Campbell, A., Klap, R., & Western, B. (1992). The deterrent effect of arrest in incidents of domestic violence: A Bayesian analysis of four field experiments. *American Sociological Review, 57,* 698–708; Dunford, F., Huizinga, D., & Elliott, D. S. (1990). The role of arrest in domestic assault: The Omaha experiment. *Criminology, 28,* 183–206; Pate, A. M., & Hamilton, E. E. (1992). Formal and informal deterrents to domestic violence: The Dade County spouse assault experiment. *American Sociological Review, 57,* 691–697; Sherman, L. W., & Berk, R. A. (1984). The specific deterrent effects of arrest for domestic assault. *American Sociological Review, 49,* 261–272; Sherman, L. W., Schmidt, J. D., Rogan, D. P., Gartin, P. R., Cohn, E. G., Collins, D. J., & Bacich, A. R. (1991). From initial deterrence to long-term escalation: Short-custody arrest for poverty ghetto domestic violence. *Criminology, 29,* 821–850; Sherman, L. W., Smith, D. A., Schmidt, J. D., & Rogan, D. P. (1992). Crime, punishment, and stake in conformity: Legal and informal control of domestic violence. *American Sociological Review, 57,* 680–690; also see, Smith, D. A., & Gartin, P. R. (1989). Specifying specific deterrence: The influence of arrest on future criminal activity. *American Sociological Review, 54,* 94–106; Williams, K. R., & Hawkins, R. (1989). The meaning of arrest for wife assault. *Criminology, 27,* 163–181.

[31]Maxwell, C. D., Garner, J. H., & Fagan, J. A. (2002). The preventive effects of arrest on intimate partner violence: Research, policy, and theory. *Criminology & Public Policy, 2,* 51–80.

[32]Roehl, J. A., Huitt, R., Wycoff, M. A., Pate, A., Rebovich, D., & Coyle, K. (1996). *National process evaluation of Operation Weed and Seed*. Washington, DC: U. S. Department of Justice, Office of Justice Programs, National Institute of Justice.

[33]Dunworth, T., Mills, G., Cordner, G., & Greene, J. R. (1999). *National evaluation of Weed and Seed cross-site analysis*. Washington, DC: U. S. Department of Justice, Office of Justice Programs, National Institute of Justice. Also see, Morrison, S., Parker, B., McLean, B., & Massey, D. M. (2004). *Weed and Seed best practices: Evaluation-based series,* volume 2. Washington, DC: U. S. Department of Justice, Office of Justice Programs, National Institute of Justice.

[34]For example, see Bordua, D. J., & Reiss, Jr., A. J. (1966). Command, control, and charisma: Reflections on police bureaucracy. *American Journal of Sociology, 72,* 68–76.

[35]For detailed reports on the various levels of law enforcement agencies, see, Reaves, B. A. (2010). *Local police departments, 2007.* Washington, DC: U. S. Department of Justice, Office of Justice Programs, Bureau of Justice Statistics; Reaves, B. A., & Hickman, M. J. (2002). *Police departments in large cities, 1990–2000.* Washington, DC: U. S. Department of Justice, Office of Justice Programs, Bureau of Justice Statistics; Reaves, B. A. (2006). *Federal law enforcement officers, 2004.* Washington, DC: U. S. Department of Justice, Office of Justice Programs, Bureau of Justice Statistics.

CHAPTER 5

[1]Nicknamed "Clubber," Williams was a notoriously corrupt New York City Police Officer during the Political Era. The famous quotation has been attributed to him albeit with no specific date.

[2]From the majority opinion in *Mapp v. Ohio*, 367 U.S. 643 (1961).

[3]Cassell, P. G., & Hayman, B. S. (1998). Police interrogation in the 1990s: An empirical study of the effects of Miranda. In R. A. Leo & G. C. Thomas (Eds.), *The Miranda debate: Law, justice, and policing* (pp. 222–235). Boston, MA: Northeastern University Press.

[4]Simon, D. (1991). *Homicide: A year on the killing streets,* (p. 219). New York: Ivy Books.

[5]Rothwax, Judge H. J. (1996). *Guilty: The collapse of criminal justice,* p. 18). New York: Warner Books.

[6]*Aguilar v. Texas,* 378 U.S. 108 (1964).

[7]*McCray v. Illinois,* 386 U.S. 300 (1967).

[8]*Spinelli v. United States,* 393 U.S. 110 (1969).

[9]*Illinois v. Gates,* 462 U.S. 213 (1983).

[10]*Weeks v. United States,* 232 U.S. 383 (1914).

[11]*Mapp v. Ohio,* 367 U.S. 643 (1961); *Wolf v. Colorado,* 338 U.S. 25 (1949).

[12]*Silverthorne Lumber Company v. United States,* 251 U.S. 385 (1920).

[13]*Wong Sun v. United States,* 371 U.S. 471 (1963).

[14]*Michigan v. Tucker,* 417 U.S. 433 (1974).

[15]*Brown v. Illinois,* 422 U.S. 590 (1975).

[16]*United States v. Crews,* 445 U.S. 463 (1980) and *United States v. Havens,* 446 U.S. 620 (1980).

[17]*Taylor v. Alabama,* 457 U.S. 687 (1982).

[18]*Lanier v. South Carolina,* 474 U.S. 25 (1985).

[19]*Schmerber v. California,* 384 U.S. 757 (1966); *Warden v. Hayden,* 387 U.S. 294 (1967); *Skinner v. Railway Labor Executives' Association,* 489 U.S. 602 (1989); *New York v. Quarles,* 467 U.S. 649 (1984); *Michigan Department of State Police v. Sitz,* 496 U.S. 444 (1990).

[20]*United States v. Leon,* 468 U.S. 897 (1984). A sister case to *Leon* is *Massachusetts v. Sheppard,* 468 U.S. 981 (1984).

[21]*Illinois v. Krull,* 480 U.S. 340 (1987).

[22]*Arizona v. Evans,* 514 U.S. 1 (1995).

[23]*Chimel v. California,* 395 U.S. 752 (1969).

[24]*Gustafson v. Florida* 414 U.S. 260 (1973).

[25]*United States v. Robinson,* 414 U.S. 218 (1973).

[26]*Maryland v. Buie,* 494 U.S. 325 (1990).

[27]See, *Harris v. United States,* 390 U.S. 234 (1968), *Texas v. Brown,* 460 U.S. 730 (1983).

[28]*California v. Ciraolo,* 476 U.S. 207 (1986).

[29]*Dow Chemical Company v. United States,* 476 U.S. 227 (1986).

[30]*United States v. Dunn,* 480 U.S. 294 (1987).

[31]*California v. Greenwood,* 486 U.S. 35 (1988).

[32]*Horton v. California,* 496 U.S. 128 (1990).

[33]*Cooper v. California,* 386 U.S. 58 (1967).

[34]*New York v. Belton,* 453 U.S. 454 (1981).

[35]*California v. Carney,* 471 U.S. 386 (1985).

[36]*Colorado v. Bertine,* 479 U.S. 367 (1987); *Florida v. Wells,* 495 U.S. 1 (1990); *California v. Acevedo,* 500 U.S. 565 (1991).

[37]*Pennsylvania v. Labron,* 518 U.S. 938 (1996).

[38]*Chambers v. Maroney,* 399 U.S. 42 (1970).

[39]*Nix v. Williams,* 467 U.S. 431 (1984).

[40]*Schneckloth v. Bustamonte,* 412 U.S. 218 (1973).

[41]*United States v. Matlock,* 415 U.S. 164 (1974).

[42]*Illinois v. Rodriguez,* 497 U.S. 177 (1990).

[43]*Florida v. Jimeno,* 500 U.S. 248 (1991); *Florida v. Bostick,* 501 U.S. 429 (1991); *Ohio v. Robinette,* 519 U.S. 33 (1996).

[44]*Terry v. Ohio,* 392 U.S. 1 (1968).

[45]*United States v. Place,* 462 U.S. 696 (1983); *Michigan v. Long,* 463 U.S. 1032 (1983); *United States v. Hensley,* 469, U.S. 221 (1985).

[46]*New Jersey v. T.L.O.,* 469 U.S. 325 (1985).

[47]*Maryland v. Wilson,* 519 U.S. 408 (1997).

[48]*Brown v. Mississippi,* 297 U.S. 278 (1936); *Chambers v. Florida,* 309 U.S. 227 (1940); *Ashcraft v. Tennessee,* 322 U.S. 143 (1944); *Spano v. New York,* 360 U.S. 315 (1959); *Haynes v. Washington,* 373 U.S. 503 (1963).

[49]Leo, R. A. (1998). From coercion to deception: The changing nature of police interrogation in America. In R. A. Leo & G. C. Thomas (Eds.), *The Miranda debate: Law, justice, and policing,* (pp. 65–74). Boston, MA: Northeastern University Press.

[50]Massiah v. United States, 377 U.S. 201 (1964); *McLeod v. Ohio*, 381 U.S. 356 (1965).

[51]*Malloy v. Hogan*, 378 U.S. 1 (1964).

[52]*Escobedo v. Illinois*, 378 U.S. 478 (1964).

[53]*Griffin v. California*, 380 U.S. 609 (1965).

[54]*Miranda v. Arizona*, 384 U.S. 436 (1966). Miranda gets all of the glory, but the decision reached in it also resolved three similar, contemporary cases, *Virginia v. New York*; *California v. Stewart*; and *Westover v. United States*.

[55]For a more complete review, see Oberlander, L. B., & Goldstein, N. E. (2001). A review and update on the practice of evaluating *Miranda* comprehension. *Behavioral Sciences and the Law, 19*, 453–471.

[56]*Orozco v. Texas*, 394 U.S. 324 (1969).

[57]*Harris v. New York*, 401 U.S. 222 (1971).

[58]*Brown v. Illinois*, 422 U.S. 590 (1975).

[59]*Michigan v. Mosley*, 423 U.S. 96 (1975).

[60]*Beckwith v. United States*, 425 U.S. 341, 345 (1976).

[61]*Edwards v. Arizona*, 451 U.S. 477 (1981).

[62]*New York v. Quarles*, 467 U.S. 649 (1984).

[63]*Minnesota v. Murphy*, 465 U.S. 420 (1984).

[64]*Berkemer v. McCarty*, 468 U.S. 420 (1984).

[65]*Oregon v. Elstad*, 470 U.S. 298 (1985). Hoover, L. A. (2005). The Supreme Court brings an end to the 'end run' around Miranda. *FBI Law Enforcement Bulletin, 74*, 26–32.

[66]*Minnick v. Mississippi*, 498 U.S. 146 (1990).

[67]*Arizona v. Fulminante*, 499 U.S. 279 (1991).

[68]*Davis v. United States*, 512 U.S. 452 (1994).

[69]*Dickerson v. United States*, 530 U.S. 428 (2000). For a critical assessment of the Dickerson ruling, see Cassell, P., & Litt, R. (2000). Will Miranda survive? *Dickerson v. United States*: The right to remain silent, the Supreme Court, and Congress. *American Criminal Law Review, 37*, 1165–1193.

[70]Cassell, P. G. (1996). Miranda's social costs: An empirical assessment. *Northwestern University Law Review, 90*, 487–499.

[71]Schulhofer, S. J. (1996). Miranda's practical effect: Substantial benefits and vanishingly small social costs. *Northwestern University Law Review, 90*, 500–551; Schulhofer, S. J. (1987). Reconsidering Miranda. *University of Chicago Law Review, 54*, 435–461.

[72]Cassell, P. G., & Fowles, R. (1998). Handcuffing the cops? A thirty-year perspective on Miranda's harmful effects on law enforcement. *Stanford Law Review, 50*, 1055–1145.

[73]Time, V. M., & Payne, B. K. (2002). Police chiefs perceptions about *Miranda*: An analysis of survey data. *Journal of Criminal Justice, 30*, 77–86. Also see, Payne, B. K., & Time, V. M. (2000). Police chiefs and Miranda: An exploratory study. *American Journal of Criminal Justice, 25*, 65–76.

[74]Leo, R. A. (1996). The impact of Miranda revisited. *Journal of Criminal Law and Criminology, 86*, 266–303.

[75]Kassin, S. M., & Norwick, R. J. (2004). Why people waive their Miranda rights: The power of innocence. *Law and Human Behavior, 28*, 211–221; Madon, S., Guyll, M., Scherr, K. C., Greathouse, S., & Wells, G. L. (2011). Temporal discounting: The differential effect of proximal and distal consequences on confession decisions. *Law and Human Behavior*, doi: 10.1007/s10979-011-9267-3.

[76]Leo, R. A. (1996). Inside the interrogation room. *Journal of Criminal Law and Criminology, 86*, 266–303.

[77]Leo, note 74.

[78]Rothwax, Judge H. J. (1996). *Guilty: The collapse of criminal justice*, (p.86). New York: Warner Books.

CHAPTER 6

[1]Bayley, D. H. (1998). *Policing in America: Assessment and prospects* (p.1). Washington, DC: Police Foundation.

[2]Bittner, E. (1967). The police on skid-row: A study of peace keeping. *American Sociological Review, 32*, 699–715, p. 715.

[3]Wilson, J. Q. (1969). *Varieties of police behavior: The management of law and order in eight communities* (p. 36). Cambridge, MA: Harvard University Press.

[4]Klockars, C. (1985). *The ideal of police* (pp. 9–10). Beverly Hills, CA: Sage.

[5]Westley, W. A. (1953). Violence and the police. *American Journal of Sociology, 59*, 34–41, p. 34.

[6]Uviller, H. R. (1996). *Virtual justice: The flawed prosecution of crime in America* (p. 28). New Haven, CT: Yale University Press.

[7]Wortley, R. K. (2003). Measuring police attitudes toward discretion. *Criminal Justice and Behavior, 30*, 538–558.

[8]Reiss, A. J., Jr. (1971). *The police and the public* (p. x). New Haven, CT: Yale University Press.

[9]Black, D. J. (1970). Production of crime rates. *American Sociological Review, 35*, 733–748; Black, D. J. (1971). The social organization of arrest. *Stanford Law Review, 23*, 1087–1111; Black, D. J., & Reiss, A. J., Jr. (1970). Police control of juveniles.

American Sociological Review, 35, 63–77; Reiss, note 8.

[10]For additional evidence, see Smith, D. A., & Visher, C. A. (1981). Street-level justice: Situational determinants of police arrest decisions. *Social Problems, 29,* 167–177.

[11]Bittner, note 2; Goldstein, J. (1960). Police discretion not to invoke the criminal process: Low visibility decisions in the administration of justice. *Yale Law Journal, 69,* 543–594; Klinger, D. A. (1995). The micro-structure of nonlethal force: Baseline data from an observational study. *Criminal Justice Review, 20,* 169–186; Piliavin, I., & Briar, S. (1964). Police encounters with juveniles. *American Journal of Sociology, 69,* 206–214; Wilson, note 3; Schafer, J. A., & Mastrofski, S. D. (2005). Police leniency in traffic enforcement encounters: Exploratory findings from observations and interviews. *Journal of Criminal Justice, 33,* 225–238.

[12]Also see, Brandl, S. G., & Frank, J. (1994). The relationship between evidence, detective effort, and the disposition of burglary and robbery investigations. *American Journal of Police, 13,* 149–168;

[13]Bittner, note 2; Stinchcombe, A. L. (1963). Institutions of privacy in the determination of police administrative practice. *American Journal of Sociology, 69,* 150–160.

[14]For additional evidence, see Smith, D. A., & Visher, C. A. (1981). Street-level justice: Situational determinants of police arrest decisions. *Social Problems, 29,* 167–177; Stinchcombe, note 13.

[15]Fyfe, J. J., Klinger, D. A., & Flavin, J. M. (1997). Differential police treatment of male-on-female spousal violence. *Criminology, 35,* 455–473.

[16]A well-known report that amplified many of the seminal police behavior findings is: Chaiken, J. M., Greenwood, P. W., & Petersilia, J. (2004). The criminal investigation process: A summary report. In S. Brandl & D. Barlow (Eds.), *The police in America: Classic and contemporary readings* (Pp. 275–299). Belmont, CA: Thomson/Wadsworth. For more work affirming the non-discrimination thesis, see DeLisi, M., & Regoli, B. (1999). Race, conventional crime, and criminal justice: The declining importance of skin color. *Journal of Criminal Justice, 27,* 549–557; Engel, R. S., Sobol, J. J., & Worden, R. E. (2000). Further exploration of the demeanor hypothesis: The interaction effects of suspects' characteristics and demeanor on police behavior. *Justice Quarterly, 17,* 235–258; Klinger,

D. A. (1996). More on demeanor and arrest in Dade County. *Criminology, 34,* 61–82; Lundman, R. J., Sykes, R. E., & Clark, J. P. (1978). Police control of juveniles: A replication. *Journal of Research in Crime and Delinquency, 15,* 74–91.

[17]Doerner, W. G. (1998). *Introduction to law enforcement: An insider's view.* Boston, MA: Butterworth-Heinemann (p. 95).

[18]Westley, W. A. (1956). Secrecy and the police. *Social Forces, 34,* 254–257.

[19]Westley, W. A. (1953). Violence and the police. *American Journal of Sociology, 59,* 34–41.

[20]Skolnick, J. H. (1966). *Justice without trial: Law enforcement in a democratic society.* New York: John Wiley & Sons.

[21]Muir, Jr., W. K. (1977). *Police: Streetcorner politicians.* Chicago: University of Chicago Press (p. 263).

[22]Van Maanen, J. (1975). Police socialization: A longitudinal examination of job attitudes in an urban police department. *Administrative Science Quarterly, 20,* 207–228; Griffin, S. P., & Bernard, T. J. (2003). Angry aggression among police officers. *Police Quarterly, 6,* 3–21; Farkas, M. A., & Manning, P. K. (1997). Occupational culture of corrections and police officers. *Journal of Crime & Justice, 20,* 51–68; Manning, P. K. (1997). *Police work: The social organization of policing,* 2nd edition. Prospect Heights, IL: Waveland Press.

[23]Niederhoffer, A. (1967). *Behind the shield: The police in urban society.* Garden City, NJ: Anchor Books, p. 9.

[24]Bennett, R. R., & Schmitt, E. L. (2002). The effect of work environment on levels of police cynicism: A comparative study. *Police Quarterly, 5,* 493–522; O'Connell, B. J., Holzman, H., & Armandi, B. R. (1986). Police cynicism and the modes of adaptation. *Journal of Police Science & Administration, 14,* 307–313; Rafky, D. M., Lawley, T., & Ingram, R. (1976). Are police recruits cynical? *Journal of Police Science & Administration, 4,* 352–360; Hickman, M. J., Piquero, N. L., & Piquero, A. R. (2004). The validity of Niederhoffer's cynicism scale. *Journal of Criminal Justice, 32,* 1–13; Langworthy, R. (1987). Police cynicism: What do we know from the Niederhoffer scale? *Journal of Criminal Justice, 15,* 17–35; Regoli, R. M. (1976). An empirical assessment of Niederhoffer's police cynicism scale. *Journal of Criminal Justice, 4,* 231–241; Regoli, R. M., Culbertson, R., & Crank, J. (1991). Using

composite measures in police cynicism research. *Journal of Quantitative Criminology, 7,* 41–58.

[25]Lundman, R. J. (1980). *Police and policing: An introduction.* New York: Holt, Rinehart and Winston; Paoline, E. A., III. (2004). Shedding light on police culture: An examination of officers' occupational attitudes. *Police Quarterly, 7,* 205–236; Paoline, E. A., III. (2003). Taking stock: Toward a richer understanding of police culture. *Journal of Criminal Justice, 31,* 199–214; Crank, J. P. (2003). Institutional theory of police: A review of the state of the art. *Policing: An International Journal of Police Strategies & Management, 26,* 186–207; Cao, L., Deng, X., & Barton, S. (2000). A test of Lundman's organizational product thesis with data on citizen complaints. *Policing: An International Journal of Police Strategies & Management, 23,* 356–373.

[26]Durose, M. R., Smith, E. L., & Langan, P. A. (2007). *Contacts between police and the public, 2005.* Washington, DC: U. S. Department of Justice, Office of Justice Programs, Bureau of Justice Statistics.

[27]Terrill, W. (2005). Police use of force: A transactional approach. *Justice Quarterly, 22,* 107–139.

[28]Terrill, W., & Reisig, M. D. (2003). Neighborhood context and police use of force. *Journal of Research in Crime and Delinquency, 40,* 291–321.

[29]Hoffman, P. B., & Hickey, E. R. (2005). Use of force by female police officers. *Journal of Criminal Justice, 33,* 145–151. For a study that produced substantively similar results from a different data set, see Alpert, G. P., Dunham, R. G., & MacDonald, J. M. (2004). Interactive police-citizen encounters that result in force. *Police Quarterly, 7,* 475–488.

[30]Adams, K. (1999). *What we know about police use of force. In Use of force by police: Overview of national and local data* (pp. 1–14). Washington, DC: U. S. Department of Justice, Office of Justice Programs, Bureau of Justice Statistics and National Institute of Justice.

[31]DeLisi, M. (2011). *The monetary costs of the murder of a law enforcement officer.* Washington, DC: U. S. Department of Justice.

[32]Brown, J. M., & Langan, P. A. (2001). *Policing and homicide, 1976-1998: Justifiable homicide by police, police officers murdered by felons.* Washington, DC: U. S. Department of Justice, Office of Justice Programs, Bureau of Justice Statistics.

[33]For assorted studies on police use of lethal force and police killings, see Brandl, S. G. (1996). In the line of duty: A descriptive analysis of police assaults and accidents. *Journal of Criminal Justice, 24,* 255–264; Brubaker, L. C. (2002). Deadly force: A 20-year study of fatal outcomes. *FBI Law Enforcement Bulletin, 71,* 6–13; Fyfe, J. J. (1979). Administrative interventions on police shooting discretion: An empirical examination. *Journal of Criminal Justice, 7,* 309–323; Hontz, T. A. (2000). Justifying the deadly force response. *Police Quarterly, 2,* 462–476; King, W. R., & Sanders, B. A. (1997). Nice guys finish last: A critical review of *Killed in the Line of Duty. Policing: An International Journal of Police Strategies & Management, 20,* 392–407; Wilbanks, W. (1994). Cops killed and cop-killers: A historical perspective. *American Journal of Police, 13,* 31–49.

[34]Klinger, D. (2001). *Police responses to officer-involved shootings.* Washington, DC: U. S. Department of Justice, Office of Justice Programs, National Institute of Justice.

[35]Klinger, D. (2004). *Into the kill zone: A cop's eye view of deadly force.* San Francisco, CA: Jossey-Bass.

[36]For history and other information about the Chicago Crime Commission, consult their web site at www.chicagocrimecommission.org.

[37]Key, Jr.,V. O. (1935) Police graft. *American Journal of Sociology, 40,* 624–636.

[38]Lersch, K. M., & Mieczkowski, T. (2005). Violent police behavior: Past, present, and future research directions. *Aggression and Violent Behavior, 10,* 552–568.

[39]*Summary Report of the Independent Commission on the Los Angeles Police Department.* (1991). Public domain.

[40]Mollen, M., Baer, H., Evans, H., Lankler, R. C., Tyler, H. R., Armao, J. P., & Cornfeld, L. U. (1994). *Commission to investigate allegations of police corruption and the anti-corruption procedures of the police department. Final report.* New York: Mollen Commission (p. 1).

[41]Mollen et al., note 40, p. 10.

[42]For example, see Priest, T. B., & Carter, D. B. (1999). Evaluations of police performance in an African American sample. *Journal of Criminal Justice, 27,* 457–465.

[43]For example, see Engel, R. S. (2003). Explaining suspects' resistance and disrespect toward police. *Journal of Criminal Justice, 31,* 475–492.

[44]Reitzel, J. D., Rice, S. K., & Piquero, A. R. (2004). Lines and shadows: Perceptions of racial profiling and the Hispanic experience. *Journal of Criminal Justice, 32,* 607–616 (p. 615).

[45]Rice, S. K., & Piquero, A. R. (2005). Perceptions of discrimination and justice in New York City. *Policing: An International Journal of Police Strategies & Management, 28,* 98–117.

[46]Becker, S. (2004). Assessing the use of profiling in searches by law enforcement personnel. *Journal of Criminal Justice, 32,* 183–193.

[47]Smith, M. R., & Petrocelli, M. (2001). Racial profiling? A multivariate analysis of police traffic stop data. *Police Quarterly, 4,* 4–27; Petrocelli, M., Piquero, A. R., & Smith, M. R. (2003). Conflict theory and racial profiling: An empirical analysis of police traffic stop data. *Journal of Criminal Justice, 31,* 1–11.

[48]Schafer, J. A., Carter, D. L., & Katz-Bannister, A. (2004). Studying traffic stop encounters. *Journal of Criminal Justice, 32,* 159–170.

[49]For variations on this theme, see Dunham, R. G., Alpert, G. P., Stroshine, M. S., & Bennett, K. (2005). Transforming citizens into suspects: Factors that influence the formation of police suspicion. *Police Quarterly, 8,* 366–393; Novak, K. J. (2004). Disparity and racial profiling in traffic enforcement. *Police Quarterly, 7,* 65–96; Rojek, J., Rosenfeld, R., & Decker, S. (2004). The influence of driver's race on traffic stops in Missouri. *Police Quarterly, 7,* 127–147.

[50]Smith, M. R., & Alpert, G. P. (2002). Searching for direction: Courts, social science, and the adjudication of racial profiling claims. *Justice Quarterly, 19,* 673–704.

[51]Mac Donald, H. (2003). *Are cops racist? How the war against the police harms black Americans.* Chicago, IL: Ivan R. Dee.

[52]Braga, A. A., Weisburd, D. L., Waring, E. J., Green Mazerolle, L., Spelman, W., & Gajewski, F. (1999). Problem-oriented policing in violent crime places: A randomized controlled experiment. *Criminology, 37,* 541–580; Katz, C. M., Webb, V. J., & Schaefer, D. R. (2001). As assessment of the impact of quality-of-life policing on crime and disorder. *Justice Quarterly, 18,* 825–876; Green, L. (1995). Cleaning up drug hot spots in Oakland, California: The displacement and diffusion effects. *Justice Quarterly, 12,* 737–754; Kelling, G. L., & Bratton, W. J. (1998). Declining crime rates: Insiders' views of the New York City story. *Journal of Criminal Law and Criminology, 88,* 1217–1231; Bratton, W. J. (1998). *The turnaround: How America's top cop reversed the crime epidemic.* New York: Random House. Not all studies have produced favorable results of aggressive policing. For an example, see Novak, K. J., Hartman, J. L., Holsinger, A. M., & Turner, M. G. (1999). The effects of aggressive policing of disorder on serious crime. *Policing: An International Journal of Police Strategies & Management, 22,* 171–190.

[53]Golub, A., Johnson, B. D., Taylor, A., & Eterno, J. (2003). Quality-of-life policing: Do offenders get the message? *Policing: An International Journal of Police Strategies & Management, 26,* 690–707.

[54]Cao, L., Frank, J., & Cullen, F. T. (1996). Race, community context and confidence in the police. *American Journal of Police, 15,* 3–22; Henderson, M., Cullen, F. T., Cao, L., & Browning, S. L., & Kopache, R. (1997). The impact of race on perceptions of criminal injustice. *Journal of Criminal Justice, 25,* 447–462; Huebner, B. M., Schafer, J. A., & Bynum, T. S. (2004). African American and white perceptions of police services: Within- and between-group variation. *Journal of Criminal Justice, 32,* 123–135; Jefferis, E. S., Kaminski, R. J., Holmes, S., & Hanley, D. E. (1997). The effect of a video-taped arrest on public perceptions of police use of force. *Journal of Criminal Justice, 25,* 381–395; Rosenbaum, D. P., Schuck, A. M., Costello, S. K., Hawkins, D. F., & Ring, M., K. (2005). Attitudes toward the police: The effects of direct and vicarious experience. *Police Quarterly, 8,* 343–365; Webb, V. J., & Marshall, C. E. (1995). The relative importance of race and ethnicity on citizen attitudes toward the police. *American Journal of Police, 14,* 45–66.

CHAPTER 7

[1]Feeley, M. M. (1992). *The process is the punishment: Handling cases in a lower criminal court* (p. 297), revised edition. New York: Russell Sage Foundation.

[2]Garofalo, J., & Clark, R. D. (1985). The inmate subculture in jails. *Criminal Justice and Behavior, 12,* 415–434, p. 431.

[3]Demuth, S., & Steffensmeier, D. (2004). The impact of gender and race-ethnicity in the pretrial release process. *Social Problems, 51,* 222–242, p. 240.

[4]Beeley, A. L. (1927). *The bail system in Chicago.* Chicago: University of Chicago Press. Quotation cited in J. S. Goldkamp, M. R. Gottfredson, P. R. Jones, & D. Weiland. (1995). *Personal liberty and*

community safety: Pretrial release in the criminal court. New York: Plenum Press, p. 3.

[5]Klofas, J. M. (1990). The jail and the community. *Justice Quarterly, 7,* 69–102, p. 69.

[6]Origin unknown.

[7]Nelson, W. R., O'Toole, M., Krauth, B., & Whitemore, C. G. (1983). *New generation jails.* Longmont, CO: U. S. Department of Justice, National Institute of Corrections, Jails Division, p.37.

[8]Conklin, J. E., & Meagher, D. (1973). The percentage deposit bail system: An alternative to the professional bondsman. *Journal of Criminal Justice, 1,* 299–317.

[9]Johnson, B. R., & Warchol, G. L. (2003). Bail agents and bounty hunters: Adversaries or allies of the justice system. *American Journal of Criminal Justice, 27,* 145–165.

[10]Goldfarb, R. L. (1965). *Ransom: A critique of the American bail system.* New York: Harper & Row.

[11]*Nicolls v. Ingersoll,* 7 Johns. 145, 154 (N.Y. 1810).

[12]*Reese v. United States,* 76 U.S. 13 (1869).

[13]*Taylor v. Taintor,* 83 U.S. (16 Wall.) 366 (1873).

[14]Vera Institute of Justice. (2003). *A short history of Vera's work on the judicial process.* New York: Vera Institute of Justice.

[15]Goldfarb, note 10, pp. 37–42.

[16]Goldfarb, note 10, p. 5.

[17]Goldfarb, note 10, p. 3.

[18]Johnson, B. R., & Warchol, G. L. (2003). Bail agents and bounty hunters: Adversaries or allies of the justice system. *American Journal of Criminal Justice, 27,* 145–165.

[19]Burns, R., Kinkade, P., & Leone, M. C. (2005). Bounty hunters: A look behind the hype. *Policing: An International Journal of Police Strategies and Management, 28,* 118–138.

[20]Clark, J., & Henry, D. A. (2003). *Pretrial services programming at the start of the 21st Century.* Washington, DC: U. S. Department of Justice, Office of Justice Programs, Bureau of Justice Assistance.

[21]Clark & Henry, note 20.

[22]Reaves, B. A., & Perez, J. (1994). *Pretrial release of felony defendants, 1992.* Washington, DC: U. S. Department of Justice, Office of Justice Program, Bureau of Justice Statistics. Substantively similar findings were produced in a follow-up report, see Cohen, T. H., & Reaves, B. A. (2007). *Pretrial release of felony defendants in state courts.* Washington, DC: U. S. Department of Justice, Office of Justice Program, Bureau of Justice Statistics.

[23]Wolf, T. J. (1997). What United States pretrial services officers do. *Federal Probation, 61,* 19–24.

[24]Scalia, J. (1999). *Federal pretrial release and detention, 1996.* Washington, DC: U. S. Department of Justice, Office of Justice Programs, Bureau of Justice Statistics.

[25]18 U.S.C. §§ 3141–3150.

[26]Goldkamp, J. S. (1993). Judicial responsibility for pretrial release decision-making and the information role of pretrial services. *Federal Probation, 57,* 28–35.

[27]Gottfredson, M. R. (1974). An empirical analysis of pretrial release decisions. *Journal of Criminal Justice, 2,* 287–303; Goldkamp, J. S. (1979). Bail decision-making and pretrial detention: Surfacing judicial policy. *Law and Human Behavior, 3,* 227–249; Gottfredson, M. R., & Gottfredson, D. M. (1980). *Decision-making in criminal justice: Toward the rational exercise of discretion.* Cambridge, MA: Ballinger Publishing Company; Goldkamp, J. S. (1983). Questioning the practice of pretrial detention: Some empirical evidence from Philadelphia. *Journal of Criminal Law and Criminology, 74,* 1556–1588; Holmes, M. D., Hosch, H. M., Daudistel, H. C., Perez, D. A., & Graves, J. B. (1996). Ethnicity, legal resources, and felony dispositions in two southwestern jurisdictions. *Justice Quarterly, 13,* 11–30; DeLisi, M., & Berg, M. T. (2006). Exploring theoretical linkages between self-control theory and criminal justice system processing. *Journal of Criminal Justice, 34,* 153–163.

[28]Maxwell, S. R. (1999). Examining the congruence between predictors or ROR and failures to appear. *Journal of Criminal Justice, 27,* 127–141.

[29]Albonetti, C. A., Hauser, R. M., Hagan, J., & Nagel, I. H. (1989). Criminal justice decision-making as a stratification process: The role of race and stratification resources in pretrial release. *Journal of Quantitative Criminology, 5,* 57–82.

[30]Demuth, S. (2003). Racial and ethnic differences in pretrial release decisions and outcomes: A comparison of Hispanic, Black, and White felony arrestees. *Criminology, 41,* 873–908; Demuth, S., & Steffensmeier, D. (2004). The impact of gender and race-ethnicity in the pretrial release process. *Social Problems, 51,* 222–242; Katz, C. M., & Spohn, C. C. (1995). The effect of race and gender on bail outcomes: A test of the interactive model. *American Journal of Criminal Justice, 19,* 161–184,

[31]Demuth, S. (2003). Racial and ethnic differences in pretrial release decisions and outcomes:

A comparison of Hispanic, Black, and White felony arrestees. *Criminology, 41,* 873–908 (p. 894); Demuth & Steffensmeier, note 3, p. 232.

[32]Goldkamp, J. S., & Jones, P. R. (1992). Pretrial drug-testing experiments in Milwaukee and Prince George's County: The context of implementation. *Journal of Research in Crime and Delinquency, 29,* 430–465; Jones, P. R., & Goldkamp, J. S. (1993). Implementing pretrial drug-testing programs in two experimental sites: Some deterrence and jail bed implications. *Prison Journal, 73,* 199–219.

[33]Goldkamp, J. S., Gottfredson, M. R., & Weiland, D. (1990). Pretrial drug testing and defendant risk. *Journal of Criminal Law and Criminology, 81,* 585–652; Britt, C. L., Gottfredson, M. R., & Goldkamp, J. S. (1992). Drug testing and pretrial misconduct: An experiment on the specific deterrent effects of drug monitoring defendants on pretrial release. *Journal of Research in Crime and Delinquency, 29,* 62–78.

[34]Goldkamp et al., note 4, pp. 307–308.

[35]Feeley, note 1.

[36]For example, see Ares, C., Rankin, A., & Sturz, H. (1963). The Manhattan Bail Project: An interim report on the use of pretrial parole. *New York University Law Review, 38,* 67–92; Eisenstein, J., & Jacob, H. (1977). *Felony justice: An organizational analysis of criminal courts.* Boston: Little, Brown; Holmes, M., Daudistel, H., & Farrell, R. (1987). Determinants of charge reductions and final dispositions in cases of burglary and robbery. *Journal of Research in Crime and Delinquency, 24,* 233–254.

[37]Williams, M. R. (2003). The effect of pretrial detention on imprisonment decisions. *Criminal Justice Review, 28,* 299–316.

[38]Minton, T. D. (2010). *Jjail inmates at midyear 2009.* Washington, DC: U. S. Department of Justice, Office of Justice Programs, Bureau of Justice Statistics.

[39]Minton, note 38, pp. 8–9.

[40]Garofalo, J., & Clark, R. D. (1985). The inmate subculture in jails. *Criminal Justice and Behavior, 12,* 415–434; Backstrand, J. A., Gibbons, D. C., & Jones, J. F. (1992). Who is in jail? An examination of the rabble hypothesis. *Crime and Delinquency, 38,* 219–229; DeLisi, M. (2000). Who is more dangerous? Comparing the criminality of homeless and domiciled jail inmates. *International Journal of Offender Therapy and Comparative Criminology, 44,* 59–69.

[41]James, D. J. (2004). *Profile of jail inmates, 2002.* Washington, DC: U. S. Department of Justice, Office of Justice Programs, Bureau of Justice Statistics.

[42]James, note 41, p. 1.

[43]James, D. J. (2000). *Drug use, testing, and treatment in jails.* Washington, DC: U. S. Department of Justice, Office of Justice Programs, Bureau of Justice Statistics.

[44]Goldfarb, A. (1976). *Jails: The ultimate ghetto of the criminal justice system.* New York: Doubleday (pp. 1–86). For assorted looks at the history of jails, see Adler, F. (1986). Jails as a repository for former mental patients. *International Journal of Offender Therapy and Comparative Criminology, 30,* 225–236; Irwin, J. (1985). *The jail: Managing the underclass in American society.* Berkeley, CA: University of California Press; Mattick, H., & Aikman, A. (1969). The cloacal region of American corrections: Prospects for jail reform. *Annals of the American Academy of Political and Social Science, 381,* 109–118.

[45]Applegate, B. K., Surette, R., & McCarthy, B. J. (1999). Detention and desistance from crime: Evaluating the influence of a new generation jail on recidivism. *Journal of Criminal Justice, 27,* 539–548; Tartaro, C. (2002). Examining implementation issues with new generation jails. *Criminal Justice Policy Review, 13,* 219–237; Williams, J. L., Rodeheaver, D. G., & Huggins, D. W. (1999). A comparative evaluation of a new generation jail. *American Journal of Criminal Justice, 23,* 223–246.

[46]Backstrand, J. A., Gibbons, D. C., & Jones, J. F. (1992). Who is in jail? An examination of the rabble hypothesis. *Crime and Delinquency, 38,* 219–229.

[47]Pogrebin, M., Dodge, M., & Katsampes, P. (2001). The collateral costs of short-term jail incarceration: The long-term social and economic disruptions. *Corrections Management Quarterly, 5,* 64–69.

[48]Hoff, R., Baranosky, M. V., Buchanan, J., Zonana, H., & Rosenheck, R. A. (1999). The effects of a jail diversion program on incarceration: A retrospective cohort study. *Journal of the American Academy of Psychiatry and the Law, 27,* 377–386; Lamb, H., Shaner, R., Elliott, D., DeCuir, W. J., & Foltz, J. T. (1995). Outcomes for psychiatric emergency patients seen by an outreach police–mental health team. *Psychiatric Services, 46,* 1267–1271; Steadman, H. J., Cocozza, J. J., & Veysey, B. M. (1999). Comparing outcomes for diverted and nondiverted jail detainees with mental illness. *Law and Human Behavior, 23,* 615–627.

[49]Steadman, H. J., & Naples, M. (2005). Assessing the effectiveness of jail diversion programs for persons with serious mental illness and co-occurring substance use disorders. *Behavioral Sciences and the Law, 23,* 163–170.

[50]Baumer, T. L., Maxfield, M. G., & Mendelsohn, R. I. (1993). A comparative analysis of three electronically monitored home detention programs. *Justice Quarterly, 10,* 121–142; Courtright, K. E., Berg, B. L., & Mutchnick, R. J. (1997). The cost effectiveness of using house arrest with electronic monitoring for drunk drivers. *Federal Probation, 61,* 19–22; Lilly, J. R., Ball, R. A., Curry, G. D., & McMullen, J. (1993). Electronic monitoring of the drunk driver: A seven-year study of the home confinement alternative. *Crime and Delinquency, 39,* 462–484; Maxfield, M. G., & Baumer, T. L. (1990). Home detention with electronic monitoring: Comparing pretrial and postconviction programs. *Crime and Delinquency, 36,* 521–536; Maxfield, M. G., & Baumer, T. L. (1992). Pretrial home detention with electronic monitoring: A non-experimental salvage evaluation. *Evaluation Review, 16,* 315–332.

[51]Stanz, R., & Tewksbury, R. (2000). Predictors of success and recidivism in a home incarceration program. *Prison Journal, 80,* 326–344.

[52]Pekins, C. A., Stephan, J. J., & Beck, A. J. (1995). *Jails and jail inmates, 1993-1994.* Washington, DC: U. S. Department of Justice, Office of Justice Programs, Bureau of Justice Statistics.

CHAPTER 8

[1]Henry VI, Part II, Act IV, Scene ii, quotation made by Dick the butcher.

[2]Uviller, H. R. (1999). *The tilted playing field: Is criminal justice unfair?* (p.2) New Haven, CT: Yale University Press.

[3]Forst, B. (2002). Prosecution. In J. Q. Wilson & J. Petersilia (Eds.), *Crime: Public policies for crime control* (pp. 509-536). Oakland, CA: Institute for Contemporary Studies Press.

[4]American Bar Association Model Rules of Professional Conduct. (1983). Rule 3.8. Chicago: American Bar Association.

[5]The Bureau of Justice Statistics a component of the Office of Justice Programs within the United States Department of Justice sponsored national surveys of American prosecutors in 1990, 1992, 1994, and 1996 that were administered by the National Opinion Research Center. The format changed to a census in 2001.

[6]Perry, S. W. (2006). *Prosecutors in state courts, 2005.* Washington, DC: U. S. Department of Justice, Office of Justice Programs, Bureau of Justice Statistics; DeFrances, C. J. (2003). *State court prosecutors in small districts, 2001.* Washington, DC: U. S. Department of Justice, Office of Justice Programs, Bureau of Justice Statistics.

[7]Forst, B. (2002). Prosecution. In J. Q. Wilson & J. Petersilia (Eds.), *Crime: Public policies for crime control* (pp. 509-536). Oakland, CA: Institute for Contemporary Studies Press.

[8]Cole, G. F. (1970). The decision to prosecute. *Law and Society Review, 4,* 313-343.

[9]Boland, B., & Forst, B. (1985). Prosecutors don't always aim to pleas. *Federal Probation, 49,* 10-15.

[10]Adams, K., & Cutshall, C. R. (1987). Refusing to prosecute minor offenses: The relative influence of legal and extralegal factors. *Justice Quarterly, 4,* 595-609. Also see, Bernstein, I., Kelley, W. R., & Doyle, P. A. (1977). Societal reaction to deviants: The case of criminal defendants. *American Sociological Review, 42,* 743-755; Wilbanks, W. (1987). *The myth of a racist criminal justice system.* Monterey, CA: Brooks/Cole; Gottfredson, M. R., & Gottfredson, D. M. (1987). *Decision-making in criminal justice: Toward the rational exercise of discretion,* 2nd edition. Cambridge, MA: Ballinger.

[11]Sanborn, J. B. (1996). Factors perceived to affect delinquent dispositions in juvenile court: Putting the sentencing decision into context. *Crime & Delinquency, 42,* 99-113.

[12]Sanborn, J. B. (1995). How parents can affect the processing of delinquents in the juvenile court. *Criminal Justice Policy Review, 7,* 1-26.

[13]Schmidt, J., & Steury. (1989). Prosecutorial discretion in filing charges in domestic violence cases. *Criminology, 27,* 487-510.

[14]Albonetti, C. A., & Hepburn, J. R. (1996). Prosecutorial discretion to defer criminalization: The effects of defendant's ascribed and achieved status characteristics. *Journal of Quantitative Criminology, 12,* 63-81.

[15]Rainville, G. (2001). An analysis of factors related to prosecutor sentencing preferences. *Criminal Justice Policy Review, 12,* 295-310.

[16]Forst, note 3, p. 512.

[17]Spears, J. W., & Spohn, C. C. (1997). The effect of evidence factors and victim characteristics on

prosecutors' charging decision in sexual assault cases. *Justice Quarterly, 14,* 501-524.

[18]Beichner, D., & Spohn, C. (2005). Prosecutorial charging decisions in sexual assault cases: Examining the impact of a specialized prosecution unit. *Criminal Justice Policy Review, 16,* 461-498.

[19]*Powell v. Alabama,* 287 U. S. 45 (1932) (pp. 68-71).

[20]Rush, G. E. (2000). *The dictionary of criminal justice* (pp. 290-291), 5th edition. New York: Dushkin/McGraw-Hill.

[21]*Johnson v. Zerbst,* 304 U. S. 458 (1938).

[22]*Griffin v. Illinois,* 351 U. S. 12 (1956).

[23]*Douglas v. California,* 372 U. S. 353 (1963); *Gideon v. Wainwright,* 372 U. S. 335 (1963).

[24]*Argesinger v. Hamlin,* 407 U. S. 25 (1972).

[25]*In re Gault,* 387 U. S. 1 (1967); *In re Winshop,* 397 U. S. 358 (1970).

[26]DeFrances, C. J., & Litras, M. F. X. (2000). *Indigent defense services in large counties, 1999.* Washington, DC: U. S. Department of Justice, Office of Justice Programs, Bureau of Justice Statistics; Farole, Jr., D. J., & Langton, L. (2010). *County-based and local public defender offices, 2007.* Washington, DC: U. S. Department of Justice, Office of Justice Programs, Bureau of Justice Statistics; Langton, L., & Farole, Jr., D. (2010). *State public defender programs, 2007.* Washington, DC: U. S. Department of Justice, Office of Justice Programs, Bureau of Justice Statistics.

[27]DeFrances & Litras, note 26, pp. 1-5.

[28]Harlow, C. W. (2000). *Defense counsel in criminal cases.* Washington, DC: U. S. Department of Justice, Office of Justice Programs, Bureau of Justice Statistics.

[29]*Dickey v. Florida,* 398 U.S. 30 (1970).

[30]*Klopfer v. North Carolina,* 386 U. S. 213 (1967).

[31]*Barker v. Wingo,* 407 U.S. 514 (1972).

[32]18 United States Code §§ 3161-3174.

[33]For an interesting look at judicial culture, see Crank, J. (1986). Legal culture: A re-examination of the legal culture. *Criminal Justice Review, 11,* 8-14.

[34]Crawford, K. A. (2001). The Sixth Amendment right to counsel: Application and limitations. *FBI Law Enforcement Bulletin, 70,* 27-33. *Kirby v. Illinois,* 406 U.S. 682 (1972) established that 6th Amendment protections are not invoked until adversarial court action is taken by the state.

[35]*United States v. Wade,* 388 U. S. 218 (1967); *Gilbert v. California,* 388 U. S. 263 (1967).

[36]*Brewer v. Williams,* 97 S. Ct. 1232 (1977). Importantly, appellate courts have determined that Sixth Amendment provisions are attached specific to the crime(s) for which a defendant has been charged, not necessarily subsequent crimes that the defendant may confess to or otherwise admit. See, *McNeil v. Wisconsin,* 111 S. Ct. 2204 (1991); *Blockburger v. United States,* 284 U. S. 299 (1932).

[37]*Hamilton v. Alabama,* 368 U. S. 52 (1961).

[38]*Coleman v. Alabama,* 399 U. S. 1 (1970).

[39]*Brady v. United States,* 397 U. S. 742 (1970).

[40]*Powell v. Alabama,* 287 U. S. 45 (1932); *Gideon v. Wainwright,* 372 U. S. 335 (1963).

[41]*Townsend v. Burke,* 334 U. S. 736 (1948).

[42]*Douglas v. California,* 372 U. S. 353 (1963).

[43]*Mempa v. Rhay,* 389 U. S. 128 (1967).

[44]*Morrisey v. Brewer,* 408 U. S. 471 (1972); *Gagnon v. Scarpelli,* 411 U. S. 778 (1973).

[45]*In re Gault,* 387 U. S. 1 (1967).

CHAPTER 9

[1]Lynch, T. (2003). The case against plea-bargaining. *Regulation, Fall,* 24–27. Washington, DC: Cato Institute.

[2]Arnold, T. (1962). *The symbols of government* (pp. 128–130). New York: Harcourt, Brace & World.

[3]Blumberg, A. S. (1967). The practice of law as a confidence game: Organizational cooperation of a profession. *Law and Society Review, 1,* 15–39, p. 27.

[4]Adams, J. (1770). Quotation cited in *Facts about the American judicial system.* (1999). American Bar Association.

[5]Cole, G. F. (1993). Performance measures for the trial courts, prosecution, and public defense. In J. J. DiIulio, G. P. Alpert, M. H. Moore, G. F. Cole, J. Petersilia, C. H. Logan, & J. Q. Wilson (Eds.) *Performance measures for the criminal justice system* (pp. 86–107). Washington, DC: U. S. Department of Justice, Office of Justice Programs, Bureau of Justice Statistics, p. 93.

[6]Zatz, M. J., & Lizotte, A. J. (1985). The timing of court processing: Towards linking theory and method. *Criminology, 23,* 313–335, pp. 330–331.

[7]Rhodes, W. M. (1978). *Plea-bargaining: Who gains? Who loses?* Washington, DC: Institute for Law and Social Research.

[8]*McNabb v. U. S.,* 318 U. S. 332 (1943).

[9]Rosenmerkel, S., Durose, M. R., & Farole, Jr., D. (2009). *Felony sentences in state courts, 2006—Statistical tables.* Washington, DC: U. S. Department of Justice, Office of Justice Programs, Bureau of Justice Statistics.

[10]Rush, G. E. (2000). *The dictionary of criminal justice* (p. 252), 5th edition. New York: Dushkin/McGraw-Hill.

[11]Alschuler, A. (1968). The prosecutor's role in plea-bargaining. *University of Chicago Law Review, 36,* 50–112.

[12]Alschuler, A. (1975). The defense attorney's role in plea-bargaining. *Yale Law Journal, 84,* 1179–1313.

[13]Lynch, D. R., & Evans, T. D. (2002). Attributes of highly effective criminal defense negotiators. *Journal of Criminal Justice, 30,* 387–396.

[14]Padgett, J. F. (1985). The emergent organization of plea-bargaining. *American Journal of Sociology, 90,* 753–802.

[15]Meyer, J., & Gray, T. (1997). Drunk drivers in the courts: Legal and extra-legal factors affecting pleas and sentences. *Journal of Criminal Justice, 25,* 155–163. Also see, Alschuler, A. (1976). The trial judge's role in plea-bargaining, part I. *Columbia Law Review, 76,* 1059–1154.

[16]Worden, A. P. (1995). The judge's role in plea-bargaining: An analysis of judges' agreement with prosecutor's sentencing recommendations. *Justice Quarterly, 12,* 257–278.

[17]Vigorita, M. S. (2003). Judicial risk assessment: The impact of risk, stakes, and jurisdiction. *Criminal Justice Policy Review, 14,* 361–376.

[18]Viljoen, J. L., Klaver, J., & Roesch, R. (2005). Legal decisions of preadolescent and adolescent defendants: Predictors of confession, pleas, communication with attorneys, and appeals. *Law and Human Behavior, 29,* 253–277.

[19]LaFree, G. D. (1985). Adversarial and non-adversarial justice: A comparison of guilty pleas and trials. *Criminology, 23,* 289–312; Walsh, A. (1990). Standing trial versus copping a plea: Is there a penalty? *Journal of Contemporary Criminal Justice, 6,* 226–237.

[20]Gillis, J. W. (2002). *Victim input into plea agreements.* Washington, DC: U. S. Department of Justice, Office of Justice Programs, Office for Victims of Crime.

[21]For investigations of legal and extra-legal factors in plea-bargaining, see Champion, D. J. (1989). Private counsels and public defenders: A look at weak cases, prior records, and leniency in plea-bargaining. *Journal of Criminal Justice, 17,* 253–263; Kellough, G., & Wortley, S. (2002). Remand for plea: Bail decisions and plea-bargaining as commensurate decisions. *British Journal of Criminology, 42,* 186–210; LaFree, G. D. (1985). Adversarial and non-adversarial justice: A comparison of guilty pleas and trials. *Criminology, 23,* 289–312; Meyer, J., & Gray, T. (1997). Drunk drivers in the courts: Legal and extra-legal factors affecting pleas and sentences. *Journal of Criminal Justice, 25,* 155–163.

[22]For a colorful symposium on plea-bargaining, see Scott, R. E., & Stuntz, W. J. (1992). Plea-bargaining as contract. *Yale Law Journal, 101,* 1909–1968; Easterbrook, F. H. (1992). Plea-bargaining as compromise. *Yale Law Journal, 101,* 1969–1978; Schulhofer, S. J. (1992). Plea-bargaining as disaster. *Yale Law Journal, 101,* 1979–2010; Scott, R. E., & Stuntz, W. J. (1992). Reply: Imperfect bargains, imperfect trials, and innocent defendants. *Yale Law Journal, 101,* 2011–2016.

[23]Gibbons, W. L. (1999). Instituting a no plea bargaining policy. *Prosecutor, 33,* 35–40.

[24]*Williams v. Florida,* 399 U. S. 78 (1970).

[25]*Witherspoon v. Illinois,* 391 U. S. 510 (1968).

[26]*Wainwright v. Witt,* 469 U. S. 412 (1985).

[27]*Lockhart v. McCree,* 476 U. S. 162 (1986).

[28]*Mu' Min v. Virginia,* 500 U. S. 415 (1991).

[29]For interesting studies of the criminology of jury selection, consult Fukurai, H. (1996). Race, social class, and jury participation: New dimensions for evaluating discrimination in jury service and jury selection. *Journal of Criminal Justice, 24,* 71–88; Fukurai, H. (1997). A quota jury: Affirmative action in jury selection. *Journal of Criminal Justice, 25,* 477–500.

[30]*Ristaino v. Ross,* 424 U. S. 589 (1976).

[31]*Turner v. Murray,* 476 U. S. 28 (1986).

[32]*Batson v. Kentucky,* 476 U. S. 79 (1986).

[33]*Powers v. Ohio,* 499 U. S. 400 (1991); also see *Georgia v. McCollum,* 505 U. S. 42 (1992).

[34]*Purkett v. Elem,* 514 U. S. 765 (1995).

[35]*J. E. B. ex rel. T. B.,* 511 U. S. 127 (1994).

[36]Federal Rules of Evidence. (2011). Retrieved February 25, 2011, from www.law.cornell.edu/rules/fre/rules.htm.

[37]*Sullivan v. Louisiana,* 508 U. S. 275 (1993).

[38]A related issue is jury nullification defined as the improper insistence on acquittal of a demonstrably guilty defendant because of some pre-existing bias on the part of one or more jurors. If a juror is successful at jury nullification, he or she produces a hung jury and subsequent mistrial. Although jury nullification is a controversial issue, it is exceedingly rare. For studies of jury nullification, see Hannaford, P. L., Hans, V. P., & Munsterman, G. T. (1999). How much justice hangs in the balance? A new look at

hung jury rates. *Judicature, 83,* 59–67; Hannaford-Agor, P. L., & Hans, V. P. (2003). Jury nullification at work? A glimpse from the National Center for State Courts Study of Hung Juries. *Chicago-Kent Law Review, 78,* 1249–1277.

[39]*Allen v. U. S.,* 164 U. S. 492 (1896).

[40]Hannaford-Agor, P., Hans, V. P., Mott, N. L., & Munsterman, G. T. (2002). *Are hung juries a problem?* Washington, DC: U. S. Department of Justice, Office of Justice Programs, National Institute of Justice.

[41]The literature of criminal sentencing is simply massive. Some well-known and interesting works on the subject include, Andenaes, J. (1974). *Punishment and deterrence.* Ann Arbor, MI: University of Michigan Press; Blumstein, A., Cohen, J., & Nagin, D. (Eds.). (1978). *Deterrence and incapacitation: Estimating the effects of criminal sanctions on crime rates.* Washington, DC: National Academy of Sciences Press; Tonry, M. (1998). Intermediate sanctions in sentencing guidelines. *Crime and Justice, 23,* 199–253; Zimring, F. E., & Hawkins, G. J. (1973). *Deterrence: The legal threat in crime control.* Chicago: University of Chicago Press; Zimring, F. E., & Hawkins, G. J. (1995). *Incapacitation: Penal confinement and the restraint of crime.* New York: Oxford University Press.

CHAPTER 10

[1]Kleiman, M. (1999). Community corrections as the front line in crime control. *UCLA Law Review, 46,* 1909–1925, p. 1917.

[2]Petersilia, J. (2002). Community corrections. In J. Q. Wilson & J. Petersilia (Eds.), *Crime: Public policies for crime control* (pp. 483–508). Oakland, CA: Institute for Contemporary Studies Press, pp. 484–485.

[3]Tonry, M. (1998). Intermediate sanctions in sentencing guidelines. *Crime & Justice, 23,* 199–254, p. 243.

[4]Quotation cited in Schneider, A. L., Ervin, L., & Snyder-Joy, Z. (1996). Further exploration of the flight from discretion: The role of risk/need instruments in probation supervision decisions. *Journal of Criminal Justice, 24,* 109–121, pp. 116–117.

[5]Skolnick, J. H. (1960). Toward a developmental theory of parole. *American Sociological Review, 25,* 542–549, p. 549.

[6]Lowenkamp, C. T., Latessa, E. J., & Holsinger, A. M. (2006). The risk principle in action: What have

we learned from 13,676 offenders and 97 correctional programs? *Crime & Delinquency, 52,* 77–93, pp. 77–78.

[7]Criminality, risk factors, and protective factors are part of a recent paradigm of research that seeks to translate criminological research findings into effective public policy. In fact, a recent issue of *Criminology & Public Policy* devoted several articles to this issue. For examples, see, Lowenkamp, C. T., & Latessa, E. J. (2005). Increasing the effectiveness of correctional programming through the risk principle: Identifying offenders for residential treatment. *Criminology & Public Policy, 4,* 263–290; Byrne, J. M., & Taxman, F. S. (2005). Crime (control) is a choice: Divergent perspectives on the role of treatment in the adult corrections system. *Criminology & Public Policy, 4,* 291–310; Harris, M. K. (2005). In search of common ground: The importance of theoretical orientations in criminology and criminal justice. *Criminology & Public Policy, 4,* 311–328; MacKenzie, D. L. (2005). The importance of using scientific evidence to make decisions about correctional programming. *Criminology & Public Policy, 4,* 249–258.

[8]Holsinger, A. M., & Latessa, E. J. (1999). An empirical evaluation of a sanction continuum: Pathways through the juvenile justice system. *Journal of Criminal Justice, 27,* 155–172.

[9]Morris, N. (1974). *The future of imprisonment.* Chicago: University of Chicago Press.

[10]Tonry, M. (1998). Intermediate sanctions in sentencing guidelines. *Crime & Justice, 23,* 199–254.

[11]Glaze, L. E. (2010). *Correctional populations in the United States, 2009.* Washington, DC: U. S. Department of Justice, Office of Justice Programs, Bureau of Justice Statistics; Glaze, L. E., & Bonczar, T. P. (2010). Probation and parole in the United States, 2009. Washington, DC: U. S. Department of Justice, Office of Justice Programs, Bureau of Justice Statistics.

[12]Petersilia, note 2, p. 493.

[13]Feeley, M., M., & Simon, J. (1992). The new penology: Notes on the emerging strategy of corrections and its implications. *Criminology, 30,* 449–474; Irwin, J., Austin, J., & Baird, C. (1998). Fanning the flames of fear. *Crime & Delinquency, 44,* 32–48; Austin, J., & Krisberg, B. (1982). The unmet promise of alternatives to incarceration. *Crime & Delinquency, 28,* 374–409; Irwin, J., & Austin, J. (2000). *It's about time: America's imprisonment binge,* 3rd edition. Belmont, CA: Wadsworth. For variations

on this theme, see Pontell, H., & Welsh, W. (1994). Incarceration as a deviant form of social control: Jail overcrowding in California. *Crime & Delinquency, 40,* 18–36; Welsh, W. (1993). Changes in arrest policies as a result of court orders against county jails. *Justice Quarterly, 10,* 89–120.

[14]For example, see DiIulio, J. J. (1991). *No escape: The future of American correctional system.* New York: Basic Books.

[15]On this "Robin Hood" approach to imposing fines, see Posner, R. A. (1980). Optimal sentences for white-collar criminals. *American Criminal Law Review, 17,* 409–418

[16]Critelli, J. W., & Crawford, R. F. (1980). The effectiveness of court-ordered punishment: Fines versus no punishment. *Criminal Justice & Behavior, 7,* 465–470; Gordon, M. A., & Glaser, D. (1991). The use and effects of financial penalties in municipal courts. *Criminology, 29,* 651–676.

[17]Gillis, J. W. (2002). *Ordering restitution to the crime victim.* Washington, DC: U. S. Department of Justice, Office of Justice Programs, Office for Victims of Crime.

[18]Outlaw, M. C., & Ruback, R. B. (1999). Predictors and outcomes of victim restitution orders. *Justice Quarterly, 16,* 847–869.

[19]Clingermayer, J. C., Hecker, J., & Madsen, S. (2005). Asset forfeiture and police priorities: The impact of program design on law enforcement activities. *Criminal Justice Policy Review, 16,* 319–335.

[20]Worrall, J. L. (2001). Addicted to the drug war: The role of civil asset forfeiture as a budgetary necessity in contemporary law enforcement. *Journal of Criminal Justice, 29,* 171–187.

[21]Clingermayer, J. C., Hecker, J., & Madsen, S. (2005). Asset forfeiture and police priorities: The impact of program design on law enforcement activities. *Criminal Justice Policy Review, 16,* 319–335.

[22]Williams, D. J., & Turnage, T. A. (2001). The success of a day reporting center program. *Corrections Compendium, 26,* 1–3, 26.

[23]Roy, S., & Grimes, J. N. (2002). Adult offenders in a day reporting center: A preliminary study. *Federal Probation, 66,* 44–50.

[24]Martin, C., Lurigio, A. J., & Olson, D. E. (2003). An examination of re-arrests and re-incarcerations among discharged day reporting center clients. *Federal Probation, 67,* 24–30.

[25]Roy & Grimes, note 23.

[26]Craddock, A. (2004). Estimating criminal justice system costs and cost-saving benefits of day reporting centers. *Journal of Offender Rehabilitation, 39,* 69–98; Craddock, A., & Graham, L. A. (2001). Recidivism as a function of day reporting center participation. *Journal of Offender Rehabilitation, 34,* 81–97.

[27]Caputo, G. A. (1999). Why not community service? *Criminal Justice Policy Review, 10,* 503–519; Harris, R. J., & Lo, T. W. (2002). Community service: Its use in criminal justice. *International Journal of Offender Therapy and Comparative Criminology, 46,* 427–444.

[28]Rackmill, S. J. (1996). Printzlien's legacy, the "Brooklyn Plan," A.K.A. deferred prosecution. *Federal Probation, 60,* 8–15.

[29]Pratt, T. C., & Winston, M. R. (1999). The search for the frugal grail: An empirical assessment of the cost-effectiveness of public versus private correctional facilities. *Criminal Justice Policy Review, 10,* 447–471.

[30]For examples, see Hartman, D. J., Friday, P. C., & Minor, K. I. (1994). Residential probation: A seven-year follow-up study of halfway house discharges. *Journal of Criminal Justice, 22,* 503–515; Dowell, D. A., Klein, C., & Krichmar, C. (1985). Evaluation of a halfway house for women. *Journal of Criminal Justice, 13,* 217–226. For more equivocal findings, see Dowdy, E. R., Lacy, M. G., & Unnithan, N. P. (2002). Correctional prediction and the Level of Supervision Inventory. *Journal of Criminal Justice, 30,* 29–39; Latessa, E. J., & Travis III, L. F. (1991). Halfway house or probation: A comparison of alternative dispositions. *Journal of Crime and Justice, 14,* 53–75.

[31]On the overuse of prison to serve minimum- and medium-risk felons, see Bonta, J., & Motiuk, L. L. (1990). Classification to halfway houses: A quasi-experimental evaluation. *Criminology, 28,* 497–506.

[32]MacKenzie, D. L., & Piquero, A. (1994). The impact of shock incarceration programs on prison crowding. *Crime & Delinquency, 40,* 222–249.

[33]Lutze, F. E., & Brody, D. C. (1999). Mental abuse as cruel and unusual punishment: Do boot camp prisons violate the 8th Amendment? *Crime & Delinquency, 45,* 242–255; Welch, M. (1997). A critical interpretation of correctional boot camps as normalizing institutions. *Journal of Contemporary Criminal Justice, 13,* 184–205.

[34]Lutze, F. E. (1998). Are shock incarceration programs more rehabilitative than traditional prisons? A survey of inmates. *Justice Quarterly, 15,* 547–63.

[35]MacKenzie, D. L. (1991). The parole performance of offender released from shock incarceration (boot camp prisons): A survival time analysis. *Journal of Quantitative Criminology, 7,* 213–236; MacKenzie, D. L., & Brame, R. (1995). Shock incarceration and positive adjustment during community supervision. *Journal of Quantitative Criminology, 11,* 111–142; Mitchell, O., MacKenzie, D. L., & Perez, D. M. (2005). A randomized evaluation of the Maryland correctional boot camp for adults: Effects on offender antisocial attitudes and cognitions. *Journal of Offender Rehabilitation, 40,* 3–4, 71–86.

[36]Stinchcomb, J. B., & Terry III, W. C. (2001). Predicting the likelihood of re-arrest among shock incarceration graduates: Moving beyond another nail in the boot camp coffin. *Crime & Delinquency, 47,* 221–242.

[37]Benda, B. B. (2003). Survival analysis of criminal recidivism of boot camp graduates using elements from general and developmental explanatory models. *International Journal of Offender Therapy and Comparative Criminology, 47,* 89–110; Benda, B. B., Toombs, N. J., & Peacock, M. (2003). Discriminators of types of recidivism among boot camp graduates in a five-year follow-up study. *Journal of Criminal Justice, 31,* 539–551; Benda, B. B., Toombs, N. J., & Peacock, M. (2006). Distinguishing graduates from dropouts and dismissals: Who fails boot camp? *Journal of Criminal Justice, 34,* in press.

[38]MacKenzie, D. L., Wilson, D. B., & Kider, S. B. (2001). Effects of correctional boot camps on offending. *Annals of the American Academy of Political and Social Science, 578,* 126–143.

[39]MacKenzie, D. L., Brame, R., McDowall, D., & Souryal, C. (1995). Boot camp prisons and recidivism in eight states. *Criminology, 33,* 327–357; MacKenzie, D. L., Wilson, D. B., & Kider, S. B. (2001). Effects of correctional boot camps on offending. *Annals of the American Academy of Political and Social Science, 578,* 126–143.

[40]Gainey, R. R., & Payne, B. K. (2000). Understanding the experience of house arrest with electronic monitoring: An analysis of quantitative and qualitative data. *International Journal of Offender Therapy and Comparative Criminology, 44,* 84–96.

[41]Vollum, S., & Hale, C. (2002). Electronic monitoring: A research review. *Corrections Compendium, 27,* 1–4, 23–27; Glaser, D., & Watts, R. (1993). The electronic monitoring of drug offenders on probation.

Journal of Offender Monitoring, 6, 1–10, 14; Courtright, K. E., Berg, B. L., & Mutchnick, R. J. (1997). The cost effectiveness of using house arrest with electronic monitoring. *Federal Probation, 61,* 19–22; Papy, J., & Nimer, R. (1991). Electronic monitoring in Florida. *Federal Probation, 55,* 31–33.

[42]Glaser, D., & Watts, R. (1993). The electronic monitoring of drug offenders on probation. *Journal of Offender Monitoring, 6,* 1–10, 14; Finn, M. A., & Muirhead-Steves, S. (2002). The effectiveness of electronic monitoring with violent male parolees. *Justice Quarterly, 19,* 293–312; Gainey, R. R., Payne, B. K., & O'Toole, M. (2000). The relationships between time in jail, time on electronic monitoring, and recidivism: An event history analysis of a jail-based program. *Justice Quarterly, 17,* 733–752.

[43]Courtright, K. E., Berg, B. L., & Mutchnick, R. J. (1997). The effects of house arrest with electronic monitoring on DUI offenders. *Journal of Offender Rehabilitation, 24,* 35–51; Courtright, K. E., Berg, B. L., & Mutchnick, R. J. (2000). Rehabilitation in the new machine? Exploring drug and alcohol use and variables related to success among DUI offenders under electronic monitoring: Some preliminary outcome results. *International Journal of Offender Therapy and Comparative Criminology, 44,* 293–311.

[44]Bonta, J., Wallace-Capretta, S., & Rooney, J. (2000). Can electronic monitoring make a difference? An evaluation of three Canadian programs. *Crime & Delinquency, 46,* 61–75. For more criticisms of this sanction, see Schmidt, A. (1991). Electronic monitors: Realistically, what can be expected? *Federal Probation, 55,* 49–57; Corbett, R. & Marx, G. T. (1991). No soul in the new machine: Technofallacies in the electronic monitoring movement. *Justice Quarterly, 8,* 399–414.

[45]Petersilia, J. (1997). Probation in the United States. *Crime & Justice, 22,* 149–200 (p. 159).

[46]Kingsnorth, R. F., MacIntosh, R. C., & Sutherland, S. (2002). Criminal charge or probation violation? Prosecutorial discretion and implications for research in criminal court processing. *Criminology, 40,* 553–578.

[47]Petersilia, note 2.

[48]Glaze, note 11.

[49]Petersilia, note 45.

[50]Cunniff, M. A., & Bergsmann, I. R. (1990). *Managing felons in the community: An administrative profile of probation.* Washington, DC: U. S. Department of

Justice, Office of Justice Programs, Bureau of Justice Statistics.

[51]Thomas, D. W. (1993). *The state of juvenile probation, 1992: Results of a nationwide survey.* Washington, DC: U. S. Department of Justice, Office of Justice Programs, Bureau of Justice Statistics.

[52]Carter, R. M., & Wilkins, L. T. (Eds.). (1970). *Probation and parole: Selected readings.* New York: John Wiley & Sons; Worrall, J. L., Schram, P., Hays, E., & Newman, M. (2004). An analysis of the relationship between probation caseloads and property crime rates in California counties. *Journal of Criminal Justice, 32,* 231–241.

[53]Cohen, R. L. (1995). *Probation and parole violators in state prison, 1991.* Washington, DC: U. S. Department of Justice, Office of Justice Programs, Bureau of Justice Statistics.

[54]Langan, P. A., & Cunniff, M. A. (1992). *Recidivism of felons on probation, 1986-1989.* Washington, DC: U. S. Department of Justice, Office of Justice Programs, Bureau of Justice Statistics; Cunniff, M. A., & Shilton, M. K. (1991). *Variations on felony probation: Persons under supervision in 32 urban and suburban counties.* Washington, DC: U. S. Department of Justice, Office of Justice Programs, Bureau of Justice Statistics.

[55]Harris, P. M., Petersen, R. D., & Rapoza, S. (2001). Between probation and revocation: A study of intermediate sanctions decision-making. *Journal of Criminal Justice, 29,* 307–318.

[56]Mayzer, R., Gray, M. K., & Maxwell, S. R. (2004). Probation absconders: A unique risk group? *Journal of Criminal Justice, 32,* 137–150; Gray, M. K., Fields, M., & Maxwell, S. R. (2001). Examining probation violations: Who, what, and when. *Crime & Delinquency, 47,* 537–557.

[57]Petersilia, J., Turner, S., Kahan, J., & Peterson, J. (1985). *Granting felons probation: Public risks and alternatives.* Santa Monica, CA: RAND.

[58]The literature on probation is voluminous, however a diverse samples of studies includes the following: Benedict, W. R., Huff-Corzine, L., & Corzine, J. (1998). 'Clean up and go straight': Effects of drug treatment on recidivism among felony probationers. *American Journal of Criminal Justice, 22,* 169–187; Griffin, M. L., & Armstrong, G. S. (2003). The effect of local life circumstances on female probationers' offending. *Justice Quarterly, 20,* 213–239; MacKenzie, D. L., & De Li, S. (2002). The impact of formal and informal social

controls on the criminal activities of probationers. *Journal of Research in Crime and Delinquency, 39,* 243–276; Minor, K. I., & Elrod, P. (1994). The effects of a probation intervention on juvenile offenders' self-concepts, loci of control, and perceptions of juvenile justice. *Youth & Society, 25,* 490–511; Petersilia, J., & Turner, S. (1992). An evaluation of ISP in California. *Journal of Criminal Law and Criminology, 82,* 610–658.

[59]Petersilia, note 2; Turner, S., Petersilia, J., & Deschenes, E. P. (1992). Evaluating ISP for drug offenders. *Crime & Delinquency, 38,* 539–556.

[60]Geerken, M. R., & Hayes, H. D. (1993). Probation and parole: Public risk and the future of incarceration. *Criminology, 31,* 549–564.

[61]Fulton, B., Latessa, E. J., Stichman, & Travis, L. F. (1997). The state of ISP: Research and policy implications. *Federal Probation, 61,* 65–75.

[62]Gendreau, P., Cullen, F. T., & Bonta, J. (1994). Intensive rehabilitation supervision: The next generation in community corrections? *Federal Probation, 58,* 72–78; also see, Clear, T. R., & Latessa, E. J. (1993). Probation officers' roles in intensive supervision: Surveillance versus treatment. *Justice Quarterly, 10,* 441–462.

[63]Hughes, T. A., Wilson, D. J., & Beck, A. J. (2001). *Trends in state parole, 1990-2000.* Washington, DC: U. S. Department of Justice, Office of Justice Programs, Bureau of Justice Statistics.

[64]Travis, J., & Lawrence, S. (2002). *Beyond the prison gates: The state of parole in America.* Washington, DC: The Urban institute, Justice Policy Center.

[65]Technically this is not correct. Once inmates are sentenced to state prison, they are first sent to a diagnostic and classification facility within the state department of corrections that will determine the most appropriate facility placement for each inmate. Some inmates are classified as so low-risk that they are immediately granted parole even though they were recently sentenced to prison by the courts, a process known as "direct sentence" or "automatic parole." These offenders ostensibly never served time in prison even though they were granted parole. However, for the lion's share of offenders, parole occurs after serving some portion of a sentence behind bars.

[66]Petersilia, J. (1998). Probation and parole. In M. Tonry (Ed.), *The handbook of crime and punishment* (pp. 563–588). New York: Oxford University Press.

[67]Travis, J., & Lawrence, S. (2002). *Beyond the prison gates: The state of parole in America.* Washington, DC: The Urban institute, Justice Policy Center.

[68]Glaze & Bonczar, note 11.

[69]Hughes, T. A., Wilson, D. J., & Beck, A. J. (2001). *Trends in state parole, 1990-2000.* Washington, DC: U. S. Department of Justice, Office of Justice Programs, Bureau of Justice Statistics.

[70]Hughes et al., note 69.

[71]Hughes et al., note 69.

[72]For studies of parole outcomes, reintegration, and parolee recidivism, see, Gottfredson, D. M., Gottfredson, M. R., & Garofalo, J. (1977). Time served in prison and parole outcomes among parolee risk categories. *Journal of Criminal Justice, 5,* 1–12; Gottfredson, M. R., & Gottfredson, D. M. (1988). *Decision-making in criminal justice: Towards the rational exercise of discretion,* 2nd edition. New York: Plenum; Hoffman, P. B. (1994). Twenty years of operational use of a risk prediction instrument: The United States Parole Commission's salient factor score. *Journal of Criminal Justice, 22,* 477–494; Hoffman, P. B., & Beck, J. L. (1985). Recidivism among released federal prisoners: Salient Factor Score and five-year follow-up. *Criminal Justice & Behavior, 12,* 501–507; Morgan, K. D., & Smith, B. (2005). Parole release decisions revisited: An analysis of parole release decisions for violent inmates in a southeastern state. *Journal of Criminal Justice, 33,* 277–287; Travis, J., & Visher, C. (Eds.). (2005). *Prisoner reentry and crime in America.* New York: Cambridge University Press.

CHAPTER 11

[1]De Beaumont, G., & de Tocqueville, A. (1994). On the penitentiary system in the United States and its application in France. In J. E. Jacoby (Ed.), *Classics of criminology,* (pp. 372–386). Prospect Heights, IL: Waveland Press.

[2]Martinson, R. (1974). What works? Questions and answers about prison reform. *The Public Interest, 35,* 22–54, p. 25.

[3]Seiter, R. P., & Kadela, K. R. (2003). Prisoner reentry: What works, what does not, and what is promising. *Crime & Delinquency, 49,* 360–388, p. 381.

[4]Allender, D. M. (2004). Offender reentry: A returning or reformed criminal? *FBI Law Enforcement Bulletin, 73,* 1–13, p. 2.

[5]Hemmens, C., & Marquart, J. W. (2000). Friend or foe? Race, age, and inmate perceptions of inmate-staff relations. *Journal of Criminal Justice, 28,* 297–312.

[6]Sorensen, J., Hope, R., & Stemen, D. (2003). Racial disproportionality in state prison admissions: Can regional variation be explained by differential arrest rates? *Journal of Criminal Justice, 31,* 73–84, p. 82.

[7]DeLisi, M. (2003). Criminal careers behind bars. *Behavioral Sciences and the Law, 21,* 653–669, p. 655.

[8]Petrosino, A., Turpin-Petrosino, C., & Buehler, J. (2003). Scared Straight and other juvenile awareness programs for preventing juvenile delinquency: A systematic review of the randomized experimental evidence. *Annals of the American Academy of Political and Social Science, 589,* 41–62.

[9]Excellent primers on the history of American prisons are Friedman, L. M. (1993). *Crime and punishment in American history.* New York: Bantam Books; Morris, N., & Rothman, D. J. (1998). *The Oxford history of the prison: The practice of punishment in Western society.* New York: Oxford University Press.

[10]Retrieved March 1, 2011, from http://www.easternstate.org/history/sixpage.html; A & E. (2002). *The big house: Eastern State Penitentiary.* A & E VHS Video.

[11]Rotman, E. (1998). The failure of reform: United States, 1865–1965. In Morris, N., & Rothman, D. J. (1998). *The Oxford history of the prison: The practice of punishment in Western society* (pp. 151–177). New York: Oxford University Press, p. 152.

[12]Brockway, Z. R. (1994). The American reformatory prison system. In J. E. Jacoby (Ed.), *Classics of criminology* (pp. 387–396). Prospect Heights, IL: Waveland Press.

[13]Federal Bureau of Prisons. (2006). *A brief history of the Bureau of Prisons.* Washington, DC: U. S. Department of Justice, Retrieved March 1, 2011, from http://www.bop.gov/about/index.jsp; West, H. C., & Sabol, W. J. (2010). *Prisoners in 2009.* Washington, DC: U. S. Department of Justice, Office of Justice Programs, Bureau of Justice Statistics.

[14]Blumstein, A., & Cohen, J. (1973). A theory of the stability of punishment. *Journal of Criminal Law and Criminology, 64,* 198–207

[15]Clemmer, D. (1940). *The prison community.* New York: Holt, Rinehart, and Winston; Clemmer, D. (1950). Observations on imprisonment as a source of criminality. *Journal of Criminal Law and Criminology, 41,* 311–19.

[16]Hayner, N. S., & Ash, E. (1940). The prison as a community. *American Sociological Review, 5,* 577–583 (p. 583).

[17]Sykes, G. M. (1958). *The society of captives: A study of a maximum-security prison.* Princeton, NJ: Princeton University Press.

[18]Akers, R., Hayner, N., & Gruninger, W. (1977). Prisonization in five countries: Type of prison and inmate characteristics. *Criminology, 14,* 527–554; Huebner, B. M. (2003). Administrative determinants of inmate violence: A multilevel analysis. *Journal of Criminal Justice, 31,* 107–117; Jiang, S., & Fisher-Giorlando, M. (2002). Inmate misconduct: A test of the deprivation, importation, and situational models. *The Prison Journal, 82,* 335–358; Poole, E. D., & Regoli, R. M. (1983). Violence in juvenile institutions: A comparative study. *Criminology, 21,* 213–232; Reisig, M. D., & Lee, Y. (2000). Prisonization in the Republic of Korea. *Journal of Criminal Justice, 28,* 23–31; Walters, G. D. (2003). Changes in criminal thinking and identity in novice and experienced inmates: Prisonization revisited. *Criminal Justice and Behavior, 30,* 399–421; Wheeler, S. (1961). Socialization in correctional communities. *American Sociological Review, 26,* 697–712.

[19]Irwin, J., & Cressey, D. (1962). Thieves, convicts, and the inmate culture. *Social Problems, 10,* 142–155.

[20]Jacobs, J. B. (1977). *Stateville: The penitentiary in mass society.* Chicago: University of Chicago Press; Wilson, J. Q. (1983). *Thinking about crime,* revised edition. New York: Vintage Books.

[21]Feeley, M. M., & Simon, J. (1992). The new penology: Notes on the emerging strategy of corrections ad its implications. *Criminology, 30,* 449–474.

[22]Conklin, J. E. (2003). *Why crime rates fell.* Boston, MA: Allyn & Bacon.

[23]Levitt, S. D. (2004). Understanding why crime fell in the 1990s: Four factors that explain the decline and six that do not. *Journal of Economic Perspectives, 18,* 163–190.

[24]On the deleterious effects of solitary confinement, see Andersen, H. S., Sestoft, D., Lillebaek, T., Gabrielsen, G., & Hemmingsen, R. (2003). A longitudinal study of prisoners on remand: Repeated measures of psychopathology in the initial phase of solitary versus non-solitary confinement. *International Journal of Law and Psychiatry, 26,* 165–177.

[25]West & Sabol, note 13.

[26]West & Sabol, note 13.

[27]Greenfeld, L. A. (1995). *Prison sentences and time served for violence.* Washington, DC: U. S. Department of Justice, Office of Justice Programs, Bureau of Justice Statistics.

[28]Ditton, P. M., & Wilson, D. J. (1999). *Truth in sentencing in state prisons.* Washington, DC: U. S. Department of Justice, Office of Justice Programs, Bureau of Justice Statistics.

[29]Sabol, W. J., & McGready, J. (1999). *Time served in prison by federal offenders, 1986-1997.* Washington, DC: U. S. Department of Justice, Office of Justice Programs, Bureau of Justice Statistics.

[30]Stephan, J. J. (2008). *Census of state and federal correctional facilities, 2005.* Washington, DC: U. S. Department of Justice, Office of Justice Programs, Bureau of Justice Statistics.

[31]Camp, S. D., & Gaes, G. G. (2002). Growth and quality of U.S. private prisons: Evidence from a national survey. *Criminology & Public Policy, 1,* 427–450.

[32]Pratt, T. C., & Maahs, J. (1999). Are private prisons more cost-effective than public prisons? A meta-analysis of evaluation research studies. *Crime & Delinquency, 45,* 358–371.

[33]Bales, W. D., Bedard, L. E., Quinn, S. T., Ensley, D. T., & Holley, G. P. (2005). Recidivism of public and private state prison inmates in Florida. *Criminology & Public Policy, 4,* 57–82.

[34]Stephan, note 30.

[35]Harlow, C. W. (2003). *Education and correctional populations.* Washington, DC: U. S. Department of Justice, Office of Justice Programs, Bureau of Justice Statistics.

[36]Harlow, note 35.

[37]Stephan, note 30.

[38]Farrington, D. P., & Welsh, B. C. (2005). Randomized experiments in criminology: What have we learned in the last two decades? *Journal of Experimental Criminology, 1,* 9–38; Allen, L. C., MacKenzie, D. L., & Hickman, L. J. (2001). The effectiveness of cognitive behavioral treatment for adult offenders: A methodological, quality-based review. *International Journal of Offender Therapy and Comparative Criminology, 45,* 498–514.

[39]For exhaustive reviews of correctional treatment or evaluations of specific programs, see Seiter, R. P., & Kadela, K. R. (2003). Prisoner reentry: What works, what does not, and what is promising. *Crime & Delinquency, 49,* 360–388; Prendergast, M. L., & Wexler, H. K. (2004). Correctional substance abuse

treatment programs in California: A historical perspective. *The Prison Journal, 84,* 8–35; Cullen, F. T. (2005). The 12 people who saved rehabilitation: How the science of criminology made a difference. *Criminology, 43,* 1–42; Anglin, M. D., & Maugh, T. H. (1992). Ensuring success in interventions with drug-abusing offenders. *Annals of the American Academy of Political and Social Science, 521,* 66–90; Gendreau, P., & Ross, R. (1987). Revivification of rehabilitation: Evidence from the 1980s. *Justice Quarterly, 4,* 349–407; Lipton, D. S. (1998). Therapeutic community treatment programming in corrections. *Psychology, Crime, and Law, 4,* 213–263; Lipsey, M. W., & Wilson, D. B. (1993). The efficacy of psychological, educational, and behavioral treatment: Confirmation from meta-analysis. *American Psychologist, 48,* 1181–1209.

[40]Mumola, C. J. (2005). *Suicide and homicide in state prisons and local jails.* Washington, DC: U. S. Department of Justice, Office of Justice Programs, Bureau of Justice Statistics.

[41]Maruschak, L. M. (2004). *HIV in prisons and jails, 2002.* Washington, DC: U. S. Department of Justice, Office of Justice Programs, Bureau of Justice Statistics.

[42]Baillargeon, J., Black, S. A., Pulvino, J., & Dunn, K. (2002). *Disease profile of Texas prison inmates.* NIJ Final Report. Washington, DC: U. S. Department of Justice, Office of Justice Programs, National Institute of Justice.

[43]Mumola, C. J. (2000). *Incarcerated parents and their children.* Washington, DC: U. S. Department of Justice, Office of Justice Programs, Bureau of Justice Statistics.

[44]Hagan, J., & Dinovitzer, R. (1999). Collateral consequences of imprisonment for children, communities, and prisoners. *Crime & Justice, 26,* 121–162.

[45]Durose, M. R., & Mumola, C. J. (2004). *Profile of nonviolent offenders existing state prisons.* Washington, DC: U. S. Department of Justice, Office of Justice Programs, Bureau of Justice Statistics.

[46]Scalia, J. (2001). *Federal drug offenders, 1999 with trends 1984-1999.* Washington, DC: U. S. Department of Justice, Office of Justice Programs, Bureau of Justice Statistics.

[47]Benda, B. B., & Tollett, C. L. (1999). A study of recidivism of serious and persistent offenders among adolescents. *Journal of Criminal Justice, 27,* 111–126.

[48]Stephan & Karberg, note 30.

[49]DeLisi, note 7.

[50]Gendreau, P., Goggin, C. E., & Law, M. A. (1997). Predicting prison misconducts. *Criminal Justice and Behavior, 24,* 414–431; Homant, R. J., & Witkowski, M. J. (2003). Prison deviance as a predictor of general deviance: Some correlational evidence from Project GANGMILL. *Journal of Gang Research, 10,* 65–75; DeLisi, M., Berg, M. T., & Hochstetler, A. (2004). Gang members, career criminals, and prison violence: Further specification of the importation model of inmate behavior. *Criminal Justice Studies, 17,* 369–383; Allender, D. M., & Marcell, F. (2003). Career criminals, security threat groups, and prison gangs: An interrelated threat. *FBI Law Enforcement Bulletin, 72,* 8–12; Hochstetler, A., & DeLisi, M. (2005). Importation, deprivation, and varieties of serving time: An integrated-lifestyle-exposure model of prison offending. *Journal of Criminal Justice, 33,* 257–266; Drury, A. J., & DeLisi, M. (2010). The past is prologue: Prior adjustment to prison and institutional misconduct. *The Prison Journal, 90,* 331–352.

[51]Langan, P. A., & Levin, D. J. (2002). *Recidivism of prisoners released in 1994.* Washington, DC: U. S. Department of Justice, Office of Justice Programs.

[52]Langan & Levin, note 51.

[53]Langan, P. A., Schmitt, E. L., & Durose, M. R. (2003). *Recidivism of sex offenders released from prison in 1994.* Washington, DC: U. S. Department of Justice, Office of Justice Programs, Bureau of Justice Statistics.

[54]DeLisi, M. (2005). *Career criminals in society.* Thousand Oaks, CA: Sage.

CHAPTER 12

[1]Sowell, T. (1997). The death penalty is a deterrent. In D. L. Bender (Ed.), *The death penalty: Opposing viewpoints* (pp. 10–107). San Diego, CA: 3 Greenhaven Press.

[2]The quotation was originally attributed to Mohandas Gandhi and later also used by Dr. Martin Luther King. The quotation matches the philosophy of nonviolence advocated by both leaders.

[3]The quotation from Marquette University political science professor appears on the home page of pro-death penalty resource, http://www.prodeathpenalty.com/.

[4]Durkheim, E. (1900). Two laws of penal evolution. *Cincinnati Law Review, 38,* 32–60, p. 35.

[5]Rosenbaum, T. (2005). *The myth of moral justice: Why our legal system fails to do what's right* (p. 59). New York: Harper Collins.

[6]Barnes, H. E. (1996). *Story of punishment: A record of man's inhumanity* cited in R. J. Simon & D. A Blaskovich (2002). *A comparative analysis of capital punishment: Statutes, policies, frequencies, and public attitudes the world over* (p. xi). Lanham, MD: Lexington Books.

[7]Mead, G. H. (1918). The psychology of punitive justice. *American Journal of Sociology, 23,* 577–602, pp. 585–586.

[8]Associated Press. (2005). Retrieved January 10, 2005, from http://www.cnn.com/2005/LAW/01/09/death-row.clemency.ap/index.html.

[9]Associated Press. (2005). Retrieved February 3, 2005, from http://www.cnn.com/2005/LAW/02/01/deathrow.syndrome.ap/index.html.

[10]Associated Press. (2005). Retrieved March 1, 2005, from http://www.cnn.com/2005/LAW/03/01/scotus.death.penalty.ap/index.html.

[11]Reuters. (2005). Retrieved February 18, 2005, from http://www.cnn.com/2005/LAW/02/17/texas.execution.reut/index.html.

[12]Mears, B. (2005). Retrieved March 10, 2005, from http://www.cnn.com/2005/LAW/03/08/scotus.deathpenalty.mexicans/index.html.

[13]Associated Press. (2005). Retrieved April 21, 2005, from http://www.cnn.com/2005/LAW/04/21/texas.execution.ap/index.html.

[14]Associated Press. (2006). Retrieved February 14, 2006, from http://www.cnn.com/2005/LAW/11/07/inmate.escapes/index.html.

[15]Snell, T. L. (2010). *Capital punishment, 2009—Statistical tables.* Washington, DC: U. S. Department of Justice, Office of Justice Programs, Bureau of Justice Statistics.

[16]*Roper v. Simmons*, 543 U. S. 551 (2005).

[17]Retrieved March 1, 2011, from http://www.tdcj.state.tx/statistics/deathrow/drowlist/bagwell.jpg.

[18]Snell, note 15.

[19]*Coker v. Georgia,* 433 U. S. 584 (1977). Erlich Coker was serving a lengthy prison term upon convictions for murder, rape, kidnapping, and assault when he escaped from prison in 1974 and subsequently committed burglary, rape, and auto theft. For these crimes (rape was the most serious charged), Coker was sentenced to death—a sentence that was held as grossly disproportionate for rape and thus unconstitutional.

[20]*Gregg v. Georgia,* 428 U. S. 153, 49 L. Ed. 2d 859, 96 S. Ct. 2909 (1976); *Jurek v. Texas*, 428 U. S. 262 (1976); *Roberts v. Louisiana,* 428 U. S. 325 (1976); *Proffitt v. Florida,* 428 U. S. 242 (1976); *Woodson v. North Carolina,* 428 U. S. 280 (1976).

[21]Rush, G. E. (2000). *The dictionary of criminal justice,* 5th edition. New York: Dushkin/McGraw-Hill (p. 275).

[22]Snell, note 15.

[23]Snell, note 15.

[24]Snell, note 15.

[25]Van Soest, D., Park, H., Johnson, T. K., & McPhail, B. (2003). Different paths to death row: A comparison of men who committed heinous and less heinous crimes. *Violence and Victims, 18,* 15–33.

[26]Cunningham, M. D., & Vigen, M. P. (2002). Death row inmate characteristics, adjustment, and confinement: A critical review of the literature. *Behavioral Sciences and the Law, 20,* 191–210 (p. 207).

[27]DeLisi, M., & Scherer, A. M. (2006). Multiple homicide offenders: Offense characteristics, social correlates, and criminal careers. *Criminal Justice and Behavior, 33,* 1–25; DeLisi, M. (2005). *Career criminals in society.* Thousand Oaks, CA: Sage.

[28]*Furman v. Georgia,* 408 U. S. 238, 33 L. Ed. 2d 346, 92 S. Ct. 2726 (1972); *Branch v. Texas*, 408 U. S. 238 (1972); *Jackson v. Georgia,* 408 U. S. 238 (1972).

[29]Mooney, C. Z., & Lee, M. (2000). The influence of values on consensus and contentious morality policy: U. S. death penalty reform, 1956–1982. *Journal of Politics, 62,* 223–239.

[30]Galliher, J. M., & Galliher, J. F. (2001). The commonsense theory of deterrence and the ideology of science: The New York State death penalty debate. *Journal of Criminal Law and Criminology, 92,* 307–333.

[31]Spurr, S. J. (2002). The future of capital punishment: Determinants of the time from death sentence to execution. *International Review of Law and Economics, 22,* 1–23.

[32]Retrieved March 1, 2011, from http://www.innocenceproject.org/; also see Scheck, B., Neufeld, P. J., & Dwyer, J. (2000). *Actual innocence: Five days to execution and other dispatches from the wrongly convicted.* New York: Doubleday; Huff, C. R., Rattner, A., & Sagarin, E. (1996). *Convicted but innocent: Wrongful conviction and public policy.* Thousand Oaks, CA: Sage.

[33]Harmon, T. R. (2001). Guilty until proven innocent: An analysis of post-Furman capital errors. *Criminal*

Justice Policy Review, 12, 113–139; Harmon, T. R. (2001). Predictors of miscarriages of justice in capital cases. *Justice Quarterly, 18,* 949–968; Harmon, T. R. (2004). Race for your life: An analysis of the role of race in erroneous capital convictions. *Criminal Justice Review, 29,* 79–96; Harmon, T. R., & Lofquist, W. S. (2005). Too late for luck: A comparison of post-Furman exonerations and executions of the innocent. *Crime & Delinquency, 51,* 498–520.

[34]Leo, R. A. (2005). Rethinking the study of miscarriages of justice: Developing a criminology of wrongful conviction. *Journal of Contemporary Criminal Justice, 20,* 201–223.

[35]Because the overwhelming preponderance of academic research is conducted from the abolitionist perspective, criminologists whose work favors the death penalty are often derided and always second guessed. For an example of this "us versus them" approach, see Bedau, H., & Radelet, M. L. (1987). Miscarriages of justice in potentially capital cases. *Stanford Law Review, 40,* 21–179; Markman, S., & Cassell, P. (1988). Protecting the innocent: A response to the Bedau-Radelet study. *Stanford Law Review, 41,* 121–160. Others contend that both liberals and conservatives due process and crime control types are guilty of bias in death penalty research. For instance, see Donohue, J. J., & Wolfers, J. (2005). Uses and abuses of empirical evidence in the death penalty debate. *Stanford Law Review, 58,* 791–846.

[36]Leo, R. A. (2005). Rethinking the study of miscarriages of justice: Developing a criminology of wrongful conviction. *Journal of Contemporary Criminal Justice, 20,* 201–223.

[37]Associated Press. (2006). DNA: Virginia executed the right man. Retrieved January 12, 2006, from www.cnn.com/2006/LAW/01/12/dna.execution.ap/index.html.

[38]DeLisi, note 27.

[39]Sorensen, J. (2004). The administration of capital punishment. *ACJS Today, 29,* 1, 5–7, p. 7.

[40]Bailey, W. C., & Peterson, R. D. (1997). Murder, capital punishment, and deterrence: A review of the literature. In H. A. Bedau (Ed.), *The death penalty in America: Current controversies* (pp. 135–161). New York: Oxford University Press.

[41]Radelet, M. L., & Borg, M. J. (2000). The changing nature of death penalty debates. *Annual Review of Sociology, 26,* 43–61; Radelet, M. L., & Akers, R. L. (1996). Deterrence and the death penalty: The views of the experts. *Journal of Criminal Law and Criminology, 87,* 1–16.

[42]Cheatwood, D. (1993). Capital punishment and the deterrence of violent crime in comparable counties. *Criminal Justice Review, 18,* 165–181; Cheatwood, D. (2002). Capital punishment for the crime of homicide in Chicago: 1870–1930. *Journal of Criminal Law and Criminology, 92,* 843–866.

[43]King, D. R. (1978). The brutalization effect: Execution publicity and the incidence of homicide in South Carolina. *Social Forces, 57,* 683–696; Bowers, W. J., & Pierce, G. L. (1980). Deterrence or brutalization: What is the effect of executions? *Crime & Delinquency, 26,* 453–484; Cochran, J. K., Chamlin, M. B., & Seth, M. (1994). Deterrence or brutalization? An impact assessment of Oklahoma's return to capital punishment. *Criminology, 32,* 107–134; Thomson, E. (1997). Deterrence versus brutalization: The case of Arizona. *Homicide Studies, 1,* 110–128.

[44]Cochran, J. K., & Chamlin, M. B. (2000). Deterrence and brutalization: The dual effects of executions. *Justice Quarterly, 17,* 685–706.

[45]Bailey, W. C. (1998). Deterrence, brutalization, and the death penalty: Another examination of Oklahoma's return to capital punishment. *Criminology, 36,* 711–733.

[46]Ehrlich, I. (1975). The deterrent effect of capital punishment: A question of life and death. *American Economic Review, 65,* 397–417.

[47]The impassioned negative responses to Ehrlich's work lend some support for the idea that some criminologists are simply ideologically unwilling to acknowledge that the death penalty has a deterrent effect. For a sampling of this area of research, see Phillips, D. P. (1980). The deterrent effect of capital punishment: New evidence on an old controversy. *American Journal of Sociology, 86,* 139–148; Phillips, D. P., & Bollen, K. (1985). Same time, last year: Selective data dredging for negative findings. *American Sociological Review, 50,* 101–116; Ehrlich, I. (1977). Capital punishment and deterrence: Some further thoughts and additional evidence. *Journal of Political Economy, 85,* 741–788; Bowers, W. J., & Pierce, G. L. (1975). The illusion of deterrence in Isaac Ehrlich's research on capital punishment. *Yale Law Journal, 85,* 187–208; Passell, P. (1975). The deterrent effect of the death penalty: A statistical test. *Stanford Law Review, 28,* 61–80; Zeisel, H. (1982). Comment on the deterrent

effect of capital punishment. *American Journal of Sociology, 88,* 167–169.

[48]Shepherd, J. M. (2004). Murders of passion, execution delays, and the deterrence of capital punishment. *Journal of Legal Studies, 33,* 283–322.

[49]Dezhbakhsh, H., Rubin, P. H., & Shepherd, J. M. (2003). Does capital punishment have a deterrent effect? New evidence from post-moratorium panel data. *American Law and Economics Review, 5,* 344–376.

[50]Dezhbakhsh, H., & Shepherd, J. M. (2006). The deterrent effect of capital punishment: Evidence from a judicial experiment. *Economic Inquiry, 44,* 1–24 (p. 21).

[51]Phillips, note 47.

[52]Stack, S. (1987). Publicized executions and homicide, 1950–1980. *American Sociological Review, 52,* 532–540.

[53]Cheatwood, D. (2002). Capital punishment for the crime of homicide in Chicago: 1870–1930. *Journal of Criminal Law and Criminology, 92,* 843–866.

[54]Levitt, S. D. (2004). Understanding why crime fell in the 1990s: Four factors that explain the decline and six that do not. *Journal of Economic Perspectives, 18,* 163–190. Because of the infrequency of executions, others have argued that prison conditions measured by the prisoner death rate are a better method of deterrence. For instance, Lawrence Katz and his colleagues found that between 30–100 violent crimes and 30–100 property crimes were saved per inmate death in prison. Katz, L., Levitt, S. D., & Shustorovich, E. (2003). Prison conditions, capital punishment, and deterrence. *American Law and Economics Review, 5,* 318–343.

[55]Kant's ethical system appeared in *Foundation for the Metaphysic of Morals* in 1785. An excellent primer on justice and desert, including Kant's work, is Pojman, L. P., & McLeod, O. (1999). *What do we deserve: A reader on justice and desert.* New York: Oxford University Press.

[56]Simon, R. J., & Blaskovich, D. A. (2002). *A comparative analysis of capital punishment: Statutes, policies, frequencies, and public attitudes the world over.* Lanham, MDA: Lexington Books.

[57]Johnson, S. L. (2000). The Bible and the death penalty: Implications for criminal justice education. *Journal of Criminal Justice Education, 11,* 15–34, p. 31.

[58]Ellsworth, P. C., & Gross, S. R. (1994). Hardening of the attitudes: Americans' views on the death penalty. *Journal of Social Issues, 50,* 19–52.

[59]Davis, M. (2002). A sound retributive argument for the death penalty. *Criminal Justice Ethics, 21,* 22–26.

[60]For studies of the correlates and predictors of retributive beliefs, see Bohm, R. M. (1992). Retribution and capital punishment: Toward a better understanding of death penalty opinion. *Journal of Criminal Justice, 20,* 227–236; Cullen, F. T., Fisher, B., & Applegate, B. K. (2000). Public opinion about punishment and corrections. *Crime & Justice, 27,* 1–79; Finckenauer, J. O. (1988). Public support for the death penalty: Retribution as just deserts or retribution as revenge? *Justice Quarterly, 5,* 81–100; Lotz, R., & Regoli, R. M. (1980). Public support for the death penalty. *Criminal Justice Review, 5,* 55–66; Schadt, A. M., & DeLisi. M. (2007). Is vigilantism on your mind? An exploratory study of nuance and contradiction in student death penalty opinion. *Criminal Justice Studies, 20,* 255–268; Unnever, J. D., & Cullen, F. T. (2005). Executing the innocent and support for capital punishment: Implications for public policy. *Criminology & Public Policy, 4,* 3–38; Barkan, S. E., & Cohn, S. F. (2005). On reducing white support for the death penalty: A pessimistic appraisal. *Criminology & Public Policy, 4,* 39–44;

[61]Several criminologists and commentators have written about the moral underpinnings of criminal justice. For a sampling of these works, see Berns, W. (1979). *For capital punishment: Crime and the morality of the death penalty.* Lanham, MD: University Press of America; Murphy, J. G. (2003). *Getting even: Forgiveness and its limits.* New York: Oxford University Press; Rosenbaum, T. (2005). *The myth of moral justice: Why our legal system fails to do what's right.* New York: Harper Collins; Wilson, J. Q. (1993). *The moral sense.* New York: The Free Press.

[62]Berns, W. (1979). *For capital punishment: Crime and the morality of the death penalty* (p. 152). Lanham, MD: University Press of America.

[63]Longmire, D. R. (2000). Race, ethnicity, and the penalty of death: The American experience. *Corrections Management Quarterly, 4,* 36–43; Schaefer, K. D., Hennessy, J. J., & Ponteretto, J. G. (1999). Race as a variable in imposing and carrying out the death penalty in the U. S. *Journal of Offender Rehabilitation, 30,* 35–45.

[64]Baldus, D. C., Pulaski, C., & Woodworth, G. (1983). Comparative review of death sentences: An empirical study of the Georgia experience.

Journal of Criminal Law and Criminology, 74, 661–753; also see Baldus, D. C., Woodworth, G., & Pulaski, C. A. (1990). *Equal justice and the death penalty: A legal and empirical analysis. Boston,* MA: Northeastern University Press; Baldus, D. C., Woodworth, G., Zuckerman, D., Weiner, N. A., & Broffitt, B. (1998). Racial discrimination and the death penalty in the post-Furman era: An empirical and legal overview, with recent findings from Philadelphia. *Cornell Law Review, 83,* 1638–1770. Earlier Baldus conducted an analysis of the findings of Thorsten Sellin and Isaac Ehrlich in which he curiously found that Sellin's work was more methodologically sound and credible than Ehrlich's. See, Baldus, D. C., & Cole, J. W. L. (1976). A comparison of the work of Thorsten Sellin and Isaac Ehrlich on the deterrent effect of capital punishment. *Yale Law Review, 85,* 170–186.

[65]*McClesky v. Kemp,* 481 U. S. 279 (1987).

[66]Radelet, M. L. (1981). Racial characteristics and the imposition of the death penalty. *American Sociological Review, 46,* 918–927.

[67]Kleck, G. (1981). Racial discrimination in criminal sentencing: A critical evaluation of the evidence with additional evidence on the death penalty. *American Sociological Review, 46,* 783–805, pp. 798–799.

[68]Berk, R., Li, A., & Hickman, L. J. (2005). Statistical difficulties in determining the role of race in capital cases: A re-analysis of data from the state of Maryland. *Journal of Quantitative Criminology, 21,* 365–390.

INDEX